Outsourcing:

All You Need To Know

Sara Cullen

Managing Director of the Cullen Group, Visitor at the University of Melbourne, and Research Associate at the London School of Economics and Political Science

Melbourne, Australia

Mary Lacity

Curators' Professor of Information Systems and International Business Fellow at the University of Missouri-St. Louis, and Visiting Professor at the London School of Economics and Political Science

St Louis, USA

Leslie P. Willcocks

Professor of Technology Work and Globalization at the London School of Economics and Political Science

London, UK

WHITE PLUME PUBLISHING

Outsourcing: All You Need To Know.

White Plume Publishing
info@whitelumepublishing.com

First Edition Published 2014.

ISBN: 978-0-9923436-1-3

NEED ASSISTANCE?

We offer professional, technical, advisory and educational support supplemented with further detailed materials for all issues highlighted within this book. Please contact info@whiteplumepublishing.com and one of our experts will contact you directly and discuss your requirements.

CONTENTS

FIGURES

TABLES

PREFACE

Acknowledgements

As ever, we sincerely thank the now over 3,500 executives across the globe who participated in our research over the past 24 years. Without them, our work just would not have been possible. Due to the sensitive nature of outsourcing, many participants requested anonymity and cannot be individually acknowledged. Participants who did not request anonymity are acknowledged in the appropriate places throughout this book. We also wish to acknowledge the supportive research environments from several institutions, not least Templeton College (now Green Templeton), Oxford, University of Missouri, Warwick University, University of Melbourne, and the London School of Economics and Political Science,

Obviously, research work of this scope over such a long period is not just a three-person effort. Several colleagues, who became friends, made significant contributions and published with us in the earlier period, in particular Rudy Hirschheim, Wendy Currie, and Guy Fitzgerald. Later we have thoroughly enjoyed researching, digesting, and writing with several colleagues who are not in the present book but who shaped and contributed to our many research agendas. These are Thomas Kern, David Feeny, Eric van Heck, Peter Seddon, Peter Reynolds, Julia Kotlarsky, Ilan Oshri, Eleni Lioliou, Jae Yong Lee, and John Hindle. All of them provided intelligence, inspiration, and hard work in equal measure and it has been a joy to collaborate with them.

Mary thanks Vice Chancellor Nasser Arshadi, Dean Charles Hoffman, Joseph Rottman, Dinesh Mirchandani, Kailash Joshi, Vicki Sauter, and Karen Walsh at the University of Missouri-St. Louis. She also thanks the PhD students she has enjoyed working recently with including Shaji Khan, Stan Solomon, and Aihua Yan. Mary thanks her parents, Dr. and Mrs. Paul Lacity, her three sisters: Karen

Longo, Diane Iudica, and Julie Owings and her son, Michael Christopher. She thanks her closest friends, Jerry Pancio, Michael McDevitt, Beth Nazemi, and Val Graeser.

Leslie would like to thank his circle of family and friends for their forbearance and humor, and especially George, Catherine, John, Joan, Phil and Chrisanthi, not least for the getaway nights at the opera, Christine for being Christine, and Andrew for persisting with the tennis, against the odds. His debt to Damaris is simple - she makes all things possible, and all things worthwhile.

Sara thanks her husband Joe, whose unwavering support is heroic. She also thanks her wonderful sons, Gianni and Dante, who understand and forgive mom for her incessant travel and (unfair) time at the computer. Her colleague at the University of Melbourne, Prof. Peter Seddon, was responsible for Sara entering the academic world after two decades of leading consulting areas within Ernst & Young and Deloitte. His relentless pursuit of the truth is an inspiration. Lastly, of course, Sara would like to thank her mother, whose love of reading is legendary, and who is still waiting for Sara to write something interesting.

We all thank our editor, Ian Rogers, for his fantastic work and insightful advice.

Professional Credits

David Feeny is emeritus professor and Fellow of Green Templeton College, Oxford University. He has published widely on CIO and retained capability, strategy and the management of information technology, especially in *Harvard Business Review* and *Sloan Management Review* as well as many highly ranked IS journals. His current research interests are in the evaluation of executive education and innovation. Previously, he was a senior executive for over 20 years at IBM.

Dr John Hindle is Outsourcing Marketing Lead at Accenture responsible for industry relationships, research partnerships, and thought leadership programs. He also serves as Vice-Chairman of the HR Outsourcing Association (HROA) and holds appointment as Adjunct Professor of Human and Organizational Development at Vanderbilt University. John has an extensive international business background, with over 30 years experience as a senior executive and adviser to companies in the US and Europe. He has published widely in trade, practice, and academic media.

Dr Ilan Oshri is Professor of Technology and Globalization at Loughborough University. Previously he was Associate Professor of Strategy and Technology Management at Rotterdam School of Management Erasmus, The Netherlands. Ilan holds a PhD in Strategic Management and Technological Innovations from Warwick Business School. He is the co-author of three recent books - *Handbook of Global Outsourcing and Offshoring* (Palgrave, 2012), *Knowledge Processes in Globally Distributed Context* (Palgrave, 2008), *Standards-Battles in Open Source Software* (Palgrave, 2008) and is co-editor of *Outsourcing Global Services* (Palgrave, 2008). His work has appeared in leading academic journals including *MISQ, MISQ Executive, Communications of the ACM,* and *Journal of Strategic Information Systems,* and also in trade press and numerous books. Ilan is the co-founder of the Global Sourcing Workshop and an associate member of the Outsourcing Unit at the LSE.

Dr. Joseph Rottman is the Director of the International Business Institute, an Associate Professor of Information Systems, and a Research Fellow in the Center for International Studies at the University of Missouri, St. Louis. He is also an Associate Researcher at The Outsourcing Unit, London School of Economics. He has conducted case studies in over 40 organizations and has been engaged by Fortune 500 companies to analyze their offshore strategies. His recent book, *Offshore Outsourcing of IT Work* (with Mary Lacity) details models and practices IT professionals can utilize to effectively engage offshore providers and explores emerging outsourcing markets such as rural sourcing and the Chinese market. His publications have appeared in *Sloan Management Review, MIS Quarterly Executive, Information Systems Frontiers, Strategic Outsourcing: An International*

Journal, IEEE Computer, the *Journal of Information Technology*, the *American Review of Public Administration* and *Information and Management* and leading practitioner outlets such as *CIO Insight* and the *Cutter Consortium*. He earned his Doctor of Science in Information Management from Washington University in St. Louis. He has conducted research and spoken internationally on global sourcing, innovation diffusion and government IT. He was a Research Fellow with the Chinese Academy of Social Sciences in 2009, received the 2006 Anheuser-Busch Excellence in Teaching award, and is on the editorial board of *MIS Quarterly Executive*.

INTRODUCTION - FROM MYTHS TO EFFECTIVE PRACTICE

"No principality is secure without having its own forces. Nothing can be so uncertain or unstable as fame or power not founded on its own strength."

Machiavelli Il Principe, 1531.

Outsourcing is the running of the management and operations of assets/activities/people by external providers. Machiavelli, as one can gather, had little time for outsourcing. On the other hand, the Italy of his day was replete with the use of mercenary troops, whose leaders were celebrities in their own right, and often the subjects of now famous paintings from that era.

Parallels with today? Some senior executives hate outsourcing; others cannot seem to get enough of it. Is outsourcing an enabling strategic tool or disabling step backwards disguised as panacea?

History is of course replete with the use of outsourcing, mainly for military purposes, going back to ancient Egypt, through the early classical era, the Roman imperial era, in Asia and Africa, right up to modern wars of the 21st century. In the 21st century, unmanned aerial vehicles are being used in combat zones, often guided by private contractors. The following example illustrates the level of sophistication now reached.

By February 2010 QinetiQ, the privatized British defence technology company, had operators working with the Royal Netherlands Army in war zones in central Afghanistan, providing a system of unmanned aerial vehicles (UAVs) that could be called upon at any time by the Dutch forces. The London Times commented that, as military chiefs looked for spending cuts, UAVs might well be a cost effective option. *"UAVs (unmanned aerial vehicles)... provided by private companies – that is systems supplied and/or installed for immediate use, sometimes including providing the necessary operators – could help the Ministry of Defence to make difficult choices on what can be afforded."* [1]

But the article also pointed to outsourcing being controversial in conflict zones because it requires qualities such as flexibility, trust, and mutual understanding that are difficult to write into a standard contract. It also raised ethical questions, since defence companies were developing combat UAVs to replace fighter aircraft. In the future, the decision to pull the trigger could be part of a commercial contract. By 2013, the use of UAVs in war zones for surveillance and attack had escalated considerably. A May 2013 Guardian article pointed to another dimension, which is that UAVs represent a move to outsource further - not just to a contractor but also to technology. As one advocate commented, *"Why should we be afraid of unmanned? We are not reinventing flying; we are simply organizing a different form of control. The pilot has not gone walkabout; he is on the ground monitoring the situation in the same way as if he was in the air... in some respects it will be safer ... and it will be more effective and cost less."* [2]

Clearly, outsourcing has come a long way! Early industrialization in a range of economies and sectors (e.g. textiles, cars, and engineering products) has been marked by a putting-out system whereby much of the work was done elsewhere and then brought together to a central urban point. This tended to evolve into a larger factory system with as much as possible under one roof to achieve scale economies, control over labor, to intensify the use of technology, and subsequently apply mass production processes - including applying most recently automation

---

[1] *The London Times*, February 2010.

[2] Ray Mann, owner of Aberporth airfield, as quoted in *The Guardian*, 7th May 2013.

and robotics. Such approaches have also been applied to service industries. However, in recent years, the economics of the organization have changed due to competitiveness issues, globalization, and technological development.

In economics, the whole question of "*why do organizations exist?*" formed the basis of transaction cost economics (TCE) theory in which the first classic paper was written by Ronald Coase in 1931.[3] Modeling the changes in many sectors, TCE suggested that increasingly, especially for smaller organizations, production costs may well be lower if outsourced (i.e. the market could do the job better and cheaper). The rising problem, then, became the transaction costs associated with outsourcing - the costs of searching for, contracting with, monitoring of, and controlling and leveraging the performance of the provider.

Take a particular product; say making a shoe for Nike, or producing a computer keyboard for Apple. Outsourcing production makes economic sense when there are high gains from lower production costs and the transaction costs are low. If transaction costs exceed the gains through outsourcing production, then production should be kept inhouse.

In his classic book *Intelligent Enterprise* (1992), James Brian Quinn demonstrates (using examples such as Apple, Honda, ServiceMaster, and Merck), that outsourcing has spread even further from the time when Coase was writing.[4] And he adds a great new idea. He makes the case for organizations, in fact all organizations, developing a deep understanding of a few highly developed knowledge and service-based 'core competencies' that derive sustainable advantage from leveraging those intellectual assets that competitors cannot reproduce. The other competencies can safely, in principle, be outsourced.

---

[3] Coase, R. H. (1937) "The Nature of the Firm," *Economica*, (4): 386-405.

[4] Quinn, J. (1992) Intelligent Enterprise: a knowledge and service based paradigm for industry. The Free Press, New York.

According to Quinn, rarely will owning the largest raw material resources, manufacturing plants, equipment bases, or integrated facilities provide a maintainable competitive edge. Such physical properties are too easily cloned or bypassed. By outsourcing less important functions to superior outside providers, clients become more responsive, decentralized, and lean. By designing and benchmarking their knowledge and service-based activities to be world class, managers can drastically reduce overhead cost and bureaucracy, while motivating personnel and creating greater value for customers and shareholders.

Since *Intelligent Enterprise* was published, outsourcing has also taken off in a big way in more service-based industries such as financial services, government agencies, legal and other professional services, as well as back office areas such as IT, HR, procurement, asset management, administration, and marketing. Throughout each service, production system or function the 'core competencies' logic tends to be applied. Identify and keep inhouse what we are best at, and what is 'core', and, if there is a cost effectiveness rationale, outsource the rest.

Quinn's book is an enthralling read, but his enthusiasm distracts from a set of problems inherent in the whole core competencies vision. One challenge is being able to define what the core competencies of an organization are, and as a party to an outsourcing contract. We have practical answers to this problem at a high level in Chapter 3, and at a more detailed level throughout Part 2 (Chapters 5 to 9) pertaining to competencies needed to design and manage outsourcing arrangements from womb to tomb.

The second problem is knowing just how sustainable core competencies are. Eventually, whatever differentiates an organization has an used-by date - that is, it commodifies over time. That is a much more difficult issue to deal with.

Thirdly, and critical for the rationale of this book, nowhere does Quinn address the complex challenges inherent in outsourcing. Unfortunately, as we have discovered from the exhaustive research we have done since, outsourcing remains far from the simple process of handing over a task and then just merely monitoring the outcomes. This handing over, or contracting out, creates multiple practical challenges for both parties - not least risk and its mitigation.

Other questions arise for clients:

- How do we control the provider's performance? How do we know the provider has the capabilities they espouse?

- What will be the true costs? What happens if we want to change our requirements?

- How far must we be involved? What capabilities do we need?

- What kind of contract work? What do we do when things go wrong?

All of these lead to the central question we address in this book, "*How does a client leverage the ever-growing external services market to gain operational, business, even strategic advantage?*"

In seeking to answer this question, it is crucial first to identify the myths that have grown up around the subject. We then need to understand the evolution of the modern outsourcing market and capabilities. The core of the book then provides a step-by-step guide to evidence-based, practical thinking, frameworks, and actions to achieve superior performance.

Myths Surrounding Outsourcing

The outsourcing market is big; make no mistake. In the UK alone, the outsourcing industry represents some 8% of the country's annual turnover (gross domestic product). In 2013, the total size of the BPO (business process outsourcing) and ITO (information technology outsourcing) segment of the market was approaching

$US952 billion. Compound annual growth from 2013-2017 is expected to be between 3.5% and 5.5% depending on the service outsourced.[5]

There are thousands of general and specialist outsourcing providers of all sizes throughout the world, amongst the biggest being Serco, Capita, Accenture, SODEXO, IBM, Colliers, CSC, ISS, CapGemini, Tata, Infosys and HP.

In terms of activities and processes outsourced, there is a wide range of practice. At one extreme, one in three help desks are outsourced at client companies. At the other extreme, only 5% of logistic/supply chain management, financial planning and analysis, and direct procurement are outsourced. The rest is sourced inhouse or as offshore captives.[6]

This suggests that outsourcing still has a long way to grow, and all the indications are that the market will only get bigger. It also suggests that although the outsourcing market is large and getting larger, people continue to find alternative forms of sourcing attractive. This fact would suggest that outsourcing is not always the answer, and that one should approach outsourcing claims with considerable caution.

Indeed, it is very important not to believe everything you hear about outsourcing. Not least because sales pitches, ideologies, beliefs, and generalizations (which we call, collectively, 'myths') are far more rampant and appear to carry far more influence than is acceptable, in our opinion.

---

[5] HFS Research (2013) *State of the Outsourcing Industry 2013*. HFS Research/KPMG, Boston. The survey covered 1355 enterprises across multiple major economic sectors. There are many sources producing figures for the size of the outsourcing market; we choose this one because we understand and support its methodology.

[6] HFS Research (2013) *State of the Outsourcing Industry 2013*. HFS Research/KPMG, Boston. The outsourcing choices mentioned here were registered by 399 buy-side enterprises.

A myth is not necessarily untrue. For example, it may be possible to reduce costs by 20% if you outsource, although most clients do not (for a plethora of reasons). A myth may be true in certain circumstances, but the danger lies when these are generalized to everyone's situation. It is dangerous to read your own specific circumstances into an outsourcing myth.

"*Let's face it,*" as a provider CEO once memorably told us, "*outsourcing contracts are agreed in concept but delivered in detail, and that's why they can break down.*" The message - don't discount the promises; but analyze them very carefully indeed, and take real steps to secure the outcomes you really need; which, by the way, may be different from the ones on offer.

Let's look at the major myths. We identify ten.

Myth 1 *"Providers have inherent advantages in economies of scale and superior management practices. Therefore, they will achieve lower costs while improving service."*

In practice, providers frequently overplay the economies of scale argument. The scale economies that providers can achieve whether in, for example, data centers, specialist labor pools, centralizing physical assets, and financing can be replicated by any large client. Economies of scale often plateau once scale reaches a certain level. This can mean diseconomies of scale (forces that cause larger companies to produce goods and services at increased per-unit costs) can occur.

Providers are often as indifferently organized internally as their clients. This lack of efficiency means, in TCE language, production costs are *not* always lower if you go to the market. For example, many providers are organized by regional 'silos, even though their global clients require seamless global delivery. Others are organized by product or service silos in separate entities or divisions, despite their clients wanting total integrated solutions. And yet, others remain a collection of undigested series of mergers and acquisitions. All these silos have transaction costs, as well as required profit margins, within a provider.

Superior management practices of the provider are a more likely, and indeed usually, the major benefit sought through outsourcing. However, reorganizing work, automating tasks, employing fewer but more able staff, and providing better managers have no magic about them. These can all be replicated inhouse, provided there is the political will and leadership to implement them.[7]

Remember also, that providers will usually take over an existing service, including its processes and people, without making substantial changes and just charge these back to the client. Providers often make their margins by 'sweating the assets' over a number of years, charging for every added service or unit, and not making investments in new technology, process improvement, or more expensive skilled labor. You do not inherently get superior management practices from outsourcing - in fact, if you do want advanced practices it is best to specify those practices in your agreement, rather than assume they will naturally occur.

Myth 2 "Long-term single-provider deals secure partnering relationships, lower transaction costs, and greater business advantage."

The idea here is that if you sign a contract of 10 years or more, this forms the basis of a long-term relationship in which the client can bring the provider into strategic discussions and actions, while the provider feels confident enough to make large investments in innovation, improvements and service quality. Synergies will also develop from superior relationships, trust and information transparency. In fact, the record on these sorts of deals has been very mixed. For example, looking at 29 deals, the authors found 38% of them met expectations, 35% were unsuccessful, and 27% of these deals got mixed results.[8] Risky business indeed.

---

[7] For IT examples see Lacity, M. and Hirschheim, R. (2005) *Beyond the Outsourcing Bandwagon.* Wiley, Chichester.

[8] Lacity, M. and Willcocks, L. (2001) *Global IT Outsourcing: In Search of Business Advantage.* Wiley, Chichester.

In the early 1990s, outsourcing deals tended to be struck to reduce costs, often for financial reasons including restructuring the balance sheet of clients in financial trouble. Leveraging the service was not uppermost in the decision-makers' minds; indeed often the service was reclassified as a commodity so that it could be easily outsourced. Providers made large initial capital outlays to buy the client's assets and take over much of the internal headcount. They then needed to recoup this investment over the life of the agreement and make a profit. As a result, clients often felt exploited in the last five years of contracts.

Moreover, industries moved on in terms of price/performance ratios (typically better performance for the same price), and clients discovered a range of necessary services or technologies outside the scope of the original contract that now have to be paid for at relatively high prices. This pattern is typical in recessionary periods, and in long-term deals in both commercial and government sectors.

Even the better designed long-term deals (both single and multiple provider) that we have looked at rarely report actual innovation, significant risk sharing, or real business advantage flowing from their deals. Some organizations also recorded withdrawing from the idea of partnering, and reported that the deal settled down into what is nothing more than a traditional fee-for-service contract, no more.

It is also clear from our evidence that long-term deals should only be undertaken by a client that has a mature ability to manage outsourcing, perhaps having managed through a series of smaller short-term deals first. It is no coincidence that the dominant practice in the leading markets of USA and UK has been *selective outsourcing,* typically between 20-38% of the relevant budget outsourced to multiple providers on shorter-term contracts. This has been the lower risk, learning-by-experience option of most clients in developed economies. It has also been the outsourcing practice that has grown most since the financial crash of 2008.

It should also be noted that single-provider deals actually often involve a lot of subcontracting on the part of the provider, in fact becoming head contractors rather than direct providers (for a description of these terms, see Configuration Attribute #2: Supplier Grouping in Chapter 4). These days, even the biggest providers cannot be good at, or even resource, everything. Sometimes 30% or more of big deals are subcontracted out. This is the case across the board, in areas as diverse as construction, special projects, healthcare hospital management, technical consulting, desktop hardware and installation, network and telecoms. This raises many questions because of the mixed responsibilities for performance, size of management fees and levels of activity by the lead provider. Do they really manage other providers better than you can? Are costs really lower by going with one provider rather than several, given the head contractor makes a margin on top of the subcontractors? What are the security issues, and true liabilities, should something go wrong? Who is liable to pay the subcontractors if the head provider doesn't? In some countries, such as Australia, this can be you, even if you have already paid the head provider.[9]

Myth 3 *"Outsourcing is about spending as little as possible and monitoring outcomes, not managing them; that can be left to the provider."*

Clients usually outsource for a mix of strategic, financial, political, technical, and tactical reasons. However, the evidence is that cost savings does figure as one of the important expectations. It always comes to the fore in recessionary periods, such as in the periods of 1989-1993, 2000-2003, and 2008-2013. There is plenty of evidence that cost savings can be achieved, but there are definite limits to providers working smarter to achieve the 'outsourcing holy trinity' of dramatic cost savings, plus a decent profit margin, as well as higher KPIs (key performance indicator) for the client.

---

[9] Many states in Australia have a 'security of payment' act that allows subcontractors, who do not receive payment from the prime contractor, to obtain it from the client. The client then, must seek the payment back from its provider. This came about because some primes were not paying their subcontractors. This enabled the prime to have better cash flow, and in some cases, caused subcontractors to become insolvent.

In practice, there will be a trade-offs between these three outcomes (e.g. significant cost savings achieved at the expense of degraded KPIs or at the expense of technology/process investment by the provider). In one large-scale deal we researched, the client's senior managers were satisfied with the cost savings, but the operational service had so degraded that some business units had started their own surrogate services out of various budgets to counteract the poor service they received. The message is not to have unrealistic expectations about what is possible. Driving hard for cost reduction may well have harmful consequences for other aspects of performance. In some big deals we have seen, an over-concentration on cost ends up creating operational inflexibility and even competitive disadvantage.

More importantly, cost savings can be at risk it the client does not undertake active management on many fronts, from the pre-contract stage onwards. Practically, the client should have four major capabilities before outsourcing:

1. able to make evidence-based sourcing decisions and formulate sustainable sourcing strategies,

2. understand the market as a whole, the strategies and capabilities of individual providers, and the unique tricks, traps and tips required when using a specific provider,

3. able to articulate, negotiate, and contract effectively to get what is required delivered, and

4. have in place post-contract skills and competencies that mitigate risk, elicit and deliver on business requirements, develop the blueprint and plans for delivery of the process/technology platform, and manage external supply to the client's advantage.

In our experience, the biggest omissions tend to be in area 4. This is a serious weakness because post-contract capability acts as an ultimate safety blanket for failures to establish points 1-3. Our research shows that managing outsourcing successfully needs much more than a caretaker function. We address this issue throughout Part 2 - The Outsourcing Lifecycle.

Myth 4 "Outsource your problems. The market is mature enough to provide superior capability to handle them."

Contrary to this claim, we would offer a different, risk-mitigating rule of thumb: Do not outsource problems. Only outsource those things you can write a detailed specification for and that you can effectively monitor performance. What is the thinking here? After all, it is when you lack capability to do something that the market most comes into its own, isn't it? Well, yes and no. It depends on the nature of the task.

In situations where the technology/process is well understood and stable, the precise objective can be delineated and a detailed specification can be given, then it becomes relatively safe to throw the task over the wall to the specialists (whether they be inhouse or external providers). Taking IT as our example, not surprisingly the most popular tasks that are outsourced are infrastructure and operational activities, followed by maintenance and support. But even things that 'should be' easy to outsource invariably have surprisingly idiosyncratic aspects. Rubbish collection, for example, in many countries is nowadays separated into types of rubbish that must be processed differently, and needs expertise in following recycling regulations.

The problems occur in conditions of low technology/process maturity. Maturity is low when the process is a new and unstable, technology has ill-defined business use, or where an existing process or technology is used in it a radical new way, or where specialist expertise with the process or technology is lacking. In these cases, throwing the task over the wall to specialists must be replaced by a multi-functional team - embracing relevant business users, managers, internal subject specialists, project managers and then buying in external resources where necessary to work under internal management direction.

Moreover, the closer the service comes to the business and to strategy, the less advisable it is to outsource the related tasks. Using an IT example, software development is an interesting test case. While many clients have outsourced development tasks, many have not, and many have brought aspects of software development capability back inhouse after a period of outsourcing. This is because development involves working closely with the business, and because having some capability here secures the client's control of its IT destiny. If this abandoned to the provider, asymmetries of power and opportunism might develop.

A further point here is that the core internal capabilities should never really be outsourced. Take internal process/technology fixing capability for example. Outsourcing providers may well be able to provide routine solutions to routine problems, but it will take inhouse capability to handle the non-routine technical issues that inevitably arise and for which knowledge of the business, high skills, and a thorough understanding of the client's idiosyncratic processes and systems, and the ways in which they connect, are needed. Internal capabilities provide the essential problem-solving capability that external resources, with the best will in the world, cannot supply in a sustainable way.

Take, as another example, innovation development capability. We have invariably found that this capability had to be developed internally three or four years into the contract because of what we term, 'mid-contract sag' and lack of innovation coming from the provider. Rarely have we found new ways of leveraging the relationship emerging from a provider's initiative. We discuss innovation in detail in Chapter 13.

Myth 5 "Partnerships secures superior relationships, innovation, risk sharing, and greater business leverage."

Partnership deals are often called 'strategic partnerships' or alliances. One of these approaches, that of taking equity in a provider or the provider taking equity in the client, has proved quite popular. In the 1990s, these were particularly fashionable in the IT sector (e.g., Delta Airlines $US2.8 billion, 10-year agreement with AT&T, Perot Systems and Swiss Bank's 25 year $US6.2 billion deal, the 1996 Telstra-ISSC (later IBM GSA) deal with Telstra taking a 26% stake in the latter, and Lend Lease taking a 35% stake in ISSC in exchange for a total outsourcing arrangement). We have been involved in or studied most of these deals and have to report that the advantages touted rarely actually came through in any sustainable way.

A more frequent finding was that taking equity shares in a provider or in each other often led to complacency that could also translate into indifferent service at the operational level. To be blunt, the motivational aspects of risk sharing over share ownership failed to translate to lower levels of the client. Moreover, when complaints were made about poor service, the provider could justifiably argue that it was devoting its efforts to securing further revenues with other clients, which was also to the advantage of the present client since it owned a substantial part of the provider! Interestingly, the Telstra deal we mentioned above came apart in the late 1990s. By 2002, Telstra had some five outsourcing contracts with providers, only one of which was IBM GSA. Another one of IBM GSA's partners, Lend Lease, terminated the outsourcing contract while retaining equity in IBM GSA. The Perot-Swiss Bank deal was negotiated down to a much shorter, selective outsourcing deal, while the equity share holding arrangement was cancelled after 2000. This is somewhat a typical pattern for all such deals, and not just in the IT sector.

A more recent partnership variant in the government sector is called Public-Private Partnerships (PPPs). Here a government service or infrastructure is funded and operated through a partnership of government and one or more commercial sector companies via a special purpose vehicle (SPV). The SPV is to assume the financial, technical, and operational risk; the government tends to provide the land, a few tax incentives to make it attractive, and calls for tenders. Most often capital investment is made by the commercial sector on the basis of a contract with the government to provide agreed long term services, with the government paying the cost of service (along with some of the cost subsidized by a user-pay system). For example, a hospital building may be financed and constructed by a private developer which is then leased to the hospital authority who collects payments from patients and doctors. The developer acts as landlord, charging rent and for non-medical services, while the hospital provides medical services. PPPs have been widely used for public infrastructure projects, and for large-scale investments in public services.

The record worldwide on such deals has been mixed. Many of the patterns witnessed in share-holding deals noted above found their way into PPP deals. Moreover, while risk and investment seemingly devolves to the commercial sector companies, when the deals run into trouble it was invariably the government sector that picked up the cost and had to take on more risk.

Some studies show that the PPP model was financially inferior to the standard model of government procurement based on competitive tenders - government can borrow capital more cheaply and does not need to return a profit. The privatization of water and electric utilities has often not seen lower prices for consumers; neither has it seen the large-scale investment anticipated from the (now) commercial sector owners. We should make the point that some PPP projects have proceeded smoothly (e.g. in India for infrastructure projects, in Canada for social and infrastructure development). However, across the world, there have also been many controversial schemes. Some examples include Airport Link and Sydney Harbor tunnel in Australia, Private Finance Initiatives in the UK, the UK's London underground PPP that was returned into public control in 2007 after 4.5 years and a cost of £2 billion.

Myth 6 "Drive the hardest commercial bargain possible. The provider will look after its own profit margin. The contract is everything."

You may now feel very wary of providers. One natural instinct would be to make sure you have a watertight contract - one that the provider cannot reinterpret or escape and one that you intend to impose to the smallest detail. There is also sometimes a lot of machismo in the negotiations, as well as in the management of the contract. Furthermore, during the 2008-2014 period, we heard several advisors and commercial research organizations pointing out that providers were having a rough time, and now was the opportunity to take advantage of this, and get the best cost deal possible. All this is fine, as long as you remember one thing: allow for, and ensure that the provider makes a reasonable profit. The truth is that slim or no profit margins drive a provider to opportunistic behavior that can harm the relationship, and ultimately the business value of the service performance.

Be clear that poor or onerous contracts can severely damage client-provider relationships. Lack of flexibility and common sense, or poor timing in the use of onerous contract terms does exactly the same thing. The contract is a clear fail-safe device, there to be used, but you will find that in practice it cannot predict and cover every eventuality and that active management and relationships on both sides are what lubricate effective outsourcing performance.

While it is almost a cliché to talk of win-win deals, be sure not to sign win-lose ones. In their article on the **'winner's curse'**, Kern, Willcocks and Van Heck show the consequences when a provider wins an outsourcing bid from which ultimately it stands to make no money.[10] How does a provider make such a mistake? Sometimes it may be a straightforward matter of miscalculation. Sometimes the inhouse costs that the provider had to bid against were in fact grossly (though unintentionally) understated by the client. In one major deal, we found such inhouse costs understated by 50%. Fortunately, this was discovered during the due diligence period, otherwise the provider would have been contractually committed to making a large loss each year for five years. Sometimes the provider is desperate for business and will undercut all other competitive bids, in the hope that once the work is secured, the money can be recovered by additional services, and reinterpreting or exploiting loopholes and

---

[10] Kern, T. and Willcocks, L. and Van Heck, E. (2002) The Winners Curse in IT Outsourcing: Strategies for Avoiding Relational Trauma. *California Management Review*, 44, 2, 47-69.

ambiguities in the contract. Whatever the cause, the effects of the winner's curse for a provider, and its client, can be devastating.

Kern, Willcocks, and Van Heck studied 85 completed contracts and found two disturbing facts. Firstly, the winner's curse existed in nearly 20% of them (i.e. it is a much more common phenomenon than one would actually credit). Secondly, in over 75% of those contracts, the winner's curse was also visited on the client. In other words, if the provider is having a bad outsourcing experience, it is highly probable that this will create negative repercussions for its client too.

Myth 7 "Contracts are self-executing. Once a contract is signed, then the hard work is over. The document will manage the provider."

The contract is merely a (often large) document that the parties have signed as evidence of their intent. As to whether that intent is carried out as envisioned, that comes down to how it is implemented and managed. And that takes knowledgeable people on both sides.

Modern outsourcing contracts are out of date even before the ink is dry. Price-performance formulae move on, as does technology, and the competition. Client needs are fluid and ever changing. All this means that contract management, as opposed to mere contract administration and monitoring, is highly important. But it cannot be approached in too legalistic a manner. In one of our studies, we found that over-reliance on the contract contributed significantly to failure in many deals - leading to inflexibility, over-legalistic interpretations, lack of responsiveness to current issues, and many more problems.

Relying on the contract is invariably a last ditch measure. Mature clients build relationships, have clear objectives, and maintain flexibility on contract in the face of dynamic market conditions and changing business demands. The wise customers review and update contracts regularly with their providers, but are also able to build relationships that serve to soften contracts when they get in the way.

Two decades of studies demonstrate that outsourcing cannot be contracted for and then not be managed by the client. Just how much a client needs to invest in ensuring benefits are achieved, costs are contained, and risks are mitigated surprises is a question far too many clients do not answer until the degree of underinvestment becomes apparent - in surprise problems, surprise costs, surprise responsibility confusion, surprise scope interpretations… the list goes on. For this reason, we have devoted Chapter 8 to helping understand that it is not the contract, in so much as it is the contract management that matters.

Myth 8 *"Expect more from the provider than you do from your own organization. After all, you are the customer and it's your money."*

We once wrote a series called 'Twenty Things a Supplier Would Tell You if They Could'. One of the big complaints providers registered was that they seem to be there to be blamed for mistakes and failures, while clients frequently were themselves recalcitrant and major contributors to disappointing performance. In our own research where we found poor performance, invariably 60% of the responsibility could be laid at the client's door. After all, the client worded the contract, selected the provider, decided on scope required, agreed on the pricing, and as one provider (only half-humorously) told us, *"they kept changing their minds, ignored our recommendations, disempowered us on decisions, and failed to heed our warnings."*

Clients, we find, need to grow into being mature customers, willing to state requirements clearly, be proactive in their own and the providers' interests, and treat the provider as professionally as they themselves wish to be treated.

However, reciprocal behaviors and expectations can be quite a challenge in practice. For example, a bank recently wanted an 'open door' policy with the provider, but would not grant such access itself. It wanted management issues responded to on the same business day, but could not give the same guarantee in return. Invoices had to be raised on time and tracked as a KPI but on time payments were not tracked. The provider was expected to be proactive about potential problems, but the bank let the provider discover the problems caused by the bank, after it was too late to prevent them. In fact, in calling the relationship a 'partnership', the bank really just wanted a master-slave relationship.

Responsibility-free outsourcing is an illusion. Both parties need to work in concert, show mutual respect, and provide smart resources. If one party does not, why should the other?

Myth 9 "Outsourcing technology, specialist, or knowledge-based activities is much like buying commodities."

Not everything is a commodity. Surprisingly even cement and coal, for example, are not 'commodities' for those working in those industries. There are different kinds of cement and coal useful for different purposes, performing in different ways in different circumstances. How much more complicated are complex services or a technologies, specialist services, or knowledge-based activities?

Think of IT. In fact, IT is not a homogeneous function, but comprises a wide variety of IT activities. IT capabilities continue to evolve at a dizzying pace. Thus predicting IT needs beyond a three-year horizon is wrought with uncertainty. There is no simple basis for gauging the economics of IT activity. Economic efficiency has more to do with IT practices than inherent economies of scale. Most distinctively of all, large switching costs are associated with ITO decisions; meaning it is difficult to reverse out of them inexpensively.

Nonetheless, we've recently observed an ITO contract issued in a government tender that was a 'cut and paste' from a construction contract…complete with five pages dedicated to the provider's responsibilities for archeological discoveries… but no IT issues were addressed.

Of course, one tries to make things as simple as possible, but oversimplification to the point of believing outsourcing can be successfully handled by copying unrelated contracts, tenders, and even management strategies misses the unique challenges and benefits that each outsourcing exercise has. We have observed thousands of deals collectively, and not one has been the same - even for similar scope, with similar providers, with similar clients. Attempting to commoditize, or make an outsourcing deal undifferentiated from any other purchase, only locks in failure, never success.

Myth 10 *"Anything is going to be better than our present internal department."*

It is true that outsourcing can be successfully used as a catalyst for improving performance and galvanizing an otherwise sleepy and complacent inhouse department. Indeed, we have participated in such change agency ourselves. However, all too often, we have seen 'the grass is greener elsewhere' syndrome operating in favor of the outsourcing decision. Usually, we see the inhouse department or activity painted as a cash sink - a black hole into which increasing expenditure disappears and from which little business value emerges. Success, or effective operation, is rarely noticed - let alone praised. Meanwhile, failures and mishaps are often very visible. Moreover, internal functions are rarely good at internal marketing.

All this plays into the hands of the superior marketing of providers who come with no 'baggage' (perceived bad track record) to the potential client's site. Against the seeming large outlays and disappointing internal performance, the provider can play the card of world-class provider and of lower cost and premium service, 'superstar' performance. However, the truth of feasible performance usually lies between these two scenarios. That is you can get low cost, but probably also degraded service, or if you want superior service from some aspects you will have to pay premium prices for it. In other words, as in so many other things, in outsourcing you tend to get what you pay for.

The outsourcing experience may also change people's minds about the previous performance of the internal service function. Following an outsourcing decision, we have frequently heard people complain of *"getting charged for everything now"* - bemoaning the lack of flexibility in what can be provided, the degree of bureaucracy, the time delays involved in securing resources from the provider, the lack of better-trained provider staff, of overall higher costs, and the constant fight for service and attention. While these issues are by no means the only experiences of outsourcing we could report on, they do concentrate people's minds somewhat on whether the problems are endemic to the service rather than just to a specific provider. In other words, you may just be changing one category or set of problems for another.

A further point here is that actually, as we indicated above, you can never really outsource all of your internal service or department. If you do, the risks are highly prohibitive. Furthermore, to this day, a predominant majority of clients still keep most of their expenditure inhouse rather than with providers. In fact, over the last seven years, in general, we have found inhouse functions improving in their performance relative to what the services market can offer. A galvanizing factor here may well have been the rising threat from outsourcing, which has also established a more visible benchmark for what the inhouse function should be attaining.

The signs have been that inhouse functions have been steadily getting their houses in order. A provider's bid may well be used to indicate areas in which the inhouse group may readily embark on a program of self-improvement. As a final point, no matter how bad an internal function is perceived to be, the function still needs to be involved and must have the opportunity to improve. Ultimately, of course, we are suggesting that to outsource properly, you need a high performance internal function in place to keep control of your destiny, even though this internal function may end up being a very different kind from the one that went before.

A Brief History of Outsourcing

The myths we have just discussed demonstrate that, when it comes to outsourcing, clients and providers alike are still on the learning curve. You will also notice that outsourcing may have rules of thumb, but there are no hard and fast rules. So much depends on the circumstances, the reasons for outsourcing, and the capabilities brought to bear by clients and providers in specific deals.

In 2013, our research established that 20% of BPO deals were high performing, 25% were good, 40% were doing okay, and 15% were poor. Why such a mixed set of experiences? The common denominator was that management made up to a 47% difference in performance.[11] 'Management' here refers to the right mix of skills, attitudes, experiences, and behaviors amongst influential players across both parties, leading to the adoption and application of the effective outsourcing practices detailed in this book.

So what does this learning curve look like? To see and understand it clearly, a little history is in order. Not only can one learn lessons from past examples (what works and what does not), one can also unpack why the present takes the form it does, and whether today's practices were developed for other contexts and problems, and so need to be changed in new contexts, in order to address new requirements. Therefore, we will look first at how the market developed and how we got to where outsourcing is today. Then we review how clients have been climbing up the outsourcing learning curve.

---

[11] The review of BPO performance appears in Lacity and Willcocks (2014) *High Performance BPO*. The 'up to 47% difference' figure is indicative, and comes from our 1993 study of organizations that outsourced to achieve cost savings. We found the outcomes ranging from 23% cost savings to 24% cost increases, and concluded that it was the quality of management that made the difference. In a further study of cases, Willcocks, Cullen, and Craig (2011) *The Outsourcing Enterprise*, Palgrave, London, concluded that *'relationship management can create a 20% to 40% difference on service, cost and other performance indicators.'*

Behind the scenes of an organization are an incredible number of horizontal and vertical business services that support operations. Horizontal services include any support services needed by all organizations, such as IT, financial and accounting, human resource (HR) management, procurement, real estate, and legal services. Vertical business services are industry-specific, such as policy administration and claims administration in an insurance company or research, development, and clinical trials in a pharmaceutical company. For the first part of the twentieth century, organizations insourced (vertically integrated) nearly all their vertical services. There was no outsourcing market for business support services.

Enter Henry and Joe Taub, the two founders of Automatic Payrolls in 1953, a manual payroll processing business. In 1957, the company changed its name to Automatic Data Processing (ADP), and began using automation, including punched card machines, check printing machines, and mainframe computers. Payroll was thus one of the first business services to be outsourced. Next enters Ross Perot — a Texan, ex-Naval officer, and frustrated salesman at IBM. He started Electronic Data Systems (EDS) in 1962 to establish a company that offered high-end electronic data processing management personnel, along with the computer hardware, by targeting large corporations and by offering long-term contracts at a time when short-term contracts were the industry norm.[12] His first big contract was with the US Federal Government for processing Medicare and Medicaid healthcare-claims. EDS marks the birth of ITO. Computer hardware providers, most notably IBM and CSC, soon began selling IT services in addition to their traditional hardware and software offerings.

Over the next twenty-five years, ITO grew to span multiple services and clients transferred a significant amount of assets, leases, licenses, and staff to providers.

---

[12] Source: Wikipedia.

The beginning date of modern ITO is usually attributed to 1989 and the landmark Eastman Kodak $US500 million outsourcing arrangement with IBM, DEC, and Businessland (now ENTEX). This was immediately followed by Enron's $750 million, ten-year contract with EDS (acquired by HP in 2008). From then, IT became the single most popular outsourcing target, with revenues moving from $10 billion in 1989, to about $50 billion revenues in 1994, $152 billion in 2000, to (on different forecasts) from $340 billion to over $660 billion by 2014.

Within the wider early-1990s debate about organizational core competence, clients increasingly looked to outsource 'commodity' IT to reduce costs, access expertise, and/or catalyze performance.

In the UK, notable deals included contracts between Inland Revenue and EDS and between BAE Systems and CSC, both ten-year deals. BP Exploration's five-year contracts with three providers in 1993 were groundbreaking because it popularized selective sourcing as a new model. Also during the 1990s, ITO contracts went global, with companies like DuPont signing $4 billion worth of contracts with CSC and Andersen Consulting (now Accenture) that operated in 22 different countries.

Interestingly, the period 1989-1997 saw some high profile large-scale, sometimes single provider, ITO deals (e.g. BP, General Dynamics, DuPont, Xerox, Commonwealth Bank, UK Inland Revenue), but these represented a minority practice. By 1999, there were globally just over 120 such deals. The dominant practice was multiple provider outsourcing with shorter-term contracts (three to seven years), which focused on outsourcing stable, discrete activities.

ITO has continued apace in the first decade of the new century. Gartner estimated that the global ITO market in 2013 was worth $325 billion. Horses for Sources (HfS) place the ITO market even higher for that year at $648 billion.[13]

During 2000-2010, a renewed, more strategic interest in multi-sourcing (e.g. the ABN Amro bank deal with four providers in 2005) was seen as the way strategic sourcing would go. At the same time, the period 2005-2010 saw more, smaller, shorter-term contracts driving market growth. With the economic downturn, an interest in consolidating provider numbers took place. On the back of this, the economic and management advantages of 'bundled' outsourcing (going with one provider for several IT and business process services) grew.[14]

After ITO, came BPO, the outsourcing of all the other business support services besides IT. As early as 1991, BP Exploration outsourced all of its European accounting operations to one provider, consolidating them in a single site at Aberdeen, Scotland. Likewise, in 1996, BP did the same for its US upstream, downstream, and chemical businesses, moving to two outsourcing providers in 1999. The Aberdeen shared services centre also attracted additional oil industry clients (e.g. Britannia Operator and Conoco). Some early BPO deals piggybacked on ITO deals. For example, Procter & Gamble initially signed a $3 billion 10-year ITO contract in 2003 with HP and then extended the contract to include global transactional accounts payable operations in 2004.

A more common practice has been to hire different providers for different ITO/BPO activities, for example BAE Systems hired Xchanging for human

---

[13] The source is HFS Research (2013) *State of the Outsourcing Industry 2013*. HFS Research/KPMG, Boston.

[14] Detailed histories of IT and business process outsourcing can be found in Lacity, M., Willcocks, L. and Rottman, J. (2008) "Global Outsourcing of Back Office Services: Lessons, Trends and Enduring Challenges." *Strategic Outsourcing* 1, 1, 13-34; Willcocks, L. and Lacity, M. (2009) *The Practice of Outsourcing: From Information Systems to BPO and Offshoring*, Palgrave, London; and Campbell, K. (2010) *Outsourcing: A New Value Proposition*. Accenture, London.

resource outsourcing (HRO) services in 2001, BP hired Exult for HRO and Accenture for accounting and finance (from 1993). Both BAE and BP had different ITO providers. However, bundling BPO - that is giving a mix of BPO activities to one provider - has been a growing practice since 2005.[15] Compared to ITO, BPO is a less mature market. ITO had over $193 billion in global revenues 2013 according to Gartner, and $304 billion according to HfS[16], but BPO is growing at a faster rate.

Then came offshoring. As a number of American and West European clients developed captive centers and outsourced some IT work in India and elsewhere (e.g. Baan, GE) while Indian providers began to develop their capabilities and markets (e.g. Infosys, TCS, Wipro). But it was the increasing, and successful, use by North American and European companies of Indian providers and locations to deal with the Y2K problem that really began to put offshore models on the map, from around 2000.

Both BPO and offshoring genuinely opened up the global outsourcing market in the new decade, offering real routes to cost savings, and greater value from outsourcing. BP were again pioneers, this time in HRO in their 1999 deal with Exult. Another new BPO 'pure play', Xchanging signed a similar deal, though on a joint venture basis, with British Aerospace in May 2001, while Bank of America contracted with Accenture. From the turn of the century, the BPO market picked up considerably. The issue for BPO, generally, was whether clients had the confidence to outsource, even transform, their back offices (e.g. HR, procurement, legal, accounting, finance, asset management), against a background of a global provider market still developing its capabilities. The outcome by 2010 was that

---

[15] See Lacity, M. and Willcocks, L. (2012) Advanced Outsourcing Practice: Rethinking ITO, BPO, and Cloud Services, Palgrave, London.

[16] Figures from Willcocks, L. Cullen, S. and Craig, A. (2011) *The Outsourcing Enterprise: From Cost Management to Collaborative Innovation.* Palgrave, London.

there had been rapid BPO expansion, but that there remained still massive untapped potential growth for the BPO market.

Of all the outsourcing variants, offshoring saw much the fastest growth in the first decade of the new century. With its head start, scale, and a group of major providers, by 2014 India continued to dominate the global market. But at the same time, other countries have been actively offering services, and developing their outsourcing services industries dynamically, most of them with government backing.

One small market, that for ASP (application service provision), is also worth commenting on here. Concerned with delivering applications, infrastructure and services on a rental basis over the internet, this phenomenon (which we dubbed 'netsourcing') grew in the 1997-2001 period. It then fell away with the bursting of the internet bubble. From about 2008, it was resurrected in newer forms with the growing interest in 'cloud computing' - including amongst big product as well as providers.[17] In the current decade, ASP has proliferated into many derivatives of 'XaaS' (e.g., SaaS - software as a service, PaaS - platform as a service, IaaS - infrastructure as a service). Business Process as a Service (BPaaS) is any type of horizontal or vertical business process delivered via the cloud services model.

We predict that BPaaS will actually take off over a longer period than many suggest, and will complement as well as partly cannibalize the BPO/ITO service industries, while simultaneously changing their configuration.

---

[17] See Willcocks, L., Venters, W. And Whitley, E. (2014) *Moving To The Cloud Corporation: Gamechange 2014-2025*. Palgrave, London.

The Evolution of Outsourcing: Still on the Learning Curve

Looking back over our short history of outsourcing, rapid growth has had several impacts.

One is that clients and providers alike have had to run very fast to catch up with the latest twists in the market and new sources of competition and value. Senior executives have been short on time to think through long-term issues and requirements, even though that is precisely what sourcing strategy requires. Finding out what works and what does not has, perhaps too often, been a 'suck-it-and-see' experience. When one is committing to what can be a long large-scale contract, this is not necessarily the optimal way to proceed. Thirdly, creating a body of knowledge about outsourcing (in terms of governance, contracting, measurement, processes, relationship practices), is still very much work in progress, although we would like to believe we have made in this book, and our previous work, substantive contributions in this area. Fourthly, and another reason why the present book has been written, the outsourcing industry is still at the early stages of professionalizing itself. The benefits of professionalization in terms of, standard practices, codes of conduct, minimum standards of competence, an understanding of roles required, and what it takes to fill them, are not really with us yet. We hope we are contributing to these developments in this book.

Throughout this short history, there has been much learning and evolution by clients and providers alike. We capture the main parameters in Figure 0-1, developed originally by Rottman and Lacity.[18]

---

[18] Rottman, J. and Lacity, M. (2006) "Proven Practices for Effectively Offshoring IT Work," *Sloan Management Review*, Vol. 47, 3, 56-63.

Figure 0-1: The Outsourcing Learning Curve

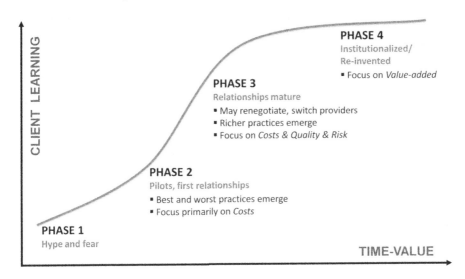

CLIENT LEARNING

PHASE 4
Institutionalized/
Re-invented
• Focus on *Value-added*

PHASE 3
Relationships mature
• May renegotiate, switch providers
• Richer practices emerge
• Focus on *Costs & Quality & Risk*

PHASE 2
Pilots, first relationships
• Best and worst practices emerge
• Focus primarily on *Costs*

PHASE 1
Hype and fear

TIME-VALUE

Figure 0-1 captures the voyage of discovery that clients have been on. A client contemplating its first generation outsourcing arrangement will typically be at Phase 1. In our research, we have seen such clients either believing far too much of what they read in marketing brochures and hear from providers pitching for work, or far too disbelieving and skeptical of what to expect. Either approach has not proven to be a sound basis for entering into an outsourcing relationship.

In Phase 2, clients tend to focus mainly on cost, and usually pass through a baptism of hard learning. In all outsourcing arrangements, at any time in a client's evolution, risk mitigation is central. Interestingly, we found what seemed at first a surprising number of the 1990s deals had been relatively, if quietly, successful. The characteristics of these deals were:

- They had limited objectives, usually just related to cost and service.

- They typically outsourced only 20-30% of the budget only, thus retaining a lot of inhouse capability.

- They outsourced stable, discrete activities they could write complete contracts for, on three to five year contracts to multiple providers.

This remains a good starting point for clients wishing to build their learning incrementally through the actual experience of outsourcing. Once requisite organizational capability has been built, much more scale, complexity, and sophistication becomes possible.

A client will learn much from its first generation outsourcing deal, and this can be put to good use for the second generation. We have found most clients sticking with incumbent providers (though sometimes bringing some work back inhouse), building up more retained capability, getting smarter on contracts, and about what was realistically attainable through outsourcing. Ironically though, some clients did not build on their learning. Scarred by their first outsourcing encounter, they did something completely different in their second, and sometimes different again in their third generation deals.

Clients that have reached Phase 3 in Figure 0-1 are older and wiser, and are able to get the balance of contract and relationship management right, have secured the right internal capabilities to keep control of their outsourcing destiny, and focus on leveraging the relationship with their providers. By 2014, we found up to 20% of clients had reached Phase 4 of their journey.

There are multiple reasons why so many clients have progressed quite slowly, often painfully up the learning curve. Key people learn, and then they leave. Organizational learning is not institutionalized. Nor is learning on one type of outsourcing routinely transferred and applied to another. Objectives change and new forms of outsourcing and contracts are entered into with new providers, and a client moves down the learning curve once more. Moreover, clients seem to prefer what we call 'hard learning'. Unless they have experienced it themselves, they never quite believe, let alone enact, the advice they get. This brief history indicates that each client will, at any one moment in time, inhabit its own distinctive place on the learning curve. Within each client, that learning will tend to be more advanced in some outsourcing areas (e.g. domestic equipment support) than it is for others (e.g. offshoring).

This book aims at getting a client to an advanced stage of Phase 3, and prepared to move to Phase 4. To achieve this, the book distills the key learnings and lessons from the comprehensive longitudinal case research we have carried out on over 2000 outsourcing arrangements on a global basis between 1989 and the end of 2013. Studying cases over time (we have research some outsourcing arrangements over three generations), gives us unique insight into what works, what does not, what outcomes are achieved, under what conditions, what people and capabilities are needed, timing issues, and how productive relationships can be constructed over several years. Moreover, when combined, this research base covers all major economic and government sectors, including financial services, energy and utilities, defence/aerospace, retail, telecoms and IT, oil, transportation, central, state and local government, health care, industrial products and chemicals, and is drawn from medium, large and multinational organizations based in Europe, USA and Asia Pacific. The key lessons and emerging practices from this research are presented in this book.

Sometimes, we are asked, "*Are you for, or against, outsourcing?*" The question ignores the pervasiveness of outsourcing practice; whether we are 'for or against' it is irrelevant. What interests us more are the bigger questions surrounding sourcing as a whole. The real managerial question we have asked ourselves for the present book, as researchers and advisers is, "*When does outsourcing become an effective approach to achieving organizational objectives?*" The answers, for us, have to be evidence-based. In this book, we have formulated the key lessons and effective practices based on what we consider as the admissible evidence. Enjoy the book, the value, and the increased performance you will get from using it.

About this Book

While 55% of the academic literature focuses on why clients make outsourcing decisions[19], this is not the focus of this book. Outsourcing has become a routine part of management, yet it remains far from easy. In general, the concept of using external providers is considered an efficient and logical way to get things done, and is indeed widely accepted in many sectors of the economy.

However, the learning curve is significant, involves considerable hard work by both parties on a daily basis, and results are highly dependent on the capabilities of the parties involved. This book has been designed to accelerate your learning curve, by focusing on crucial activities that make a difference between success and disappointment.

This book offers real solutions, requiring real work - no silver bullets here.

The book is set out into three parts:

Part 1 - Key Concepts, Chapter 1 summarizes the last 20 years of research into outsourcing and its determinants. Chapter 2 moves outsourcing up the CEO's agenda as a strategic issue. Chapter 3 provides the latest research on core competences, both of the client and provider organizations. Chapter 4 runs through the seven vital structural decisions that you must make regarding outsourcing.

Part 2 - Action Program is dedicated to the critical actions throughout the Outsourcing Lifecycle. Chapter 5 introduces the concept. Chapter 6 covers the first Architect Phase where you make the key outsourcing decisions and design the deal. Chapter 7 is the Engage Phase, where you select the provider/s and negotiate the deal. Chapter 8 is about transition and management, where all the work done

---

[19] Dibbern, J., et al. (2004) "Information Systems Outsourcing: A Survey and Analysis of the Literature", *The Data Base for Advances in Information Systems*, 35:4, 6-102.

in the previous phases come to fruition (or not, if work in the previous phases were lacking). Chapter 9, the Regenerate Phase, helps you plan the end of one lifecycle and the start of the next, and decide on the options for the next generation. Chapter 10 presents the journey of seven organizations through the lifecycle and the lessons they learnt.

Part 3 - Emerging Areas, we highlight a few of the most interesting areas of current research that are emerging. Chapter 11 explains the human side of outsourcing, with the latest research on individual values and behaviors, showing clear 'personality' divergence between the parties, and between clients. Chapter 12 examines bundling up work to sole providers. Innovation, and how to achieve it comprises Chapter 13. The frontlines of offshoring - the fastest growing segment of the outsourcing market - are examined in Chapter 14. In Chapter 15, we highlight ideas whose time has come including diamond versus pyramid organizational structures, the cloud, and impact sourcing.

PART 1: KEY CONCEPTS

Part 1 presents, what we believe, to be 'perennials' - the enduring concepts that have changed little in the 30 years we have been researching and practicing.

We begin by summarizing the last 20 years of academic research in Chapter 1, focusing on the outsourcing decisions and determinants of success. The importance of outsourcing in achieving organizational goals requires top management focus and capabilities; thus, in Chapter 2 we lay out the role of the CEO in driving successful outsourcing.

It is not just the CEO of the client organizations, of course, that drives successful outsourcing. It requires management capabilities at all levels within both the client and the provider. Chapter 3 addresses these capabilities.

Our final key concept, that of configuration, is explained in Chapter 4. Configuration represents the seven vital structural decisions that all outsourcing arrangements require; and which must be made early, strategically, and at the highest level.

Chapter 1   Compilation of Research from the Last 20 Years

"Take nothing as it looks, take everything on evidence"

Charles Dickens

In this chapter, we review the research conducted into outsourcing. We will examine sourcing decisions for products first, because that topic was what economists studied first. So, how do manufacturing companies decide whether to make or buy component parts? During the 1970s, economists studied sourcing decisions in the U.S. automobile industry. One study examined the sourcing for 133 automotive components by General Motors and Ford for U.S. production in 1976. Based on data from these two automotive manufacturers, the researchers found that both companies preferred making their own components when the components were firm-specific (i.e. highly customized) and when their design must be highly coordinated with other systems.[20] Another study of sourcing decisions in 69 manufacturing companies for four years of data (1958, 1963, 1967, and 1972), found that companies insource when the product is 'research intensive' and when there are a small number of providers in the market.[21]

---

[20] Source: Monteverde, K. and Treece, D. (1982) "Supplier Switching Costs and Vertical Integration in the Automobile Industry," *The Bell Journal of Economics*, Vol. 13, 1, 206-213.

[21] Source: Levy, D. (1985) "The Transactions Cost Approach to Vertical Integration: An Empirical Examination," *The Review of Economics and Statistics*, Vol. 67, 3, 438-445.

These studies tell us that the attributes of the product (organization-specific, degree of customization, and research intensity) and attributes of the market (availability and quality of providers) are important factors in making sourcing decisions for products. They are also important factors in making outsourcing decisions for services.

Outsourcing is not just shifting from internal provision to providers; it is also about sourcing for the first time with providers. Cloud services provide one great example. Increasingly, many new enterprises we are studying are simply 'born in the cloud'. Since the dot.com bubble burst, investors are reluctant to dole out large amounts of cash for start-ups to build an IT infrastructure. Increasingly, venture capitalists and angel investors expect start-ups to acquire IT capabilities as a service. Cloud services help entrepreneurs avoid capital costs, enable rapid business deployment, and reserve funding for staff focused on the core business.

Finally, outsourcing is not limited to component parts or to business support services. Sometimes entire operations are outsourced. Consider, for example, governments that outsource everything they do from policy to services for prisons, hospitals, aged care, parks, and even entire islands. With banks, all of the operations for cash management, ATMs, mortgage initiations and settlements, front office (branches), treasury, in addition to the standard back office (processing, document management, and call centers) may be outsourced.

Thus far, we have discussed that clients make sourcing decisions about products and services and the simple choice between make or buy. Of course, reality is much more complex than this. In this chapter, we answer the fundamental questions, "*What are the sourcing options besides make or buy? What determines the likelihood an organization will choose each option?*" All of these questions have been rigorously examined by scholars across many disciplines, including economics, business strategy, information systems, and international business. We present the most recent and robust findings from research.

Academics have thoroughly studied the motivations, influences, and attributes of the product or service that determine sourcing decisions. Researchers have also thoroughly studied the outcomes of outsourcing. Overall, the academic evidence finds that outsourcing can deliver value to clients, but that it takes a tremendous amount of detailed management by both parties to realize expected benefits.

Researchers have identified that the capabilities of both parties, configuration, and the quality of both the contract and relationship all determine outsourcing outcomes. Despite all that researchers do know about outsourcing, there are still knowledge gaps and enduring practitioner challenges. We address many of these challenges throughout this book.

In this chapter, we examine the research relating to three research streams as shown in Figure 1-1:

- sourcing choices - internal, external and hybrid service provision,

- determinants of sourcing choices - that affect the likelihood that a client would outsource, and

- determinants of sourcing outcomes - that affect the degree of success that outsourcing achieves.

Figure 1-1: Sourcing Choices and Outcomes

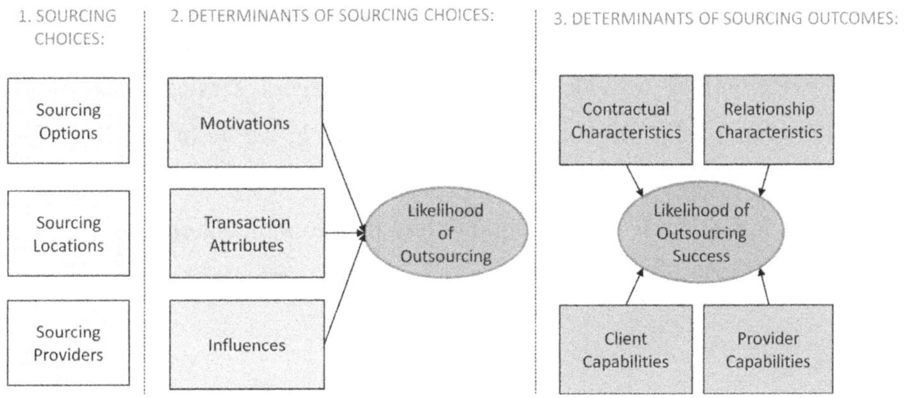

1.1   Sourcing Choices

The most fundamental sourcing decision is the 'make-or-buy' decision, *"Should we insource or outsource business services?"* In reality, this decision is more complex because there are many sourcing options, sourcing locations, and providers to be considered. For over two decades, we have argued that a better question is, *"How can organizations leverage the external services market for business advantage?"* Many academics, informed closely by both theory and practice, have good answers to this question. In this section, we discuss sourcing options, sourcing locations, and other decisions executives consider when making sourcing decisions. These choices have different benefits and risks and may require unique practices to ensure positive outcomes.

1.1.1   Sourcing Options

Executives have numerous sourcing options to consider including insourcing, staff augmentation, management consulting, shared services, traditional outsourcing, cloud services, and joint ventures/partnerships.

The sourcing options are not mutually exclusive and many clients use hybrids. Many internal shared services organizations, for example, rely heavily on external providers. Many traditional outsourcing arrangements include both staff augmentation as well as fee-for-service pricing components. Many joint ventures also have fee-for-service components for services the venture delivers to the client investor. Executives provide a portfolio of business services that, in turn, necessitate a portfolio of sourcing options (which we term **configuration**). Chapter 4 lays out the high level configuration options when considering outsourcing, but for now we highlight a few of the main internal, external, and hybrid options as shown in Table 1-1, and explain in some detail below it.

Table 1-1: Sourcing Options

	Sourcing Options	Description
Internal	Inhouse provision, insourcing	A sourcing option in which a client owns the assets and employs their own staff.
	Shared services	A sourcing option in which a client centralizes and standardizes delivery of business services that are shared among several business units.
Hybrid	Staff augmentation, contract labor	A sourcing option in which a client buys in low to mid-level labor to supplement inhouse capabilities; the client manages the people, usually at the client site.
	Management consulting	A sourcing option in which a client buys in high-level expertise to supplement inhouse capabilities.
	Joint ventures, strategic partnerships	A specific type of arrangement entered into by two or more parties in which each agrees to furnish a part of the capital and labor for a business enterprise in a separate entity (joint venture) or under a contract (partnership).
External	Traditional outsourcing, fee-for-service outsourcing	A sourcing option in which a client pays a fee to a provider in exchange for the management and delivery of specified products or services. The client is in charge of specifying needs and the provider is in charge of managing the resources to deliver those needs.
	Cloud services	With this utility model, clients pay a usage-based fee to providers in exchange for services being delivered over the Internet.
	Crowdsourcing	A sourcing option that invites open calls to an unknown population to perform tasks; the crowd may be rewarded with financial compensation and/or personal recognition.

Insourcing is still the most common sourcing option. In 2012, the research firm IDC estimated that among Fortune 500 companies, only $68 billion of $1.3 trillion of non-core cost base was outsourced. For IT spend, the Society of Information Management's annual survey of Chief Information Officers (CIOs) conducted by Jerry Luftman typically found that about 33% of an annual IT budget was for internal staff, compared to 9% for consulting services, 15% for domestic contractors/providers and 3%-4% for offshore providers.[22] Increased use of

---

[22] Luftman's surveys may be found in: Luftman, J. and Derkson, B. (2012) "Key Issues for IT Executives 2012: Doing More with Less," *MIS Quarterly Executive*, Vol. 11, 4, 207-218; Luftman, J. and Zadeh, H. (2011) "Key information technology and management issues 2010–11: an

Continues on next page.

external staff (domestic and offshore) is growing and gains more public attention than the quieter, yet larger, insourcing practice. In some clients, the sheer threat of outsourcing empowered executives to make sweeping, yet unpopular, changes to reduce internal costs through consolidation, standardization, and rationalization of resources to avoid outsourcing. The lesson for practitioners is that the external services market serves as a viable competitor that keeps inhouse staff motivated.

Shared services is defined by Accenture as, *"the consolidation of support functions (such as HR, finance, IT, and procurement) from several departments into a standalone organizational entity whose only mission is to provide services as efficiently and effectively as possible."*[23] Shared services is an important management trend and was listed as one of the seven habits of effective CIOs.[24] Economic downturns intensify pressure for organizations in both the government and commercial sectors to reduce costs, shed staff, and to 'do more with less'. Shared services are seen as a powerful practice for relieving this pressure - offering promises of lower costs, tighter controls, improved KPIs, and scalability.

However, studies have shown that not all clients achieve the benefits they expect from shared services. Many shared service initiatives take years to implement and result in meager cost savings. Among all the advanced practices for successfully implementing shared services, change management may be the most important and the most lacking in practice. Based on our case research, we found that creating shared services requires a coordinated integration of four change programs:

---

international study", *Journal of Information Technology*, Vol. 26, 193–204; Luftman, J. and Kempaiah, R. (2008) "Key Issues for IS Executives," *MIS Quarterly Executive*, Vol. 7, 2, 99-112.

[23] Accenture (2005) Driving High Performance in Government: Maximizing the Value of Public-Sector Shared Services.

[24] Andriole, S. (2007) "The 7 Habits of Highly Effective Technology Leaders" *Communications of the ACM*, Vol. 50, 67-72.

business process redesign, organizational redesign, sourcing redesign and technology enablement.[25]

With **staff augmentation,** a client buys in labor to supplement inhouse capabilities. In one of our global surveys involving 73 organizations, there was a 50/50 split between employed labor and labor under contract.[26] In any Fortune 500 company headquarters, up to 40% of the IT staff may be domestic contract laborers who works alongside employees. Clients use a staff augmentation model to meet fluctuations in demand for work, to access scarce technical skills, and to avoid the HR headaches associated with employment. Staff augmentation is one of the most expensive options bought from urban cities in developed countries. It is one of the least expensive options if bought offshore or from non-urban (rural) areas. One of the best studies on staff augmentation compared contractors to permanent employees. Overall, contract workers had lower levels of loyalty, trustworthiness, obedience, and performance than permanent workers. Contract workers also had lower task variety, identity, significance, autonomy, and feedback relative to permanent workers.[27] For our discussion on the additional options for contracting in service delivery resources, in addition to labor, see Configuration Attribute #6: Resource Ownership in Chapter 4.

Management consulting is a short-term sourcing option in which a client hires an advisory or consulting firm, typically for help with new strategic initiatives. This option brings in external energy, signals clear commitment to the strategic

---

[25] For more information on shared services, see Lacity, M. and Fox, J. (2008) "Creating Global Shared Services: Lessons from Reuters," *MIS Quarterly Executive*, Vol. 7, 1, 17-32; Lacity, M. (2012) "Creating Shared Services in Private and Public Sectors," in *Advanced Outsourcing Practice: Rethinking ITO, BPO, and Cloud Services*, Palgrave, London, 69-95.

[26] Cullen, S. (2007) "The Configuration Concept: Resource Ownership", Sourcing and Vendor Relationships Executive Update, Vol 8 No 6. Cutter Consortium, Arlington.

[27] Source: Ang, S. and Slaughter, S. (2001) "Work Outcomes and Job Design for Contract Versus Permanent Information Systems Professionals on Software Development Teams," *MIS Quarterly*, Vol. 25, 3, 321-350.

initiative, and reduces political resistance. However, management consultancy has several major risks. The two most significant ones are potential cost escalation and lack of sustainability because the consultant has no long-term commitment. The result can be a lessened sense of accountability and a lack of alignment between the parties. Furthermore, expertise and knowledge may leave when the consultant leaves.[28]

Joint Ventures/Strategic Partnerships are not very common (at 5% of outsourcing spend[29]), but the scale and scope of these deals garnered significant media attention, particularly during the 1990s. In joint ventures, the provider investor intends to sell the client's excess capacity to third parties and share the revenues with the client investor. Examples of these deals included Swiss Bank and Perot Systems, Commonwealth Bank and EDS, Xerox and EDS, and Delta Airlines and AT&T. These deals did not work as planned. The providers had their hands full just servicing the client investors' operational needs. In addition, clients frequently oversold the value and portability of their assets. The deals we studied all either reverted to traditional outsourcing relationships or were terminated. However, we have found more success with joint ventures/strategic partnerships in other areas, including procurement, HR, claims, and policy administration.[30] For our discussion on the additional options for commercial relationship structures, in addition to equity forms, see Configuration Attribute #7: Commercial Relationship in Chapter 4.

---

[28] Lacity, M., Feeny, D. and Willcocks, L. (2003) "Transforming a back-office function: Lessons from BAE Systems' experience with an enterprise partnership," *MIS Quarterly Executive*, 2, 2, 86-103.

[29] Cullen, S. (2007) "The Configuration Concept: Commercial Relationship", *Sourcing and Vendor Relationships Executive Update*, Vol 8 No 10. Cutter Consortium, Arlington.

[30] The following articles discuss successful partnerships at BAE and Lloyd's: Lacity, M., Feeny, D. and Willcocks, L. (2003) "Transforming a back-office function: Lessons from BAE Systems' Experience With an Enterprise Partnership," *MIS Quarterly Executive*, 2, 2, 86-103; Lacity, M., Feeny, D. and Willcocks, L. (2004) "Commercializing the Back Office at Lloyds of London: Outsourcing and Strategic Partnerships Revisited," *European Management Journal*, 22, 2, 127-140.

Traditional outsourcing is the most common form of outsourcing and has grown each year it has been tracked as we discussed in the Introduction. With this option, a client pays a fee to a provider in exchange for the management and delivery of specified services. The client is in charge of specifying needs (typically in a service level agreement), and the provider is in charge of managing the resources to deliver those needs. Much of the academic literature on outsourcing falls under this category, and there have been hundreds of published studies, which we reviewed. The model works best when: (a) clients have a good understanding of their current baseline and future requirements, (b) requirements are stable, (c) a capable provider is selected, and (d) the contract is designed to benefit both parties. However, outsourcing contracts are notoriously inflexible, and changes are difficult to handle because parties' incentives are not aligned. Change will usually harm one of the parties. In successful relationships, both parties resolve disputes caused by change by focusing on what is fair, rather than by what the contract decrees.

The cloud is the idea of buying business services like a utility. The concept is not new; time-sharing was the first outsourcing model back in the 1960s. During the dot.com boom, application service provision (ASP) was a business model in which providers hosted and rented standard applications to clients over the Internet. ASP was one way small clients could access expensive software while avoiding high infrastructure costs, support costs, or hefty software license fees. ASP burst when the dot.com bubble popped. Clients liked the idea of renting rather than owning resources, but providers had difficulty generating revenues because the value of contracts were too small, the duration too short, the marketing costs to educate clients about ASP too high, the margins from reselling propriety software too thin, and the transaction costs of serving so many needy clients too high.[31] Today, cloud services are the reincarnated, super-charged version of ASP. Cloud is one of

---

[31] Kern, T., Lacity, M. and Willcocks, L. (2002) *Netsourcing: Renting Business Applications and Services over a Network*, Prentice Hall, New York.

the fastest growing markets in the ITO/BPO space. According to Gartner, the cloud was a $68.3 billion industry in 2010 and predicts it will reach $148.8 billion by 2014. Despite the tremendous public attention to cloud computing, it cannot yet achieve the 'plug-and-play' simplicity of electricity.[32] See our discussion of the cloud and other developments in our Technology Spotlight (section 15.4).

Crowdsourcing is the process by which organizations source crowds of people outside the organization to perform tasks ranging from the simple to the complex. Google's use of reCAPTCHA is an example of using crowds for simple tasks like translating books, one word at a time. reCAPTCHA asks a user to type two words seen in distorted text images onscreen. One word Google already translated and one word is a distorted version of a word that an automated optical character recognition could not translate. If the user gets the known word correct, the software assumes the unknown word is also correct, and viola, the user has helped to digitize a word from a book. There are other good examples of firms using crowdsourcing to help solve complex problems, like Gold Corp's contest to help determine best opportunities to mine for gold based on very sophisticated seismic studies. Although crowdsourcing is not normally considered a viable choice to manage business services, crowdsourcing is emerging as an option to spawn innovation, build brand image, and to meaningfully engage customers. See our discussion of crowdsourcing, in addition to other rising markets, in section 15.5.

1.1.2   Sourcing Locations

Executives have to make location decisions, for example where will staff be located. Options include domestic, offshore, nearshore, rural, or global (Table 1-2). Note that location strategies may or may not involve outsourcing. For

---

[32] Willcocks, L., Venters, W. and Whitley, E. (2011) *Cloud and the Future of Business 1 - The Promise*. Accenture/LSE Outsourcing Unit, London.

example, offshore may involve outsourcing, joint ventures, strategic partnerships, or wholly-owned captive centers.

Table 1-2: Sourcing Location Decisions

Sourcing Locations	Provider Staff Location
Domestic	In the same country as the client's business users
Offshore	On a different continent than the client's business users
Nearshore	In a nearby country (such as a US client being serviced from a Canadian delivery center)
Rural	In a rural community.
Global	In several countries

Location decisions are often based on a country's business, financial, and human resource attractiveness (**location attractiveness**). A country's **business attractiveness** is the degree to which a country is attractive to clients because of favorable business environmental factors such as economic stability, political stability, cultural compatibility, infrastructure quality, and security of intellectual property. A country's **financial attractiveness** is the degree to which a country is attractive because of favorable financial factors such as labor costs, taxes, regulatory, and other costs. A country's **human resource attractiveness** is the degree to which a country is attractive because of favorable people skills and availability factors such as size of labor pool, education, language skills, experience, and attrition rates.[33]

A country's attractiveness can change rapidly, as happened with the political upheavals in Egypt in 2011 to 2013, which halted international investment in Egypt's ITO and BPO services export market. For this reason, we have advised

---

[33] For examples of location attractiveness studies, see: Malos (2009) "Regulatory Effects and Strategic Global Staffing Profiles: Beyond Cost Concerns in Evaluating Offshore Location Attractiveness," *Employee Responsibilities and Rights Journal*, Vol. 22, 113-131; Willcocks, L., Lacity, M. and Craig, A. (2013) "Compass Points: Assessing Countries," *Professional Outsourcing*, Issue 13, 22-31.

that clients base location their decisions on the organization's strategic objectives and overall commitment to certain destinations. For example, one aerospace company selected Malaysia as their IT offshore destination because they hoped to sell planes in that country. The Malaysian government requires that some of the manufacturing be done in Malaysia, and the IT presence would certainly help to meet that requirement. Another hardware company selected China because they hoped to sell computers there. Others selected offshore locations where they have existing manufacturing or R&D facilities. The existing facilities serve as a launch pad, with current employees serving as guides to the country, providers, and culture.[34]

Domestic location of staff is pursued when clients value close proximity between its service users and service delivery staff. Close physical proximity is associated with better service quality, faster response time, better domain understanding, easier communications, and lower transaction costs. However, domestic staff - whether employees, contract labor, or domestic outsourcing - is the most expensive location option in high-cost locations like urban US or UK cities.

Offshore location of staff is pursued when clients seek lower costs, sunrise-to-sunrise services, access to talent, and/or geographical risk mitigation. Western-based clients frequently select India, the Philippines, Eastern Europe, or China as offshore destinations, particularly for the lower cost and talent availability. The offshore market has been estimated to be about US$80 million to $100 billion, with India representing the largest share. Despite noise suggesting that India will lose its edge due to rising wages, the Everest Group predicted in 2011 that India would maintain its lead for 12 years under a pessimistic scenario and for 23 years under an optimistic scenario. Preferred venues change, based on a mix of location attractiveness factors, and a recent development that has seen offshore venues such

---

[34] Rottman, J. and Lacity, M. (2006) "Proven Practices for Effectively Offshoring IT Work," *Sloan Management Review,* Vol. 47, 3, 56-63.

as India subcontract work to countries like South Africa and China. Research has found that locating staff offshore can deliver on many of its promised benefits, but researchers have also found that it poses additional challenges when compared to domestic locations. For example, captive centers or offshore outsourcing are more challenging because of time zone differences, increased efforts in knowledge coordination, and boundary spanning, the need for more controls, cultural differences, defining requirements more rigorously, and difficulties in managing dispersed teams. Some of these issues are so difficult to manage that practitioners are turning to nearshore alternatives.[35] See Chapter 14 for a discussion of our research regarding offshoring.

Nearshore location of staff is pursued when the client expects to benefit from one or more of the following proximity constructs: economic, geographic, temporal (time zone), cultural, linguistic, political, and historical linkages. Nearshore locations are selected primarily because of lower costs, but are preferred to offshoring as the proximity requires less time and money to travel and provides time zone overlap between the parties. For US organizations, NAFTA (North American Free Trade Agreement) facilitates nearshoring because it is easier to obtain visas from NAFTA partners than it is to obtain visas for India-based staff.[36]

Rural location of staff is an emerging niche trend in several countries, including the US, India, China, and Israel. The Rockefeller Foundation valued the global impact sourcing market - which is primarily a rural market - at US$4.6 billion in 2010. The main appeal of rural locations stems from their lower wages and higher

---

[35] A number of studies have examined the challenges of offshoring including: Carmel, E. (2006) "Building Your Information Systems from the Other Side of the World: How Infosys Manages Time Zone Differences," *MIS Quarterly Executive*, Vol. 5, 1, 43-53; Levina, N. and Vaast, E. (2008) "Innovating or Doing as Told? Status Differences and Overlapping Boundaries in Offshore Collaboration", *MIS Quarterly*, Vol. 32, 2, 307-332; Kotlarsky, J., van Fenema, P. and Willcocks L. (2008) "Developing a Knowledge-based Perspective on Coordination: The Case of Global Software Projects," *Information and Management*, Vol. 45, 2, 96-108.

[36] Carmel, E. and Abbot, P. (2007) "Why Nearshore Means that Distance Matters," *Communications of the ACM*, Vol. 50, 10, 40-46.

retention rates because few or no competitors exist to poach talent. Within the US, rural locations can reduce costs by up to half as compared to urban locations like New York City. In India, despite the global economic recession, global demand for Indian ITO and BPO services is still very strong and consequently Indian providers are still experiencing 14% to 22% turnover in urban areas. By building delivery centers in Tier 3 cities, Indian organizations achieve lower costs and attrition rates. Chinese providers also cited lower costs, but not necessarily lower attrition rates, by locating in Tier 3 cities. Specifically, they reported that labor costs are up to 50% lower and real estate costs are 70% to 90% lower in Tier 3 cities compared to Tier 1 cities. The major downsides of rural locations are scalability and workforce availability.[37] We discuss rural sourcing, and other rising markets, in more detail in section 15.5.

Global location, having staff located delivery centers based in several countries, is the norm for large, international companies. Large global companies locate operations globally using a combination of sourcing options discussed above, including captive centers, fee-for-service outsourcing, and joint partnerships. One U.S. global financial services company we studied has various captive centers, joint ventures, and fee-for-service relationships with 14 Indian providers. This network of providers enabled the company to adapt quickly to the immense surge in mortgage applications during the refinancing boom. As the refinancing boom burst, the company was able to immediately scale back resources--all without affecting their domestic headcount. Global providers like Accenture and IBM can provide vast geographic coverage for their clients. For example, Accenture provides Microsoft with coverage in 94 countries and 37 languages, as the following case discusses.

---

[37] Lacity, M., Rottman, J. and Carmel, E. (2012) Emerging ITO and BPO Markets: Rural Sourcing and Impact Sourcing, *IEEE Readynotes*, IEEE Computer Society.

Case: Microsoft global shared services and global outsourcing[38]

Microsoft is an American multinational software corporation headquartered in Washington State that develops, manufactures, licenses, and supports a range of software products and services. In 2006, Microsoft was achieving extraordinary growth, partly by allowing a high degree of autonomy for its subsidiaries. But autonomy also resulted in high fragmentation of the company's finance, accounting, and procurement functions. Microsoft sought to standardize these processes globally with aims to reduce costs, improve service and compliance, and focus internal roles on more strategic activities. To assist Microsoft in this shared services initiative (called *OneFinance*), it partnered with Accenture in 2007.

The initial seven-year agreement spanned 90 countries and 450 individual roles. Within 18 months, the parties designed and implemented a global set of standardized processes across 92 countries, improved internal controls and compliance, improved scalability, and reduced costs by 35%. Microsoft's financial controllers were able to focus on more strategic activities. Prior to this, the controllers spent 75% of their time and resources on transactions and compliance; this dropped to 23% after outsourcing. In 2009, the scope was extended to include more accounts payable and buying center processes. The contract, now worth US$330 million, was extended until 2018. The parties then delivered an additional 20% in savings by streamlining and/or automating key procurement and accounts payable processes. The parties implemented new tools that increased transparency by allowing Microsoft's business users to see every dollar spent and timely measures on performance.

Five years in and the parties continue to innovate Microsoft's financial, accounting, and procurement processes. In 2010-2011, for example, the parties moved 25 international subsidiaries from manual invoicing to electronic invoicing, so generating millions in savings and improving accuracy. New transformation projects are planned each year.

1.1.3   Sourcing Providers

If executives decide to outsource, there are two additional decisions that follow regarding the use of providers, *"How many providers?"* and *"Do we continue this same configuration when the contract expires?"*

---

[38] Excerpt from Lacity, M. and Willcocks, L. (2012) "Mastering High-Performance: The Case of Microsoft's OneFinance".

Multi-sourcing or bundled services. When outsourcing, clients have to decide about the number of providers to engage. In one of our global surveys, the 73 respondents had 866 outsourcing providers between them. While the average number of providers was 13, the range was from 1 to 200; quite a large spread.[39] Multi-sourcing has many advantages and disadvantages, as does sole-sourcing. We discuss these in Chapter 4: Configuration along with the other forms of many versus few providers. Then in Chapter 12, we discuss a trend involving the bundling up of work into large sole-sourced BPO packages, rather than have many interdependent providers.

Next Generation. Most clients are in their second, third, and even fourth generation of outsourcing relationships. As contracts begin to mature, clients need to decide what to do next, "*Should we renegotiate the contract with the incumbent provider? Split up a sole-sourced deal? Rationalize providers? Switch providers? Backsource by bringing operations back inhouse?*" In Chapter 9, we devote considerably more attention to next generation decision-making, but there are emerging some interesting research findings.

Both economic and relationship constructs are important determinants of next generation decisions. For a provider to keep a contract, merely performing is not enough. There needs to be a good relationship and prohibitive switching. Clients renewing contracts reported high levels of product quality, service quality, relationship quality, and switching costs. Clients that switched providers reported high product and service quality, but low relationship quality and switching costs. Clients that backsourced reported low levels on all four variables.[40]

---

[39] Cullen, S. (2006) "The Configuration Concept: Supplier Grouping", *Sourcing and Vendor Relationships Executive Update*, Vol 7 No 18. Cutter Consortium, Arlington.

[40] Whitten, D. and Leidner, D. (2006) "Bringing IT Back: An Analysis of the Decision to Backsource or Switch Vendors," *Decision Sciences*, 37, 4, 605 – 621.

In one of our early surveys of US and UK CIOs, we found that 32% of clients had canceled one or more outsourcing contracts. Of these, half switched providers, a third brought the work back inhouse, and 11% ended up renegotiating the contract with the incumbent provider due to prohibitive switching costs.[41] More recently, we surveyed Australian CIOs and found that 65% re-negotiated with the incumbent, 30% switched providers, and 5% backsourced.[42]

1.2   Determinants of Sourcing Choices Made

In addition to studying the types of sourcing decisions organizations make, academics have thoroughly studied the determinants of sourcing decisions, including the motives, transaction attributes, and influence sources. These determinants are introduced below.

1.2.1   Motivations

Researchers have studied at least 27 motives or reasons driving sourcing decisions. The most frequently found motives are listed in Table 1-3.

Research has consistently found that sourcing decisions are primarily driven by the desire to reduce overall costs (usually to try to save at least 10% to 15%). Research has also found that the greater the fear of losing control, fear of losing intellectual property, or concern for security, then the more likely an organization chose insourcing.

---

[41] Lacity, M. and Willcocks, L. (2001) *Global Information Technology Outsourcing: In Search of Business Advantage*. Palgrave, UK.

[42] Willcocks, L., Cullen, S. and Craig, A. (2011) *The Outsourcing Enterprise: From Cost Management to Collaborative Innovation*, Palgrave, UK.

Table 1-3: Top Motives for Sourcing Decisions

Motives	Description
Cost reduction	A client's desire or need to reduce or control costs.
Core focus	A client's desire or need to focus on its core capabilities.
Access to skills	A client's desire or need to access provider skills / expertise.
Business process improvements	A client's desire or need to help improve an organization's business, processes, or capabilities.
Technical reasons	A client's desire or need to gain access to leading edge technology available through the providers but not available inhouse.
Political reasons	A client stakeholder's desire or need to promote personal agendas such as eliminating a burdensome function, enhancing their career, or maximizing personal financial benefits.
Concern for security/ Intellectual property	A client's concerns about security of information, trans-border data flow issues, and protection of intellectual property.
Fear of losing control	A client's concerns about losing control over the business service.

Besides cost savings, research has found that clients expect outsourcing to deliver a number of additional business benefits, including one or more of the following (see Figure 1-2):

- ability to redirect inhouse staff on more strategic activities,

- access to scarce skill sets,

- service quality improvements,

- business process improvements, and

- technology upgrades.

Figure 1-2: Motivations to Outsource[43]

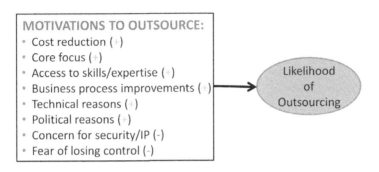

1.2.2   Transaction Attributes

Researchers have examined at least 14 transaction attributes as potential determinants of sourcing decisions. Four attributes were commonly found to drive sourcing decisions: uncertainty, critical role of the product or service, transaction costs, and business risks (Table 1-4). Higher values placed on any of these four attributes by organizations in the research were associated with higher frequencies of insourcing (Figure 1-3).

Table 1-4: Transaction Attributes Affecting Sourcing Decisions

Attributes	Description
Uncertainty	The degree of unpredictability / volatility as it relates to the requirements, emerging technologies, and/or environmental factors.
Critical Role of Product or Service	The degree to which a client views the product or service as a critical enabler of business success.
Transaction Costs	The effort, time, and costs incurred in searching, creating, negotiating, monitoring, and enforcing a contract between the parties.
Business Risk	The probability that an action will adversely affect a client

---

[43] A '+' denotes that research has consistently found a positive relationship between this and a client outsourcing (i.e. a client that had this objective, had outsourced). A '-' denotes a negative relationship to a client outsourcing.

Figure 1-3: Transaction Attributes

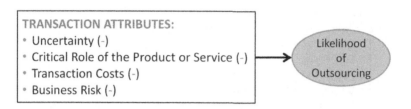

1.2.3   Influences

Researchers have studied the extent to which mimetic, normative, and coercive influences determine clients' sourcing decisions (Table 1-5).[44] Among these, only mimetic influences were repeatedly examined and found to significantly influence sourcing decisions.   Mimetic influences arise from the perception that peer organizations are more successful, and that by modeling itself on peer organizations, the mimicking client aims to achieve similar results.   In the ITO context, researchers found that clients were influenced to outsource based on peer institutions that successfully outsourced IT.[45]

Table 1-5: Influence Sources

Type	Description
Mimetic	Influences that arise from the perception that peer organizations are more successful.
Normative	Influences arising from norms of professionalism, including formal education and professional and trade associations.
Coercive	Influences that result from both formal and informal pressures exerted on a client by other organizations upon which they are dependent.

[44] For a discussion on the three types of influence sources, see DiMaggio, P. and Powell, W. (1991) "The Iron Cage Revisited: Institutional Isomorphism and Collective Rationality in Organizational Fields," in *The New Institutionalism in Organizational Analysis*, University of Chicago Press, 63-82.

[45] For an example of an empirical test of influence sources on ITO decisions, see: Ang, S. and Cummings, L. (1997) "Strategic Response to Institutional Influences on Information Systems Outsourcing," *Organization Science*, Vol. 8, 3, 235-256.

1.3 Determinants of Outsourcing Outcomes

Based on our review of the empirical research, we extracted what we call robust practices - practices that have been academically tested and proven effective. These practices are grouped into four categories: Contractual Characteristics, Relational Characteristics, Client Retained Capabilities, and Provider Capabilities.

1.3.1 Contractual Characteristics

Contractual characteristics are the formal, written rules embodied in the outsourcing contract. In the scholarly works we reviewed, contractual characteristics (see Table 1-6) were frequently described as degree of **contract detail** (e.g. the types of clauses, number of KPIs), **contract duration** (how long the contract is to run for), **contract value** (how much it is worth), and **price model** (e.g. fixed price, time and materials).

Table 1-6: Contractual Characteristics

Characteristic	Description
Contract Detail	The number or degree of detailed clauses in the outsourcing contract, such as clauses that specify prices, service levels, benchmarking, warranties, and penalties for non-performance.
Contract Duration	The duration of the contract in terms of time.
Contract Value	The contract's financial value usually measured as the total value over its duration (see Configuration Attribute #3: Financial Scale).
Price Model	A term denoting different forms of contracts used in outsourcing, predominately based on the price model (see Configuration Attribute #4: Pricing Framework).

Substantial evidence finds that (a) more detailed contracts, (b) mid-term contracts and (c) higher-dollar valued contracts are significantly associated with positive outsourcing outcomes (see Figure 1-4).

Figure 1-4 : Contract Characteristics Effect

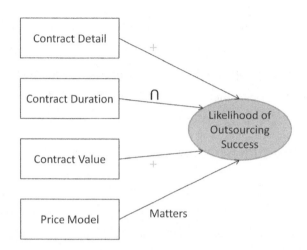

Contract Details. Detailed contracts that defined the service scope, prices, KPIs, responsibilities of both parties, and prescribed how parties would adapt to changes in character, volume, or best practices had better outcomes than contracts with fewer details. One study used three categories and found that clients who signed 'tight' contracts had higher rates of success than clients who signed strategic alliances or 'loose' contracts.[46] In this book, Building Block 4 - Design in the Outsourcing Lifecycle (Chapter 6) is devoted to designing good contract details.

Contract Duration. Mid-term contracts in the three-to-five-year range experienced successful outcomes more frequently than contracts with greater than five years duration or contracts shorter than three years (see Figure 1-5). Contracts that are too short in duration may not attract serious bids because providers know they cannot recoup upfront investment, transaction, and transition costs in such a brief period of time. Contracts can also be too long in that relationships can become stale and the initial operating agreements can become obsolete as business and technologies evolve over time.

---

[46] Lacity, M. and Willcocks, L. (1998) "An empirical investigation of information technology sourcing practices: Lessons from experience," *MIS Quarterly,* Vol. 22, 3, 363-408.

Figure 1-5: Contract Duration and Outsourcing Performance

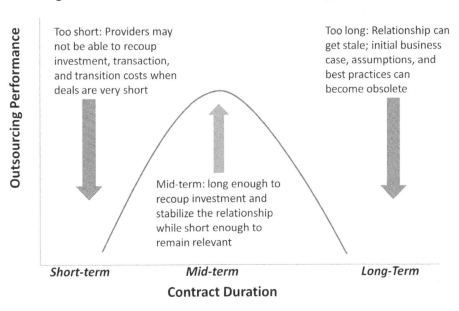

Too short: Providers may not be able to recoup investment, transaction, and transition costs when deals are very short

Too long: Relationship can get stale; initial business case, assumptions, and best practices can become obsolete

Mid-term: long enough to recoup investment and stabilize the relationship while short enough to remain relevant

Outsourcing Performance

Short-term   Mid-term   Long-Term

Contract Duration

Contract Value. Higher-valued contracts perform better than lesser-valued contracts because the transaction costs associated with outsourcing are spread over a greater volume of work.

Price Model. Denotes different forms of contracts according to the price model adopted. Examples from the literature include fixed-price, time & materials (T&M), and fee-for-service. Various researchers describe contracts differently across a number of studies, so it is difficult to generalize the likelihood of success other than to say that the price model mattered in many studies. In one study, different price models motivated providers differently. In the offshore context, clients reported that T&M contracts produced better work, but at greater expense to the client. Providers were not pressured to take shortcuts in order to protect their profit margins as they were with fixed-price deals. But some providers placed new staff on client accounts because the client (in effect) subsidized the employee's learning curve under T&M contracts. Ironically, provider staff who are unproductive take more hours to complete a task, which generates greater provider revenues.[47] In another study, the price model was either fixed price or T&M and the authors found that uncertainty about the client's requirements were associated with T&M contracts. They also found that provider profits were higher for T&M contracts than for fixed-priced ones.[48]

1.3.2   Relationship Characteristics

Relational characteristics reflect how the relationship is viewed and operates. In the scholarly works we reviewed, this was most frequently seen as effective knowledge sharing, communication, trust, and viewing the provider as a partner (see Table 1-7 and Figure 1-6).

Table 1-7: Relationship Characteristics

Characteristic	Description
Effective Knowledge Sharing	The degree to which the parties are successful in sharing and transferring knowledge.
Partnership View	The client's view of providers as trusted partners rather than as opportunistic providers.
Prior Working Relationship	The situation under which the parties have previously worked.
Communication	The degree to which parties are willing to openly discuss their expectations, directions for the future, their capabilities, and/or their strengths and weaknesses.
Trust	The confidence in the other party's benevolence.

---

[47] Lacity, M. and Rottman, J. (2008) *Offshore Outsourcing of IT Work*, Palgrave, UK.

[48] Gopal, A., et al. (2003) "Contracts in Offshore Software Development: An Empirical Analysis," *Management Science,* 49, 12, 1671-1683.

Figure 1-6: Relationship Characteristics Effects

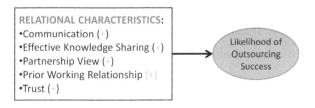

In 94% of the findings, the research showed that better relationships were associated with higher levels of success. In some ways, the findings are trivial. Few people would argue that withholding knowledge, closed communications, or distrust would lead to better relationships. A more interesting research finding is that contracts and relationships serve as complements, in that both need to be strong to produce positive outsourcing outcomes.[49]   In general, they are not substitutes in that a poorly crafted contract cannot be overcome with friendly, communicative, and trusting account managers. Poor contracts, we have found, generally make for poor relationships.

1.3.3   Client Capabilities

Research has found that clients must learn to manage differently after outsourcing in order to achieve expected benefits and have many capabilities (see Table 1-8). Clients must become good at managing providers by shifting their capabilities from managing resources and processes to managing inputs and outputs. This is not an easy transition for many clients. The **supplier management capability**

---

[49] Many excellent studies have examined the effects of relational governance on outsourcing outcomes, including: Goo, J., et al. (2009) "The role of service level agreements in relational management of information technology outsourcing: An empirical study," *MIS Quarterly,* Vol. 33, 1, 1-28; Poppo, L. and Zenger, T. (2002) "Do Formal Contracts and Relational Governance Function as Substitutes or Complements?" *Strategic Management Journal,* Vol. 23, 707-725; Wüllenweber, K., et al. (2008) "The Impact of Process Standardization on Business Process Outsourcing Success," *Information Systems Frontiers,* Vol. 10, 2, 211-224.

was often found to be lacking in clients and seen as a major reason to explain negative outsourcing outcomes. Clients also need a strong **contract negotiation capability**, which is frequently supplemented with the aid of advisory firms. **Technical and methodological capability** is another important client retained capability. This is an operational capability needed by both parties in order to coordinate work effectively. Indeed, process standardization and maturity are two of the key enablers of global outsourcing.[50]

Clients must learn to understand, accept, and adapt to cultural differences between themselves and their providers (**cultural distance management capability**). Clients also need to be able to identify, rate, and mitigate potential risks associated with outsourcing (**risk management capability**). Other client capabilities have been identified as affecting outsourcing decisions and outcomes: absorptive capacity, readiness, change management capability, HR management capability, and transition management capability. Clearly, outsourcing is not about abdicating management responsibility, but about managing differently.

Table 1-8: Client Capabilities

Capability	Description
Supplier management	The extent to which a client is able to effectively manage providers.
Contract negotiation	The extent to which a client is able to effectively bid, select, and negotiate effective contracts with providers.
Technical/ methodological	A client's maturity level regarding technical or process related standards (e.g. the Capability Maturity Model (CMM), Capability Maturity Model Integrated (CMMI), IT Infrastructure Library (ITIL), and best practices such as component reuse and playbook development.
Cultural distance management	The extent to which the client understands, accepts, and adapts to cultural differences between the parties.
Risk management	A client's practice of identifying, rating, and mitigating potential risks associated with outsourcing.

---

[50] Davenport, T. (2005) "The Coming Commoditization of Processes," *Harvard Business Review*, Vol. 83, 6, 101-108.

1.3.4 Provider Capabilities

Which provider capabilities contribute to positive outsourcing outcomes? The three most frequently studied and most important provider firm capabilities were **human resource management capability, technical and methodological capability**, and **domain understanding** (see Table 1.10). A provider's ability to identify, acquire, develop, and deploy human resources to achieve both provider's and client's organizational objectives was found to positively and significantly affect client outcomes 95% of the time it was examined. Clients often engage providers because of their superior human resources in terms of both number and quality of staff. The provider's Technical and Methodological Capability was the second most frequently studied capability, and it was found to affect outcomes positively. Domain Understanding is the extent to which a provider has prior experience and/or understanding of the client organization's business and technical contexts, processes, practices, and requirements.

Other provider capabilities were also found to be important: client management capability, managing client expectations, provider employee performance, risk management capability, security, privacy and confidentiality capability, provider's core competencies, absorptive capacity, environmental capability, and corporate social responsibility capability. Providers are unlikely to excel in all of these areas, but better capabilities lead to better outcomes.

Table 1-9: Provider Capabilities

Capability	Description
Human resource management	A provider's ability to identify, acquire, develop, and deploy human resources to achieve both parties' organizational objectives.
Technical/ methodological	A provider's level of maturity in terms of technical or process related standards (e.g. CMM, CMMI, ITIL), and best practices such as component reuse and development of playbooks.
Domain understanding	The extent to which a provider has prior experience and/or understanding of the client's business and technical contexts, processes, practices, and requirements.

In considering both client and provider capabilities, the one overlapping capability identified in the prior research was the technical/methodological capability (see Figure 1-7). Both parties benefit from a maturity and standardization of technologies and methods, so that work can be readily coordinated among parties.

Figure 1-7: Client and Provider Capabilities Identified by Prior Research

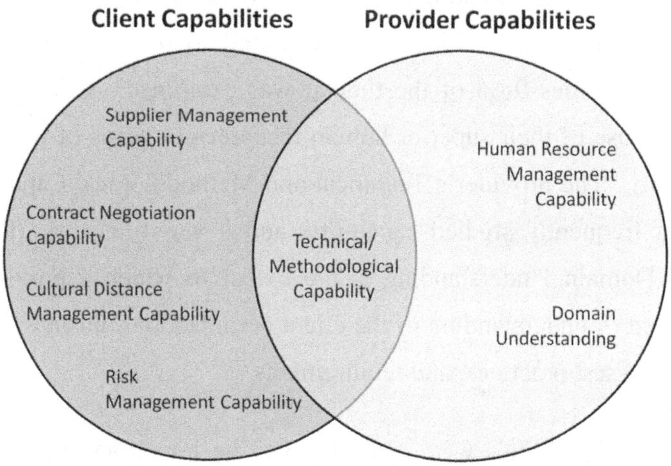

Our own research suggests that clients and providers need more than just the seven capabilities identified in Figure 1-7. In Chapter 3, we present a comprehensive set of management capabilities for both clients and providers which leads to the ultimate goal of competence.

1.4   Summary

We have consistent evidence as to what motivates sourcing decisions:

- Executives want to reduce costs, to focus on core capabilities, and to inject organizations with provider resources such as skills, expertise, and superior technology to improve client performance.

- Executives are more likely to insource activities that have high levels of uncertainty, criticality, business risks, and transaction costs.

On the determinants of outcomes, overall we know that the characteristics of the contract and the relationship are important, and that both clients and providers need strong complementary capabilities to make outsourcing successful.

Outsourcing has almost become a routine part of management. Twenty years of research establishes the common denominator that outsourcing requires detailed oversight. Outsourcing itself is not a panacea to a client's challenges, but represents a different way of managing products and services. Much depends on experiential learning and sheer hard work by clients and providers alike on a daily basis.

Our own work on management practice suggests that executives must climb a significant learning curve (see Figure 0-1 in the Introduction) and build key inhouse capabilities in order to successfully exploit outsourcing opportunities. They need to accept that outsourcing is not about giving up management but managing in a different way. Outsourcing also needs focus at the highest level of organizations right up to the CEO. The benefits that outsourcing can bring, and the risks that it can harbor, requires that the CEO plays a key role; and this provides us with the subject of the next chapter.

Chapter 2   Moving to the CEO's Strategic Agenda

"He that would be a leader, must be a bridge"

Welsh Proverb

2.1   Reasons Outsourcing must Move up the CEO Agenda

Why should hard-pressed CEOs devote attention to outsourcing? Because a substantial, and rapidly rising, amount of most large organizations' cost base is already with outsourcing providers. Because getting large-scale outsourcing wrong can seriously damage the business. And because, from now, outsourcing is part of any future strategy.

The evidence from our research shows clearly that outsourcing (properly planned, resourced, and managed) can deliver significant competitive advantage to companies and organizations in all sectors. But only when the CEO plays a key role by taking crucial strategic decisions, creating vital capabilities, putting in place integrated management processes and applying effective monitoring and evaluating mechanisms. Let's look at these issues in more detail.

Our research points to five reasons why outsourcing must now move up the CEO agenda.[51]

Reason 1 - Outsourcing affects market value

Share price is a fundamental barometer of company performance. Previous research,[52] as well as our own case histories, has identified a significant correlation between companies that outsource their infrastructure or back offices and a positive stock market response. Investors consider outsourcing as an important, and generally favorable, variable when assessing a company's worth. In our experience, the announcement of large-scale outsourcing regularly has a positive effect on share price that can last between three and ten months. Outsourcing is seen as a sign of active investment and management on the part of the firm.

That said, the opposite can occur if the market perceives outsourcing to be an inadequate measure given the scale of difficulties involved, where the deal seems to be flawed or hastily contrived, or where the CEO and organization ultimately fail to deliver the financial results stated (or implied) in the initial announcement. The danger for the CEO is being swayed by short-term share price concerns and signing a large, long-term deal in order to try to shift the share price or to buy time, rather than focusing on the fundamental business logic of the outsourcing deal. Long-term contracts signed for short-term reasons invariably bring about major disappointments for CEOs, their companies, and their shareholders.

---

[51] Recent distillations of this research include Willcocks, L. and Lacity, M. (2009) *The Practice of Outsourcing: from Information Systems To BPO and Offshoring* (Palgrave, London); Lacity, M. and Willcocks, L. (2009) *Information Systems and Outsourcing: Studies In Theory and Practice* (Palgrave, London); Oshri, I., Kotlarsky, J. and Willcocks, L. (2012) *Handbook of Global Outsourcing and Offshoring* (Palgrave, London).

[52] See for example. Loh, L. and Venkatraman, N. (1992) *Stock Market Reaction to IT Outsourcing: An Event Study*, MIT Working Paper 3499-92BPS.

Reason 2 - Outsourcing is pervasive and growing. The spend alone needs attention

Outsourcing makes up a substantial and rapidly increasing proportion of expenditure in corporations and government agencies alike. On our figures, global ITO outsourcing revenues exceeded $US270 billion by end of 2010 and are scheduled to rise at 5-8% per annum to 2015. Global BPO revenues, in areas such as HR, procurement, back office administration, call centers, finance and accounting, were over $165 billion by 2010 and likely to rise by 8-12% per annum through 2011-2014. Meanwhile, as part of this, offshore outsourcing exceeded $60 billion revenues in 2010, and is set to grow at a faster rate over the next five years. By 2013, as we saw in the Introduction, the total size of the BPO and ITO services markets was approaching $952 billion, with ITO worth $648 billion and BPO $304 billion in revenues that year. Compound annual growth between 2013-2017 is expected to be between 3.5% and 5.5%.

Clients are choosing to outsource more and more and for a variety of reasons: to get more quickly to market, to cut costs, or to leverage the increasing capabilities of providers, to name a few. For many clients, outsourcing is well above the parapet in sheer expenditure terms. Outsourcing is not a fad, but a substantial part of corporate and government expenditure, needing top team oversight and management. However, too often in practice, this process happens incrementally, as a response to immediate market conditions and specific opportunities to cut costs, rather than based on long-term strategic thinking. CEOs, if they have not already done so, need to put such large spending on to a much more strategic footing.

Reason 3 - Outsourcing can enable or disable business strategy

The outsourcing highway is littered with casualties. We have seen even experienced clients repeatedly running into massive problems, suffering from slow organizational learning, and working in a reactive rather than an anticipatory mode.[53]

Here are some 21st century examples:

- In 2000, UK retailer Sainsburys signed a 7-year $US3.25 billion deal with Accenture to outsource its IT operations. By late 2004, the deal had been renegotiated twice, and Sainsbury had announced a 2004/2005 write-off of $254 million of IT assets, and a further $218 million write-off of automated depot and supply chain IT. The way forward was to reduce costs and simplify systems. [54]

- In the face of poor financial results, the CEO of one of our cases signed a 10-year $520 million ITO deal with a single provider. Within 17 months, he had been removed and the contract was then terminated prematurely. As well as paying the provider's fees, the company incurred $50 million implementation and $30 million termination costs. More money was then swallowed up in rebuilding inhouse capability and shifting to a multi-supplier model.

---

[53] For evidence see Cullen, S. and Willcocks, L. (2003) *Intelligent IT Outsourcing*, Butterworth Heinemann, Oxford; Kern, T. and Willcocks, L. (2001) *The Relationship Advantage: Information Technology, Outsourcing and Management*, Oxford University Press, Oxford; Kern, T., Willcocks, L. and Van Heck, E. "The Winner's Curse in IT Outsourcing: How to Avoid Relational Trauma," *California Management Review*, 44, 2, 47-69; Lacity, M. and Willcocks, L. (2003) "Information Technology Sourcing Reflections," *Wirtschaftsinformatik*, Special Issue on Outsourcing, Vol. 45, 2, p. 115.

[54] Reported in Rohde, L. (2004) "Sainsbury, Accenture To Redo Outsourcing Pact", *Computer Weekly* October 25th 2004.

- A 2003 report into 182 outsourcing deals found more than a fifth ended prematurely.[55]

- In 2004, JP Morgan and Chase scrapped its $5 billion contract with IBM two years into a 7-year deal, concluding that much of the work could be better handled inhouse. Also in 2004, Dupont was reported to have discovered $150 million in over-charges relating to outsourcing services with its provider.[56]

- In autumn 2004, the Child Support Agency-EDS deal surfaced as the latest in a long catalogue of outsourcing failures in the UK public sector. The pattern continued across the rest of the decade as revealed by a series of House of Commons Public Accounts Committee reports.[57]

- In January 2010, media company BSkyB won a judgment against EDS (now owned by HP), which was contracted to develop and implement a £50 million customer relationship management system at BSkyB's contact centers in Scotland in 2000. Two years in, EDS was removed for poor performance. The system was finally completed by another provider in March 2006. The interim judgment gave BSkyB damages of £270 million (the cost to complete the project) for fraudulent misrepresentation despite the limited liability in the contract of £30 million.[58]

---

[55] Reported in Earle, A. (2004) 'End of The Affair: Bringing Outsourced Operations Back in-house'. *Computerworld,* May 31st, 2004.

[56] Wighton, D. (2004) "JP Morgan Scraps IT Deal With IBM", *Financial Times*, September 16th 2004. Dupont reported by Miller, A, "Outsourcing Options and Performance Management in the Private and Public Sectors". Presentation at *the Outsourcing Summit*, London, 22nd November 2004.

[57] Collins, T. (2004) "MPs Given Little Comfort on State of Child Support Agency Systems", *Computer Weekly*, 28th October 2004. As an example of parliamentary reports, see House of Commons Public Accounts Committee (2009) Central Government's Management of Service Contracts. Stationery Office, London.

[58] Herbert Smith (2010) The Sky's the Limit: Liability for IT and Outsourcing Projects. *Herbert Smith Bulletin*, February 2010.

One should also note the often-sizeable hidden costs of management for outsourcing. In re-analyzing our multiple research bases - by 2013 representing over 2100 deals, we made three findings. First is that the **costs of getting to contract** is between **0.4% and 2.5%** of total contract value (or 16% of its per annum value, on average). As one example, in 1997 Dupont spent $US100 million when signing their seven year, $4 billion deals with CSC and Andersen Consulting (now Accenture). These costs rise as a percentage as the size of the deal increases. Second, we found **ongoing outsourcing management costs** ranging from **3% to 10%** of annual contract value (6% on average). Third, is the increasing cost of managing offshoring: ranging from 10% to 12% of the annual contract value in 2000, from 10% to 15% in 2003-2004, and ranging from 12% to 16% from 2005-2009.[59]

As outsourcing becomes a core competency, wise CEOs invest more in its management, even though spending more runs counter to most Boards' goal of spending less. The CEO should also monitor the costs of management as a key indicator. Too low and it could be symptomatic of under-managing contracts. Rapid growth in management costs will be symptomatic of rising problems and loss of control being encountered with outsourcing.

Why should the CEO and Board members be involved? Because in outsourcing, strategic risk mitigation is fundamental. Furthermore, pursuing an operational, cost-reducing outsourcing strategy can drive costs down but often at the expense of other expected benefits. Strategic and even operational inflexibilities can result. As one example, while the Xerox-EDS 1994-2004 ITO deal successfully achieved

---

[59] In one of our studies, the deals that outsourced over 65% of the IT budget averaged a 10% management cost, while those under 25% of the IT budget averaged 3%; reflecting the difference between professionally managing a contract versus merely administrating it. Detailed case study research allows us to make some judgments about effective spend. If one excludes from these figures the clients having poor experiences, those doing contract administration rather than effective management, and those playing catch-up due to early lack of investment, the figures of 3% to 10% are reliable for domestic outsourcing, checked across all our separate studies.

cost reductions, at one point it damaged Xerox's ability to respond to a major change in market structure. In late 1999, Xerox lost control of its billing and sales commission systems which had major consequences for profitability. In one year, Xerox's value per share had dropped from above $90 to below $20.[60]

The CEO must also care because, as the examples above show, strategic decisions to merge, acquire, or enter new markets can incur substantial unforeseen damage, delays and costs, if existing outsourcing arrangements need to be refocused.

Reason Four - Outsourcing can play a positive, strategic role

We are increasingly seeing leading clients utilize forms of outsourcing to:

* penetrate new markets quickly,

* operate in new regions (e.g. Boeing sourcing IT to Malaysia in order to sell core products there, or Dell looking to sell into China),

* achieve strategic agility (e.g. adjusting volumes in response to business cycles or to provide business continuity in times of crisis),

* achieve strategic sourcing (e.g. using offshore competition to get better prices and service; best-of-breed sourcing), and

* enhance strategic capabilities by teaming with a complementary provider.

In our research and advisory work, we have also seen CEOs using outsourcing to pursue the following strategies:

* **Financial restructuring** - improving the business's financial position while reducing or at least containing costs.

* **Core focus** - redirecting the business into core competencies.

---

[60] Kern, T. and Willcocks, L. (2001) *The Relationship Advantage* (OUP, Oxford).

- **Capability building** - strengthening resources, services, and flexibility in technologies and/or business processes to underpin business's strategic direction.

- **Catalyst** - facilitating and supporting major organizational change.

- **Innovation** - using outsourcing to innovate processes, skills and technology (while mediating financial risk) to achieve competitive advantage.

- **New market** - direct profit generation through joint venturing with providers.

All of these need meticulous CEO attention. In fact, for these moves to pay off in any way, the CEO needs to shift from a tactical hands-off view, to a strategic and much more personally involved approach to outsourcing. If one becomes increasingly reliant, as a business, on an array of providers, the practices described in this book become the only secure foundation for the CEO to ensure future business strategy is leveraged, rather than crippled.

Reason Five - CEOs alone possess the crucial bargaining power

There is one element in outsourcing which the CEO alone can bring to bear on the massive scale that is required: bargaining power. Organizationally and strategically, the CEO is the ultimate pivot of bargaining power.

In Part 2 of this book we detail a program of action we call the **Outsourcing Lifecycle**. This covers the sourcing decisions from inception through implementation to termination. The constant aim during the lifecycle is to build and manage relative bargaining power. Understanding it is the first step in the lifecycle (see Action 1). Enter the lifecycle without having first amassed the best possible bargaining power prior to starting negotiations and you will find it almost impossible thereafter to improve your position.

A key CEO role, therefore, is to ensure that the organization's bargaining power is sustained; both through their personal influence with the provider's power brokers and by putting in place the strategies, processes and people needed to keep the relationship with the provider sharply competitive and productively leveraged. As one canny senior executive told us, *"Bargaining power was something we planned for from the beginning. We always saw ourselves in competition for the supplier's attention and resources against all its other customers."*

2.2   Sourcing - Becoming Strategic

According to the CEO (in 2001) of Capital One, the US Credit Card Group, *"If you have a business that churns out products then outsourcing makes sense. But in the case of IT, it's actually our central nervous system. If I outsourced tomorrow, I might save a dollar or two on each account, but I would lose flexibility, and value and service levels."*

Contrast this with Cisco Systems at much the same time. It had outsourced much of its production to 37 factories. Suppliers made all components and carried out 55% of sub-assembly and final assembly work. According to one senior executive, *"We can go from quote to cash without ever touching a physical asset or piece of paper. You've heard of JIT manufacturing, well this is not-at-all manufacturing."*

Two different businesses, both successful, each with a completely different philosophy on outsourcing. What explains this? Are there then no obviously adoptable outsourcing strategies? For the CEO, there is work to do in arriving at strategic sourcing decisions, configuring outsourcing deals, and ensuring these continue to underpin strategic direction of the business.

There are CEOs who outsource because they are not willing to invest in, or have given up on, the ability of a particular business function (e.g. IT, HR, procurement, legal) to keep costs down, deliver required service, or significantly improve. As we will explain, there are ways of making such outsourcing work. Nevertheless, even if such outsourcing is successful it can only achieve so much. This is because fundamental strategic flaws in the organization cannot be sold off - they must be understood and addressed. Applying outsourcing to a flawed business model can, only result, at best, in a more efficient version of that flawed model. As one vice-president commented to us, *"The belief is if you give the problem away, the third party will make it magically disappear. This tactic doesn't succeed because the client has not invested the time to address the underlying business processes or model."*

Management must be able to provide the answers to the perennial question, *"Where are we now, where do we want to be, and how do we get there?"* Outsourcing is then a management tool that can be used to leverage the resulting answers. Without such an analysis, and without integrating the outsourcing strategy with business strategy, outsourcing becomes at best a tactical device for achieving lower level goals.

In 1994 John Browne, CEO of BP stated, *"Failure to outsource our commodity IT will permanently impair the future competitiveness of our business."* From 1993, when BP Exploration signed five-year total outsourcing contracts with three providers, BP itself has risen to be consistently one of the top three oil companies in the world. Our own analysis shows how BP made strategic sourcing decisions that underpinning business strategy over many years into the new century.[61] How can this be achieved?

---

[61] See Lacity, M. and Willcocks, L. (2001) op. cit. and Kern and Willcocks (2001) op. cit.

Our root-cause research regarding outsourcing failures suggests strongly that it can easily fail if you:

- see the area to be outsourced (e.g. IT, HR, procurement) as an undifferentiated commodity that can be outsourced in its entirety,

- outsource for dramatic cost reductions

- outsource because you have given up on the inhouse ability to deliver,

- buy what is on offer rather than what you need,

- sign long-term contracts for short-term, tactical reasons,

- draw up adversarial contracts; and/or

- do not put in place the necessary management capability throughout the lifecycle.

There is another way.

One company, Dell, a top performer in the early 1990s for a decade, is worth using as an example.

Case: Dell as a virtual integrator

From the late 1990s, Dell explicitly described its strategy as virtual integration. Its success was invariably put down to customer focus and attention to detail. However, an underlying vital component was sourcing strategy and management. Commenting on the company's growth through the 1990s into the new century Michael Dell said, *"I don't think we could have created a $12 billion business if we had tried to be vertically integrated."*

With fewer physical assets and people, there were fewer things to manage and fewer barriers to change. Through IT-enabled coordination of its value network of suppliers and partners, Dell could operate with a 20,000 rather than an 80,000 member workforce. In the supply arena, it focused on making long-term deals with as few leading suppliers as possible. Datalinks measured and fed back supplier performance in real time. Close ties with suppliers *("their engineers are part of our design and implementation teams")* meant that Dell bought in innovation from its suppliers. Information technologies allowed speed and information sharing and much more intense forms of collaboration. It also meant that suppliers could be notified precisely of Dell's product requirements. This also allowed Dell to focus on inventory velocity and keeping inventory levels low.

Dell also, throughout its short history, sought strong partnering relationships with key customers. Seen as *"complementors,"* customers are often involved in research and development, where Dell's focus is on relevant, easy-to-use technology, improvements in the customer buying process, keeping costs down, and superior quality in manufacturing. Dell also offered service centers in large organizations to be close to the customer. Thus, in the early 2000s, Boeing had over 100,000 Dell PCs and over 30 dedicated Dell staff on the premises.

How are such effective sourcing decisions made? We provide two matrices (Figure 2-1 and Figure 2-2), born of experience and research, to facilitate decision-making. Sourcing must start with the business imperative.

2.2.1   Sourcing Decisions by Business Contribution

Figure 2-1: Sourcing Decision Matrix - by Business Contribution

Figure 2-1 indicates two ways of defining activities. The first is in terms of a business activity's contribution to business positioning. Some activities are frequently categorized as 'commodities' that need to be done, but do not differentiate the organization competitively. On the other hand, British Airways'

yield management system gave the company a competitive edge in ticket pricing for many years and has been regarded as a 'differentiator'.

The vertical axis allows us to assess whether a business activity critically underpins strategic direction and its delivery, or merely makes incremental contributions to the bottom line.

Let us use the well-known history of Dell to illustrate the thinking here. **Order Winners** are those business activities that critically and advantageously differentiate a firm from its competitors. Looking at Dell around 2002, the company had six such order winners or 'critical differentiators':

1. Dell focused its attention on all activities that create customer value. This included research and development involving over 1500 people and a $250 million plus budget that focused on customer-facing activity and the identification of relevant technology. It tended to outsource as much as possible all other activities that needed to be done.

2. At the time, Dell defined its core capability as a solutions provider and technology navigator. It used providers as much as possible to deal with such matters as products, components technology development, assembly.

3. A key task was coordination, rather than doing tasks such as manufacturing and delivery.

4. A core capability was control of the network through financial and informational means to ensure requisite speed, cost, and quality. Dell appointed and monitored reliable, responsive, leading edge providers of technology and quality.

5. Dell took responsibility for seeking and improving all arrangements that gave it speed and focus in the marketplace.

6. Dell treated (and still does) information management and orchestration as a critical differentiator. This is an outcome of two strategic moves on its part. The first is to convert as much of the physical assets it manages into digital form. The second is to outsource as much as possible of the remaining physical assets and tasks, while rendering management of the digital world a core set of tasks.

One secret of Dell's success, we would suggest, was its absolute clarity about what was core, and what was not. It also recognized that this might change dynamically with circumstances. This enabled it to authoritatively place 'non-core' activities as candidates for outsourcing, and make decisions on the best models types, and on suitable candidates.

Qualifiers are business activities that must be carried out as a necessary minimum-entry requirement to compete in a specific sector. For airlines, aircraft maintenance systems are such a requirement, but do not differentiate one from another. One can see in Dell's strategy their preference to outsource as many critical commodities as possible. Often critical differentiators can become commodities and move to this quadrant. One task of the CEO is to monitor and act upon such value migration. During 2003, Dell defined assembly, manufacturing, and delivery as 'Qualifiers'. These should be 'best sourced' - done by third parties where they meet the right cost and competence criteria.

Necessary Evils are tasks that have to be done, but are not core activities and there is no strategic gain from their fulfillment. Dell has tended to cut down on administration, payroll and inventory tasks for example, but would seek to outsource as much of these activities as possible.

Distractions are failed or failing attempts to differentiate the organization form its competitors. The goal here must be to eliminate the activity, or migrate it to another quadrant. Thus in 1989, Dell opened retail outlets but soon discovered this development was not going to be successful, and fell back on its direct business model. A more profound mistake is not to notice until too late the value shifts in a specific competitive arena, for example IBM against Microsoft and Intel in the late 1980s/early 1990s. Dell had made few such mistakes in its rise to being one of the best global performers in the 1990-2003 period. Perhaps this resulted from its CEO's explicit recognition that, *"looking for value shifts is perhaps the most important dimension of leadership."*

2.2.2   Sourcing Decisions by Market Comparisons

It is not enough, however, to identify a potential use for providers or other business allies. What is available in the market also requires detailed analysis. If the market is not cheap, capable or mature enough then the organization will need to seek a largely inhouse solution. A second matrix is needed to capture fully the major elements for consideration (Figure 2-2).

Figure 2-2: Sourcing Decision Matrix - by Market Comparisons

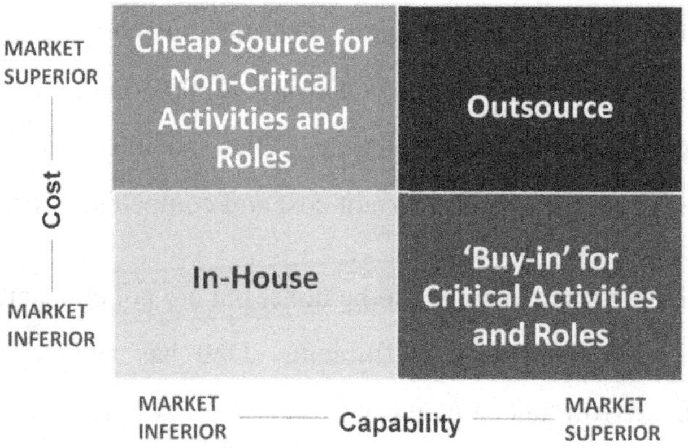

In Figure 2-2, we plot the cost efficiencies and capabilities the market can offer against carrying out tasks and functions internally. Where the market is cheaper and better, then outsourcing is the obvious decision, but only for Qualifiers and Necessary Evils. An example is Federal Express providing customer delivery for

Dell. Another example is in the London Insurance Market using Xchanging since 2001 for back-office processing and services for policy and claims settlement. Major US and European companies offshore software development and call centers for similar reasons.

Where the market offers an inferior cost and capability, then inhouse sourcing will be the best alternative (assuming Distractions are best not sourced at all). Where the market offers a better cost deal then this should be taken, but only for non-key activities (Necessary Evils). Where the market offers superior capability, but at a premium price above what the inhouse cost might be, then there still may be good reasons for buying-in or close partnering with the third party, not least to leverage and learn from their expertise, and apply it to Qualifying and Order Winning activities.

Thus, the two figures help to summarize the main criteria for making sourcing decisions. Use of the matrices requires decisions on trade-offs in order to establish the least risky ways providers can be leveraged. However, making the right sourcing decisions does not guarantee their successful implementation - that requires sound management of the entire lifecycle (Part 2 of this book).

2.3   Lessons on Moving to the Strategic Agenda

In this chapter, we have provided an overview of why the CEO, and Board, should care about sourcing strategy and large-scale outsourcing. The strategic lessons are:

1. Clients fail because they outsource problems, messes, and things they do not understand. The lower risk option is to outsource activities you understand and can write detailed contracts for, and can monitor. Partnering arrangements are for mature clients to undertake. Buying-in resources to operate under your management is also a viable lower risk way to use the external services market.

2. Outsourcing disappoints where the CEO and senior management see it as about spending a little as possible, and about stepping aside from management. In fact, outsourcing is still about managing but in a different way, with different skill sets, if the organization is to retain control of its own destiny.

3. Signing long-term outsourcing contracts for short-term reasons has been, and will continue to be a regular source of serious disappointment.

4. Providers still tend to be better at selling their services than clients are at buying them. This book is dedicated to developing better buyers, as well as providers.

5. Client organizations, and their CEOs, still expect too much from providers, and not enough from themselves.

So what should they be able to do?

- Formulate and monitor a sourcing strategy that fits with dynamically changing strategic and operational business needs for the next five years.

- Configure outsourcing deals that are optimal; making judicious, complementary choices across the seven configuration structures (discussed in Chapter 4).

- Understand in detail the external services market, provider strategies and capabilities, where providers are coming from, and what a good deal with *this* provider looks like.

- Put in place a process for managing across the lifecycle of all the organization's outsourcing arrangements.

- Arrive at a contract that delivers what you expect and need without sustaining high hidden or switching costs over the next 3-5 years.

- Put in place and sustain a post-contract inhouse management capability (Chapter 3) that keeps control while leveraging provider capabilities and performance to mutual advantage.

In this book, we cover these issues in detail.

Why should the CEO be involved? A provider's CEO put it succinctly, *"The customer from hell is the naïve buyer."* He was referring to senior client executives who did not know what they wanted, kept changing their minds, had disputes amongst themselves, and did not do the detailed work up front.

It is not just the CEO of course, who is crucial to outsourcing being a success. In the next chapter, we examine the importance of middle management; the conduit between strategy and results.

Chapter 3   Core Capabilities and Middle Management in Outsourcing

"We are what we repeatedly do. Excellence, then, is not an act, but a habit."

Aristotle

Nothing much is delivered through outsourcing unless the parties possess certain complementary, essentially human, skills-based core competencies.   In this chapter, we detail what these competencies are, how they are composed of capabilities, and how they are made up of sets of skills, behaviors and attitudes that (when operationalized) lead to effective performance.

We focus in this chapter on the middle management (MM) level; a broad spectrum of management that sits between Board level senior executives and the operators and specialists.

Recent researchers give strong endorsement for the vital role middle managers (MMs) play in modern corporations and government agencies.[62]   In fact, developments in technology, the increase in outsourcing, and dramatically changing economic circumstances have all contributed to a revival and

---

[62] Huy, Q. (2001) "In Praise of Middle Managers", *Harvard Business Review*, 79, September, 72-79; Kanter, R. (2004) "The Middle Manager as Innovator", *Harvard Business Review,*82, July, 150-161; Osterman, P. (2009) *The Truth About Middle Managers*, Harvard Business Press, Boston.

strengthening of the role of the MM. Our own research shows that the MM has now become one of the key factors determining whether an outsourcing arrangement is effective or whether it simply adds to the overall cost base.[63]

3.1 The Importance of Middle Managers

3.1.1 Influence

The middle manager has been described in the Collins Dictionary as "*a level of management in an organization or business consisting of executives or senior supervisory staff in charge of the detailed running of an organization or business and reporting to top management.*"

This definition is now far too narrow, because it only describes an inward looking focus - the main reason why so many management layers could be removed previously. Working in technologically and organizationally more complex, globalized environments, MMs are found to be, in Osterman's words, "*the glue that hold organizations together… responsible for accomplishing the core tasks of their organizations.*"[64]

So exactly how do MMs have so much influence on outsourcing effectiveness? Senior executives will make the agenda-setting decisions that determine an organization's course, but MMs have considerable influence on the long road to implementation - because MMs interpret, modify, and execute those decisions. Osterman's study of MMs found them in greater demand, with a broader range of

---

[63] Lacity, M. and Willcocks, L. (2009) *Information Systems and Outsourcing: Studies in Theory and Practice*, Palgrave, London; Oshri, I, Kotlarsky, J. and Willcocks, L. (2009) *The Handbook of Global Outsourcing and Offshoring*, Palgrave, London; Willcocks, L. and Lacity, M. (2009) *The Practice of Outsourcing: From Information Systems To BPO and Offshoring*, Palgrave, London.

[64] See Osterman, P. (2009) op. cit.

tasks and responsibilities than the past. [65]   They are ambassadors between top management and the workforce, between the many teams that make a client and its providers function effectively.   They are the key resource for coordination, whether interfacing, scheduling, or managing flow of materials, activity, funds, and ideas through an enterprise or project.

At the basic level, the MM still has the historic role of acting as the transmission belt between the top and bottom of organizations, but in addition, the MM now has scope to manage internal and external teams and relationships, and be fundamentally involved in managing risk. They make day-to-day choices and key trade-offs that escape top management attention, know-how, and interest, yet are central to an organization's performance.

In service companies in particular, MMs are Janus-like personalities (looking both ways) externally to the customers and other providers, and internally both to their senior management to obtain and interpret direction, and to their junior management where they provide the necessary mentoring and training. Interestingly, as organizations have de-layered, introduced technology, and outsourced, increasingly MMs have taken on the roles and experiences (and additional stress) ascribed for general managers thirty to forty years ago.

Additionally, outsourcing changes the management model further and amplifies the importance of MM for both clients and providers alike.

---

[65] Osterman found the 'business side' becoming as important as the technical dimensions of the role (pages 61-62). Our own research endorses this strongly - See Oshri, I, Kotlarsky, J. and Willcocks, L. (2012) *The Handbook of Global Outsourcing and Offshoring*. Palgrave, London.

3.1.2   As the 'Glue' for Outsourcing

In many clients, there continues to be a blindly held belief that outsourcing is a straightforward transaction involving the simple transfer of services to a provider, and that benefits will automatically follow according to the contract. But outsourcing is not a straightforward transaction; it is a complex strategy for managing the delivery of a range of services against changing economic backgrounds and then delivering to precise targets. The MM is the means to do this because their role is to implement the company's vision and to ensure the operations of the company go smoothly according to the defined plan and objectives. This is not as easy as it may seem.

Relationships have to be established both within and across the client and provider organization, and at every level. This is where MMs and their skills, knowledge, and experience - become key. Individual people can get in the way of outsourcing success. At one major oil company, the CXO commented, *"When 'Tom' was in place as a demand manager nothing got done; when 'Harry' took his place it all began to happen."*

In one major arrangement we researched, both client and provider contract managers fought as adversaries over the contract for the first 18 months. Eventually both of them were replaced by people who were more able to build and sustain the ten year-relationship.

The MM's flexibility and leadership skills will determine how well they are able to tailor and adapt initiatives to the company's changing circumstances. Their ability to do this and manage the customer as well as build the relationship absolutely drives the bottom line of any business. In addition, major strategic initiatives have to be executed by MMs and a strong MM team can produce outstanding operational results, easing the need for top managers to oversee and intervene directly in day-to-day operations. A well-functioning MM team will also proactively create a stream of new initiatives to remedy problems and seize new opportunities. As a result, strong MM performance becomes a key leverage point as well as a scarce resource. In practice, MMs ensure a smoother transfer of knowledge and therefore helps to ensure greater efficiency in terms of time by solving immediate problems.

In the context of offshore outsourcing, MMs must acquire another dimension of skills. These are the skills of dealing across significant boundaries, countries and perhaps cultures where there can be distinct status differences. The building of 'virtual teams' across these boundaries, the development of trust and the necessity of effective communication, are crucial if team leaders or project managers are to achieve effective outcomes. This is particularly complex where for example, a company has offshoring of BPO say in India, customer services in Egypt, manufacturing in China and software development in the Czech Republic.

Given the importance of such skills and the difficulty in how they are acquired (experientially over time), it is not surprising to discover that they are in short supply, especially in offshore outsourcing sites. This has led to a strong market in these skills across the globe. The result? Countries and companies that acquire MMs, or run training schemes to develop them, are still faced with considerable retention challenges.[66]

But there are deeper issues than this, which we will address in this chapter:

- What should organizations be training people in?

- Is it enough to create MM resources or is something more needed?

---

[66] See Willcocks, L. Griffiths, C. and Kotlarsky, J. (2009) *Beyond BRIC – Offshoring in Non-BRIC Countries: Egypt a New Growth Market*. LSE Enterprise/ITIDA, London. Here we researched 14 countries that were developing their offshoring industries and found middle managers a scarce, and valued resource in all of them. The countries were Belarus, Bulgaria, Costa Rica , Czech Republic, Egypt, Mexico, Morocco, Poland, Romania, Slovakia, Tunisia, Venezuela and Vietnam.

3.1.3   The Offshore Dimension

Our recent research[67] has shown that international offshoring to a particular host country may only be profitable if the production facility in the host country is composed of two layers of human resources rather than one: (1) a set of workers specialized in production and (2) a set of MMs in charge of supervision. MMs thus shield top management in the home country from having to deal with routine problems faced by workers in the host country. The presence of MMs allows a more efficient timesaving transmission of knowledge across countries.

However, the speed with which many countries are developing their outsourcing and offshoring industries has often meant that growth has come without the necessary corporate competencies, roles and structures to sustain either the speed or size of growth in the long term. This means that without the necessary MMs to hold the company together, smooth operational issues, and build a corporate knowledge repository, many providers quickly reach a growth plateau. The problem of lack of MM in offshore providers has quietly dogged the industry from the late 1990s, but has been exacerbated with growth and with more sophisticated work being outsourced.

In India, often looked to as a model of a dynamic outsourcing country, the lack of middle management and the low staff retention rates are causes of concern. This means that there is only limited experience from which graduates can learn. As one example, in September 2009 India's Commission on Information and Communications Technology registered concern over the lack of skilled workers needed to sustain growth, in particular pointing to the lack of viable mid-level managers needed to efficiently resource outsourcing operations. Indian universities were upgrading their courses to address rising demand for middle and project managers.

---

[67] Willcocks, L., Lacity, M. and Craig, A. (2012) *Becoming Strategic: South Africa's BPO Service |Advantage*. LSE, London.

Given our findings on the fundamental role MMs play in making outsourcing and offshoring arrangements effective, it is important to better understand the distinctive capabilities (as opposed to just resources) that both parties need to acquire and sustain.

3.2   Moving from Resources to Capabilities to Competencies

When clients outsource, it is all too usual for them to think of the people they need to keep or acquire as individual resources, rather than what such resources need to add up to collectively. We find clients often following the same pattern when evaluating prospective providers. Resources receive attention because they are highly visible, for example on site tours, in resumes received in provider bids, and in interviews and presentations. But clients should be much more interested in their own and a provider's ability to develop resources into capabilities that, in turn, can be developed into high-level competencies.

Figure 3-1 illustrates the relationship between these resources, capabilities, and competencies. Clearly, it is not enough to just employ people as resources with certain skills. Organizations need resources with human capabilities that collect into organizational competencies.

Figure 3-1: From Resources to Competencies

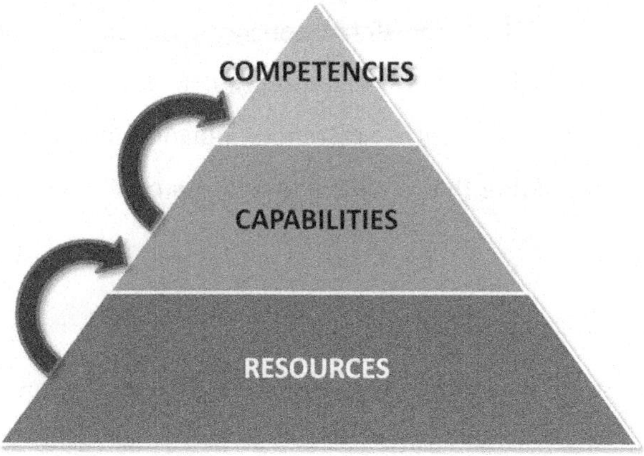

COMPETENCIES

CAPABILITIES

RESOURCES

The following definitions help to frame the more detailed discussion of client and provider capabilities in later sections of this chapter:

- A **role** refers to an individual person formally enacting a capability. For example, in the role of CFO a person enacts the leadership capability. In the role of procurement manager, the role holder will enact informed buying.

- **Resources** are physical and human assets such as physical facilities, technologies, tools, and workforce.

- A **capability** is a distinctive set of human-based skills, orientations, attitudes, motivations and behaviors within a team that, when applied, can transform resources into specific business activities.

- Collections of capabilities, in turn, create strategic organizational **competencies** that positively influence business performance.

We will look first at the most important, and ironically, most overlooked set of MM capabilities needed in outsourcing, namely those of the retained capability in the client (section 3.3). Next, we turn the spotlight on the provider's capabilities (3.4). We then present four general MM roles as a framework for thinking about both client and provider capabilities, followed by some guidelines for the leaders within clients to achieve these capabilities (section 3.6).

3.3   Managing the Demand Side - the Client's Competencies and Capabilities

All too often, we find that clients underrate the amount of MM capability needed to operate outsourcing arrangements effectively. Our research demonstrates that a high-performing internal function that manages outsourcing arrangements is managed by a team of highly capable, demand-led and mainly strategy-focused people.

In this section, we provide a framework for describing and discussing the competences and capabilities required. As shown in Figure 3-2, there are four competencies comprised of nine capabilities in a high-performing client team.

Figure 3-2: The Client's Four Competencies and Nine Capabilities

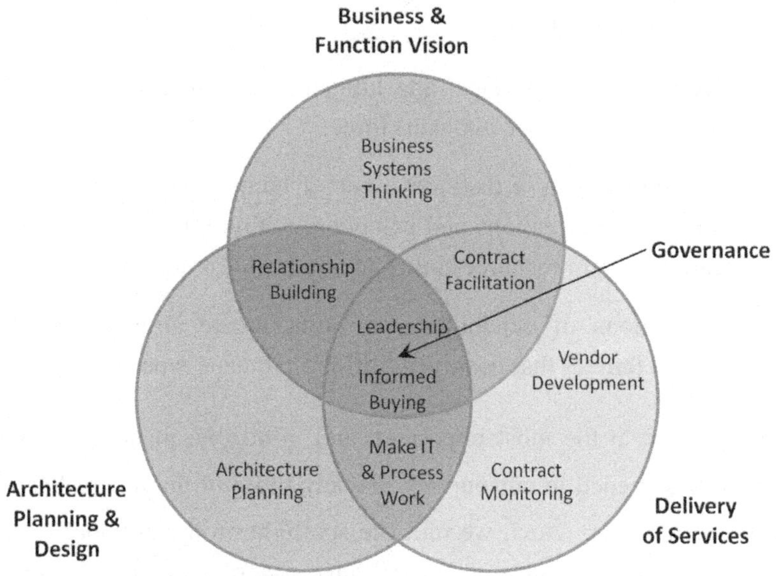

3.3.1   Client Competencies

Our work has identified four competencies needed by a high-performing function:

- **Governance,** including leadership and coordination. This involves dynamically aligning the function's activities internally, and with those of the organization as a whole.

- **Business and Function Vision**. A demand-driven competence concerned with defining business requirements, and how systems and capabilities can be leveraged for business purpose.

- **Architecture Planning and Design**. A supply-focused competence that defines systems, information, and processes to be provided to support business requirements, and deals with risks inherent in non-routine issues.

- **Delivery of Services** concerns arriving at and managing sourcing strategy. It requires understanding of the provider markets, and the ability to select, engage, and manage internal and external resources and services over time.

3.3.2   Client Capabilities

The nine capabilities (Table 3-1) all demand high performers who can develop into a high performance team. In contrast to the more traditional skills found in service functions, there needs to be a much greater emphasis on business skills and business orientation in nearly all roles. There is also a significantly increased requirement for 'soft' skills across all roles.

Table 3-1: The Nine Client Capabilities

Capability	Reason the Capability is Required
1. Leadership	To integrate the effort with business purpose and activity.
2. Informed buying	To manage the sourcing strategy to meet the needs of the business.
3. Business systems thinking	To ensure that capabilities are envisioned in every business process.
4. Relationship building	To get the business constructively engaged in operational issues.
5. Contract facilitation	To ensure the success of contracts for external services.
6. Architecture planning	To create the coherent blueprint for a technical platform that responds to present and future needs.
7. Vendor development	To identify the potential added value from the providers.
8. Contract monitoring	To protect the business' contractual position now and in the future.
9. Making IT and process work	To rapidly troubleshoot problems being disowned by others across the technical supply chain.

Let's now examine each of the capabilities in terms of the competencies, as well as in terms of integration between competencies.

Capabilities for Governance Competence

This competence is delivered through leadership and informed buying capabilities. The central **Leadership** task is to devise and engage in organizational arrangements (governance, structures, processes, and staffing), that successfully manage internal and business interdependencies, in ways that ensure the function delivers business value for money.

One leader in charge of a seven-year $US900 million outsourcing contract for a mineral resources multinational commented on his role, "*What keeps me up at night? It changes! When we first outsourced, it was all external issues: negotiating, getting the price right, getting the service delivered. We got a bit overtaken by that...and missed things we needed to do internally. I think our challenge now is probably more internal than external. And that is how to get all of our internal stakeholders lined up behind whatever we execute. Get them to understand this is the way we need to manage. What does governance success look like? How do you measure governance success? What is the right way of measuring the goodness of any of these deals? And what is the right kind of framework to pull this together?*"

In a client that has decides to outsource most of a function's services (whether it be procurement, IT, marketing, etc.), the **Informed buying** capability is the most prominent to support the CxO (e.g. CIO, COO, CFO, etc.) who heads the function. Informed buyers:

- analyze and benchmark regularly the external market for relevant services,

- select the 5-10 year sourcing strategy to meet business needs, and

- lead the tendering, contracting, and service management processes.

Informed buying also requires an intimate knowledge of providers, their strategies, financial strength, and their capabilities (and incapabilities) in different sectors, services, and regions. One informed buyer also described the pragmatic aspect to the capability, *"If you are a senior manager... and you want something done, you come to me and I will... go outside, select and draw up the contract with the outsourcer, and if anything goes wrong, it's my butt that gets kicked by you."*

Capabilities for Vision Competence

In leading-practice clients that we have studied, **Business systems thinking** is an important contribution to teams charged with business problem solving, process re-engineering, strategic development, and delivering e-business. Such leading-practice organizations recognize that business processes should be redesigned in the light of technology potential. The case below, concerning an insurance company, illustrates the problems faced when this capability was not in place.

Case: Insurance company

Without such staffing and vision, a major insurance company contracted a provider to deliver a strategic IT system aimed at transforming administrative and customer service systems. However, the business transformation was misconceived as an IT project, and the provider was given primary responsibility and aggressive deadlines. The provider failed to deliver the detailed business requirements on time and the project was cancelled nine months into the two-year implementation. The CEO learned from this. In later projects he insisted that internal 'business systems thinking' MMs were in place.

Capabilities for Architecture Competence

Let us again use the example of the IT function. The principal challenge to the **Architect planning** capability is, through insight into process and technology, providers and business directions, to anticipate technology trends so that the client is consistently able to operate from an effective and efficient IT platform – without major investments into major migration efforts. This capability shapes the IT architecture and infrastructure through developing the vision of an appropriate technical platform, and through formulating associated policies that ensure necessary integration and flexibility in services. All outsourcing arrangements provide a strong test of the value of retaining this capability. When looking at organizing new contracts, a water utility executive said, "*We need internal knowledge to make decisions about where we are going rather than having to rely on the provider to say: this new technology has come up, how are we going to deal with it?*"

We saw a bank and a manufacturer give away their architects, assuming that the task of architecture planning was technical and therefore one for the providers and not their own people. Three years into outsourcing found both of these clients rebuilding this capability because they could not understand, let alone talk with and influence, the providers about how to address existing and fresh demand through a new technology platform with better economics.

Capabilities for Service Delivery Competence

Here, **Contract monitoring** involves inputting into the development and maintenance of a robust contract as the basis for a sound governance framework. The capability then leads onto holding providers to account against the contracts and comparing the contracts to the performance standards of the relevant markets.

Not all potential issues and expectations can be identified at the onset of a relationship, and the contract will be subject to differing interpretations as issues arise. While all the clients that we have studied recognized the importance of contract monitoring, and staffed it at the beginning of their outsourcing deals, they all too frequently put the wrong people in place, especially in the large deals, underestimating the dynamic nature and extent of the task.

Vendor development is concerned with leveraging the long-term potential for providers to add value, creating the 'win-win' situations in which the provider increases its revenues while also providing services that increase business benefits. Given the prohibitive size of switching costs, it is in the client's interest to maximize the contribution from existing providers.

It is important to guard against what we call 'mid-contract sag' where the provider delivers to the contract, but only to the letter. As the Service Director of an aerospace company said, *"Yes the supplier can achieve all the things that were proposed. But where is the famous 'value-added service'? We are not getting anything over and above what any old outsourcer could provide."* Compare this with a retail multinational that meets providers formally at senior levels to find new ways forward, *"There are certain things we force on our suppliers like understanding our business and growing the business together."*

Capabilities that Integrate the Competencies

The interfaces in Figure 3-2 are crucial to facilitate the integration of effort across the competencies. Operating in the overlap between the challenges of Architecture design and Services delivery is the capability of **Making IT and process work**. If we use the example of the IT function, this capability troubleshoots problems and identifies how to address business needs that cannot be satisfied by standard technical approaches. People with this capability understand the idiosyncrasies of the infrastructure and applications, enabling them to make rapid technical/specialist progress (by one means or another). Such 'fixers' have a high degree of technical knowledge, and also domain expertise (i.e. knowledge of the business, processes, systems and how things work locally).

In outsourced environments, they also assess and challenge third party suppliers' claims about technical problems and proposed solutions. The need to retain good 'doing' capability was widely recognized amongst the clients we studied. For example, the lead IT executive in a government agency in charge of a five-year deal stated, *"We can't retain too much skill because we will be paying twice for it. But we are retaining a modicum in the systems analysis and requirements definition area, and, for example, rapid application development, prototyping, and hybrid skills."*

The **Contract facilitation** interface capability is crucial for lubricating the relationship between providers and the client's businesses, not least by ensuring that problems and conflicts are seen to be resolved fairly and promptly within, what are usually, long-term relationships. It is an action-orientated capability.

Interestingly, the need for this capability is rarely spotted straight away when a client outsources. Instead, recognition tends to grow in response to ongoing issues (e.g. the business demanding work outside the scope of the contract and incurring excessive charges, the provider or client's businesses demand it to improve efficiency, and managing the coordination between multiple providers).

The **Relationship building** interface capability is an integrating, operational capability, facilitating the wider dialogue, and establishing understanding, trust and cooperation amongst business users and function specialists. People with this capability develop users' understanding of the function and its potential for their lines of business. They help users and specialists to work together, help to identify business requirements, ensure user ownership and build user satisfaction.

3.4   Managing the Supply Side - the Provider's Competencies and Capabilities

MMs within providers are fundamental to ensuring that a provider's resources turn into capabilities and three higher competencies concerning delivery, relationship, and transformation (Figure 3-3).

Figure 3-3: The Provider's Three Competencies and Twelve Capabilities

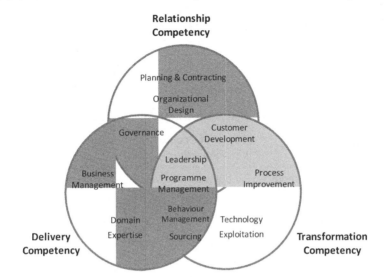

3.4.1 Provider Competencies

Providers need to demonstrate and utilize a mix of competencies to deliver different types of contracts:

- **Delivery competency** provides a cost-effective, improved performance against contractual terms and conditions and against KPIs.

- **Relationship competency** is vital when a client wishes to engage the provider's full capacities and expects the provider to align itself with the client's values, goals, and needs in order to support its long-term, business direction. We have seen many companies in retail, manufacturing and financial services increasingly looking for this level of commitment in their providers.

- **Transformation competency** is needed where a provider has agreed to deliver radically improved services in terms of cost and quality.

3.4.2   Provider Capabilities

Our research demonstrates that MMs have crucial roles to play in delivering the 12 key provider capabilities (Table 3-2) that create the competencies.[68]

Table 3-2: The Twelve Provider Capabilities

Role	Reason the Capability is Required
1. Leadership	To identify, coordinate, and deliver overall success throughout the lifecycle.
2. Business management	To deliver in line with SLAs and business plans.
3. Domain expertise	To retain and apply professional, technical and domain knowledge.
4. Behavior management	To motivate and inspire people to change and deliver high-level service.
5. Sourcing	To access resources cost effectively as needed.
6. Program management	To deliver a series of inter-related projects.
7. Governance	To define, track, take responsibility for performance.
8. Process improvement	To identify and incorporate changes to the service process to meet dramatic improvement targets.
9. Technology exploitation	To swiftly and effectively deploys technology for business purpose.
10. Customer development	To help customers make informed decisions about KPIs, costs, and functionality.
11. Planning and contracting	To design contracts to deliver win-win results for both parties.
12. Organizational design	To design and implement successful organizational arrangements.

Before discussing these in detail, it is useful comment on the leadership and interfacing capabilities. The leadership capability in the provider involves governance and coordination, and, as in the client, performs lynchpin activities. Our formal definition of the leader's role is "*responsibility for identifying,*

---

[68] Supplier capabilities and the supporting research is explained in more detail in Willcocks, L. and Lacity, M. (2006) *Global Sourcing of Business and IT Services,* Palgrave, London.

communicating, and delivering the balance of delivery, transformation, and relationship activities necessary to achieve present and future success for both parties."[69] Less formally, we have found that leadership capability requires individuals who have the vision, experience, ability, and political influence and credibility within both parties to serve as 'CEO' of the relationship. The other interfacing capabilities (Program management, Sourcing, Behavior management, Customer development, and Governance), are crucial for integrating and balancing effort and sustaining relationships across multiple teams and objectives.

The Delivery Competency

Seven capabilities are needed if the provider is to deliver an improved cost-service equation to the client.

- **Leadership** identifies and delivers success. In practice, leadership is required at middle, as well as top, management levels because modern outsourcing is full of adaptive challenges that require experiments, discoveries, adjustments, and innovations from many different parts of the organizations involved.

- **Business management** delivers in line with SLAs and both parties' business plans.

- **Domain expertise** retains and applies professional knowledge. For this, one should look not just for technical know-how but for the much harder to acquire experience in the client's specific function receiving outsourced services (e.g., example procurement, IT, or HR in a manufacturing environment).

- **Behavior management** capability is used to motivate and inspire people to deliver high-level service, to encourage staff to transition from the client to the provider, to recruit new staff as well as retain

---

[69] See Willcocks, L., Cullen, S. and Craig, A. (2010) *The Outsourcing Enterprise: From Cost Management To Collaborative Innovation*. Palgrave, London.

current staff. **Sourcing** accesses resources (e.g. technology, people, other suppliers) as needed. **Program management** capability is used to deliver a series of interrelated projects, both within a single client and between clients. **Governance** capability is used to track and measure performance. In practice, good governance has been found to make a big difference in outsourcing arrangements, so it is vital that the governance capability is not only well structured, but also well resourced by appropriately skilled MMs.

The Relationship Competency

Outsourcing arrangements invariably require the provider, together with the client, to have the ability to establish appropriate relationships at all levels of the relevant organizations. As Figure 3-3 shows, clients that are looking for a strong relationship need to find two more capabilities in the provider in addition to governance, program management, leadership and customer development capabilities. These are:

- **Planning and contracting** that is required to deliver 'win/win' results for both parties. Clients need to ask the question "Does the provider share with you its vision of the potential prize for both parties, and a coherent process for achieving it?"

- **Organizational design** that creates and implements successful organizational arrangements. In practice, providers vary greatly in their flexibility here. Some emphasize a 'thin' front-end client team, interfacing with consolidated service units. This could constrain the ability to customize service and deliver to a specific client business plan. As a client, what degree of flexibility do you need? The provider's MMs with organizational design capability are vital repositories of knowledge and experience on what designs will work in what circumstances.

The Transformation Competency

To deliver a transformation agenda to a client, the provider needs three additional capabilities other than leadership, program management, sourcing, and behavior (change) management.

Process engineering designs and incorporates improvements to client processes and procedures. MMs with this capability incorporate changes to the service process to meet dramatic improvement targets.

When working well, the **Technology exploitation** capability allows swift and effective deployment of new technology on the client's behalf. A major reason for the adoption of BPO is harnessing the provider's IT capability, and getting the provider to make the IT investment that clients are usually reluctant to make.

Finally, **Customer development** helps clients make informed decisions. This may sound odd, but in practice, we regularly find that client staff accustomed to an internally delivered service invariably need provider support to be able to make informed choices about service levels, functionality, and costs. As the Leader in one provider told us, when taking over a major contract in a financial services institution, *"I found I had 200 users who complained about everything. A critical task was to change their mind-sets so that they became customers."*

3.5   Middle Managers: The Four Primary Roles in Outsourcing

MM roles in outsourcing arrangements (as in contemporary organizations generally) seem incredibly diverse. But one thing is abundantly clear. MMs emerge from the research as the key means by which strategic direction and executive decisions are converted into completed work.

The major shift we have been observing in organizations such as Esso, ICI, DuPont, Commonwealth Bank, Lloyds of London, BP, and GE is toward fewer personnel, but ensuring those it has are of very high quality.

In practice, recruitment and retention of this small high quality MM group is a major HR challenge for both parties. Two solutions that need to be addressed are upskilling and hiring. As one multinational oil company executive commented, *"You've got to be able to upskill your organization and to have a HR policy which provides such training to people in your organization."* The logistics manager at a major retailer said, *"To be honest, we had to recruit a few people."* Moreover, the parties will need to pay them at a level within striking distance of that provided by alternative employers, provide them consistently with the level of challenge they look for in the job and develop career paths for them.

The research we have carried out on outsourcing extends and enriches the broader work on modern middle management, and assists in visualizing a small high quality MM group, by pointing to four general roles for MMs that need to exist in each party when managing outsourcing arrangements. These roles require a mix of the client and provider capabilities (see Table 3-3).

Table 3-3: Middle Manager Roles

Role	Capabilities Required	
	Client	**Provider**
Co-ordinator	• Business systems thinking • Contract facilitation • Informed buying • Leadership • Relationship building	• Business management • Governance • Leadership • Organizational design • Program management • Sourcing
Knowledge repository	• Architecture planning • Contract monitoring • Making IT and process work	• Domain expertise • Planning and contracting • Technology exploitation

| Role | Capabilities Required | |
	Client	Provider
Social capitalist	• Contract facilitation • Informed buying • Leadership • Relationship building	• Behavior management • Customer development • Governance • Leadership • Planning and contracting • Process improvement • Program management • Sourcing • Technology exploitation
Change agent	• Contract facilitation • Making IT and process work • Relationship building	• Behavior management • Leadership • Organizational design • Planning and contracting • Process engineering • Program management • Technology exploitation

The *Coordinator* provides 'glue' that holds a company together, performing vital linking work up and down and across the organization, and with external providers and allies. Both parties need lynchpin roles that hold the relationship together, manage logistics and progress activity. The client capabilities of Leadership, Informed buying, Business systems thinking, Relationship building and Contract facilitation are particularly crucial for coordination, though each for different reasons and in different contexts. On the provider side, coordination is the primary role for the Leadership, Business management, Sourcing, Program management, Governance, and Organization design.

The *Knowledge Repository* retains information and knowledge repositories of corporate memory and experience. Utilizes and communicates contents. Without this, every new piece of work becomes an exercise in reinventing the wheel. Formal knowledge bases can only get a client and provider so far. On the client side Architecture planning, together with Contract monitoring and Making IT and process work are particularly important capabilities as sources of knowledge that carried in human, rather than 'hardcopy' or 'softcopy' form. On the provider side,

Domain expertise, Technology exploitation and Planning and Contracting capabilities rank highest with such a role, each for different types of knowledge.

The *Social Capitalist* creates vital social capital through relationship management, as well as through team and project leadership. This role is particularly important in founding a provider's relationship competency, but in fact, nine of the 12 provider capabilities have important relationship building dimensions. On the client side, we see that the relationship building, contract facilitation, leadership and informed buying capabilities must all be present to fulfill this general role.

The *Change Agent* work in dynamic contexts, with frequently changing demands, in search of business results in adaptive ways. In providers, such MMs are heavily involved in transitioning work from clients and in transformation efforts and project work on clients' behalf. Such a general role is primary or highly important for the Process engineering, Technology exploitation, Program management, Behavior management, Planning and contracting, and Organization design. Leadership on the provider side is, of course, about being such a Change Agent. These MMs need their counterparts on the client side in all such activities.

Ensuring Adaptability and Relationship Chemistry with MM Capabilities

Much of outsourcing work is about transitioning, stabilizing a service, and then delivering it cost-effectively.   Typically, technical work (e.g. desktop maintenance, or payroll) requires the application of existing specialist know-how and techniques and can be outsourced relatively safely, assuming competent specialists can be hired. Even so, outsourcing always involves getting two or more organizations to operate together, differently, with little or no experience of how the other party works, or what its capabilities really are.

It is all too easy to underestimate how much of an adaptive challenge, as opposed to 'business-as-usual' this represents to the organizations involved, but especially to the client organization. Immediately one can see why the four MM roles become vital ingredients in the levels of adaptability and success achieved by the parties.

Furthermore, the more that the technical work outsourced becomes ambiguous and complex (that is, where solutions are not clear and problems are complex), then the more that leadership and middle management is required, the more multiple stakeholders need to be engaged with defining the problem, and the more that the parties working together is required to arrive at and implement a solution. And in fact, even fee-for-service outsourcing has many adaptive challenges mixed in with, and often mistaken for, technical challenges.

The obvious case is when outsourcing IT tasks. For example, tried and tested technology introduced into a new client environment impacts on existing technical and social systems and presents adaptive challenges. The provider will need to collaborate with the client's business users and inhouse IT people to get it to work.

This is particularly the case in offshore work involving, for example, applications development projects, or where new and innovatory initiatives are being attempted. The development of suitable teams across organizational boundaries and functional silos is vital for ensuring adaptivity. The MM capabilities needed to achieve relationship chemistry become a vital component in such teaming success.

A new ERP system development and implementation project we researched required not only senior executive support (as project sponsors and champions) but also a multi-functional team including a project manager, potential users of the system, inhouse IT-specialists, external supply management and technical staff, and senior user managers brought in as needed. If we add in the fact that the providers operated on all shores (onshore, nearshore, and offshore) and there was a strong 'virtual teaming' component, it becomes clear that the MM capabilities described in this paper were absolutely vital to the project's success.

3.6   Guidelines for Client Leaders

The evidence suggests that MMs are now no longer easily replaced by technology. A new role has been carved out which is multi-dimensional and critical for outsourcing, offshoring, and virtual teaming. Our work suggests that MMs are now to be found wherever outsourcing is successful. In this section, we provide four guidelines for leaders in client firms.

1. Assess the provider's competencies that are most important. These depends on your objectives, for example focus on the provider's delivery competency if you want to maintain or slightly improve existing services, or on the provider's transformation competency when you are seeking radical improvements in costs and services, and on the relationship competency when you require a substantial and long term commitment from the provider. Ensure you draw up contracts that reflect these objectives and reward performance on the relevant competencies. Analyze a provider's track record against the twelve capabilities in Table 3-2. But remember that you will not necessarily need your provider to have all the 12 capabilities. However, also remember our finding that a provider's lack of the requisite MM capability will translate into significant hidden costs and problems for you as a client.

2. Retain core client capabilities. Plan for the nine client capabilities in Table 3-1. You will need to diagnose which existing staff fulfill the distinctive skills mix required for each role. You will likely need to hire some new people as well. Look to create a small, but high performance team. You will need to evolve these roles over time. Start first with the leadership role and with those that underpin delivery (the relationship building, technology/process fixing, and contract facilitation roles). Next, ensure that the technical/process architecture is in place. Do not take on more outsourcing than you can manage at this stage. Certainly, do not outsource on a large-scale unless the informed buying, contract facilitation, vendor development, and contract monitoring capabilities are fully staffed at MM levels.

3. Reward client and provider adaptability. This needs to be done both contractually and relationally. Planning and contracting are vital starting points for outsourcing and offshoring, but that is all they are. The plan becomes rapidly outmoded and there is an immense amount of adaptive work in outsourcing that MMs are vital for fulfilling. Remember that the contract is out-of-date on the day you sign it. This means that governance and relationships are keys to fulfilling all those promises you and the provider made to each other. And the MMs on both sides are vital to ensuring that the promises and concepts are delivered in the necessary detail to secure success.

4. Invest in ways to help providers develop MM capabilities. The mature clients that we researched saw the importance of ensuring their providers had the requisite MMs to deliver something more than a straight technical service of a certain quality assessed against an SLA (service level agreement) or job specification. In 2003, we found a major pharmaceutical company seconding MMs to their Indian provider to help develop their MM expertise. While the provider had cheaper and superior technical and process expertise, the lack of MMs might have caused their performance to flounder in vital, unmeasurable ways. We found large US-based multinationals running transition programs for their providers, designed not just to pass on knowledge of the business, but also to develop relationships, and identify potential MMs in the provider they could help develop and work with. When clients complain about the lack of value-added from their outsourcing relationships, it is invariably useful to ask the question, "*How much have you invested in the MMs needed to achieve such value-added, not just in your own organizations, but in your providers as well?*

The MM cadre must be able to function as an integrated team of complementary capabilities if high performance is to be achieved. New MM roles in both the client and the provider have been carved out which are multi-dimensional and critical for successful outsourcing, offshoring, and virtual teaming. MMs on both sides are the keys to ensuring that relationships are secured, evolve, and are leveraged to business purpose; that work is coordinated; that experience and knowledge are applied in a sustained and practical manner, and that the stakeholder organizations remain ever responsive to changes in objectives, resources, external dynamics, and internal disruptions.

Modern dynamic complex, risky business environments challenge client and provider alike, and the act of outsourcing carries with it its own risks. In these circumstances, MMs provide the vital absorptive capacities that are all too often unheralded, but are nevertheless vital to any modern outsourcing enterprise.

In the next chapter, we turn to a very important set of overarching structural decisions that are made by CEOs and MMs, relating to what sort of outsourcing deals are constructed. This is known as **configuration**. The configuration decisions made have a pervasive and enduring effect on all outsourcing initiatives - now and in the future. And these decisions will require all of the capabilities we have discussed.

Chapter 4   Configuration

"The whole is greater than the sum of the parts."

Euclid

4.1   The Concept of Configuration

Every client uses different outsourcing structures, depending on the specific situation and the perceptions and preferences of its decision makers. Disparate strategies may result in different, yet equally desirable outcomes, and each client uses a different outsourcing configuration for different reasons.

Configuration is like looking out from a high vantage point over the buildings of a city and saying, *"We have one deal over here, the tall, thin, brown one. We have another deal over there, the long, squat, blue one,"* and so on. Each building represents an individual deal. Zooming in one any one 'building', the deal can be described in enormous detail, (e.g., by the contract clauses, the KPIs, the volume of work, etc.). Configuration takes a 'zoomed out' view.

Note also that a client's outsourcing configuration is not static. Just as a city's skyline changes over time, so too does an organization's configuration. Although it may cost them dearly, both parties have the right to request renegotiation of any deal at any time. Furthermore, the next generation deals are rarely reconfigured the same as the previous generation.

Why is configuration so important? It matters because you must make numerous structural choices and choose the optimum configuration attributes to balance the goals sought, with the risks presented, within the context of your organization. It matters because outsourcing is high risk, often irreversible if not done properly, and certain configurations are more risky than others are. Lastly, configuration matters because outsourcing is now a core competence required of management.

The reason that you will want a more precise, and granular, understanding of your outsourcing arrangements is because outsourcing is extraordinarily complex. Your organization has so many choices when outsourcing (what to outsource, to whom, where, how they are charged, the duration of the deal, etc.) that each deal in your portfolio is different. When you have numerous deals to decide, or already have in place, it can become difficult to meaningfully compare them as well as manage the entire portfolio.

In fact, the resulting portfolio of sourcing decisions makes each client's approach to outsourcing very different. This is one reason why management consultancy templates for outsourcing often run into problems, and why understanding configuration is vital to successful outsourcing.

4.1.1   The Seven Configuration Attributes

Each deal is made up of seven attributes as shown in Figure 4-1. These attributes are:

- **Scope grouping** - what work is being provided to whom, and where,
- **Supplier grouping** - how many providers, and in what form,
- **Financial scale** - what the deal will cost and how relatively important it is in dollar value,
- **Duration** - how long a deal will run, including extension options,
- **Pricing framework** - how payment to the provider is calculated,
- **Resource ownership** - which party controls what resources, and
- **Commercial relationship** - how the high-level relationship is structured.

Figure 4-1: The Seven Key Attributes of Configuration

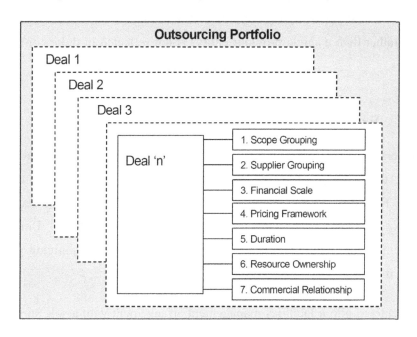

Since many, if not most, clients use a number of providers under differing arrangements, we use the term **'portfolio'** to describe the collection of deals in force at any one time for a given organization and the term **'deal'** to mean the outsourcing arrangement with a given provider. A typical outsourcing portfolio will have many deals, 14 deals on average[70], with different service scopes covering different functional and geographic areas of the business. Homogeneous scope (similar service, recipients, and regions) between clients is improbable. And decisions on what to outsource, in which areas of the business, and where, are not simple ones to make.

Each of these seven configuration attributes will be discussed in turn shortly. Note that the concept of configuration represents the client's perspective. It does not represent the provider, although such a concept might very well be applied. For

---

[70] Cullen, S. (2006) "The Configuration Concept: Scope Grouping", Sourcing and Vendor Relationships Executive Update, Vol 7 No 17. Cutter Consortium, Arlington.

that reason, the provider's structural characteristics (e.g. if the provider offshores some of the work, or if service delivery occurs through a number of equity-related entities rather than a single provider entity) is not reflected in these configuration attributes.

4.1.2   Example of the Configuration Concept

To understand why not all outsourcing should be treated as homogeneous, consider the following two organizations.   One is a manufacturing company, MAN1. The other is a national provider, SERV1. Both operate in all states of the country.   Both have annual revenues in the range $2-5 billion.   Both started outsourcing over five years ago for cost savings, but their outsourcing portfolios are very different.

MAN1 entered into a facilities management arrangement with a sole supplier in a 3+2 term[71] $10M per annum fixed-price deal. It sold its assets and facilities to the provider at a high price, agreeing in return to pay relatively high rates for services contracted back, and transferred its facilities management staff to the provider. Five years later, it backsourced its assets and awarded a tender-for-service contract, so saving 70% of the original contract's value.

By contrast, SERV1 entered into a series of labor contracts with various providers whose job was to provide different levels of staff to be under the direct supervision of SERV1's management.   SERV1's contracts were for five years with a combined estimated value of $30M per annum, but were variable-priced at specified labor rates.

The main issues MAN1 had was the sale of the facilities, transfer of staff, and contracted costs greater than current market prices. The main issue SERV1 had

---

[71] A '3+2' year deal means that the initial contract term was for 3 years with the option to extend it for another 2 years.

revolved around the extent to which the providers were expected to do more than just show up - whether they were to project manage as well as provide methodologies and intellectual property.

The point of this example is simply that while both clients described their activities as outsourcing, the nature of the services they are purchasing, their contractual arrangements, their choice of providers, and the issues they faced as a result, are very different.

Using the configuration concept will allow you to make meaningful comparisons between your organization and other organizations, as well as provide insight into the various structural choices and the implications for management.

4.2   Attribute #1: Scope Grouping

Scope Grouping describes **what** services are provided to **whom**, and **where**. This is also known as the *scope footprint*. The three scope footprints are Service, Recipient, and Geographic (see Table 4-1):

- **Service scope** - logical segmentation of work. For example, in an HR function the services of payroll, recruitment, training and development, and remuneration setting are all services that can be outsourced separately or bundled.

- **Recipient scope** - business groups marked to receive outsourced services. These can be divisions, departments, subsidiaries, and joint ventures.

- **Geographic scope** - physical locations that receive outsourced services. The scope can be local footprint (e.g. operations within a city), regional (e.g. state-based), national (e.g. US), and cross border (e.g. Europe).

Table 4-1: Scope Grouping

	Options	Rationale	Risk	Management Issues
Service Scope	Bundled	Conducive to a sole or prime supplier	Maintaining knowledge and control	• Retaining appropriate core competencies • Providing strategy and direction • Providing management focus and time
	Unbundled	Conducive to best-of-bread and/or panels	End-to-end process integration and metrics	• Total cost of ownership (TCO) management • Detailed scope performance metrics that aggregate to overall performance metrics
Recipient	All units	• Consistency, standardization • Potential economies of scale	Unique needs not met cost-effectively	• Getting buy-in from business units • Tailoring agreement to meet unique needs while keeping standards
	Units self select	Accountability and ownership	Integration between business units	Contract flexibility rights (e.g. to merge or eliminate business units, chop and change requirements or KPIs)
Geographic	All areas	• Consistency, standardization • Potential economies of scale	Inconsistent market capabilities between regions	• Getting buy-in from regional management • Tailoring contract to meet unique needs while keeping necessary items standard
	Areas self-select	Accountability and ownership	Integration between regions	Contract flexibility (e.g. rights to merge regions, chop and change service scope, move under a prime supplier)

Service Scope

Service Scope describes the service bundles, often aligned with the traditional segmentation of a function. Many functional areas think of themselves as a collection of services that provide value, or alternatively, of occupying a certain position within the organizational structure. Recognizing this, the **portfolio view** of scope configuration breaks down the entire client into a segmented model that represents the collection of the entire operations of the client and the degree to which they are outsourced, while the **deal-level view** focuses on the service scope within a given contract.

A client may outsource different aspects of a function. Some outsource nearly everything, retaining a minimum of inhouse capability, whilst others perform selective outsourcing of portions of the function. For example, some may outsource an entire help desk, while other outsource only 1st level functions (first contact), while others retain this level and outsource only 2nd level (requires resources and experience) and 3rd level (requiring detailed subject matter expertise).

Recipient Scope

Recipient Scope refers to the business groups that have been identified to receive specific outsourcing services. A contract tailored to the various recipients in a client has been sometimes referred to 'creative contracting' in which special contractual provisions are created to meet each recipient's unique needs.

This is particularly applicable to decentralized clients, which often allow business units to selectively participate in outsourcing initiatives. In that case, the client is likely to have a different SLA for each of its business units in the recipient scope, but all operating under an umbrella contract.

The recipient footprint can also cover organizations outside of the particular client, which is something we see in the government sector whereby a number of departments or agencies are bundled into a single contract.

Geographic Scope

Geographic Scope refers to the physical locations marked to receive particular outsourcing services. For domestic outsourcing, the geographic footprint is decided by city, state, or regions.

However, geographic scope can be quite complex for global clients. Each geographical area in which the client operates may have a different service scope, as well a different supplier grouping and different providers within that grouping. For example, when Ericsson first decided to outsource its back-office IT back in the 1990's, it selected three preferred global providers; but it let each country decide what (if any) services were to be outsourced and to whom.[72]

4.3   Attribute #2: Supplier Grouping

Supplier Grouping refers to the structuring of the number of providers that are to provide the scope. Managers must be aware that there are more options than the traditional dyad (two parties to the contract) when outsourcing. The provider configurations range from simple (a single 'one-stop-shop' provider) to complex (many providers in different forms).

There are four possible options:

- **Sole Supplier** - a single provider provides all the outsourced services, without any subcontracting.

- **Prime Contractor** - a head provider subcontracts work to any number of third-party providers, but is still accountable for all the scope.

---

[72] Cullen, S. and Willcocks, L. (2003) *Intelligent IT Outsourcing*. Butterworth-Heinemann, Oxford. Korean version (2007), Elsevier.

- **Multiple/Best of Breed** - more than one provider, each providing interdependent services often as the 'best in class' for its particular service scope.

- **Panel** - multiple providers providing similar services under continuous competition. Typically, the panel members operate under the same contractual terms and conditions, none are guaranteed work, and work opportunities are quoted upon by all members as the need arises. Examples include a panel of preferred legal firms, training companies, application developers, and so on.

Any or all of these options can be in place in any given outsourcing portfolio. It is common that different recipients choose different supplier groupings (e.g. one geographic region could use a sole supplier for a given service, but another region might use a multiple-supplier approach for the same service. It is also common that different service scope has different supplier groupings based on how the market operates (e.g. construction is nearly always performed by a prime supplier, legal work performed by multiple providers specific to their expertise, and so on).

We have summarized the rationale, risks, and issues in Table 4-2. In Chapter 12 we debate two of these groupings (Sole Supplier verses Multiple Supplier) because of the trend towards rationalizing providers through aggregating scope into a sole-source arrangement - which is known as **bundling**. We have experienced numerous debates on all these supplier groupings for the last two decades, but the most controversial one remains whether to use a few wide-scope providers or many specialists. That debate is far from finished.

Table 4-2: Supplier Grouping

	Rationale	Risks	Management Issues
Sole Supplier	• Single accountability • Potential to pass on economies of scale • Streamlined delivery • End-to-end KPIs	• Monopolistic behaviors by the sole provider • Compromised quality where the sole supplier is not best of breed (in certain services, businesses, or geographic areas)	• Extensive contract flexibility and rights due to the dependence on one provider • Having independent expertise to avoid solution channeling and to ensure ongoing value for money
Prime Contractor	• Single accountability • Allows potential for best-of-breed subcontracting • More complex contracting • End-to-end KPIs	• Prime must be good at subcontracting (selection, management, exit) • Client may desire different subcontractors • Client having to resolve issues between the prime and subcontractors • Primes and subcontractors can encroach on each other's territory	• Contract ensuring various rights over subcontracting (access, selection, veto, etc.) • Compliance auditing ensuring the prime passes on obligations to the subcontractors • Ensuring all parties operate as an efficient front
Multiple/ Best of Breed	• Greater control • Flexibility to chop and change • Promotes competition and prevents complacency	• Attracting the market for smaller 'slices' of work • Keeping providers interested, giving focus and allocating staff • Interdependent services and contracts • Integration complexity • Tracing accountability	• Design of inter-dependent contracts between independent providers • Multi-party interfaces and handovers • End-to-end process management • Interdependent lifecycles
Panel	• Buy services / products as required • Promotes ongoing competition • Prevents complacency	• Attracting providers when there is no guarantee work • Adding new panel members • Use of providers not on the panel	• Bidding process of panel members for work orders • Continuous ranking of panel members • Managing and evaluating the total panel program

Sole Supplier

Sole Supplier is the simplest relationship, whereby a single provider supplies the entire scope. This is commonly also knows as the 'one-stop-shop'. It is preferred by clients who want one point of accountability. However, these clients often compromise superior service quality across the entirety of the scope, because the sole supplier is rarely pre-eminent in all areas. While this supplier configuration might lower communication costs, it is very costly to switch a provider that has a large scope, and can make the client vulnerable to opportunistic behavior because of the client's dependence on the one provider.

Prime Contractor

A Prime Contractor arrangement is another supplier configuration is used to overcome the issue with quality in the sole supplier model, while also overcoming the communication issues in the multiple supplier model. Accordingly, it acts as a hybrid between sole-sourcing and multi-sourcing. In this model, one head provider (the 'Prime') is held accountable and contractually liable for all outsourced services, but uses any number of subcontractors to deliver the scope. These subcontractors are chosen either by you, or by the Prime, or a combination of both of you.

The subcontractors tend to have expertise, or operate in regions that the Prime does not so that the Prime can contract for the full scope of work. But that is not always the case. On occasion, even though the Prime does not need to subcontract, specific subcontractors may be required by your organization for a particular reason (e.g. previous work done), or you may require a specified number of local subcontractors as part of an industry development program.

Note that, at a minimum, this supplier configuration requires contract provisions to limit what can be subcontracted, to which companies, and how the subcontractors will be controlled.

Multiple/Best-of-Breed

This approach is where you have a number of providers. You can configure this so that each provides a unique service (best of breed) or have interchangeable, loosely coupled providers that may be doing similar work (multiple). In such arrangements, your organization is, in effect, the 'head contractor' for the supply chain.

This approach may be preferred if you want the most qualified providers doing work, want control over the relationship, or you do not want to become over dependent on any particular provider. However, the approach becomes difficult when the various providers need to work together. The benefits and problems with this option relate to the competitive element - it is difficult to manage providers that may be competing with one another, but this tension can also yield continuous improvement and allows for cost effective benchmarking.

Panel

A Panel arrangement involves a list of preferred providers that continuously compete for work. Typically, no provider is guaranteed work and each must compete on a regular basis for various contracts or 'work orders' over a defined period. A panel is common where the work is periodic and/or and your requirements vary extensively with each new initiative.

In one of our ITO studies in 2006, we found that, while panels were only used by 12% of the 76 organizations in the study, panels resulted in the most amount of clients that were very satisfied.[73] The explanation is simple. Panels offer the most flexibility, the greatest range of choice, and maintain the client's bargaining power.

---

[73] See Figure 12-1 in Chapter 12 from Cullen, S. (2006) "The Configuration Concept: Scope Grouping", *Sourcing and Vendor Relationships Executive Update*, Vol 7 No 17. Cutter Consortium, Arlington.

On the providers' side, it offers more opportunities to work with clients that might have otherwise formed exclusive arrangements.

4.4   Attribute #3: Financial Scale

Financial Scale indicates the degree of outsourcing performed in a financial sense, describing its financial value to the client, using both the *relative* and *absolute* dimensions, as well as its financial value within the industry using the absolute dimension.

- Relative spend - the percent of operating spend represented by the outsourcing portfolio.

- Absolute value - the dollar value of the contract, expressed as either a per annum value, but often as the total value over the contract's duration (e.g. a five-year contract worth $10 million per year expressed as a $50 million deal).

Relative Financial Scale

If a client outsources 80% or more of the operating budget for a function, it is usually considered a total outsourcing of that function. Total outsourcing is rare, risky if not done properly, and the stakes are high. Large relative-scale deals require considerable time, effort, and money to execute the complex contracting process. This is why having many small-scale contracts has been the norm. But small-scale outsourcing may not attract many providers, and have been known to receive less than the desired attention by many providers.[74]

---

[74] Cullen, S., Seddon, P. and Willcocks, L. (2005) "ITO Configuration: Research into Defining and Designing Outsourcing Arrangements", *Journal of Strategic Information Systems*. December, 14.

Absolute Financial Scale

In order to invoke greater competition, clients often turn to a deal's absolute value and try to make it a large number. Provider's use this as well to their advantage, by reporting the total possible income stream rather than its annual value or relative financial scale. It is interesting that when we began practicing and researching in the late 80's/early 90's a 'mega deal' worthy of making the global press was $100 million, but now must be $1 billion or more. These and other issues are laid out in Table 4-3.

Table 4-3: Financial Scale

	Option	Rationale	Risks	Management Issues
Relative Scale	Large relative scale	• Enable focus on core business • Allow major transformations	• High risk and impact • Consumes significant senior resources • Knowledge retention	• Managing large-scale change • Management of outsourcing must be a core competence
	Small relative scale	• Retain operational knowledge • Manage at lower levels • Outsource tasks, not functions	• Management responsibility 'bolted on' to existing roles. • Expertise and/or attention may be absent.	• Ensuring risks are managed, since the dollar value is low and can be overlooked • Ensuring those responsible know how to manage contracts
Absolute Scale	Large absolute scale	• Attract many providers and/or large providers • Attract volume discounts	• Winner's curse (provider bids too low to make a profit) • Subcontractors likely to be required	• Getting expertise equal to the provider/s • Ensuring costs do not overrun
	Small absolute scale	• Target small providers and be an important client • Approve and manage at lower ranks	• May need to get the market's attention • Can receive scant attention from either, or both, parties • Lots of 'little' deals can quickly add up to large relative scale	• Managing the overall small-scale deals as a portfolio

4.5   Attribute #4: Pricing Framework

Early outsourcing deals were typically fixed price, but today there are many more options. The Pricing Framework describes the method by which the payment to the provider/s is calculated. There are three basic options: Lump Sum, Unit Rate, and Cost-based.

- **Lump Sum** - a fixed price for a specific scope (e.g. $20 million per year for customer call including a contract centre and CRM (customer relationship management) system).

- **Unit Rate** - a price per specific transaction unit (e.g. price per call, rate per hour, cost per machine).

- **Cost-based** - invoiced at the provider's actual costs plus a percentage mark up or fixed management fee (e.g. equipment cost + 30% mark-up or equipment cost + $330k per annum administration fee).

Which one is best? In one study, in the offshore context, clients reported that unit rates produced better work. Providers were not pressured to take shortcuts in order to protect their profit margins as they were with lump-sum deals.[75] But in another study, the authors found that provider profits were higher for time & materials unit rate configurations (a labor rate plus a cost-based charge for products and supplies) than for lump sum contracts.[76] This was due to some providers placing new employees on client accounts because the client (in effect) subsidizes the providers' employee learning curve by pay the same labor rates for new employees as for existing ones, but even more so was that employees who are unproductive take more hours to complete tasks, which then generates greater revenues. In one case, concerning the maintenance of a major port, the only aspect of configuration that changed in the second-generation deal was the movement

---

[75] Lacity, M. and Rottman, J. (2008) *Offshore Outsourcing of IT Work*, Palgrave, UK.

[76] Gopal, A., et al. (2003) "Contracts in Offshore Software Development: An Empirical Analysis," *Management Science*, Vol. 49, 12, 1671-1683.

from a cost-based configuration to a lump sum. The incumbent provider increased the price by 30% (which was still much lower than the other new entrant bidders). This was to hedge risk and cost increases, which used to be borne by the client at the point it occurred, but now had to be 'priced in' whether it occurred or not.

However, you will rarely see a single contract being invoiced using only one of these frameworks. Pricing combinations, or hybrids, are more common than a pure form, particularly with experienced clients who have been through many generations of sourcing decisions. They know that there is no simple answer and each model must be chosen carefully, for different parts of the scope. The rationale, risks, and management issues of each option are in Table 4-4.

Table 4-4: Pricing Framework

	Rationale	Risk	Management Issues
Lump Sum	• Potential to lock in cost • Predictable costs within the specified volume bands • Explicit financial goal	• Misinterpretations over what is 'in' and 'out' of the price • Can lose track of individual cost drivers, as everything is lumped into one figure • Can be difficult to obtain reduced price if less volume is required • Portion of the fixed price relates to the risk determined by the provider in terms of the volatility of cost to supply	• Continuous forecasting • Monitoring price limitations (e.g. volumes) • Defining and managing scope • Agreeing charges for out-of-scope work • Ability to unbundle prices, and assess cost drivers and benchmarks
Unit rates	• Ability to 'chop and change' services • Volume discounts • Reduce costs by reducing demand • Track unit costs • Assists chargeback systems	• Can be a premium if provider does not have a base guaranteed workload • Exceeding budget - supply is effectively 'unlimited', particularly if there has been pent up demand or latent demand created	Tracking and managing demand, as price is directed related to usage

	Rationale	Risk	Management Issues
Cost-based	• Full knowledge of cost dynamics • Retain knowledge of operations • Can track unit costs, in particular when calculating TCO (total cost of operations)	• Costs are known, but in the control of the provider • Costs are incurred prior to client audits, thus client cannot recoup past 'losses' • Provider often reliant upon client directions • Provider without motivation to reduce cost	• Maintaining a detailed understanding of cost drivers and market prices • Directing provider's efficiency • Auditing and benchmarking of provider's costs and efficiency

Lump Sum

Lump Sum models charge a fixed amount for a fixed period for a fixed amount of work. The conditions for a lump-sum contract require certainty of demand, as well as certainty of cost to supply. Otherwise, the price will be anything but the 'fixed price' because such contracts are only fixed under specified conditions. As was found by many of the early clients, the quoted price was rarely the actual one paid as volumes fluctuated and controversial 'out-of-scope' work attracted additional fees. Variations become the norm, not the envisioned price stability.

Unit-based Price

Unit-based models charge a price per specific transaction unit (either an input unit such as labor, or an output unit such as calls responded to). This is the 'utility form' of outsourcing, whereby you only pay for what you use. Issues arise over the need to guarantee a minimum base load in order to cover any permanent resources the provider requires, your ability to accurately forecast demand, and the degree of volume discounts available.

Cost-based Price

Cost-based, or 'cost plus', models have the provider pass through actual costs to the client, plus a provision for profit. This profit component can come either as a percentage markup (e.g. materials at cost with a 10% markup) or part of a fixed management fee (e.g. $1M per annum). Reimbursables are covered this model as well, but do not have a profit component. This approach has value when the demand and cost to supply are uncertain. However, you will have high management overheads due to the time and effort in verifying that 'best cost' was actually achieved (e.g. auditing invoices, timesheets, and the like).

4.6   Attribute #5: Duration

The duration reflects the agreed length of the contract. This can be expressed as one duration term, multiple terms or a never-ending term. Accordingly, there are three options (see Table 4-5):

- **Single Term** - a contract fixed for a single term

- **Rollover** - fixed initial term with options to extend.

- **Evergreen** - no defined contract expiry date, either party can invoke various termination rights.

Table 4-5: Duration

	Rationale	Risk	Management Issues
Single term	Can be aligned to life of assets or to other contracts	Results in a retender even if the provider has performed well	Preparing for end of contract
Rollover	• Pre-set conditions for extending the contract • Motivates provider to do well to get the extension	• Extension occurs due to inadequate planning, performance • No competition from other providers	• Assessing adequacy of rollover conditions • Assessing current market conditions to decide if a retender is warranted
Ever-green	• Never out of contract • Parties continue as long as mutually beneficial	Complacency in either or both parties	• Continuous assessment of contract • An unforeseen termination by a party

Conflicting advice over long versus short-term contracts abound. Some believe the endemic uncertainty involving business today and the requirement for clients to experiment and learn precludes having long-term contracts. Others argue that long-term contracts enable the provider to learn about the client and for the parties to establish mutual trust. Longer-term contracts enable set-up costs to be distributed over a longer period. Furthermore, in certain cultures, like those across Asia Pacific, longer-term contracts are a reflection of the value that the culture places on long-term relationships.

Any of these duration configurations can be short or long-term deals. For example, a single-term deal could be for one or ten years and likewise an evergreen deal could end after one year or go on for ten years. A rollover could be any number of years in duration, (e.g., a 3+2+2 deal could be three, five, or seven years depending upon whether the two extensions are taken up).

Single-Term

Single-Term deals are fixed-duration contracts that expire on a specified date and do not provide for extensions. Extensions, of course, can be negotiated and the contract varied accordingly. However, the party with the greatest negotiation power at the time of the extension will be able to exert that power over the extension conditions - and this may not be you.

Rollover

Rollover contracts have a fixed initial term and multiple shorter-term extension options. The extension/s can be either automatic (extension automatically occurs unless the client notified the provider otherwise by the notice deadline) - the most common form, or by agreement (the contract ends unless the extension is agreed).

Today, rollover is the most common form of duration because of the flexibility it offers. Unfortunately, most contracts using this form end up extending because the client did not give itself enough time to do anything other than extend.

Evergreen

Less common, but still popular, is the use *of evergreen* contracts. Evergreen deals have no expiry date. Instead, the contract continues until either party invokes its termination rights, or the goal has been achieved. An example of the former type is a labor contract (it continues as long as the client still wants the contractor and the contractor still wants the work). An example of the latter type is for construction or applications development (the contract ends at completion of the build, although there may be liquidating damages for missing a deadline).

4.7   Attribute #6: Resource Ownership

Resource Ownership describes which party controls or 'owns' the service delivery resources. These resources are the service delivery assets, facilities, and labor - any of which can be owned by either party. This 'ownership' is not literal; it merely identifies the party holding, for example, a facility or asset lease, or the party holding the labor agreement with contracted staff.

Table 4-6 shows a matrix of the various ownership alternatives, and highlights what each party contributes to each form of resource ownership. Table 4-7 summarizes the rationale, risks, and issues.

Table 4-6: Resource Ownership Options

Resource	Party 'Owning' the Resource (P = provider, C = client)												
	P	C	P	C	P	C	P	C	P	C	P	C	P
Assets (e.g. plant, software)	✓		✓			✓	✓			✓		✓	✓
Facilities (e.g. site, call center)	✓			✓	✓			✓	✓			✓	✓
Labor (direct & management)		✓	✓			✓	✓			✓	✓		✓
	Infra-structure		Onsite		Service & Facility		Asset Buy-in		Facility Host		Labor Buy-in		Total

Resource Ownership Options

The degree of *specifity* (how specialized a resource is) plays a key role in resource ownership decisions. If a resource is specific to an organization, if necessary knowledge is unable to be separated from specific people, or if it requires a certain asset unable to be used for other purposes - then the switching costs to get in another provider become immense, and you can become hostage (held to a disadvantage) by the provider.

Table 4-7: Resource Ownership

	Rationale	Risk	Management Issues
Infrastructure	• Access to infrastructure without capital investment • Pay for required capacity • Potential for volume discounts	• High switching costs • Often requires commodity assets (vanilla solutions) • Contract duration reflect asset life, not business cycle	• Capacity planning • Ensuring security and disaster recovery at provider • Ensuring asset refreshment is at market standard and price
Onsite	• Co-location promotes interaction and understanding • Greater degree of confidentiality • Can observe staff • More seamless services	• No economies of scale from shared facilities with other clients • Provider's staff adopt client's culture rather than provider's	• Ensuring facility security and maintenance • Maintaining a relationship

	Rationale	Risk	Management Issues
Service and facility	• Assets portable to a successor at minimal cost • No novation of asset leases or software licenses required	• Assets must be maintained in accord with warranty • No economies of scale from shared assets with others	• Ongoing performance and compliance reviews • Ensuring site security and disaster recovery
Asset Buy-in	• Direct control over what is bought and what it costs • Pay for required assets • Competition for each buy-in round	Provider may veto assets it does not want to support	Asset specification, implementation, integration, and management
Facility host	• Control of services and outcomes • No need to support and maintain facility	• Network link to host – potential node fault • Limited physical access to site	• Interface and access management • Ensuring site security and disaster recovery
Labor/ Staff Augmentation	• Access to skill base and expertise • Lower switching costs, if no specific knowledge	• Accountability split between parties • Provider's staff need site accommodation and access	• Providing directions to the provider's staff and managing their time • Resolving conflicting needs of the 'two bosses' - one in each party
Total	• Focus on core business • Access to facilities and assets without capital investment • Centralized support • End-to-end performance metrics • Less integration issues	• Loss of control • Over-dependence on provider • High exit barriers and disengagement costs • Significant transition requirements • Extensive rights required in contract	• Ongoing performance and compliance reviews • Obtaining operational knowledge • Ensuring viable alternatives and termination options • Auditing provider's internal controls

4.8   Attribute #7: Commercial Relationship

The commercial relationship summarizes the high-level, inter-organizational structure (that is, organization to organization, as opposed to individuals within the parties), nature of relationship structure. Options are *Arms-length, Value-add, Co-sourced*, and *Equity* listed below. Table 4-8 summarizes the rationale, risks, and issues.

- **Arms-length** - independent parties for which the relationship is solely fee-for-service.

- **Value add** - independent parties with a combination of arms-length contracts and shared business initiatives.

- **Co-sourced** - independent parties providing a mix of labor and assets, with integrated end accountability.

- **Equity** - parties owning equity in the same service providing entity (e.g. the client owning shares in the provider, or both owning a portion of a joint venture).

Note that 'partnering' is not defined as an option. Partnering is a term used today to express a trust-based relationship that various parties have attempted to engender in any of the commercial relationship options. Such trust, and the ability to rely on the other party not behaving opportunistically, is often sought in all forms of commercial relationships, rather than it being a discrete form of structure.

Partnering relationships describe a collection of intangible characteristics such as compatible cultures, working toward common goals, proactive and strategic management, and so on. It is a description of the desired behaviors between the parties, and not a unique structure per se. Partnering-style behaviors can be achieved under any of the structures, if both parties are willing to invest more than usual in the relationship, put in the right sort of people (e.g. proactive, strategic-thinking, relationship orientated), and put in the necessary underlying business practices (innovation workshops, competitive scanning/ benchmarking, etc.).

Table 4-8: Commercial Relationship

	Rationale	Risk	Management Issues
Arms length	• Distinct accountabilities • Transparency	Can result in a more adversarial approach	Defining accountabilities
Value-add	Ability to derive greater mutual value from the relationship	• The value-added element can get left behind in the need to deliver 'core' scope • Potential initiatives are often good concepts but difficult to implement	Delivery of accountabilities plus planning and executing initiatives
Co-sourced	• Both parties contribute valuable expertise • Co-location facilitates staff commitment • Client can maintain directional control	• Shared accountability decreases 'answerability' • Often means client bears majority of risk • Disengagement turmoil	• Establishing and ensuring shared values when provider wants profit and client cost control • Cost savings and overrun sharing
Equity	• Shared governance • Possible board representation • Eases transition transfers - asset, facility, and staff • May receive a return on investment	• Partners with different agendas - provider to make profits and client to have low costs • Unwinding equity to cancel contract, or vice versa • Use of alternative providers politically difficult	• Managing the contract as well as the entity vehicle • Ensuring balance of power such that one party is not more dominant than the other

Arms-Length

Arms-length is where the deal is between independent parties representing mutually exclusive accountabilities. This structure is the most common where the provider has a discrete scope of work and the client's main responsibility is to pay on time. This form makes both parties' jobs straightforward (although not necessarily any easier!).

Value-add

Value-add is where the parties have a combination of arms-length services as well as shared business initiatives, such as the commercialization of intellectual property that is being jointly developed under the contract. Under these arrangements, although there is typically one contract, there are distinct and unique components that will have different contractual obligations and remuneration approaches. On occasion, the parties combine in an attempt to market new products and services, or have a gainsharing arrangement whereby the provider receives additional revenue for doing something outside the service scope (e.g. finding a tenant for underutilized space at the client).

Co-sourced

The Co-sourced approach is where both parties provide a mix of resources (service labor, assets, and/or facilities) and have integrated accountability for the end result. Often, these involve co-location of staff and management, typically at the client's site. It is common that the provider's staff cannot be readily identified as such (e.g. they do not wear branded clothing) to facilitate the desired teamwork or so that the client's end customers do not know who is the actual employer of the individual at the front line.

Equity

Equity relationships have the parties share equity in a service delivery entity. The entity can be a joint venture or the client may have an ownership stake in the provider, often with board representation (or vice versa with the provider owning shares in the client). On occasion, it may be a related entity providing services to other related entities (e.g. a wholly owned, shared-service subsidiary). However, some people do not consider the related-entity relationship structure as outsourcing at all - it is merely a different way to structure an insourced operation.

The model has been identified as a major vehicle for business growth, where both parties pair their complementary strengths to undertake ventures that neither may have attempted independently. However, research into the joint venture equity structure has generally found that this form of commercial relationship structure leads to complacency and indifference at the operational level from the service delivery entity. Moreover, when complaints are made about poor service, the delivery entity justifiably argues that it was devoting its efforts to securing further revenues with other clients, which is to the advantage of the parent/customer entity since it owns part of the delivery entity. While some parent/customer entities have been able to exert some control over the delivery entity, many end up subsidizing other clients of the entity.

4.9   A Case Study

The following case, from one particular client that outsourced its IT function, is presented to demonstrate how configuration, and more importantly careful re-configuration, has worked in practice. In this case, the numbers in square brackets [...] correspond to the seven configuration attributes.

Case: Configuration changes get the results

GOV1 is a state owned enterprise with annual revenue of around $1B. The initial outsourcing deal was negotiated in 1994. It was supposedly a "*partnering*" deal, under which the provider agreed to full cost disclosure. However, the provider later subcontracted out 70% of service provision to another party that refused (and was not contractually obliged) to disclose its costs. GOV1 was therefore unable to gain access to the costs of service provision for the majority of its services.

Viewing the configuration at the portfolio level, GOV1 outsourced [1] all its IT function to [2] a single prime provider. This was [3a] a moderately large contract of $20M per annum, with [3b] 100% of the budget outsourced. Viewed at the contract level, this configuration involved [4] a five + five year [5] fixed-price contract. Resource ownership [6] was such that the provider owned the assets (bought from the client), and was responsible for supplying and managing labor. The facilities ownership was split in that the client owned the helpdesk facilities and the provider subcontracted the data center facilities. While this was intended to be a partnering deal, the contract was distinctly arms-length in nature [7].

The result of this configuration (and that the client did not retain any expertise) was that costs rose, service dropped, and the promised strategic leadership from the provider never materialized. GOV1 was unable to renegotiate the contract with either the prime or the subcontractor, and suffered under this configuration for the full five years.

Near the end of the first contract, the GOV1 hired a new CIO to reconfigure the outsourcing arrangement. Viewed at the portfolio level, he [1] re-scoped service provision into three groups of services, which he [2] contracted out to three different best-of-breed providers. As with the first single contract, this group of contracts [3a] amounted to a moderately large arrangement, with [3b] almost 100% of the IT budget outsourced. Viewed at the deal level, each of the three contracts had a different term [4]. One was 3+2, one was 6+3+3, and one was evergreen. Pricing was [5] hybrid in all three contracts, combining fixed price elements and variable priced elements. Resource ownership changed so that [6] each provider provided and managed the entirety of the resource base (facilities, assets, and labor). Each contract was [7] an arm's length deal.

At the end of year 1, the cost saving for all three contracts were satisfactory, service quality was judged adequate for two of the three providers, and strategic leadership was absent in all three. In other words, two of the three deals were judged successful in accordance with expectations. The third was much less so from a service view, but had the greatest cost savings (which made the CIO, but not his internal customers, very happy).

The CIO attributed the much greater success of the second-generation deals to changes in the outsourcing configuration. He reported that the old contract made IT very difficult to manage, and that these problems reduced significantly with the new configuration. Particularly important changes were the moves from a prime contract to best-of-breed contracts, from a relationship that assumed (but did not articulate) partnering to explicit arm's length deals, to hybrid pricing, and changing resource ownership to GOV1 owning the bulk of the assets.

These are all configuration issues. Configuration decisions, as he discovered, are the most crucial decisions to make.

PART 2: A PROGRAM OF ACTION - THE OUTSOURCING LIFECYCLE

Organizations have sought to attribute outsourcing success to particular variables that management believes can be easily imitated. Debates often centre on particular contractual variables (e.g. fixed price vs. time and materials, penalties vs. rewards, short-term vs. long-term), or scope variables (e.g. outsourcing infrastructure vs. services), or even the number of providers (e.g. sole-sourcing vs. multi-sourcing).

However, clients that outsourced the same things, with similar contracts, similar pricing models, etc. have had different results. The answer is quite simple. Clients have gone about outsourcing in very different ways. Success lies within in how clients manage the entire outsourcing lifecycle from womb to tomb.

In this Part 2, we provide you with all you need to know about the entire journey. We have written this as a series of actions addressed to you, as the leader of an outsourcing initiative.

We begin in Chapter 5 with an overview of the lifecycle. Figure 5-3, in particular, gives you the entire roadmap. In Chapter 6, we explain the **Architect Phase** where the smart strategic decisions need to be made and the deal designed in detail. Chapter 7, the **Engage Phase**, is all about buying and negotiating wisely - choosing the best provider under fair terms. Chapter 8, the **Operate Phase** is where the results design to occur (from the previous two phases) actually transpire through good ongoing management; or, alternatively, defects from taking shortcuts are painfully and laboriously attempted to be rectified. Chapter 9, the **Regenerate Phase** where the next generation of sourcing decisions are made and a new lifecycle begins. But this time, as in each new generation, better and faster.

Chapter 5   Overview of the Lifecycle

"Things should be made as simple as possible, but no simpler"

Albert Einstein

The Outsourcing Lifecycle is a structured way for you to make decisions, prepare for, and manage outsourcing from pre-contract to contract end. It incorporates two decades of learning and hindsight gained from 107 organizations, in 51 countries, covering deals spanning up to a decade, and ranging in value from US$200,000 to $1.5 billion per year.[77] Clients that followed the phases and building blocks in this lifecycle had more success, and fewer problems, than those that followed other sequences.

The lifecycle consists of four phases, divided into nine building blocks (BB1 to BB9), and further broken down into key actions per building block. Figure 5-1 shows the lifecycle at its highest level, highlighting the circular nature of the process as it repeats itself with each new generation. Figure 5-3 shows the lifecycle in more detail, providing the key goals and outputs along the journey.

The lifecycle shows what actions should take place, and the best time to conduct them. In the lifecycle, each phase, and its building blocks, prepares the way for the ones that follow. Likewise, the success of each one depends on the success of the preceding actions, with the last phase paving the way for the next-generation sourcing strategy and its lifecycle.

---

[77] Cullen, S., Seddon, P. and Willcocks, L. (2005) "Managing Outsourcing: The Lifecycle Imperative", *MISQ Executive*, June.

Figure 5-1: The Outsourcing Lifecycle

BUILDING BLOCK 9 REFRESH
BUILDING BLOCK 1 INVESTIGATE
BUILDING BLOCK 8 MANAGE
BUILDING BLOCK 2 TARGET
REGENERATE
OPERATE
ARCHITECT
OUTSOURCING LIFECYCLE
BUILDING BLOCK 7 TRANSITION
BUILDING BLOCK 3 STRATEGIZE
ENGAGE
BUILDING BLOCK 6 NEGOTIATE
BUILDING BLOCK 4 DESIGN
BUILDING BLOCK 5 SELECT

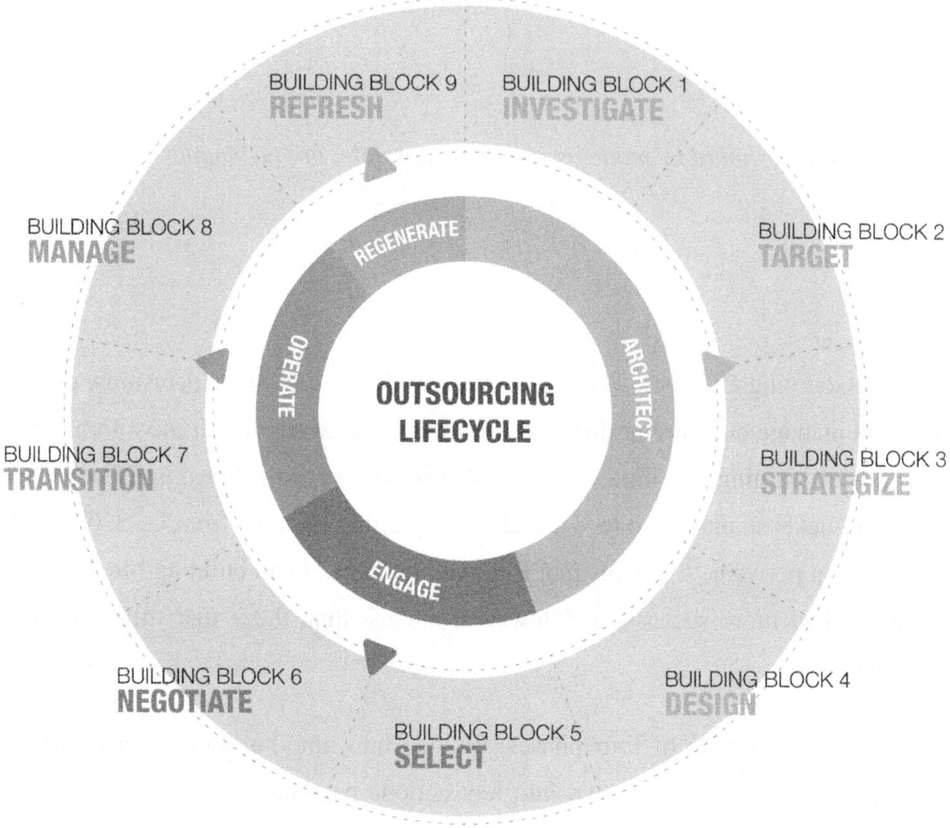

It is not unusual that you may need to loop back because you may find that you need to know more about something that you were not aware of until later on in the lifecycle. For example, you may not have investigated how performance measures really work in BB1: Investigate, but found that in BB4: Design, you do really need to know this. So, you loop back to BB1 and gain acumen on this subject before moving on through the lifecycle once more.

Many clients only plan the activities within the building blocks immediately before conducting them - in effect, looking at outsourcing as few discrete tasks, not as an interdependent lifecycle. As depicted in Figure 5-2, disjointed teams then often produce interrelated outputs, without integration and communication.

This, more often than not, results in conflicts, overlap, and contradictions in the contract documents, as well as in the conduct of the entire lifecycle.

For example, without planning the entire lifecycle, a general manager may determine what is going to be outsourced, a legal team prepares the contract, an operational team prepares the SLA, an evaluation panel selects the provider, and a different team altogether formed to manage the deal and so on. One team is rarely privy to the debates and issue resolutions that took place with other teams; thus, lack a thorough understanding of the implications of other teams' work and, eventually the basis for the final arrangement.

Figure 5-2: Haphazard vs. Streamlined Approach

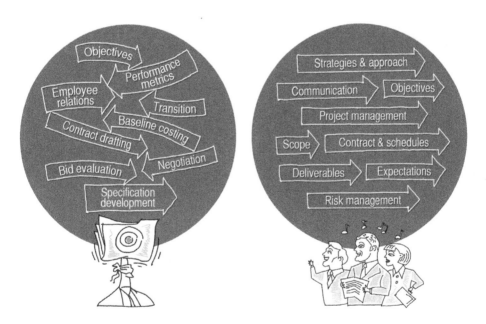

The remainder of Part 2 explains all the phases, building blocks, and key actions along with over 60 cases to demonstrate why these actions are so important. To keep things brief, we have allocated roughly one to two pages per action, although many of these actions have entire books dedicated to the subject (e.g. the Contract Scorecard, which is Action 17).

Figure 5-3: The Lifecycle: Goals and Key Outputs

ARCHITECT PHASE				ENGAGE PHASE		OPERATE PHASE		REGENERATE PHASE
BUILDING BLOCK 1 **INVESTIGATE**	BUILDING BLOCK 2 **TARGET**	BUILDING BLOCK 3 **STRATEGIZE**	BUILDING BLOCK 4 **DESIGN**	BUILDING BLOCK 5 **SELECT**	BUILDING BLOCK 6 **NEGOTIATE**	BUILDING BLOCK 7 **TRANSITION**	BUILDING BLOCK 8 **MANAGE**	BUILDING BLOCK 9 **REFRESH**
OUTCOME	**OUTCOME**	**OUTCOME**	**OUTCOME**	**OUTCOME**	**OUTCOME**	**OUTCOME**	**OUTCOME**	**OUTCOME**
Acumen	Focus	Long-term strategies	Detailed future	Best value for money	Sealed deal	Adept start	Results	Better, faster
Key Actions	**Key Actions**	**Key Actions**	**Key Actions**	**Key Actions**	**Key Actions**	**Key Actions**	**Key Actions**	**Key Actions**
↗ Understood lifecycle	↗ Sourcing map	↗ Configuration strategy	↗ Contract scorecard	↗ Evaluation team	↗ Negotiation team	↗ Final plans	↗ CM network	↗ Next gen capability
↗ Core expertise	↗ Prioritized scope	↗ Business case & approach	↗ Contract blueprint	↗ Selection criteria	↗ Analyzed issues	↗ Transition team	↗ Compliance audits	↗ Outcomes & lessons
↗ Insight from others	↗ Rollout approach	↗ Tender approach	↗ SLA	↗ Market package	↗ Negotiation strategy	↗ Managed staff	↗ Continuous improvement	↗ Next gen decision
↗ Tested expectations	↗ Profiles	↗ Transitions (in & out) strategy	↗ Financial schedule	↗ Facilitated bids		↗ Transfers	↗ Controlled finances	↗ Next gen lifecycle roadmap
↗ Market intelligence		↗ Contract mgmt & retained org strategy	↗ Governance charter	↗ Evaluation		↗ Re-engineered & integrated practices	↗ Performance mgmt	
		↗ Lifecycle communications plan	↗ Mobilization & exit schedules	↗ Due diligence		↗ Acceptance	↗ Ongoing forecasts	
			↗ Conditions of contract				↗ Relationship mgmt	
							↗ Remain informed	
							↗ Managed issues, variations & disputes	
							↗ Record keeping & reporting	

Chapter 6   Make Smart Decisions - the Architect Phase

The Architect Phase is where the foundation for successful outsourcing is set up. It is here that you gather the expertise and deep knowledge required to outsource successfully, do the long-term strategic thinking, and carefully craft the deal that will work.

The Architect Phase consists of the first four building blocks:

- BB1: Investigate - during which you acquire acumen,

- BB2: Target - during which you get focused,

- BB3: Strategize - during which you craft long-term solutions, and

- BB4: Design - during which you build clear and sharp commercial documents.

At the end of this phase, you are able go to the market in a highly professional and focused manner, demonstrating equal knowledge to providers, with fair and practical contractual documents that focus on real, sustainable solutions. You collect, analyze, and prepare information so that your organizational stakeholders can make rational and informed decisions while they have the greatest leverage with the prospective providers.

This Phase begins with the Investigate Building Block, where idealistic notions and concepts that have not been proven to deliver results are jettisoned. These are replaced with evidence-based knowledge to ensure that all the decisions required throughout entire lifecycle will be made, not from theories and beliefs, but from known successful practices.

Building Block 1: Investigate - Gain Acumen

"We are drowning in information and starving for knowledge"

Rutherford D. Roger

| ARCHITECT PHASE | ENGAGE PHASE | OPERATE PHASE | REGENERATE PHASE |

BUILDING BLOCK 1
INVESTIGATE

Outsourcing was long ago established as a highly imitative behavior, where clients attempt to repeat the success of others, but without doing the hard work. Researchers at the Massachusetts' Institute of Technology studied 60 US contracts from 1985 to 1990, and found that Kodak's act of outsourcing started the prevailing push for the practice.[78]

In this case, the prominence of the parties involved (namely Kodak and IBM) and the size of the contract (US$500 million) gave a higher level of visibility than existed previously. Kodak, as an opinion leader, was a symbol of legitimacy to potential adopters and so the imitation process began. This led the researchers to name the outsourcing bandwagon that subsequently occurred as the 'Kodak effect'. Envious clients attempted to copy the imperfectly observed feat, without achieving the expected results.

It was not the act of outsourcing itself that drove success, it was Kodak's years of preparation beforehand. The imitators rushed to outsource, but did not perform the five studies (each six to nine months), and the years of re-engineering, that took place before Kodak made its decision to outsource. Furthermore, it is only

---

[78] Loh, L. and Venkatraman, N. (1992) "Diffusion of Information Technology Outsourcing Influence Sources and the Kodak Effect," *Information Systems Research*, December, 334-358.

the honeymoon period of these historic deals that is discussed amongst the imitators, not the later history. Parts of the deals proved to be not that successful at all.

Outsourcing as an imitative behavior still occurs. In the interest of trying to get the anticipated benefits of outsourcing as quickly as possible, copycat behavior is rampant. Organizations copy what other organizations outsource, copy their strategies, copy their tenders and contracts, copy their contract management techniques...and the list goes on. We have observed over the decades that many who partake in this 'copy and paste' activity have chosen to do this in lieu of acquiring any real understanding of outsourcing and how it works. Myths and wishful thinking drive decisions, not acumen.

Successful outsourcing requires:

- know the lifecycle, and why management of it is so critical (Action 1),

- get the expertise (Action 2),

- gather insights gained from experience (Action 3),

- form realistic stakeholder expectations (Action 4), and

- know the market (Action 5).

The goal of the building block is, in a nutshell, to get smart. Clients with unrealistic expectations of how the deal will operate in practice, what its responsibilities are, and what the provider will actually be doing for the price, quickly become disillusioned and tend to blame the provider for "*not telling them*". For this reason, a client well positioned before selecting the provider(s) works to the benefit of both parties. As one provider's CEO stated, "*the customer from hell is the naïve buyer.*"

Action 1. Know the lifecycle

Clients that put in more effort up front consistently have better results. The key reason for this is that they do all the critical actions while they have bargaining power, not after they lose it. Figure 6-1 shows how bargaining power typically operates throughout the outsourcing lifecycle.

Figure 6-1: Bargaining Power and the Lifecycle

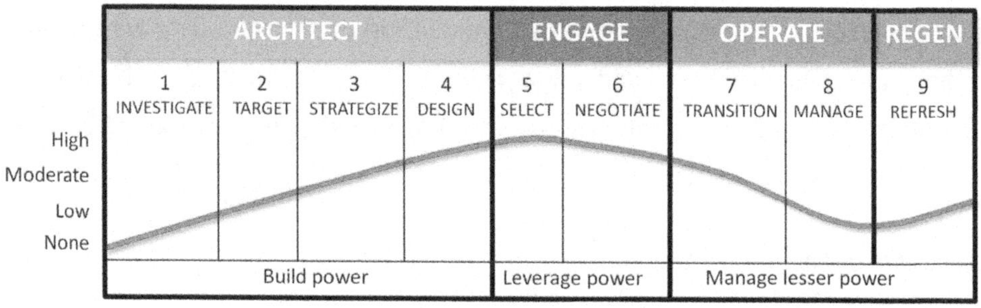

Client Bargaining Power

We begin the conversation on bargaining power, not at the beginning, but in the middle, when the client typically becomes aware of the power curve. This is during BB6: Negotiate.

The power curve begins its downward tilt away from you, and in favor of the preferred provider, once you notify them of their status and begin negotiations. This is because competition has been eliminated and you are now effectively entering into a monopolistic situation regarding the scope of the outsourcing deal. This is the case even if other bidders are 'on call' in the event negotiations fall through. You will rarely be in a genuine position to throw out the preferred provider and start negotiating with the second place bidder (even if you have retained the right to do so), because you will probably be under time and cost constraints to execute the arrangement. Also, remember that second place was awarded to them for a reason and that reason has not changed. Moreover, the next in line will probably know that you have walked away from your preferred provider (there are very few secrets that can be kept from the market), and are running out of options, which lessens your negotiating power even further.

Naturally enough, providers know all this, and many clients have experienced their preferred providers beginning to change tack once negotiations begin. It is the end of the courtship and the beginning of the (outsourcing) marriage. You will no longer hear the unconditional promises made, that the provider believed was necessary to win, during the bidding process. Promises will now be qualified, and you will start to hear things like, "*what we meant in the bid was not quite how you've interpreted it*", or "*our lawyers can't really accept what you have put in the contract*", "*we can certainly do that, would you like us to add it to the scope?*", and so on. While frustrating to clients, this is not a poor reflection on providers, just a natural occurrence as the power shifts.

Then begins the long power slide - after you have signed the contract and during the Operate Phase which comprises BB7: Transition and BB8: Manage.

BB7 is where the mobilization activities take place. Your bargaining power erodes further once the contract has been signed and you enter this building block. This is because of the switching costs. Outsourcing deals are normally prohibitively expensive to renegotiate, terminate and either backsource (bring back inhouse) or transfer to another provider. Besides, the deal is just getting started and most clients do not want to repeat the lengthy process it took to get it in place so soon after it has begun. While it is highly unusual that a client removes a provider during this building block, you will hear of it from time to time. For example, Sears terminated their ten-year agreement with CSC in the first year, (the resulting legal dispute over the US$96 million termination fee was settled in 2007 for an undisclosed sum paid to CSC).[79] It takes a great deal of economic and

---

[79] "CSC and Sears Settle Contract Dispute" *PRNewswire*, October 22 2007, and Sliwa, C. (2005) "Sears, CSC fighting over IT contract termination fees", *Computerworld*, May 23 2005.

political will to exit at this stage, and so the dominating strategy tends to be optimism about the deal improving in the future.

Once the agreement has been transitioned and is in place during BB8, your power is at the lowest point. A monopolistic situation is now in full effect due to the increased switching barriers that prevents easy changing of providers. These barriers include time and cost mentioned earlier, but now that the contract has been in effect for a while, obstacles that were not as serious during the transition, now become much more significant. These include poor disengagement clauses and plans, poor intellectual property ownership and license clauses and recording processes, and inadequate asset purchase and transfer clauses (and related identification and valuation processes), to name just a few.

Your power does begin to build back up slightly during the Refresh Phase (BB9). The contract is nearing its end and the provider will want to gain an extension or renew the contract. As one CEO told us, "*It is amazing the level of attention and service you get when contract renewal is close.*" You will experience only a slight increase in power; you will not have the full power you had during the Architect Phase. This is because, from a number of our next generation studies, the majority of next generation decisions result in the incumbent provider retaining most of the original scope, whether it was put to retender or not.[80] And most providers know this, thus the fear of losing the contract does not motivate them as much as you would hope.

In the first four building blocks you have optimal influence over the deal and getting what you want. The most important work must take place while you are in a position of power before the curve begins its slide away from you.

---

[80] Since many of the outsourcing contracts formed in the early 1990s were long term (7-10 years), we didn't begin research next generation until the late 1990s beginning with Cullen, S. (1997) *Information Technology Outsourcing Survey: A Comprehensive Analysis of IT Outsourcing in Australia.* Deloitte, Melbourne.

Unfortunately, many clients start their outsourcing preparations at BB5 by drafting a tender document in which the market is to respond (typically using a template with onerous conditions, but a loose specification). But skipping the Architect Phase and beginning at BB5 is equivalent to starting to build a house before you have designed it and hoping everything will turn out right in the end.

Note that this power curve does not apply if you are the only, or a very large, buyer and there are many sellers who all want your money. You will always have power if you can easily switch between providers. Conversely, if there are many buyers and only one seller, the provider will be in power no matter what you do. If you want their product, you need to do it on their terms, their way. But these are not normal situations for most outsourcing deals. There are many buyers and sellers of outsourcing services. Buyers have choices with whom to buy, and under what conditions. And sellers are free to choose their clients, and what to charge. However, once a contract is signed, your choices become quite limited, thus you want to ensure you have built up your power to the highest possible point before it begins to erode.

Accordingly, an upfront investment is required during the power-building stages to ensure that later, when power declines, costs are contained and quality is maintained. Those who avoid making the necessary early investment end up spending at least as much, and often quite a bit more, to manage the resultant problems.

There is a recommended investment path and a flawed path in Figure 6-2. The difference is what is invested at what time. The recommended path invests in success (e.g. knowledge, strategies, contracts) while you are in power. The flawed path invests in managing failure (e.g. service failures, surprise charges, renegotiations) after you lose power.

Fundamentally, if you do not have an in-depth understanding of what you are outsourcing, why you are doing it, and how you intend to go about it from start to finish, then it will cost you increasing amounts of time and money later on. More pertinently, if you do not put resources and effort into deals up-front, then you run the risk of being one of the many who have disappointing results, no cost savings, and lower than expected quality.

Figure 6-2: The Two Cost Curves

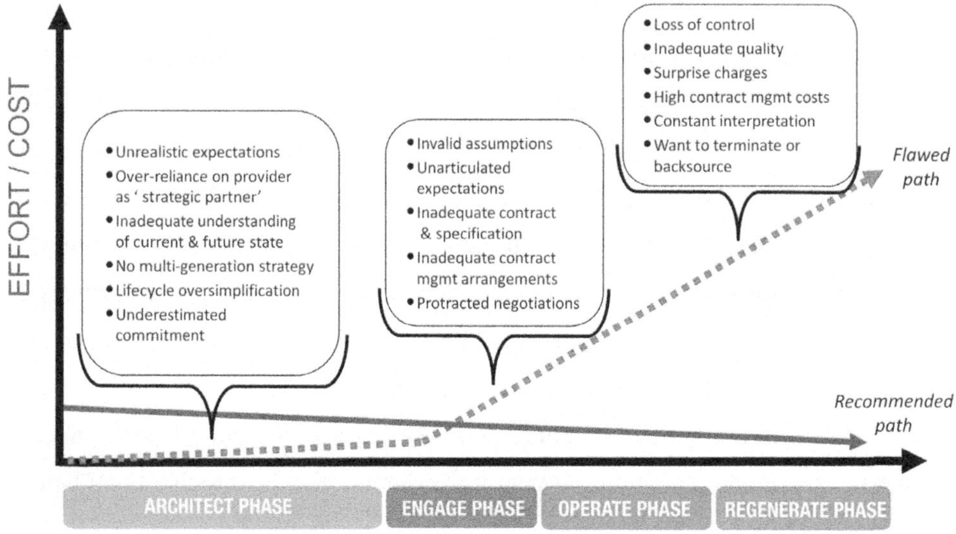

Figure 6-2 illustrates the crux of this issue. The cost of contract (invoices paid to the provider plus the client's cost of managing the arrangements) can get way out of control if shortcuts are taken early in the lifecycle to try to get a deal done fast.

Action 2. Get the core expertise onboard

One person cannot conduct the outsourcing journey alone because the range of expertise required. To give one example, on the UK Inland Revenue's first generation ten-year £1 billion deal with EDS (now owned by HP), there were over 20 people involved on the client side in just in Phases 1 and 2 of the lifecycle.

There are two categories of expertise: core and periodic. We have defined expertise here, as "*the knowledge of a person in an area or topic due to his or her study or experience in the subject matter that distinguish his or her from novices and less experienced people.*" Core expertise is required in every phase and every building block, albeit not necessarily in equal capacities. Periodic expertise is important, but only required for limited periods.

There are five core sets of expertise required throughout the lifecycle:

1. **Commercial expertise** - deep knowledge of the market and how it operates, global and industry trends, customers, supply chains, etc. This expertise is core because it establishes the client as a continuously informed buyer during all phases of the lifecycle.

2. **Program management expertise** - in planning and delivering multiple outsourcing lifecycles. This expertise is core because the lifecycle is, in effect, a long-term program of many interdependent projects with numerous deliverables, resources, and timeframes. Now multiply this by as many contracts as your organization has and you can see the multi-lifecycle/multi-generational thinking and coordination required.

3. **Domain/technical expertise** - deep knowledge of the activity being outsourced (e.g. operations, assets and workforce). This expertise ensures the right things have been specified, are occurring, and are keeping up to the industry. Perhaps most importantly, is that it prevents opportunism by providers who try to take advantage of a client who doesn't know much about what they have bought.

4. **Financial expertise** - including costing and pricing, accounting, billing and payment cycles, insurance, and liability calculations and caps. This is core, not only because there are many financial-related actions throughout the lifecycle, but also because nearly all decisions will have a financial impact.

5. **Contract management expertise** - about provider and relationship management, administration and control, planning and forecasting, performance measurement and evaluation. This is core since it ensures the deal is designed to work in practice and does so in this generation and the next.

The core expertise areas all work together throughout the lifecycle. For example, take one action, formulating the configuration strategy (Action 10) in BB3. Commercial expertise provides knowledge of the configuration strategies used in the industry and drives the supplier grouping. Domain expertise drives the scope grouping, duration, and resource ownership. Financial expertise drives sound price and value configurations. Contract management expertise contributes to the supplier grouping decision and drives the commercial relationship. And program management expertise ensures the whole configuration strategy is delivered.

There are other areas of expertise that are important, but only used periodically throughout the lifecycle. For example, this includes but is not limited to:

- **Audit expertise** (used in BB8) - in preparing and executing audit plans, gathering and examining evidence, reporting findings, making recommendations, and conducting follow-up.

- **Business analysis expertise** (used in BB1) - in researching markets, identifying requirements, analyzing and modeling processes, re-engineering, benchmarking, etc.

- **Commercial documents expertise** (used in BB4) - in preparing the exchanged documents (e.g. tendering and contractual documents) in a commercially sound manner.

- **Communication expertise** (used in BB3) - in formal and informal means of relaying information (one-way communication) and obtaining feedback (two-way communication).

- **Legal expertise** (used in BB4) - in outsourcing deals like the one you are envisioning, including what are industry norms, relevant court judgments, and the management practices required to make clauses enforceable (as merely signing a contract will not be enough).

- **Negotiation expertise** (used in BB6) - across the five styles (see Figure 7-6 in BB6).

- **Procurement expertise** (used in BB5) - in getting best value for money, while promoting fair and open competition and minimizing exposure to fraud and collusion.

- **Risk management expertise** (used in BB4 and BB8) - in identifying risks as attributed by outsourcing, by providers, and by your organization, carrying out probability and mitigation assessments, and implementing prevention techniques.

Of course, you may find you require additional areas of expertise not listed here because your deal, your industry, or your organization requires them. For example, you may want public relations expertise involved in media announcements and industrial relation expertise involved when a unionized workforce may be affected.

The purpose of this action is to identify and gather all the expertise for the entire outsourcing program well in advance, rather than making do with the staff available at the time. When clients did not stop to assess whether the people involved in the outsourcing initiative had the requisite expertise, typically because outsourcing was looked at as a task (and not a long-term program requiring a collection of expertise), serious issues arose; as the following case demonstrates.

Case: HR expertise deficiency causes crisis

A government agency had no expertise remaining in HR after the first generation of its HRO contract. This was by design. The agency's management decided back then that HR expertise would no longer be required, because it would be supplied by the provider.

The second-generation team of four people had only financial skills; no commercial, no domain (HR), nor any contract management expertise. It planned to retender (due to corporate policy) and choose on price. The team was tasked with getting through the Architect and Engage Phases quickly, so it copied a different organization's tendering and contractual documents (from a state government department) and went to market with those. It also had very vague evaluation criteria in which to guide the team in its non-financial assessment. The team was hoping a clear winner would stand out and not need too much evaluation.

After receiving the bids, the team determined it could not evaluate them in any meaningful way since the RFT (Request for Tender) was effectively designed for the other client and not their own needs. Moreover, no one in the team had the necessary expertise to evaluate the representations, approaches, options, departures, or even the prices in the bids. After the decision deadline had passed, in what was now an emergency, it obtained a group of experts with the core expertise who quickly ascertained the actual needs of the organization and evaluated the bids on its behalf, enabling it to choose a preferred provider. However, substantial negotiation and rewriting of the contractual documents was required, as the deal submitted to the market did not fit the agency, and had to be completely re-engineered during negotiation (as was the corresponding price).

Ideally, many different areas of expertise may be present in one individual. However, this is rare. The focus of this action now is to ensure that the required core and periodic expertise is represented in an effective team whose membership will change throughout the lifecycle.

Action 3. Gather insight via experts and experienced organizations

Naivety, often coupled with unrealistic timeframes and effort expectations, has been the root cause of many outsourcing blunders. We have often heard the leading statement, *"if only we had known…"* when people described the lessons learnt. It is amazing some of the deals parties get themselves locked into unnecessarily, when they decide to go cheap, quick, and with limited investigation.

Very few clients conduct their second outsourcing initiative in the same manner as their first, or for that matter any of their future outsourcing initiatives in the same manner as their past. Their experience and hindsight gained from each generation is invaluable to others contemplating outsourcing. Accordingly, it is advantageous for you to cast your net widely across diverse sources when gathering experiential knowledge for your outsourcing deals.

No conversation will be a waste of time, whether it is with other clients, potential providers, expert consultants, or academics researching the field - anyone who has hindsight, evidence, and experience. There is an old military maxim that *"time spent in reconnaissance is seldom wasted,"* and one would be wise to adopt that philosophy here. The next case demonstrates this well.

Case: An insightful investigation

A state government agency beginning a BPO initiative over its property management function had formed some preliminary ideas and expectations, but believed it was prudent to investigate further. It investigated two state government agencies like itself, a federal agency, and two companies, studying in particular the service structure and strategy in each case, the sourcing decisions and lessons, and implications for itself. The agency studied public records and contacted key personnel at the client and their providers.

This investigation changed its previous thinking. The agency learned, for example, that market offerings did not have IT systems up to their expectations. Therefore, they required the bidders to use the client's existing system that was no better or worse than the providers' had. This approach caused very little disruption to operations during transition, and allowed the client to fully retain all information during the term of the contract.

The agency also found the outsourcing market to be immature and disparate. So it opted for a staged open tender rather than a closed tender (invitation only), which had been the original plan. The winning bid ended up being from a provider it would not have invited.

In its investigation, the agency also observed the importance of having both a dedicated transition team and a dedicated contract management team. When these were missing, they saw significant problems. So the agency identified the team members and formed the core lifecycle project team quickly. It also gave the other affected employees significant professional and personal assistance to make the transition. As a result, this agency did not suffer the staff morale plunge and loss of key personnel that many others experienced.

Most importantly, the investigation taught management the value of the SLA schedule in the contract and the need to develop KPIs, which it had not known about. Management invested two months in getting the SLAs and KPIs right. Both parties credit that preparation with making the deal work smoothly over the entire term of the contract.

The goal of this action within the lifecycle is to gather intelligence from those who have already travelled this road. Many have embarked on outsourcing strategies well explored by others, ignorant of the common issues and obstacles that await them. The next case describes one such client, which did little to investigate how deals like the one it was entering into actually work.

Case: A joint venture learns the hard way

A logistics joint venture (JV) between a ground transport and an air transport company outsourced all of its IT to one of the parents as part of the JV formation deal. Management at the JV had little understanding on how such arrangements work in practice, particularly where the parent stakeholders have different objectives (the parent that provided IT wanted as much income out of the outsourcing deal as possible rather than from the JV itself, the other parent wanted a return from the JV). Nor did it seek such knowledge.

Accordingly, there was no separate outsourcing contract, no requirement that the services be provided at market prices and KPIs, and no strategy on how manage the arrangement. The JV paid more and more over the market rates for substandard services as the supplier parent continuously exerted its stronger bargaining power over the JV. Over many years, the JV collected enough examples of market prices and KPIs, such that eventually it had sufficient objective evidence to be able to renegotiate a more reasonable deal (with support from the other parent), particularly as the IT cost base was substantially affecting the return on investment of the JV for the non-supplier parent.

Action 4. Define and test stakeholder goals/expectations

There are many myths and unfounded beliefs when it comes to outsourcing. Unfortunately, these are not articulated and evidenced before the decision-makers act on those beliefs. A good example is whether outsourcing saves money or not. We have heard throughout the decades a common belief, stated again and again, that outsourcing saves 20% or more. But there is no evidence to support this belief. In fact, so many studies have such contradictory findings on this matter that there is sufficient evidence to support whatever one chooses to believe. Our studies over the years have shown cost savings to be notoriously difficult to measure, let alone achieve. Yet, the myth of the 20% cost savings lives on.

Outsourcing is often over-simplified and emotive, based on the beliefs of the decision-makers. One of the most controversial aspects of outsourcing is the degree to which the espoused benefits are real. A lesson repeatedly learnt is that the results do not inherently occur merely through the act of outsourcing; the goals need to be articulated and the means by which they will be achieved worked through. Otherwise, there may be some unanticipated consequences, like those illustrated in the next case.

Case: A strategy defect

In a law enforcement agency that outsourced its help desk (but kept it onsite), one of the key drivers was to demonstrate, through the provider, a new mentality towards working. The agency specified the type of people the supplier was to provide ranging from education levels, dress, attitude, and job dedication. Management believed that if its staff witnessed such *"professionalism,"* they would adopt it as a matter of course. No culture-change program was designed to go along with the desired behaviors; the existence of the provider's staff at the agency alone was to provide the impetus to change.

What actually occurred was an entrenching of the existing culture further, as staff quickly asserted an 'us and them' mentality and, in fact, ignored the provider's staff all together.

Most clients believe that ultimate success has only been moderate. Likewise, the degree of failure has been moderate as well. Rarely is outsourcing seen as a total success or total failure, and a number of our studies have found a noticeable gap between anticipated and actual benefits. In most cases, clients were getting benefits, but invariably less than they had expected.

It is not just expected benefits that can be unrealistic and unproven, it is also the investment required to obtain the benefits. We have conducted a number of studies regarding the cost of managing the lifecycle. Our research base of nearly 2100 outsourcing deals shows that the cost of getting to contract (the work done in BB1 to BB6) is 2.5% of the total contract value on average (or 16% of the annual value of the contract). The ongoing cost of managing domestic outsourcing contracts is 6% per year on average (double that or more for offshoring).

Yet, when we ask management at the BB1 stage what the planned investment is, the most common response is close to zero. The plan is to copy and paste tenders and contracts (or use the provider's), and then use existing (already busy) resources to manage the contract. We have found too many instances where a contract manager was managing hundreds of contracts, and some cases where a single manager was solely responsible for over a thousand.

Low contract management investors do not perform proactive and professional contract management (see BB8: Manage); they perform what we call *contract administration*. Simply administering an outsourcing contract (e.g. filing reports and invoices), ultimately leads to an erosion of control, an accumulation of unresolved issues, and a slow but steady wearing away of value for money. Ironically, this usually results in a rapid growth in management cost as problems arise and the client tries to claw back lost ground.

If stakeholders, particularly executives, are not realistic on what can be achieved and what it takes to achieve it, then theoretical assumptions become the driving force for the lifecycle and the deal. And the old lessons so well known by others, become the new lessons for your organization. The important activities here are to identify the stakeholders' expectations and present evidence as to the degree these expectations have been achieved in practice or not. Most importantly, you need to identify actual results and what it took to get them. Replace idealistic notions with evidence-based thinking.

Action 5. Collect intelligence on market conditions and potential providers

Early investigation into potential providers is often overlooked, particularly if a client assumes that there is a strong market of interested providers. In many cases, clients have gone to great expense in preparing a Request for Tender, only to get one, or even no, response. This shows a severe misunderstanding of the market - either of its existence or of how to engage it.

Collecting market intelligence becomes more imperative when the client does not have intimate knowledge of the industry and experience with the type of providers who may be potential candidates. This is one reason why we advocate the client building a core capability in *informed buying* in Chapter 3.

Informed buying can be as simple as gathering basic information about potential providers (e.g. their industries, customers, and services). Even in mature markets, most of the providers are constantly undertaking new initiatives, targeting new markets, and developing new products and services. Their strategies and capabilities need constant monitoring.

And be careful about 'casting your net' too small by assuming that providers will not be interested in your deal, you do not want to artificially reduce competition and opportunities. The next case almost missed out, on what proved to be, a very successful relationship.

Case: A technology manufacturer expands its narrow view

After failing to attract any outside customers to its commercialized IT services division, an international manufacturer of technology components decided to outsource the operations and concentrate on core business. It was not going to be a major outsourcing deal, but still worth millions per year to a provider. Because of the moderate size, the client had originally intended to invite only the second tier providers, ignoring the major international companies. Management believed that a contract would need to be worth hundreds of millions of dollars to gain the attention and focus that they wanted of its provider. However, the forthcoming opportunity hit the industry grapevine and the majors were able to convince management that this belief was unfounded. After a competitive process, one of the majors won the deal and the relationship has been deemed quite successful, even years after the honeymoon period.

For any client looking at outsourcing across different countries, it is critical to realize that provider capabilities tend to vary geographically. The structure, culture, and services of a provider in the US can be very different from the same provider in Europe, Asia Pacific, etc., and it is worth investigating how these geographic variances may affect your preliminary sourcing concepts. Global companies that have allowed their various regionally-based offices to select their own providers, have found that the regions often chose different ones due to the vast differences in the market's local capabilities and prices.

Just like Action 2 (gather insight), no discussion with providers will be a waste of time. These discussions can generate sourcing concepts you have not even thought about, can introduce new ideas for pricing and gain sharing, and help form your view on the nature of the providers' culture and strategies.

Building Block 2: Target - Get Focused

"What is conceived well is expressed clearly."

Nicholas Boileau

| ARCHITECT PHASE | ENGAGE PHASE | OPERATE PHASE | REGENERATE PHASE |

BUILDING BLOCK 2
TARGET

We know that the reasons clients outsource, and what they want to achieve from outsourcing, varies widely between clients, and then again varies over time within any given client.[81]   Likewise, exactly what clients choose to outsource varies widely as well.

There are no hard and fast rules about what should and should not be outsourced. Certainly, some types of services have been more popular, especially those with mature markets, predictable client demand, predictable provider costs, and well-known performance standards.   The key actions to choose what to outsource are to:

- prepare an initial sourcing map at a strategic level (Action 6),
- identify and prioritize candidates activities for outsourcing (Action 7),
- decide the rollout approach (Action 8), and
- fully understand the nature and extent of the activities (Action 9).

---

[81] Cullen, S., Seddon, P. and Willcocks, L. (2008) *Outsourcing Success: Unique, Shifting, and Hard to Copy*, Research and Markets, Dublin.

Action 6. Determine the initial sourcing map

Many people have the view that you can let go of commodity functions, but must not let providers get their hands on strategic areas. Others call that nonsense, and you should use third parties wherever you think you can. Both of these arguments are inappropriate generalizations.

Outsourcing is not so simple a matter that it can be categorized as a binary (yes/no) issue. There are many forms of outsourcing and many ways to employ it strategically as a management tool and to use it to shape the contract.

To help you understand some of this complexity, we have developed a high-level model known as the MAC (Maturity, Advantage, and Competence) Model shown in Figure 6-3. This model helps you determine what form of outsourcing to consider by looking through three 'lenses': (1) your organization's competence relative to its peers, (2) the maturity of the supply market, and (3) the degree to which activities contribute to your organization's competitive advantage.

Figure 6-3: The MAC Model

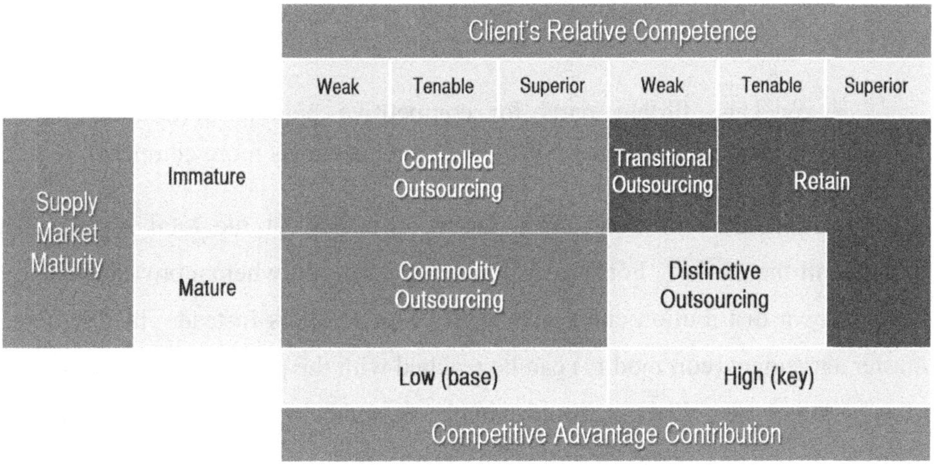

Supply Market Maturity		Client's Relative Competence					
		Weak	Tenable	Superior	Weak	Tenable	Superior
	Immature	Controlled Outsourcing			Transitional Outsourcing	Retain	
	Mature	Commodity Outsourcing			Distinctive Outsourcing		
		Low (base)			High (key)		
		Competitive Advantage Contribution					

When you look at your organization's activities through these three lenses, the model directs you to a particular form of outsourcing or recommends you consider retaining that activity. The forms of outsourcing, and the retaining option, are discussed after the three lenses are explained, and comprise (1) commodity (2) controlled (3) transitional and (4) distinctive outsourcing.

The lenses

Look at the maturity of the market.   In a mature market there are many experienced providers, switching costs are low, and switching timeframes are short.   If the market is mature, a commodity outsourcing arrangement can be the starting point.

If the market is immature (few providers or evolving capabilities), a greater degree of control is required to ensure benefits, accelerate the market's capabilities, and to develop alternative competitive supply.   Hence, a more controlled style of outsourcing is required.   Control can be obtained through numerous means, for example:

- multi-sourcing (the use of more than one substitutable provider) whereby one provider be replaced by another if need be,

- a panel whereby each provider must regularly compete for work, and/or

- package further parts for competitive bidding at a later stage as capabilities mature and/or the market becomes more competitive.

When looking at market maturity, ensure you look at the total supply chain footprint of the market.   For example, take the situation where a provider does not have its own distribution chain and it relies on resellers instead.   In this case, a master agreement (commodity) can be reached with the provider on price, but each of your locations is likely to need another agreement (controlled) with the local resellers on delivery dates, recall, and warranty fixes.

Look at activities not critical for competitive advantage. Outsourcing any part of your organization fundamentally implies an in-depth understanding of the core competencies and technologies on which your organization intends to build its future competitive advantage (key activities). For example, Apple outsources the majority of manufacturing, assembly and logistics but not design.[82]

If an activity does not create competitive advantage (known as a base activity), are you overly investing in it? There may be better investments you can make with your organization's human and asset capital for greater effect. In fact, retaining base activities may result in disadvantage if competitors are better at leveraging scarce resources. Being the best at non-advantage activities is easy to be proud of, but shouldn't your organization really be best at something else?

Look at the organization's relative competence. The third lens looks at your organization's relative competence in the area compared to the market, and your competitors in terms of effectiveness, cost, and value.

Are there activities that can deliver competitive advantage, but your organization does not possess the competence? Transitional outsourcing can bring skills and knowledge to your organization until your competence reaches the stage where the activity can be backsourced (brought in house).

If you are considering outsourcing activities that create competitive advantage (key activities) and your organization is superior to the market (regardless of its maturity); you really need to ask yourself why. Just because something can be outsourced does not mean it should (even if you believe the 20% cost savings myth). In fact, some use this superiority to offer value to others through commercializing the inhouse activity. For example, Philips Electronics forming Origin B.V. in 1996 with 16000 employees in 30 countries (acquired by Atos in 2000) to sell its IT capability in the services market.[83]

---

[82] See, for example Duhigg, et al. (2012) "How the U.S. Lost Out on iPhone Work." *The New York Times*, January 21, 2012.

[83] http://atos.net/en-us/home/contact-us/netherlands.html

Does your organization have at least a tenable position in key activities where the market is not mature? You may want to retain these inhouse and not let your organization's competitors have access via its providers.

The four forms of outsourcing

Commodity outsourcing is characterized by having industry standard performance metrics with market prices and specifications that are well known and understood by the players (buyers and sellers). This covers things like mobile phones, staff uniforms, and office stationary.

To make commodity outsourcing work, you should avoid wanting anything outside the mainstream and you must have very clear and stable requirements. This allows you to consider using standard/template contracts, which are a very basic tool for very basic needs. A word of caution is appropriate here, however. We have not seen a template contract that satisfactorily meets either party's needs, thus you must know the limitations of any template you intend to use. Never follow these blindly as a form-filling exercise. Use them merely as a starting point.

Controlled outsourcing is used when there are specific market risks. For example, where there are only a few providers, coupled with high switching costs, and long switching periods. In this case, you are unlikely to invoke any termination rights you might have because there are few alternative supply sources and a long set-up time. Alternative solutions that you really can employ must be included in your contract (e.g. benchmarking provisions).

Transitional outsourcing helps you obtain something you do not currently have. A common transitional type arrangement is one where you want to gain internal expertise not currently present in your organization. You use the market to gain it and can then backsource the work (bring it back inhouse). Knowledge transfer techniques are key elements in this case (e.g. personnel secondments, training, procedure manuals, and intellectual property licenses).

Alternatively, you may want to put in technologies without having to outlay a huge capital investment. If so, you 'piggyback' on existing platforms of providers (e.g. the cloud) until the price point of the technology means you can economically afford to set up your own operations. In this case, disengagement provisions are vital; whereby the provider has a contractual obligation to help you set up your shop, sell the technology to you at fair market value, and provide post-termination support at agreed rates.

Distinctive outsourcing is used when your organization has needs that are unique to it that necessitates carefully constructed contracts which standard templates do not cater for.

One example of distinctive outsourcing is choosing to contract multiple providers to deliver end-to-end solutions when they are not accustomed to collaborating with each other, and would not naturally do so. While becoming more common, it is still an immature capability amongst most providers. Accordingly, you will have to create solutions where there is no template and little longitudinal evidence of what consistently works. These solutions can include:

- having an inhouse integration unit ensure seamless workflows and act as the project manager with responsibility for handovers between providers;

- a cross-provider management agreement (signed by all providers and the client) stating how all the providers are expected to work together, collaborate, and innovate (and what happens if one does not); and

- satisfaction surveys of each provider with the others.

Of course, all four forms can be found in a single contract. For example, a helpdesk arrangement for standard level one support (commodity outsourcing) may be offshored (controlled outsourcing), while also actively seeking to diagnose caller issues and reduce dependence on the helpdesk (distinctive), and during which a new IVR (interactive voice response) system is being developed (transitional) designed to replace level one support.

Action 7. Identify and prioritize scope

Clients often combine and convolute the reasons for and against outsourcing, never looking at the whole in a structured manner. The objective of this action is to identify activities suitable for outsourcing, in a systematic and holistic manner across the entire assets/activity portfolio, and then package them appropriately.

Consider first breaking down the organization (or function) into what work is done where. Then identify short-term and long-term rationale for, and the barriers against, outsourcing and apply this across the area. Lastly, determine the bundles and priorities. This sounds simple, and it is, even for big companies like airlines, as the following case demonstrates.

Case: An airline gets the big picture

As part of a two-year review process at an international airline, the division chiefs were instructed by the CEO to decide what to outsource. In lieu of an objective framework, the journey began with each executive telling the others what "*could go*." Each executive believed his/her silo was core to the business and should not be outsourced. Sometimes their opinion was based solely on, "*We've always done it so it must be core, or we wouldn't be doing it*." However, when consultants were brought in, the process changed significantly. The business was mapped into processes (what took place) and silos (where processes took place). The group based its criteria on the business benefits sought from outsourcing, in the short and long term, and the apparent barriers that could preclude a service from being outsourced. The final criteria are shown in the table on the following page.

Benefits Sought		Barriers
Short-term (by year one)	Long-term	
• A proven, competitive market exists in the industry. • We can align supply to demand, particularly where we have a work backlog or cannot satisfy demand. • We can upgrade services without incurring capital investment. • We can gain a cash infusion from asset sales or staff transfers. • We can reduce costs where our costs are currently above industry standards. • We can access staff and skills in short supply.	• We can focus on strategic work inhouse, not day-to-day operations. • We can improve our customer focus. • We can make positive cultural changes within the airline.	• The service is core to our airline; we will not outsource it. • Outsourcing the area will create adverse customer perceptions. • Regulatory restrictions prevent outsourcing (e.g. chief pilot). • We might create a monopolistic situation due to the specifity of the assets and/ or the knowledge required. • We obtain a sustainable competitive advantage by performing this service.

Based on those criteria, 18 business processes and 12 business functions became the strongest candidates for outsourcing. The diagram shows the strength of candidacy for the 12 business functions, as an example. To create the graph, the airline had the criteria carry equal weight: each rationale had +1 point and each barrier -1 point.

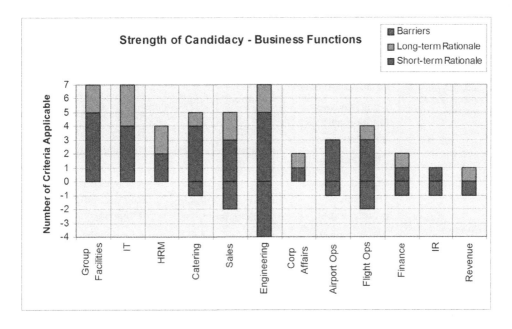

This benefits-and-barriers listing allowed the airline to systematically identify services to outsource, rather than rely on the persuasiveness of individual executives. Having the consultants facilitate the process also helped make it more objective. A clear picture of what to outsource emerged. The to-be-outsourced activities were then prioritized based on benefits, business needs, and risk management.

Action 8. Decide the rollout approach

There is no one approach to rolling out an outsourcing initiative. In practice, clients use the approaches in Table 6-1, typically in a hybrid fashion. Like most actions in the lifecycle, there is no one 'right' way. Regarding rollout, each method has its own advantages and disadvantages as summarized in the table.

Table 6-1: Rollout Approaches

Approach	Common Rationale	Risks	Critical Success Factors
Big Bang Significant portions of activities are outsourced at one time.	• Generate market interest • Centralized program with one point of contact • Lower lifecycle coordination costs • Company-wide learning and adoption • End-to-end KPIs	• Greater risk and impact • Resource intensive • More stakeholders • Can attract public and media attention • Complex project	• Re-engineering to make it work • Change program and communication strategy due to wide impact • Expertise in outsourcing critical to ensure a big success, not a big failure • Requires significant management attention
Phased One or more providers are selected for pilot/s with planned escalation of outsourcing.	• Staged approach and evolved prototyping • Allows time to learn and incorporate lessons • Immediate needs met through pilots • Providers have to prove themselves to obtain more work	• Longer period to implement sourcing solution • Providers likely to seek escalation of outsourcing irrespective of the client's readiness • Maintaining program momentum	• A continuous program with a 'champion' to keep it thriving • Articulating what further outsourcing will occur, under what conditions • Client must have commitment to further outsourcing or lose provider commitment • Each deal designed to be refreshed when better practice is learnt
Piecemeal Each activity is outsourced separately over time and a variety of providers is used.	• Best provider and price for each deal at the time • Less complex • Staggers disruption • Solve needs as they arise • Manageable at lower levels • Incorporate lessons into future deals, if knowledge is shared	• May not be best value over time • High co-ordination costs • Duplication of effort / 'wheel reinvention' • Synergies difficult • Adversity between providers • Isolated lessons • Piecemeal KPIs	• Organizational mechanism for sharing best practices and lessons learnt • Well articulated inter-dependencies between deals • Clear responsibilities between all parties that may interact • Each deal needs 'chop and change' provisions to allow re-bundling at later stages

The important issue is that you determine the rollout as part of a carefully crafted strategy to achieve the benefits you are seeking, rather than choosing one haphazardly, and consequently exposing your organization to risks you may not be aware of. The benefits of a carefully crafted rollout is given in the case below.

Case: Reconfiguration rollout for second-generation deal

A federal government department was retendering a BPO contract for its HR function. It reconfigured its second-generation deal into three service scopes from the original full scope. It further reconfigured the supplier grouping into two best of breed providers for two service packages, and a panel for the last package. In order to execute the three deals with limited resources, it assessed its rollout options and determined it needed to adopt a phased approach, issuing one tender after the other, while simultaneously disengaging the incumbent provider as the contracts were awarded to other providers. In doing so, it was able to focus on each package and transition situation, while minimizing disruptions to staff.

Action 9. Prepare the profiles

Once the candidates have been identified, a detailed understanding of them is essential so you can approach the market knowledgeably, with a clear picture of your organizations current and desired future state. Obtaining this detailed understanding is called *profiling*, and there are seven profiles listed in Table 6-2.

Table 6-2: The Seven Profiles

Profile Type	Components
Services	• Current and future service requirements • Volume, trend and load data (i.e. number of users, calls, transactions) • Performance metrics and measurement methods • Customer satisfaction indices
Costs (direct and indirect)	• Costs at current KPIs and loads • Estimated costs at required or future KPIs • Future capital expenditure program
Balance Sheet	• Assets (including intellectual property) - type, age, quantity, location • Liabilities - who is owed what and under what conditions

Profile Type	Components
Staff	• Organization chart • Job descriptions/qualifications • Staff numbers and full time equivalents • Remuneration, on costs, and conditions • Accrued and contingent liabilities • Statistics - average age, length of service, pay, etc.
Existing Contracts/ Commercial Relationships	For each current contract, license, lease, etc.: • Scope and value • Commencement and end dates • Assignment, novation and termination options • Desire or need to continue the arrangement
Stakeholders	• Internal to your organization (e.g. users, management, departments) • External to your organization (e.g. customers, affiliated entities, other providers, media, governments)
Governance	• Current management structure and authorities • Administration and control • Reporting • Quality assurance, audit and control

Some clients make the mistake of assuming a service is standard or is well known, and therefore easy to put to the market without performing the necessary investigations to verify the current state. This fatal flaw has resulted in significant cost increases when the actual scope of work is exposed, then redefined, by the provider when there is no pressure to have competitive pricing.

If your organization is currently performing something, the time to find out what it is actually doing, what it owns, its obligations, and so on, is not after a provider takes it over. This is invaluable information for one's own piece of mind, but also for when dealing with the provider's sales pitch. Being fact-based is vital; this enables you to sit down and calculate, rather than have to negotiate in an ill-informed way.

The client discussed in the next case had just this issue, but fortunately discovered that it did not know the true scope before it went to tender.

Case: Profiling pays off

A very large welfare client was outsourcing most of its IT function. It embarked on a profiling exercise to prepare the information required for the Engage Phase. The scoping study found significant errors in current state, particularly regarding the helpdesk.

Management had long ago set up one centralized helpdesk and naturally assumed it was the only one. But the profiling study discovered many 'skunk work' regional and local centers put in place by the business units over time due because of the poor response times and unfriendliness of the centralized one. The cost of these local centers was concealed in other budgets, and thus hidden from management. The tender had to be called off until the client could address the underlying issues, get the true number and nature of calls (estimated at double the known data), and ensure that the business units were on board.

Building Block 3: Strategize - Think Long Term

"Envisioning the end is enough to put the means in motion"

Dorothea Brande

| ARCHITECT PHASE | ENGAGE PHASE | OPERATE PHASE | REGENERATE PHASE |

BUILDING BLOCK 3
STRATEGIZE

This building block is crucial for effective navigation through the Outsourcing Lifecycle. Your strategy sets the parameters for what subsequently happens. Frequently, key decisions regarding outsourcing projects are delegated to lower management. When corporate guidance on a few key strategic issues is lacking, you run the danger of making decisions without the holistic view required.

The purpose of this building block is to conduct the planning that enables knowledgeable decisions to be made throughout the remainder of the lifecycle. It is important to get this right. The wrong strategies create inflexible pathways that are difficult and expensive to change later.

The recommended strategies to be developed in this building block are:

- **Configuration strategy** - your key structural decisions from Chapter 3 (Action 10),

- **Business case and approach** - your initial business case and the business case rules for the key 'go/no go' decisions (Action 11),

- **Competitive approach** - your engagement of the market (Action 12),

- **Transitions strategies** - your high level plan for the transition in and out of the agreement (Action 13),

- **Contract management strategy** - how your organization's contract management network will be structured and the deal will be managed (Action 14),

- **Retained organization** - the remaining structure after outsourcing (Action 15), and

- **Lifecycle communications strategy** - the plan for communication with internal and external stakeholders throughout the lifecycle (Action 16).

Action 10. Determine the configuration strategy

An outsourcing configuration describes what will be outsourced, where, for how long, by what type of provider model, how work will be priced, who will own which assets, and which governance structures will be put in place. Because of the critical nature of these decisions, and because we have found that awareness of them still lacking in many clients, we devoted Chapter 4: Configuration to the subject. The configuration strategy documents the decisions made and why. A best practice configuration strategy also documents why options were rejected - not just to support the decisions made, but also because this becomes very useful in making the next generation decisions in the last Refresh Phase.

Action 11. Develop the initial business case and approach

Before you invest heavily in an outsourcing initiative, you must ensure there is a compelling rationale based on sound economic analysis. The general approach to business cases covers an assessment of the expected benefits (both tangible and intangible), risks, and expected financial payback. But first, you must understand that to be of any real value, a business case has to be an ongoing analysis, and not simply an exercise you complete, then put on the shelf, and forget.

If you are considering outsourcing, then there are at least three 'go/no-go' decisions that your evolving business case must address in terms of the benefits, risks, and finances (and the rules surrounding how they are to be calculated and represented):

- **Feasibility** - the initial business case examines the feasibility of outsourcing. This business case is speculative because it is based on your best estimates. You don't have any bids yet, so you won't know what providers will actually charge; you won't have the mobilization plan from the bidders, so the costs of transition will also be speculative; and so on. But if you have investigated the market well in BB1 (Action 5), you will have a reasonable basis for this case.

- **The Winner** - the next business case concerns the selection of the preferred provider in BB5. Once you receive the bids, you will have all the 'real' numbers (what has been officially offered). This business case analyzes the bids and bidders, recommending a winner (or not going ahead).

- **The Deal** - Following negotiations, when the final numbers, deliverables, conditions, etc. have all been agreed, you update the business case to determine whether you should sign the contract in BB6.

Without a clear business case at the start, and clear rules surrounding the ongoing evolution of the business case, strange things can happen, as the following case demonstrates.

Case: No business case rules resulted in no rules at all

Mid-way through a federal government agency's market testing of a financial and records management contract, a manager new to the client was put in charge of the project. The bids had already been received, and a preferred provider chosen (but not announced). There existed within the client, a faction of management that did not want the deal to go ahead and this was their time to move. The new manager quickly teamed up with the faction determined to keep services inhouse. The manager hired a consulting firm and removed the original evaluation team. The only outcome required from the firm was to give its decision, which was to keep everything inhouse. The methodology and processes followed were put under a confidentiality restriction to avoid disclosure.

When preparing numbers for your business case, you must begin by deciding on one basic principle; whether the numbers you use will be optimistic (that is, the results you hope for) or pessimistic (a conservative estimate).

Without an explicit decision here, it is almost certain that your organization will suffer from the well-known corporate malady of *optimism bias*. This is the demonstrated systematic tendency for people to be over-optimistic about the outcome of planned actions including over-estimating the extent and likelihood of positive events and under-estimating the negative events.[84] It must be explicitly accounted for in appraisals, if these are to be realistic. Optimism bias typically results in cost overruns, time delays, and benefit shortfalls.

A good way to find out the extent of optimism bias in your organization is to examine previous business cases and the extent to which they were actually achieved. Check the degree to which assumptions were proven to be valid, that costs were accurately estimated, that expected risks were correctly foreseen and mitigated, and that expected benefits were realized. Once you know this, you can factor in your organization's optimism bias into your business cases. Or even better, you can learn where your organization has proven to be defective in formulating its business cases, so you can avoid repeating the errors of the past.

In complex deals, you may want to prepare two estimates - the best and worst cases. If the business case holds up under the worst case, it is a very strong case indeed.

Action 12. Decide the competitive process (tender approach)

Some people believe that it is most efficient to go to the market just once via a request for tender (or equivalent), rather than multiple times via a staged process. This belief often comes from inexperienced management, or from procurement specialists, both of whom can oversimplify the outsourcing tendering process as if it is akin to commodity purchasing based mostly on price.

---

[84] See, for example, Lovallo, D. and Kahnema, D. (2003) "Delusions of Success: How Optimism Undermines Executives' Decisions," *Harvard Business Review*, July, 56-63.

There are four reasons why outsourcing tends to be much more complex, and success is highly dependent on the state of the client's outsourcing maturity (how advanced the client is at successfully managing the entire lifecycle).

First is the complexity of the three different parts involved in every outsourcing transaction:

- transition-in, or mobilization, which starts from the time the contract is signed to when all start-up activities have completed and normal operations begin, then

- the routine normal operations, and then lastly

- the transition-out, which is from the time that the provider is notified that the contract will be ended through to the post-termination period (the period after the contract has ended but the provider is still on call).

Each of these three different parts can involve any number of transactions within them. For example, the transitions (in and out) are, in fact, projects that can have any number of milestones and corresponding payments. 'Normal operations' represents the length of time between those two periods of transitions. It involves routine operations, but also involves non-routine, ad hoc services, any number of re-engineering, transformation, or continuous improvement projects, potential asset refreshes, and so on.

Second, providers can be quite different in terms of capabilities, approaches, and experience, making the evaluation more intricate that just buying a product. You need to understand more about how they manage their business and what markets they operate in. The provider needs to be financially resilient and relatively stable. How the provider manages its workforce is critical in labor-intensive work. How the provider refreshes and upgrades technology is critical for technology-dependent outsourcing deals. Safety management is critical for industrial work. And the list goes on.

Thirdly, more uncertainties need to be considered since outsourcing deals tend to go over many years. They can also involve a blend of services and solutions that takes time to explore before your optimum arrangement is determined. There is also a range of price frameworks employed in any deal, including a mix of lump sum prices, unit prices, and cost-based prices (e.g. at cost plus a markup) - not to mention the reimbursable expenses.

Lastly, outsourcing deals are very different from commodity purchasing because such deals are difficult to renegotiate or terminate once the deal is signed and run for a long time. These are not spot transactions. You will have to live with your mistakes for a long time.

For these reasons, and to leverage competition in the market, we generally recommend that you take a carefully constructed, multi-staged tendering approach. A multi-stage tendering process functions primarily to filter the potential pool of providers with the least amount of effort at each stage, leaving you with a manageable number of bids to conduct your detailed evaluation.

The selection of providers via competitive tendering can involve any number of stages. The appropriate utilization of each stage depends upon:

- your **knowledge of the market** - if you are on learning curve and need a more exploratory process,

- the **stability of the market offerings** - short product/service-method lifecycles may require you to update knowledge and scan offerings,

- the **degree of influx of new entrants** - can change market dynamics,

- the **number of potential providers** - too many require culling,

- the **degree that you know what you want** - you may want to explore options and alternatives, and

- the **quality of the bids in the preceding stages** - additional stages may be required or unnecessary stages removed.

The typical tender stages you may choose to embark upon are listed in Table 6-3.

Table 6-3: The Competitive Stages

Stage	Purpose	Sought by Client	Provided by Client
ROI (Registration of Interest)	• Determine market size and makeup • Find out who is interested in bidding	General information (e.g. size, locations, offerings)	Basic characteristics sought (e.g. capabilities, locations)
RFI (Request for Information)	• Gather data about potential bidders • Shortlist, when there is a large market	• Detailed business information • High-level experience relevant to scope	• Capabilities sought • High-level work scope • Geographic scope
EOI (Expression of Interest)	• Explore options • Obtain indicative prices • Shortlist, when there are many capable providers	• Viability data • Specific scope-related experience • Indicative price • Potential options and approaches • Use of subcontractors	• Specific scope requirements • Potential price frameworks
RFT, RFO, RFP, RFQ (Request for Tender, Offer, Proposal, Quotation)	• Obtain firm price • Select preferred provider/s	• Detailed approach - plans, staff, assets, sub-contractors, etc. • Customer references • Contract departures • Firm pricing with detailed assumptions	Draft schedules and contract
BAFO (Best and Final Offer)	• Decide between equal bidders • Conduct final negotiations with competitive tension	All aspects of final bid	• Final clarifications • Final agreement revised to integrate bid

A table of indicative timings is provided in Table 6-4, to give you an idea of the amount of time these activities require. These timings are a very rough guide only.

Table 6-4: Indicative Timing of Each Competitive Stage

Stage	Client Preparation	Bid Response Period	Client Bid Evaluation (per response)
ROI	1 day	2 weeks	2 hours
RFI	3 days	2 weeks	4 hours
EOI	2 weeks	4 weeks	2 days
RFT (etc.)	4 weeks	6 weeks	5 days
BAFO	1 week	2 weeks	1 day

All parties tend to gain from a gating process (pre-qualification and then progressive short listing). Benefits of a staged approach include:

- Providers with a slim chance of winning are spared the cost and time of preparing a full proposal (and you having to evaluating bids that do not have realistic prospects of success).

- It is less expensive for bidders to respond progressively, with the full proposal costs incurred only if the provider has a relatively equal or greater probability of winning. A 'one hit' process can act as a disincentive due to the high cost of bidding, the lower probability of winning the contract, and the lower level of client engagement.

- It allows exploration of options and an evolution of your requirements as the stages progress and allows you to withdraw from the process, if required, before significant investment is made by your organization.

Action 13. Craft the transitions strategies

All contracts need a period of getting up and running, known as a *mobilization* or *transition-in*. Moreover, all contracts end one day; and the period of disengaging the incumbent provider is known as the *transition-out*. These two transitions are the 'bookends' to normal operations (Figure 6-4), the much longer period, and are self-contained projects at the start and end of every contract.

Figure 6-4: Transition Bookends

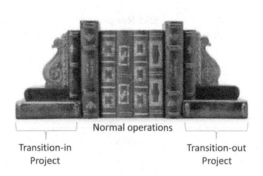

Normal operations

Transition-in   Transition-out
Project   Project

The transition-in plan focuses on the initial setup activities and responsibilities of the parties, any transfers (staff, assets, etc.). A key part of the strategy is the acceptance process and criteria, as it is at that point that mobilization is officially over and normal operations (with its different pricing and KPIs) begins. To familiarize yourself with the process and issues, refer to BB7: Transition.

The transition-out plan contains the procedures, processes, responsibilities, and obligations that arise after your organization gives a notice of termination or upon expiry of a term. Most importantly, it specifies the obligations of the parties (three parties, in the case of a handover to another provider) and the resources that they are to provide. To familiarize yourself with the process and issues, refer to BB9: Refresh. A strategy outline for each of these transitions is in Figure 6-5.

Planning for these transitions begins here in BB3 and then is used in future actions:

- transitions schedules to the contract and related contract clauses in BB4: Design (see Action 22),

- competitive process in BB5: Select where you provide the initial (incomplete) plans to the bidders to add information and revise as needed,

- BB7: Transition implements the transition-in plan, and

- BB9: Refresh implements the transition-out plan if the incumbent will not be continuing.

Figure 6-5: Transitions Strategy Outlines

Transition-in Strategy	Transition-out Strategy

1. **Kickoff**
 	
2. **Setup**
  2.1. Relationship formation
  2.2. Accommodation required (temporary, permanent)
  2.3. Access required (site, technology)
  2.4. Recruiting
  2.5. Induction and training
 	
3. **Possible Transfers**
  3.1. Assets
  3.2. Knowledge
  3.3. Staff
  3.4. Third party contracts
  3.5. WIP (work-in-progress)
 	
4. **Integration and Re-engineering**
  4.1. Current operations and documentation review
  4.2. Business processes and document-ation to be redesigned or created
 	
5. **Acceptance**
 	
6. **Anticipated Costs**
 	
7. **Project Management**
  7.1. Mobilization teams and roles
  7.2. Meetings and communication
  7.3. Estimated timetable
	1. **Tri-party Obligations**
	  1.1. Incumbent provider
	  1.2. Successor provider
	  1.3. Client
	
	2. **Disengagement**
	  2.1. Delivery-up
	  2.2. Vacation of premises
	  2.3. Redeployment and redundancies
	
	3. **Handover to a Successor**
	  3.1. Assets
	  3.2. Knowledge
	  3.3. WIP (work in progress)
	
	4. **Contract Closeout**
	  4.1. Documentation
	  4.2. Finalization of accounts
	  4.3. Final meeting
	  4.4. Acceptance of closeout
	
	5. **Anticipated Costs**
	
	6. **Project Management**
	  6.1. Exit teams and roles
	  6.2. Meetings and communication
	  6.3. Estimated timetable

Action 14. Construct the contract management (CM) strategy

As clients increasingly move towards contracting, contract management is becoming one of the core activities of overall business management. The use of outsourcing does not imply less effort in managing, only a different emphasis. Outsourcing changes the emphasis from managing day-to-day operations to a focus on ensuring providers deliver what has been outsourced.

The time to decide what needs to be done, and by whom, is not after the deal has been signed. It is tempting for some clients to wait and try to 'make a go of it' with current staff, but this approach assumes a level of effortlessness in managing outsourcing arrangements that rarely exists. This fatal flaw has left some clients with out-of-control costs, high staff turnover, and poor compliance with contracts.

The **contract management strategy** documents how your organization will manage its agreement/s. Do this now in the lifecycle, and you will be able to design a contract that will work in practice by ensuring that the contract has the provisions the CMs need to deliver the strategy. In this way, you are able to decide the way you want to manage the contract and design it accordingly, rather that the reverse: having a contract that gave no thought as to whether, and how, it would actually be managed. The key elements include those listed below and an example outline is shown in Figure 6-6:

- **The CM network** - the network of individuals involved with managing the deal *after* the contract is signed (refer to BB8, Action 40, for the discussion of these networks).

- **Protocols** - CM network or rules involving notifications, communications, consultations, and approvals.

- **Key milestones** - key dates representing both parties' obligations plus the CM milestones.

- **Plans** - the supply continuity plan (plan 'B' if the provider becomes insolvent or otherwise cannot, or does not, deliver) and the rights plan regarding the contract rights that your organization will really be depending on.

- **CM network activities** - how the CM network is to conduct the vital CM activities (see BB8 for the list and details).

- **Investment** - the CM investment (budget) that will be made (see BB8, Action 43).

- **Role descriptions** - the description of CM network roles (which are then used in job descriptions and for performance reviews).

Figure 6-6: Contract Management Strategy Outline

1. **CM Network**
   1.1. Structure
   1.2. Accountabilities

2. **Key Protocols**
   2.1. Communication
   2.2. Authorizations/Approvals

3. **Key Milestones (Gantt chart)**
   3.1. Party Milestones
   3.2. CM Milestones

4. **Plans**
   4.1. Supply Continuity Plan
   4.2. Contract Rights Plan (invocation and exercise)

5. **CM Network Activities**
   5.1. CM Network Management
   5.2. Compliance Audits
   5.3. Continuous Improvement
   5.4. Financial Management
   5.5. Performance Management
   5.6. Forecasting
   5.7. Relationship Management
   5.8. Keep informed
   5.9. Issues and Risk Management
   5.10. Variations Management
   5.11. Disagreement and Dispute Management
   5.12. Recordkeeping and Reporting

6. **CM Investment/Budget**

7. **Attachment - Role Descriptions**

Many of the reviews we have performed for various organizations over the past two decades have highlighted the need to design the CM function well. Some of the more disturbing findings include a contract manager who:

- believed he needed to 'earn' penalties from the providers at least equal to his salary to justify his existence,

- did not know what her role was and didn't understand the contract, thus rubber-stamped the invoices without any verification, and

- never reviewed performance, and by contract end, only 40% of the performance measures were being reported upon.

The following case is another instance of what can happen without a CM strategy.

Case: No strategy puts the provider in charge

A state-based insurance company had entered into a *"strategic partnership"* with an IT provider. The board, believing that the provider was now its official IT department and would act accordingly, saw no need to retain any IT capability. Accordingly, it outsourced all of its IT people, processes, technology, and strategy to the provider.

After the transition was completed, the soon-to-be exiting CIO realized that no thinking had taken place regarding managing the provider, let alone managing the utilization of IT in the company. He commissioned a study to determine what prudent management should be in place and was startled with the level of basic management required alone. He proposed the resultant IT and contract management strategy to the Board, but was overruled. Instead, the Board put the provider in charge of its own contract on behalf of the insurer. Five years later, IT strategy was non-existent and IT costs were demonstrably higher than the market. The client had to rebuild its IT organization again, beginning with the hiring of a CIO.

Action 15. Design the retained organization

Outsourcing effectively creates an inter-dependent hybrid organization combining internal and external providers that deliver an often complex array of services to the business, ideally in a seamless manner.

To exemplify this, we use the example of one of our global surveys into ITO that found that the 73 respondents (from 26 countries) had, on average, 13 providers.[85] Only 4% outsourced all of their spend, while 9% did not outsource anything, leaving the vast majority somewhere in between. Not only were the two extremes of total insourcing or total outsourcing uncommon, it was also uncommon to see any particular area totally outsourced. Partial outsourcing exceeded full outsourcing in every area by a 4 to 1 ratio, on average. So a typical organization is

---

[85] This study was done in 2006-2007 with the Cutter Consortium, a membership-based research firm.

a hybrid of many providers, as well as the client organization, delivering various degrees of interdependent scope.

While many clients that embark on outsourcing initiatives spend significant resources on defining the scope of the providers' responsibilities, the same level of effort is seldom put into defining the responsibilities to be kept within the client (known as the *retained organization*). The retained organization represents the people, process, and technology that are necessary to remain in your organization to perform the activities retained by it.

Accordingly, the retained organization strategy documents the:

- retained services, functions and work processes that will continue to be performed by your organization,

- revised organizational structure, incorporating all interfaces internal and external to your organization,

- roles and responsibilities of the retained organization, and

- costs for the retained organization, including investment in new skills.

One of the key roles of your retained organization is to act as a supply chain integrator for the internal and external services. Although the performance of activities outsourced is the domain of the providers, they are your organization's agents at the end of the day and accountability for the ultimate outcome always ends with your organization.

Action 16. Plan the lifecycle communications

All organizations need to communicate with a variety of people over the course of the outsourcing lifecycle. The word 'outsourcing' spreads like wildfire, with a plethora of rumors about your motives for doing so. The 'FUD' factor is created (fear, uncertainty, and doubt); not only with client staff, but also with current providers, the client's end customers, even outside organizations such as regulators, politicians, and the media.

As shown in Figure 6-7, there are three phases that stakeholders need to be moved through from preparation to acceptance to commitment.[86]

Figure 6-7: Stages of Commitment Model

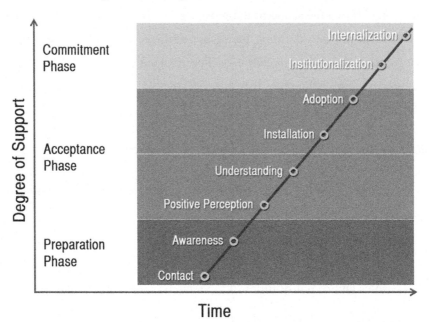

The main purpose of the communications strategy is to move the stakeholders through the degrees of support (the x axis in Figure 6-7), by providing the appropriate communications at the appropriate times. You will need to know where stakeholders are on the graph at any moment, in order to know how to pitch your communication and strategy-selling activities.

Even though all stakeholders will require some form of communication, consider focusing the efforts on individuals and groups who are critical to success, and who will take a major effort on your part to get them to 'buy in'. Figure 6-8 explains where to target your efforts here. 'Woo and Win' and 'Maintain Confidence'

---

[86] Conner, Daryl R. and Patterson, Robert (1982) "Building commitment to organizational change", *Training and Development Journal,* April Vol 36(4) 18-30.

require giving stakeholders continuous access to information and quick resolution of their questions/ issues. Use frequent face-to-face interactions and formal processes for soliciting feedback and monitoring effectiveness. For audiences less critical to the outsourcing project, you can use a variety of media, with less emphasis on face-to-face communication.

Figure 6-8: Communication Focus

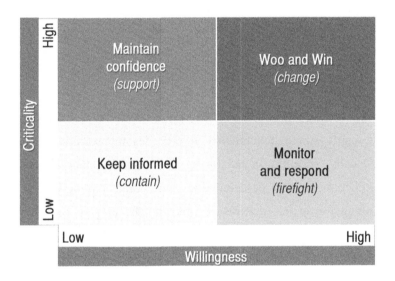

The degree of communication required often comes as a surprise to the client's teams involved at any phase during the lifecycle. Time after time, it had not been appropriately planned for and resourced. In the following case, the client found it is a full-time role.

Case: Need for a dedicated communications manager

Within a telecommunications company, the degree of communication was so great that the project manager was dedicated to it full time, in addition to consuming a third of the project's resources and necessitating the hiring of a public relations expert. In hindsight, as this initiative was going to affect 7000 staff directly and the entire organization indirectly, the substantial depth and breadth of communications required perhaps should not have been such a surprise.

Building Block 4: Design - Detail the Future

"There is nothing worse than a sharp image of a fuzzy concept"

Ansel Adams

| ARCHITECT PHASE | ENGAGE PHASE | OPERATE PHASE | REGENERATE PHASE |

BUILDING BLOCK 4
DESIGN

This building block builds on the previous ones to convert the desired arrangement into commercially sound documents. It precedes the selection process (BB5) because, logically, accepting a bid for an ill-defined 'product' is unsound. The contractual documents must be detailed at some point; leaving it until later, after your bargaining power has diminished, may not be in your organization's best interest. As those experienced with outsourcing are aware, there is a huge amount of variables that must be handled in any outsourcing deal. This is why planning and articulating the detail matters. This includes developing the:

- desired results via the Contract Scorecard (Action 17),

- skeleton of the contract in the Contract Blueprint (Action 18),

- specifications, quality KPIs, and resultant remedy/reward scheme via the SLA (Action 19),

- financial obligations and KPIs in the Financial Schedule (Action 20),

- interparty management obligations and relationship KPIs in the Governance Charter (Action 21),

- transition in and out obligations and plans (Action 22), and

- legal obligations, rights, and recourse via the contract (Action 23).

Too often, we have seen clients disappointed that some of their expectations have not been met (e.g. the introduction of innovations, exposure to global expertise, and access to the latest research). However, these expectations were never articulated and agreed to, let alone set out in a plan devised for meeting them. The benefits sought by outsourcing are not inherent in the act of outsourcing. They must be designed to occur.

This building block wraps up the Architect phase. The intent is to balance the often-competing interests of client and providers, while, at the same time, motivating the providers to provide the services and quality its client desires.

BB4 results in detailed documents that articulate the future arrangement using commercial language, that is, in language potential providers understand and can bid on. If these key documents are prepared in as close to final form as possible, and used as the baseline for the bidding process (in BB5), you increase the probability of obtaining exactly the services you require, under the conditions you require. And by leaving little to chance or opportunism, you gain considerable negotiating advantage and efficiency. This was learnt too late in the case below, and the client eventually declared bankruptcy due in part to the 'sweetheart deals'[87] it arranged, in which this case is just one example.

Case: A handshake costs plenty

The general manager of an international airline made an agreement with the top executive of a provider because they had worked together before and trusted each other. The deal was simple enough. The provider would take over inbound and outbound call centers operations (the provider's core business), so that the airline could focus on its own core business. This was to be a strategic partnership, so the parties believed they only needed a brief, high-level memorandum of understanding (MOU). The specifications, and the contract, would be developed over time.

---

[87] A 'sweetheart deal', in the lexicon, is a commercial arrangement devised by a few close individuals within the parties, typified by an informal understanding rather than a carefully crafted contract. It is also rarely subject to competition while those individuals remain in their respective parties.

Years later, after both executives had left their respective companies, an internal audit revealed that there was never a signed contract or a specification, and the provider had been over-billing for years. Each business unit was being charged a price per call, and simultaneously, the centralized accounts payable section was being charged for full cost recovery (ranging from major items such as 'management fees' from the provider's head office in the US to even minor items as toilet paper at the provider's facility). The over-billing resulted from there being no detailed specification of what was to be included in price per call and what items were permitted to be charged as reimbursable costs. The MOU merely stated both would be paid by the client.

The lesson this airline learned, and mature outsourcing clients know, is that you should never give providers complete discretion over what to charge or how to charge. Prepare your contractual documents *before* selecting your providers so that the deal that you want is put to market. In that way, negotiation (when your bargaining power starts its downward slide) is constrained to just a few elements, rather than the entire deal.

Action 17. Develop the Contract Scorecard

What is a successful contract? Different people have diverse beliefs as to what successful contracts are. Some would consider a contract successful if it did not end up in court. Others believe it to be successful if they did not need to manage the contractor too much. In our opinion, "*success means that the people in your organization got the results they were seeking.*"

To assess the myriad of results that an outsourcing deal may need to demonstrate to be deemed successful, organizations are recognizing the value of applying a balanced scorecard approach and the Contract Scorecard is a tool that has proven successful.

The Balanced Scorecard hit the corporate scene in the early 1990s, designed for companies to measure financial as well as non-financial attributes of their performance.[88] If you employ a form of the Balanced Scorecard for your internal operations, that is fine. However, if you pay a large portion of your expenditures to external parties, you may be leaving a great deal of your structure un-scored, as illustrated in the next case.

Case: A regional bank scores only part of the picture

A fast-growing regional bank had a decentralized management style, empowering staff to contract with whom, and how, each staff member saw fit. These contracted expenditures were not systematically tracked or controlled; it was up to the buyer to manage whatever they bought however they wished.

An insightful manager, after gaining substantial cost savings from better design and management of the contracts in her area, thought the techniques she employed could be useful in other contracts in the bank. Her initial guess at external spend with providers was approximately 30% of the bank's annual outgoings. A brief assessment of the accounts payable ledger found that the actual spend was about 80%.

The bank had been investing very heavily in a minor component of its outgoings including staff, but nothing on its major outgoings. It had a very large HR department and employed many leading HR techniques, such as 360-degree evaluations (assessments of an individual's performance by staff, colleagues, and supervisors), leadership training and capability assessments, mentoring programs, and the like. Meanwhile, it had no contract management area, no 'informed buying' capabilities, and did not track any form of results from the over 400 providers it engaged.

The Contract Scorecard quadrants, shown in Figure 6-9, are:

- **Quality** - getting what you paid for.

- **Financial** - the monetary outcomes your organization is seeking.

- **Relationship** - the 'right' behaviors between the parties.

- **Strategic** - the strategic goals going beyond the letter of the agreement.

---

[88] For more information on this subject, see their first work: Kaplan, R. and Norton, D. (1992) "The Balanced Scorecard - Measures that Drive Performance", *Harvard Business Review*, Jan/Feb, 71-79.

Figure 6-9: Contract Scorecard - Quadrants

Quality metrics (the most common metric type in outsourcing arrangements) are the provider's operational metrics such as timeliness, reliability, and accuracy. The detail is most commonly articulated in the *SLA* or other work specification.

Financial metrics are the monetary metrics comparing amounts paid over different fiscal points or comparatives. These fiscal points can be historical (e.g. total paid last year), percent over/under budget, variation to current market rates, and/or TCO (total cost of ownership) or its variants (total cost of asset, total cost of supply, etc.). These metrics are commonly part of the *Financial Arrangement* schedule to the contract. In that schedule, for example, you may set a KPI for reducing expenditures by 5% per year or keeping to +/- 5% of a specified budget.

Relationship goals represent the 'soft' or perception-based attributes of the working relationship. These are expressed as part of the *Governance Charter* schedule to the contract. They are not metrics, as such, but are a series of statements such as, "*we will communicate frequently and openly.*" The parties then assess the degree to which these behaviors are exhibited by the parties on a regular basis (typically at least annually).

Strategic metrics measure results that go beyond the letter of the agreement and represent more of an alliance-type situation, warranting a separate schedule in their own right. Examples include:

- **Innovation** - degree of introduction of better practices, new technologies, etc.

- **Business contribution** - degree that the deal has helped your business (e.g. core focus, mutual initiatives outside of the scope).

- **Alignment** with corporate values - extent that the provider acts in line with your organization's values and needs (e.g. local employment, carbon footprint).

- Underlying **business practices** - manner that the provider runs its business (e.g. safety, workforce management)

Besides the quadrants, it is important to be aware that there are three KPI threshold types (Figure 6-10) that you might apply to any given performance measure:

- **Target** - goals for which the provider is rewarded if achieved. It is used when you would be delighted if the target is achieved and are willing to reward the provider to do so. Rarely do clients have targets for all KPIs, only the few areas where superior results really matter.

- **Minimum standard** - the base standard to be achieved, which may have recourse for failure. This is the expected level of service that, if not achieved, means you are not getting the value you have paid for. Most clients start here, setting their basic expectations for what they want for their money.

- **Material breach** - anything at or below this level will be deemed a complete failure. It is defined as a material breach of the contract that invokes the client's right to terminate, in addition to other recourse. This usually applies only in a few areas. As it is expensive and time consuming to find a new provider, make sure that this threshold is a 'no brainer' with regard to the need to replace the provider.

Figure 6-10: KPI Thresholds

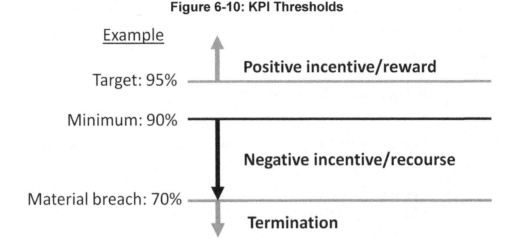

The following case shows why it is important to choose your words rather carefully when setting these thresholds in your contractual documents.

Case: What is a service level?

A manufacturing company was new to contracting out its operations. It knew that performance-based contracts needed KPIs and so established a few, some of which are shown in the table below.

Service Area	KPI	Service Level
On-Site Support Services	Availability of On-site Support Contact - Critical	Available to provide support within 30 minutes for 100% of Critical Requests
	Availability of On-site Support Contact - all Other Requests	Available to provide support within 1 hour for 80% of All Other Requests
	Device Relocation	>95% within 48 hours
	Installation of SOE Device	>95% within 48 hours

There were many problems with these KPIs. Foremost was that the client did not bother to define what it meant by 'Service Level' in the contract and didn't set up any sort of actions required in the event that the service levels were met, not met, or exceeded. Most bidders assumed the client meant service levels to be a minimum performance standard, however some did not. The cheaper bids used the least-cost assumption, that service levels were merely "*nice to meet targets*" to be achieved when convenient. The more expensive bids used the more costly assumption, that service levels must be met.

Unfortunately, the client chose a cheaper bid that did not resource to meet the KPIs, since it assumed the KPIs were merely goals as opposed to an actual requirement. In order to get the KPIs, the client was forced to pay more (and more than the most expensive bid).

Action 18. Blueprint the contractual documents

Imagine we are building a house without drawings or specifications, instead relying on various tradespeople to use their experience to build what we have in mind. So the concreter lays the slab where he thinks is best, given his experience; the plumber puts the piping where he think it should go, the electrician wires the house how she deems it should be, and so on. They have all done this before, so there is no need for a plan, really. You and I do not know how to build a house anyway, and I am sure we can both live in whatever they come up with, right?

This of course will sound extremely silly to anyone who has ever built a house, and probably to most of you who have not; the place would simply be unlivable.

Nevertheless, this is exactly how outsourcing contracts are usually constructed. Lawyers write the 'legal bits', technical folks write up a specification of some sort, a financial type writes up the pricing and invoicing portion and a bit about insurances, and the list goes on. Everyone works independently without a 'blueprint' to guide them. The result is exactly what would happen if these people were building a house; it becomes unlivable for the occupants.

This is perhaps why the majority of contract managers on both sides (client and provider) tell us they just put the contract in the drawer. The contract is just too big, too complex, too hard to decipher, and too full of conflicting and ambiguous statements … a paper-based maze that is impossible to navigate one's way out.

Case: Trying to understanding the contract is a full time job

The governing documents (contract, numerous SLAs, and schedules) for one major outsourcing arrangement were so complex, poorly written, and structured it took the new Contract Manager a year to fully understand the contract, the full extent of the arrangement, and how things were to get done between the two parties well enough to be effective at his job. Then he was transferred. His replacement also lasted slightly over a year. For years, there was no one at the client who was able to discuss the arrangement without having to rewrite the contract in a manner he or she could understand.

But it is not difficult to construct a contract that is useful in practice. It begins with the master plan, or the **contract blueprint.** The blueprint begins quite simply with an overview (see the example in Figure 6-11) listing the intended schedules and attachments, and then the clause headings (see the example in Figure 6-12).

Figure 6-11: Example Contract Blueprint (overview)

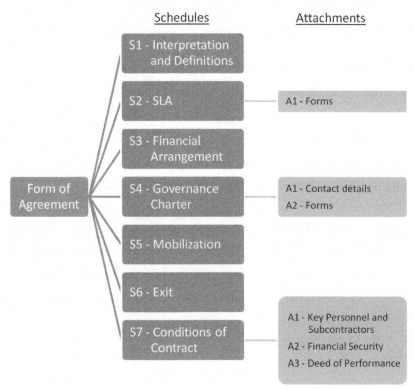

Figure 6-12: Example Contract Blueprint (schedules)

FORM OF AGREEMENT (FOA)	**S3 - FINANCIAL ARRANGEMENT**
Clause 1 Recital	Clause 1 About this schedule
Clause 2 Form of this Contract	Clause 2 Amounts in general
Clause 3 Commencement and Termination Dates	Clause 3 Charges
Clause 4 Authorized Representatives	Clause 4 Invoicing
Clause 5 Signatories	Clause 5 Payment
	Clause 6 Costs and reimbursables
S1 - INTERPRETATION AND DEFINITIONS	Clause 7 Financial KPIs
Clause 1 About this schedule	
Clause 2 Interpretation	**S4 - GOVERNANCE CHARTER**
Clause 3 Definitions	Clause 1 About this schedule
	Clause 2 Roles and responsibilities
S2 - Service Level Agreement (SLA)	Clause 3 Meetings
Clause 1 About this schedule	Clause 4 Reviews and assessments
Clause 2 Scope overview	Clause 5 Issue management
Clause 3 Specifications	Clause 6 Dispute management
Clause 4 Quality KPIs	Clause 7 Variation management
Clause 5 Reporting	Clause 8 Code of Conduct (Relationship KPIs)
Attachment – Requests and notices forms	Attachment A – Contact details
	Attachment B – Issue, dispute and variation forms

Planning and laying out the contract content in a manner like a blueprint is important. All of the countless contracts that we have reviewed over the last few decades had conflicting statements and a great deal of repetition. Examples include a performance reward system defined in the SLA and a performance recourse system defined in the general conditions; one with intellectual property owned by the provider in the general conditions, but by the client in the special conditions; another with different pricing mechanisms dispersed throughout the entirety of the document. The list of examples is nearly endless.

It is not that people set out to intentionally write incomprehensible, contradictory, and repetitive contracts. It is merely a function of who is involved, how much time and skills they have, and what they think they are supposed to do (in the absence of a blueprint).

In designing, and then bringing, all of these pieces together to form a contract, it is important to introduce the role of a *contract architect*. This person has the responsibility of drafting the blueprint and making sure the actual contents of the contract comply with it. The best person for this role would ideally be someone with commercial, financial, operational, and legal understanding of the deal at hand (both strategically and in detail).

Action 19. Draft the Service Level Agreement (SLA) schedule

The SLA is a document that defines work responsibilities of each party, defines what good work (and poor) is through the quality KPIs, and states what will be done about good and poor quality work/products.

In practice, however, the term 'Service Level Agreement' has had many meanings for different organizations. Sometime it refers to the entire contract. Towards the other extreme, it sometimes only reflects the KPIs. Because of these different meanings, it is vital that all parties to your SLA have a common definition of exactly what the SLA is, and what its components are. To aid this understanding, the key components of a typical SLA are provided in outline form in Figure 6-13.

Figure 6-13: SLA Outline

1. **About this schedule**
   1.1. Purpose
   1.2. Format

2. **Scope Overview**
   2.1. Responsibility matrix
   2.2. Possible variations to scope during the term (optional)
   2.3. Value added services (optional)

3. **Specification**
   3.1. Item #1 (from responsibility matrix)
   3.2. Item #2 (from responsibility matrix)
   3.3. Item #n (from responsibility matrix)

4. **Quality KPIs**
   4.1. KPI #1
   4.2. KPI #2
   4.3. KPI #n

5. **Effect of KPI Performance**
   5.1. Effect of good results
   5.2. Effect of poor results

Attachment - Forms

The SLA is arguably the most commercially important document in the suite of contractual documents because it clearly lays down what you expect for your money. However, if it is written poorly (unclear, ambiguous, incomplete, etc.), it will affect the initial price offered and be the main contributor to subsequent variations.

You write the SLA to be quoted from, and complied with, by providers. Having the provider draft the SLA, something we saw frequently 20 years ago, is now rare. Most clients want to be in control of defining their expectations so their needs are met and ensuring the scope is complete so that prices are accurate. To finalize the document, you update it with the final details resulting from the winning bid (BB5) and the results of any negotiation (BB6).

As the KPIs in the SLA are the ones that most typically have some form of recourse/reward framework, it is worth discussing some options here. KPI schemes encourage providers to deliver to expectation and, where desired, to deliver outstanding work. Schemes can come in the form of positive 'incentives' (rewards) for good performance, or negative 'disincentives' (recourse) for poor performance. While it is commonly assumed that the KPI effects are monetary, that does not have to be the case.

Recourse has long been an accepted consequence of not meeting KPIs. However, in recent years, there is an increasing use of rewards as well. Rewards are rarely applied carte blanche across all KPIs. With these, the increased performance delivered should bring about a business benefit, but it is often difficult to measure the benefit gained. In practice, rewards have work best when KPI targets are set for only the few services for which exceeding the minimum standard has value to your organization and are worth paying extra for (e.g. fault call reductions, backlog clearance, improved installation times, and higher satisfaction ratings).

At a minimum, you want KPIs that set the base level standard of performance to be achieved, which may have recourse for failure. Not all KPIs will necessarily attract a disincentive. However, if failing a KPI has no consequence, you may need to consider its importance since there is no explicit motivation for the provider not to fail it. This KPI should be dropped, or relegated to just a 'Performance Indicator' which are reported, but may not be part of the KPI performance scheme.

Unfortunately, many clients have lost sight of the central purpose of financial disincentives, which is to motivate the behavior of the provider so that the KPI is met. The goal of any financial disincentive scheme should never be to actually obtain the penalties, but rather to ensure that your minimum expectations are met. The sometimes strange relationship between recourse systems and the client's contract management behavior is illustrated by the following case.

Case: A regional bank 'extracts value' from its contracts

The management responsibilities for the outsourcing of IT services had been delegated to the finance department of a small regional bank. As IT was now to be outsourced, it was considered to be primarily a procurement issue rather than a service issue.

The finance department had little IT experience, but knew how to 'extract value' from procurement contracts. Accordingly, it set a budget for the achievement of financial recourse for poor performance. In this manner, the department believed it would demonstrate prudent financial management by continually reducing costs.

The development of processes and resolution of service issues giving rise to performance issues were never considered. In fact, the contract manager had a personal goal to achieve penalties at least equal to his salary. Over time, the bank eventually brought all the services back inhouse as outsourcing was deemed to result in inadequate control over quality.

There are two ways in which KPI recourse/reward programs operate: (1) an ongoing regular basis (e.g. monthly), or (2) an intermittent basis (e.g. annually). Regular schemes are nearly always a monetary scheme that adjusts value-for-money. The premise of a regular monetary scheme is that the price will have adjustments, up or down, based on the quality received. The minimum standard KPI thresholds set the base performance to be achieved for the price paid; a lesser degree of service then results in a lower price for that period. Meeting KPI targets attracts a higher price.

Intermittent schemes are not applied every month; rather on an annual basis or less frequently (i.e. near the end of the contract). These schemes offer a high-impact, low-cost incentive program. The high impact comes from having a large carrot or stick, and the low cost comes from the minimal administrative overheads incurred in operating the scheme.

The rewards typically offered under a non-monetary scheme can include:

- **Contract extension** - a smaller length of the original term is awarded for a specified period of good KPI results. For example, a three-year contract may have a performance-based extension of 12 months.

- **Active promotion as a reference site** - you open your site to the potential clients of the provider to tour, perform periodic road shows with the provider visiting potential clients, and/or speak with the provider at conferences.

- **Issue a certificate or letter** - you issue a certificate of performance, a letter of commendation or write a reference letter for the provider to use in marketing materials, bids with potential clients, frame and put in their office, etc.

- **Automatically shortlist for further work** - the provider gains automatic entry into a competitive process and bypasses any prequalification stage, thus saving some tendering costs. Note, however, winning is far from guaranteed; the provider merely gets to skip through a few hoops based on previous good performance.

The deterrents typically offered under an intermittent scheme include:

- **Warning notice** - this operates very similar to a staff warning policy. After a certain number of warnings, then you have the right to terminate.

- **Withhold payment** - you hold the part of the payment related to the defective work until the performance has improved.

- **Withdraw as a reference site** - an explicit obligation that the provider cannot use your organization's name as a reference site, in any marketing materials, or represent the contract as successful.

- **Remove from preferred provider list** - ban the provider from future work until performance has improved. Note that some governments do not allow this because it restricts trade; no matter how poorly a provider has performed, they are always entitled to bid for more work.

- **Step-in** - a successor steps in to perform the work when the original provider is failing KPIs.

- **Termination** (full or part) - at some stage, as a last resort, you may want the right to terminate for poor performance. This can be termination of the entire contract (full termination) or just the work for which the KPIs are failing (part termination).

Intermittent schemes can act as the sole program or in conjunction with a regular monetary scheme. For example, failure to meet a minimum standard KPI may result in a rebate in each month of occurrence, but three continuous months of failure may lead to possible termination (in whole or in part).

Action 20. Draft the Financial Arrangement schedule

The Financial Arrangement schedule (see Figure 6-14) tends to cover all pricing, invoicing, and payment related issues - at a minimum. The purpose of this schedule is to make it easy to bill, verify bills, and pay without having to refer to the (bulky) contract. One way to think of this is to imagine what your accounts payable function and the provider's accounts receivable functions need to know.

You write the Financial Schedule (with blanks for the providers to fill in the numbers). You want all bidders to reply using the same template because it makes it so much easier for you, as anyone who has evaluated a lump-sum contract, vs. a unit-priced contract, vs. a cost-plus contract will attest. When bidders are allowed to quote 'free-form', it makes the financial evaluation almost impossible. After you have selected the provider (BB5) and completed negotiations if any (BB6), you then complete the Financial Schedule with the final numbers.

Figure 6-14: Financial Arrangement Schedule Outline

1. **About this schedule**
   1.1. Purpose
   1.2. Format

2. **Costs to be Born by the Parties**
   2.1. Each Party to bear own costs
   2.2. Client to bear costs
   2.3. Provider to bear costs

3. **Provider's Charges**
   3.1. Lump sum charges
   3.2. Unit rate charges
   3.3. Cost-plus charges and reimbursables

4. **Charges for Additional Work** (if applicable)

5. **Mobilization and Exit charges** (if applicable)

6. **Indexing** (if applicable)[89]

7. **Invoicing**
   7.1. Submission
   7.2. Incorrect invoices
   7.3. Time limitation

8. **Payment**
   8.1. Due date
   8.2. Discounts for early payment and (if applicable)
   8.3. Charges for late payment (if applicable)
   8.4. Right to offset[90]
   8.5. Payment as acceptance (if applicable)

9. **Financial KPIs** (if applicable)
   9.1. KPI #1
   9.2. KPI #2
   9.3. KPI #n

10. **Effect of KPI Performance**
    10.1. Effect of good results
    10.2. Effect of poor results

Attachment - Forms

---

[89] The indexing section details the use of 'ratchets' that can trigger price increases/decreases such as fluctuations in CPI (Consumer Price Index) and/or other published indices.

[90] Offset is the right to deduct monies owed against monies due.

Action 21. Draft the Governance Charter schedule

A Governance Charter is a relatively simple document that facilitates successful management of the deal for both parties because it forces the parties to think about, and agree on, how they will work together. It imposes a commitment on both sides to manage the deal in a diligent and agreed manner thereby ensuring strong controls as well as facilitating an efficient working relationship.

Case: Lack of control resulting in high costs

A state-based insurance company had its costs blow out 500% from the planned expenditure after the first year of outsourcing. A brief analysis found that one of the contributing causes was the lack of control over the relationship. Anyone in either party could contact anyone in the other party for any reason. Thus, the insurance company staff were requesting and getting many more services than were provided for in the contract, and the provider never said no. In fact, the provider quickly realized it could offer many more services and the company's staff would never turn them down. It was not until rules governing out-of-scope work were put in place by the accounting department that the finances were brought back under control.

The Governance Charter provides the 'one-stop-shop' document providing the agreed governance mechanisms (see Figure 6-15). After you have selected the provider (BB5) and completed negotiations if any (BB6), you then complete the Governance Charter with the final individuals and their details.

Not all arrangements warrant a Governance Charter. If the deal is a short-term, once-off transaction, and/or is of low risk and low value, then the cost of preparing and complying with a Governance Charter may outweigh the benefits.

Typical reasons to consider the use of a Governance Charter include:

- **Importance** - if the deal is long-term, high value, or high risk.

- **Complexity** - if the management activities involve a number of personnel in either party, or the tasks are complicated or extensive.

- **Accountability** - to ensure everyone in both parties understands their roles and the roles of others.

- **Conflict resolution** - to provide an agreed process for resolution.

- **User-friendly contract document** - to have the agreed interparty management 'rules' in a useable form (i.e. easily understood and referenced).

Figure 6-15: Governance Charter Outline

1. **About this Schedule**
   1.1. Purpose
   1.2. Format of this document

2. **Governance Structure**
   2.1. Interparty management structure
   2.2. Client roles and responsibilities
   2.3. Provider roles and responsibilities

3. **Governance Operations**
   3.1. Meetings
   3.2. Reports
   3.3. Reviews and audits
   3.4. Issue management
   3.5. Dispute resolution
   3.6. Variation management

4. **Code of Conduct**
   4.1. Agreed conduct/relationship values
   4.2. Assessing perceptions

5. **Relationship KPIs** (if applicable)
   5.1. Governance operations
   5.2. Code of conduct

6. **Effect of KPI Performance** (if applicable)
   6.1. Effect of good results
   6.2. Effect of poor results

Attachments
   A.   Contact details
   B.   Forms

Action 22. Draft the Transitions schedules

If you have followed the lifecycle approach, you have already planned your approach to the two pertinent building blocks (BB7 and BB9) - the transition strategies prepared in BB3 (Action 13). This action takes those strategies and turns them into detailed contract schedules, along with the related contract clauses (see Table 6-5). The difference between a strategy and a contract schedule is that the former is a high-level concept and approach, while the latter is an enforceable undertaking (and much more detailed). The transitions are separate schedules because they are self-contained projects within an outsourcing initiative. Each schedule is only used for a short, but important period - one at the start of a contract and the other at its end.

One thing we have observed, too often, is severe neglect of contractual provisions addressing the next generation options. Yet, we have not found mobilization be such as issue. We suspect this is because mobilization it is the first thing that needs to be done and this perhaps makes it more urgent. But it is equally important to make certain the next generation options can occur with few surprises. This means planning, and making provisions, for renewal, retendering, handover, and backsourcing provisions.

In many cases, particularly first generation contracts, the lack of forethought in the original contract resulted in the client needing to negotiate such provisions while the current contract was in effect (and without much bargaining power). That was just the situation with the following case.

Case: Forgetting the contract will end one day

In the outsourcing of the HR function at a federal government department, no provisions had been made in the contract to prepare for the end of the deal. The client was planning to retender and expected the provider not to be successful due to poor past performance and a maturation of the marketplace. An urgent project was formed to create a Deed of Disengagement that covered the missing obligations and rights. The client obtained many of the needed provisions, because the provider did not want to adversely affect the relationship during the retender. However, in return, the client had to agree to an extension of the current contract and additional fees for the "*new*" exit activities.

Action 23. Draft the Conditions of Contract

We have observed in recent times an alarming trend to forego investment in a prudent contract, the rationale being that the parties desire a 'partnership' based on trust, and the perception that a comprehensive contract is at odds with this desire. However, this is a high-risk strategy, particularly where trust has not been earned over many years of the parties working with one another.

For each client, the value of drafting the contract is that it forces the people involved to go through a process of deciding and understanding the many options and issues, not just to have a signed piece of paper; or worse - to operate under a false interpretation like the next case.

Case: Understanding the impact of force majeure

A stock broking firm had no understanding of standard force majeure provisions that release the provider from its obligations due to uncontrollable events such as fire, flood, etc., (in the old days known as the 'acts of God' clause). Management assumed the services were guaranteed no matter what and nothing could interfere with that obligation. For this reason, the service scope did not include any disaster recovery provisions.

An external audit discovered the missing scope during the first year of the contract. Management immediately requested the provider to quote on providing services in the event of a disaster at the firm's site, as well as being a prioritized recover customer if a disaster occurred at the provider's site. The provider quoted a price that was equal to the current contract price (doubling the original contract's price), far beyond the current market prices of a recovery service. The client chose instead to set up its own recovery arrangement at a fraction of the price. The client learnt a valuable lesson on checking its assumptions about what the contract actually says (too late). The opportunistic behavior displayed by the provider damaged the relationship irreparably, and it was never trusted again. A very bad, and easily avoidable, start to a five-year contract.

We recommend that you start out by deciding your organization's (reasonable) position on the standard headings listed in Table 6-5. The point of starting from the headings is to decide, particular to this arrangement, what is appropriate from the plethora of options available.

Table 6-5: List of Conditions of Contract

General Conditions	Special Conditions/ Contract Operations	Financial
1. Recital	31. Compliance with the SLA and Governance Charter	66. Compliance with the Financial Arrangement
2. Duration and extensions	32. Exclusivity or non-exclusivity	67. Currency and foreign exchange
3. Conditions precedent	33. Additional/out of scope services	68. Changes to taxes and duties
4. Definitions		69. Indexing
5. Interpretation	34. Applicable standards, policies, and guidelines	70. Offset rights
6. Governing law	35. Occupational health, safety, and environment	71. Effect of KPI performance (rebates/bonuses)
7. Entire agreement		72. Gainsharing/painsharing
8. Severability of provisions	36. Subcontracting	73. Innovation funding
9. Priority of documents	37. Contractor as prime contractor	74. Liability/damages and limitations
10. Nature of the relationship	38. Contractor as agent	75. Insurances
11. General conduct of the Contract	39. Management of third-party contracts on Client's behalf	76. Financial guarantee/security
12. Assignment/novation	40. Performance guarantee	**Mobilization**
13. Change of control	41. Performance improvement	77. Party obligations during Mobilization
14. Waivers	42. Industry development	78. Compliance with the Mobilization Plan
15. Representations, warranties, and undertakings	43. Benchmarking	
	44. Shadowing	79. Asset transfer/sales
	45. Title transfers	80. Staff transfers /employment offers
16. Contractor indemnities	46. Asset refreshment/ upgrades	81. Secondments during Mobilization
17. Third party indemnities and claim management	47. Asset disposal/ salvage	82. Novation/assignment of third-party contracts
	48. Minimum resource commitment	83. Cutover/Acceptance Certificate
18. Contractor not to encumber itself	49. Contractor personnel	**Termination and Exit**
19. Intellectual property rights	50. Key Contractor personnel and Subcontractors	84. Termination for cause (Material Breach)
20. Intellectual property in escrow	51. Staff secondments	85. Termination for convenience
	52. Poaching of staff	86. Partial termination
21. Copyright/ Moral rights	53. Access to site/s	87. Right of cross-termination
22. Confidentiality	54. Records/ documentation	88. Effect of termination
23. Privacy	55. Data ownership and security	89. Redundancies and redeployment
24. Freedom of information	56. Computer viruses	90. Party obligations during Exit
25. Official enquiries	57. Audit rights, records, and access	91. Compliance with the Exit Plan
26. Media and public relations	58. Force majeure	92. Asset transfer-backs or purchases
27. Use of Client name, logo, and testimonials	59. Latent conditions/ discoveries	93. Offers of employment
	60. Temporary suspension	94. Settlement of accounts
28. Conflict of interest	61. Correction of defects	95. Closeout Certificate
29. Authorized Representatives	62. Client step-in rights	96. Post Exit services by Contractor
	63. Alternative dispute resolution	97. No representation after termination
30. Notices	64. Amendments and variations	98. Clauses surviving termination
	65. Renegotiation	

Here, in BB3, you create 'version 1' of the contract, the first in a series of versions that is created during the lifecycle journey. This draft version is provided to the bidders in BB5 for them to declare their exact preferred alternatives. **Version** 2 is created when you update with the winning bidder's bid information and is then used in negotiation. The third version, **version 3**, is the one agreed and signed by the parties at the conclusion of negotiations in BB5. You may think that version 3 is it, but there is another, **version 4**, which includes the variations that occur throughout BB8.

We do not intend to provide a comprehensive guide to contracts in this book, for there are many readily available books on the subject. One useful tip here, though, is to make sure that commercial, not legal priorities dictate the shape of the contract. Lawyers should be there to translate the agreed commercial arrangements into legally sound documents, not interfere with the commercial outcomes and practicalities of the agreement.

Chapter 7   Buy Wisely - the Engage Phase

The Engage Phase, where providers are selected and the deal is negotiated, consists of the fifth and sixth building blocks:

- BB5: Select - during which you choose the best value for money provider, and

- BB6: Negotiate - during which you finalize the best deal.

Prior to embarking on this phase, you should have conducted the following processes.

- From **BB1: Investigate** - Collected all the information needed to be an informed buyer. Do not use a tender to learn about what you want to buy!

- From **BB2: Target** - Targeted the areas to be considered for outsourcing including the preparation of profiles. Knowing what you have now, and what you want, is imperative to selecting the best provider.

- From **BB3: Strategize** - Planned and resourced your approach to the remainder of the entire lifecycle. In doing so, you will have worked out the major aspects of the deal and the keys to its success.

- From **BB4: Design** - Designed, in detail, the future arrangement and the contractual documents. This process articulated your requirements in a commercially astute manner to ensure the deal will get the desired results and minimize identified risks.

Building Block 5: Select - Get the Best Value for Money

"Round numbers are always false"

Samuel Johnson

| ARCHITECT PHASE | ENGAGE PHASE | OPERATE PHASE | REGENERATE PHASE |

BUILDING BLOCK 5
SELECT

A competitive process is the most common technique employed to select a provider. Such an approach provides pressure on the competing providers to deliver best value for money against their industry peers, exposes the client to a variety of capabilities and potential solutions, and allows an informed selection decision to evolve and mature. Of course, entering into direct negotiation is an alternative approach, but one that has had inconsistent results. In our earlier research on proven practices, we found that non-competed bids had a very mixed track record. [91]

Back in BB3 - Strategize (Action 12- Decide the competitive process), you chose how many of the five competitive stages were appropriate given your knowledge of the market, the number of potential providers, and the degree to which you know exactly what you want. This Building Block represents the one competitive stage that nearly all client do conduct. This is the fourth stage - which goes by many names, most often being a RFx derivative (Request for tender, offer, proposal, quotation, etc) or a IFx derivative (Invitation to bid, offer, etc.), but

---

[91] Lacity, M and Willcocks, L (2001). *Global Information Technology Outsourcing: In Search of Business Advantage.* Wiley, Chichester.

otherwise known as "the big one". To run a successful tender, this building block has the following actions:

- determine the evaluation team who will be making the decision (Action 24),

- determine the selection criteria the evaluation team debates and agrees will result in the best decision (Action 25),

- prepare a succinct market package (what you provide to the bidders) which is driven by the evaluation criteria (Action 26),

- facilitate the bidders being able to provide their best responses (Action 27),

- conduct interactive evaluations, rather than just rely on a written bid (Action 28),

- select the provider based on best value for money (Action 29), and

- conduct due diligence investigations to verify all representations (Action 30).

Action 24. Determine the evaluation team

Determining what provider/s you are going to live with and depend upon for many years is akin to an arranged marriage, albeit one in which you have sole discretion. The individuals involved in the evaluation are paramount to selecting the most appropriate provider. A good team determines robust criteria, which drives a high-quality request for proposal that facilitates superior bids and a good result. You first select the evaluation team, and then have that team decide the evaluation criteria and weights and then write the questions to ask the bidders based on each criterion and its importance.

The evaluation team's responsibilities usually include the following:

- develop the evaluation strategy and detailed evaluation criteria,

- gather all information necessary to enable a thorough evaluation,

- select the winner/s and conduct due diligence,

- prepare the evaluation report and business case, and

- note potential negotiation and operational issues that came to light.

A diverse evaluation team has a greater probability of developing a robust selection process. A wide range of experiences and values will promote debate on what is most important for the particular arrangement and why. This helps ensure the right questions are asked of the market and the right reasons are used to pick the winner. It is the evaluation team's unique experiences, perceptions, and values that drive the selection process. If they choose poorly, for whatever reason, it could be years before the client can unwind the outcome.

Accordingly, it is critical to the long-term success of your outsourcing arrangement to have a broad, cross-functional team with the core expertise and many of the period expertise as well (refer Action 2):

The evaluation team may need additional help to conduct a thorough and meaningful evaluation if the individuals do not have sufficient expertise in certain areas. Furthermore, not every individual on the team needs to evaluate every item. It is not uncommon for part of an evaluation to be entrusted to a working group that will report to the evaluation team.

There are two types of specialist working groups that can assist the evaluation team to make an efficient and effective evaluation. These are:

- **expertise-based** - required for a particular subject matter (e.g. financial viability, security solutions); and

- **task-based** - dedicated to a specific task for efficiency (e.g. reference checks, price analysis).

There may be certain subject areas in which the evaluation team is not the best qualified to conduct the in-depth evaluation, leading to the use of expertise-based working groups. In these instances, the evaluation of that particular area may be delegated to a working group that reports their evaluation to the evaluation team. Figure 7-1 gives an example of this kind of team structure.

Figure 7-1: Example Evaluation Team Structure

Action 25. Determine selection criteria

It is critical for the effectiveness of the entire competitive process to decide how you will evaluate bids before issuing a request to bidders, and prior to drafting the request in the first place. If a request to bidder providers (e.g. ROI, EOI, RFP) is issued before deciding how to evaluate it, the probability of a faulty request increases dramatically, as the case below illustrates.

Case: One evaluator takes over

In one evaluation team, one team member was directed to prepare the part of the RFP concerning his subject matter. This member was a quality expert, as he was the project manager who led the quality certification process of the client. It therefore made sense for him to prepare the questions to the bidders that covered quality issues. He had nearly five pages of questions, more than any other topic to be addressed. When the bidders received the RFP, they believed the sheer number of questions meant that the quality processes were a key criterion, and so invested great effort in preparing that portion of their responses. While the RFP was out in the market, the evaluation team then decided to weight the criteria. Quality certification was deemed mandatory and bidders who did not have it were to be disregarded. The nature of the quality systems they had in place were then weighted at 0.5%; hardly worth the huge effort they put into answering those five pages of questions!

Organizations that have waited until the bids are received to figure out how to evaluate them have:

- omitted critical data, thus had widely varying responses because of the assumptions that had to be made by each bidder;

- not requested appropriate information to form part of the response, thus needed to continually ask for further information and setback the timeline;

- over emphasized non-critical areas, accordingly had responses that concentrated on the non-critical aspects their bid; and

- received 'free-for-all' bids preventing an efficient evaluation by the evaluation team working without 'apples to apples' bids.

Where the price is the sole criterion, the evaluation process is relatively straightforward. However, where 'value for money' is vital, the tender evaluation becomes more complex. The 'value' is often intangible and subject to the perceptions of the valuer, thus each client must develop different selection criteria.

There are three types of selection criteria:

1. **Mandatory** - the first gate that the bidders must pass through and is typically binary (yes/no), such as having specified certifications, audited financial statements, etc.

2. **Qualitative** - the 'value' in the value-for-money equation, comprising general capability, demonstrated experience, and proposed approach.

3. **Quantitative** - the 'money' (prices bid) in the value for money equation.

Which of these criteria you apply, and how you use them, will depend upon what stage of the competitive process you are going through. However, it is critical to design your criteria before issuing any market package as the next case demonstrates.

Case: No criteria, no decision

A bank went to the open market (open to any provider), starting at the EOI (Expression of Interest) stage with advertisements in major newspapers. It sent out extensive data about its operations to all interested providers, and, in return, requested extensive information about them.

It received 14 widely different responses. Some providers bid for part of the scope; some bid for only certain geographic regions; some did not provide all the information; and some replied in a different format. Some bid fixed price; others unit prices; others a combination; and others at cost plus a margin.

After two weeks attempting to determine a short-list without reaching consensus amongst the evaluation team, the bank determined that it could only conclude its evaluation by having a structured evaluation methodology. This was particularly necessary because the evaluation team of 11 management personnel did not have much experience in assessing bids, and they were all using different criteria to nominate their individual preferences.

Consultants were hired to develop the evaluation criteria via workshops with the evaluation team. The consultants discovered that only 30% of the information required by the evaluation team to make a shortlist was actually requested in the EOI. Accordingly, no decision could be made.

Rather than suffer any credibility loss, all 14 providers were invited to the BAFO (Best and Final Offer) phase. This added two months to the evaluation period and an extra $200,000 to the project budget without having made any progress towards choosing a provider (not to mention the additional cost to the providers). It took only one day to develop the criteria and the evaluation methodology, which would have prevented this excessive cost.

While each of these categories is important, in each case you will need to decide what is more important to you. You will find that each evaluation team member has a different opinion. Some may believe it is more important to go with a long-standing brand name that has broad capabilities (general capabilities), others may believe it is more important to go with the most experienced in the actual work, in your industry (specific experience), yet others believe the best approach should win. For this reason, it is common to weight the qualitative criteria, after a robust team debate, but less so to weigh price.

If you do not weigh price, the value-for-money equation is balanced; that is, 'value' and 'money' are, in effect, weighed equally. The 'value' component is represented by the qualitative criteria and the 'money' component by the price (or total cost of contract). The evaluation is not skewed toward one or the other. However, some clients do weigh price and you may want to consider this.

A weight of over 50% ensures that price is the foremost consideration, which may be appropriate in more commodity-type purchasing where risks are low and providers undifferentiated or where cost is paramount. The result is skewed to the lowest priced bid. In instances where you wish to steer the evaluation team away from choosing the lowest price no matter what the value, you usually weight price at something less than 50%. For example, the overall decision might be based 30% on price and value at 70%, or even more extreme as illustrated in the following case.

Case: A state government department chooses value over high cost

One of the largest state departments had about 250 contracts in place at any given time. For the most part, these contracts were nightmares to manage. A key root cause was that it had selected providers very poorly in the past, choosing only on price. As a result, the department made a corporate decision to disallow evaluation teams from looking at price at all. They did not assess the price until the best quality provider had been chosen. Then the department paid that price, or attempted to obtain whatever discounts they could negotiate.

The deals done under the new selection protocol were the best the department had done; they worked better, were not adversarial, and the total cost of contracts was less than similar deals in the past.

Action 26. Prepare the market package

The market package is the set of information you submit to the market that potential providers then use to base their bids and offers on. The offers that your organization receives will reflect the quality of information it provided in its market package - in other words, 'garbage in - garbage out'.

Many clients have different ways of structuring a market package. The simplest way to look at it is that there are only two parts: (1) the things you want the bidders to know and (2) the things you want to know from the bidders (see Figure 7-2).

- **Part One: Information for Tenderers** - background information, conditions of tendering and information on work as it is currently performed. The contract is attached to it, along with any information on which the provider is going to base their offer.

- **Part Two: The Response Framework** - constitutes the bidders' official submission. It is structured so that each question asked of the respondent maps directly to the evaluation criteria developed in Action 25 so the bids are efficient and easy to score and the evaluation team will have all the information required (see Figure 7-3 showing how the criteria drives the bulk of the response questions).

Traditional market packages use a scattergun approach; oscillating between descriptions (e.g. background information) and bid response requirements (e.g. questions to be answered by the bidder). This is difficult for bidder to prepare their response and, later, for evaluators to map the response. The most efficient use of time and intellect of both parties is to develop the information requirements based on the criteria driving the selection. This results in a win-win outcome. Bidders do not waste time on low priority items, and the task of evaluation was simplified.

Case: Garbage in, garbage out

A federal government department rushed its market package out to the bidders to meet a deadline. After receiving the bids and being dismayed at the responses, the evaluation team looked more closely at what they had requested and realized the bids *did* provide what was asked for in the request for tender. The request for tender, however, was poorly written, ambiguous, and in some instances wrong. Nearly 50 clarifications were then issued (effectively redrafting the market package).

Figure 7-2: Outline of a Market Package

Part 1: Information for Tenderers	Part 2: The Response Framework
1 Structure of this RFP	**1. Part Two information**
2 Background	**2. Acknowledgment/ Statutory Declaration** (optional)
2.1 About our organization	
2.2 About the RFP	**3. Company Details**
3 The RFP Process	**4. General Capability**
3.1 Planned timetable	4.1. Subcriterion #1 questions
3.2 RFP briefing	4.2. Subcriterion #2 questions
3.3 Site visits	4.3. Subcriterion #n questions
3.4 Evaluation	**5. Specific Demonstrated Experience**
3.5 Shortlisting (optional)	5.1. Subcriterion #1 questions
3.6 Clarifications and further information	5.2. Subcriterion #2 questions
3.7 Unsuccessful tenderers	5.3. Subcriterion #n questions
4 Proposal Instructions	**6. Proposed Approach**
4.1 Lodgment	6.1. Approach to the Contract (Statement of Departure)
4.2 Alternative proposals	6.2. Subcriterion #2 questions
5 RFP Terms and Conditions	6.3. Subcriterion #n questions
5.1 Confidentiality	**7. Charges**
5.2 Document ownership	7.1. Lump sum charges
5.3 Client's rights	7.2. Unit charges
5.4 Creation of contract	7.3. Cost+ charges
5.5 Costs incurred	7.4. Mobilization charges
5.6 Probity (optional)	7.5. Disengagement charges
Attachments	7.6. Pricing information (e.g. assumptions)
A. Profiles (as appropriate)	
B. Contractual documents	

Figure 7-3: Evaluation Criteria Feeding the Response Framework

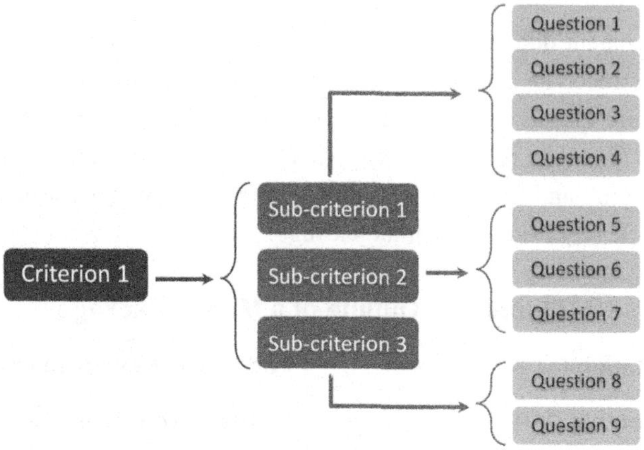

Action 27. Facilitate best responses from bidders

Just issuing paper documentation and expecting a skillful and comprehensive response is naive. Bidders require interaction to be effective. The more your organization assists providers in understanding it, its strategies and viewpoints, its preferred way of operating, and so on, the better the responses will be.

There are a number of common techniques used to facilitate getting good bids.

- **Data room** - a secure room containing bulk information and, if appropriate, a secure terminal so that the bidders can access large amounts of information, or information not allowed off your site.

- **Briefing** - a formal opportunity to meet stakeholders and obtain information. Because it is also useful for you to gauge the level of interest and competition, many clients have attendance at a market briefing a mandatory condition of submitting a bid.

- **Site visit** - when documentation cannot adequately convey information to bidders, they can be offered the chance to visit sites. In physically observing your operations, bidders can see how your business works, the challenges it faces, and ask questions at the coalface.

- **Questions and answers** (Q&A) - a written request/response process following one of two approaches. The **full disclosure method** shares all Q&As with all bidders to ensure each has identical information. But, by giving everyone all the answers, it has the perverse effect of resulting in few questions (no bidder wants want to help competitors improve their bids). The result is more caveats and assumptions in bids. The **factual disclosure method** distributes only the Q&As that correct errors.

- **Workshops** - can take any number of formats (e.g. brainstorming, idea generation, problem) to enable the provider to explore issues, solutions and options with you, so that they can better tailor their bid.

- **Bidder's discovery** - an opportunity for bidders to verify the information provided by your organization to help limit potential caveats, disclaimers, and risk contingencies contained within the bids.

Case: Two cases with different approaches and different results

A water utility wanted the metering operations outsourced fast and cheap in order to reduce its headcount. They did nothing to assist the market prepare bids and issued an onerous contract with poor specifications As a result, all bids were higher than the inhouse cost because the bidders had to price in a great deal of uncertainty and ambiguity. The work was kept inhouse with massive layoffs instead.

A telco approached things quite differently. They encouraged the bidders to prepare their best possible response. They arranged meetings with the contract management teams in all the regions, as well as site visits so that the bidders knew who and what they would be dealing with. They also set up a data room with a terminal giving access to all required operational information. The difference in offers between the bidders who took up these options and those that did not was striking.

Action 28. Conduct interactive evaluation

Assessing the written response is the typical starting point for the competitive evaluation. However, remember that a good written response may simply reflect how good a provider is at writing bids, not necessarily how good they are at delivering. This was the situation in the next case.

Case: Seeing is believing

A government department's evaluation team decided to visit the operations of the two finalists to an RFP. The first finalist (the preferred provider at that stage) had described its operations in glowing terms, and the team wanted to see it in practice. However, upon visiting the provider, reality proved a bit different. Operations were in shambles, the facility run-down and there was little security. In addition, staff could not seem to answer questions in a competent manner.

In visiting the other finalist, the bid had not done it justice. It was a very professionally ran facility with state of the art equipment and fitout, and staffed with very knowledgeable people. As a result, the team reviewed both bids with new insight gained from firsthand experience and re-scored all their evaluations. The new insight also made them more effective in interviews as they did not automatically accept the written words as fact, and sought evidence for key representations.

Situations like this case stress why the bid, as the formal response, is only one source of evaluation information. Moreover, a market package and the resultant bid/s are all paper-based communications, and may not be the best means of communicating complex information.

In addition to the formal bids, there are a number of additional information-gathering methods to consider (see Table 7-1). These various interactive techniques allow personnel from the client and provider teams to work together, to converse, and get to know one another. They provide the evaluation team with the provider's interpretations of their bid, impart clarifications and additional information, and help determine whether the proposed team is what you had expected from the information given in the bid.

Table 7-1: Options for Interactive Evaluations

	Description
Interviews	Interviews with the key individuals who will form the account and delivery teams helps gauge how well they understand your needs and understand what they have proposed. It also allows you to assess their personal capabilities and your ability to work with them.
Presentations	The best communication between people is primarily verbal. Consider having the bidders present their proposal to the client, so that each provider can highlight the bid 'in its own words'. This provides an insight into what the provider deems important, where its strengths are, and offers a chance to 'eyeball' the people.
Reference checks	In-depth reference checking is a critical procedure, particularly when a bidder is not one of your organization's current providers. Reference checking is designed to determine if the bidder has demonstrated in practice what it has stated in its bid. The best references are from those customers that most closely resemble your organization, with an arrangement that most resembles the nature of your arrangement, and that have been exposed to similar issues to those you might be facing (e.g. implementation, integration, pricing, staff transitions, etc). Do not limit the reference checks to only the provider as an entity, however. The people that you will be working with are pivotal to having an effective relationship and you should consider reference checking the proposed key personnel as well.
Site visits	Touring the provider's operations is invaluable in obtaining an understanding of how they conduct their business in practice. Touring its' customer sites gives you a chance to observe their relationship management in action. Things to look for include: • to what extent your visit is 'stage-managed' - the freedom you have to go and look at what you want to and whether you are free to chat with people you might encounter, • cultural indictors (e.g. a client with an egalitarian culture may want to be wary of a provider with an overt command and control environment), and • security and safety of the site.
Workshops or field experiments	Workshops (or field experiments) provide an opportunity to assess how well the parties work together and solve problems. Opportunities to problem-solve and exchange views, particularly where there will be interdependence, can be invaluable. Workshops can be centered on solving real-life issues you are facing, or hypothetical ones that maybe encountered. For example, a client seeking a sole provider for a technology conversion decided that before they would commit to one provider, they would have two providers do small pieces of the conversion. As a result, the client experienced much better project leadership from one in terms of onsite coordination, project status reporting, technical fit with the specification, and daily communications. The client then selected this provider to complete the entire conversion. Three months later, when the technology went live, the provider was granted the ongoing maintenance contract.

The case below show how important these techniques are.

Case: The disparity between a good bid and a good provider

In an evaluation of a BPO deal, a clear winner emerged after the evaluation of the formal written responses. However, this provider was not the one chosen after the evaluation team witnessed the bid presentation and conducted a site visit.

The presentation highlighted serious issues between sales, management, and service delivery personnel. Only the managing director spoke unless a question was specifically addressed to an individual. Even then, the managing director frequently answered on their behalf or corrected their answers. Many times, the service delivery people and the sales people contradicted each other on what could be done, sometimes aggressively. The presentations by other bidders showed superior levels of respect to one another and answers were far less filtered through one individual.

The site visit showed more problems. The client's evaluation team was not permitted to ask questions of anyone other than the escorts. Even eye contact by the provider's employees was difficult to obtain. Furthermore, the team was only allowed into limited showcase areas, rather than the total operations. Site visits to other bidders were completely open, the evaluation team was encouraged to ask anyone any question they wanted, and little of the visit appeared scripted or controlled; the evaluation team was allowed to be in charge.

This led the team to be increasingly uncomfortable with the preferred provider. The final *"nail in the coffin"* was driven in by the customer reference checks which indicated that arrogant, non-customer orientated behavior was the norm, promises made were often not kept, and that issues went unresolved for inordinate lengths of time. They chose the second provider who had a superior presentation, site visit and reference checks.

Action 29. Select provider based on value for money

Successful outsourcing is not about getting the lowest price at any cost. It is about getting the lowest accurate price with a superior provider offering sustainable solutions under a fair contract. It is not a single, isolated economic transaction that automatically executes itself after the parties sign an agreement, but an ongoing commercial relationship with economic and strategic consequences that depend upon how the parties conduct themselves. If the client selects wisely, these consequences can be good; if not, they can be very bad.

This means you should not automatically select the least expensive option, or the best quality. Instead, you weigh price against quality to determine value for money. Selecting the provider on 'best value for money' attributes rather than price alone has become the norm, particularly as clients have learnt that lowest price does not equal lower overall cost. In fact, the opposite is often the case - the lowest price results in the highest overall cost. The cost of greater oversight, out-of-scope charges, constant renegotiation, dispute resolution, rework, backsourcing, or step-in all can make the original price immaterial.

The following experience demonstrates that the lowest bid is not always where the real value is.

Case: A major retailer gets the lowest price at a high cost

The IT department of a retailing company had recently been transferred to the Corporate Services division. The general manager believed that commodity functions should be outsourced so that the division could focus on adding value to the operational business units. She targeted the *"commodity"* IT services and went to tender for the data centre operations, charging $500 to potential bidders to receive the RFT to *"weed out non-contenders."*

The emphasis was placed on the price, as she believed the services, and the providers themselves, were undifferentiated. Accordingly, the lowest priced bid was awarded the contract, rather than any sort of assessment of value for money. This bid was 30% below the nearest bid.

Things began to go awry very quickly. Scope and price variations were the norm. Eventually, a person had to be dedicated to variation management. KPIs were rarely achieved, because they were set up as targets and not as minimum standards which was due to the client allowing the provider's standard SLA to be used rather than developing one that represented the client's needs. The provider capped the number of resources they would provide for the price and would only bring in more for more money. In time, the general manager had to hire specialists to work in the data centre to raise KPIs back to what they had been and to meet demand peaks.

Within a year, the total cost of contract was higher than the highest bid, higher than the inhouse baseline. Moreover, and most telling, the division's remaining IT people were focused on fighting the contract, not on *"adding value to the business."*

There can be severe consequences when a provider wins a bid from which ultimately it stands to make no money - called the '**Winner's Curse**'. The effects of this can be devastating for both parties. The Winner's Curse has, at its core, a provider bidding a price it believes necessary to win the tender ($P1 in Figure 7-4). Not the higher price required to do the work at a reasonable margin ($P2 in Figure 7-4); and certainly not the highest price of all - the one required to interpret SLAs and contracts in the client's favor ($P3 in Figure 7-4).

Figure 7-4: The Iron Triangle and the Winner's Curse

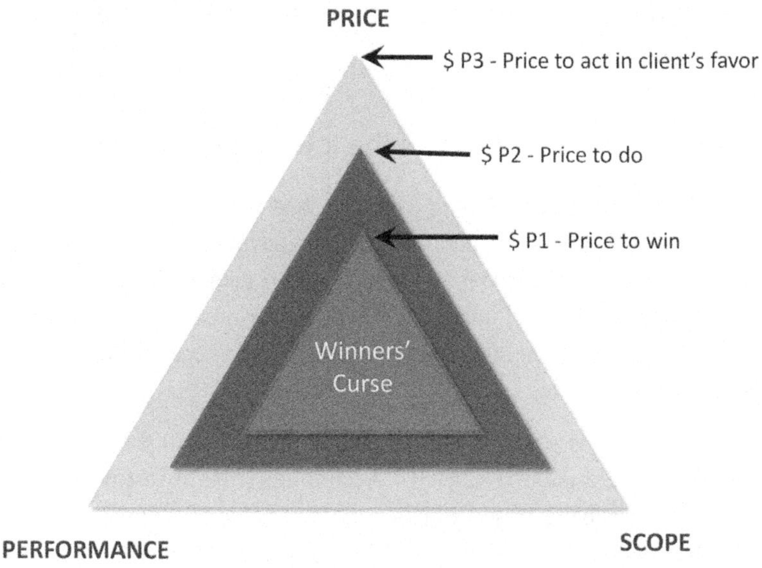

PRICE

$ P3 - Price to act in client's favor

$ P2 - Price to do

$ P1 - Price to win

Winners' Curse

PERFORMANCE   SCOPE

What Figure 7-4, a modified version of the '**Iron Triangle**'[92], shows is that these pricing decisions do not yield the same outcomes in terms of actual work performed (scope) and the quality (performance). To obtain cost recovery under the Winner's Curse (or possibly make a profit), the provider must cut corners and be aggressive in how it interprets scope and performance as specified in the

---

[92] The 'Iron Triangle' depicting the constraints of cost, time, and quality in project management was first described by Dr Martin Barnes in an UK engineering project in 1969. We've adapted his concept in that 'price' (what the client pays) differs from 'cost' (what the provider incurs), the provider's 'performance' replaces 'quality and time', and 'scope' represents the actual amount of work performed.

contract (resulting in the smallest triangle in Figure 7-4) or attempt extract more money from the client to afford to do more work at better quality.

The effect on the client of the winner's curse is that variations become the norm, disagreements become frequent, and constant vigilance in monitoring the provider is required. This results in an adversarial relationship and it raises the total cost of contract far beyond what is necessary to obtain the scope and performance.

A 2002 study of 85 contracts found, amongst other things, two disturbing facts. Firstly, the winner's curse existed in nearly 20% of the cases studied, so it was much more common than one might assume. Secondly, in over 75% of those cases the Winner's Curse was also inflicted on the client.[93] In other words, both parties are cursed, as the next case illustrates.

Case: A global manufacturer gets a good deal that goes bad

A well-known equipment manufacturer based out of Germany had a successful outsourcing business in Europe and wanted to enter the Asia-Pacific market. It cut a deal with a local industrial manufacturer that wanted to outsource its IT function. The provider created a new wholly owned subsidiary for the region, and the client's deal was the first, of what was planned to be, many deals.

In order to get that first critical deal, the provider's sales team bid a price that was under cost. It did not know that at the time however, since it was the first client and the sales team had no idea as to what the cost would actually be. It basically bid a price it deemed crucial to win; without having a firm grasp of what price was needed to have a reasonable profit. The client knew the provider could not be making money from their deal, but took comfort in the strength of the well-known global brand.

After 18 months, the provider still did not win any further clients. A review of the subsidiary by its German parent showed that it was making an unacceptable loss, with little potential for a turnaround. It had to start making money off its only client. The provider assigned a new account manager, a lawyer. He was to reinterpret the contract and reclaim any money possible.

---

[93] Kern, T., Willcocks, L. and Van Heck, E. (2002) "The Winner's Curse in IT Outsourcing: Strategies for Avoiding Relational Trauma". *California Management Review*, 44, 2, 47-69.

Nine months of intensive dispute ensued. Invoices were raised for work deemed out of scope, a number of additional charges and reimbursements were claimed dating back to contract inception. Work that the client had been obtaining was stopped if the account manager interpreted the work to be out-of-scope. The parties reached a settlement through an intermediary. The subsidiary was wound-up and the client had to find a new provider.

Once the formal bids, clarifications, and interactive sources have been scored and the price range established, you are in a position to determine the preferred provider. Before you start plotting the results, you may want to consider having thresholds. There are two thresholds to consider:

1. **cost threshold** - the maximum you will pay, acting as the cost 'ceiling' typically capped at a budget or a level equal to current costs, and

2. **quality threshold** - the worst quality you will accept, acting as the quality 'floor' represented by the minimum acceptable score.

The acceptable bids are arranged within those thresholds. The best value-for-money bid offers the *lowest price* with the *highest qualitative score*. Figure 7-5 shows the process at work.

Figure 7-5: Value for Money Diagram

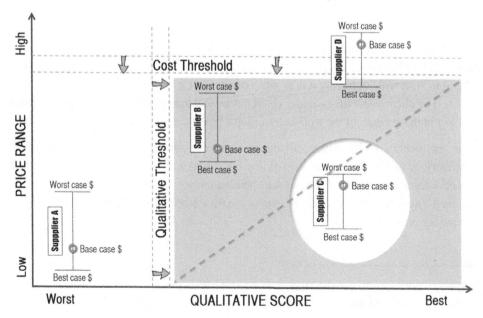

Action 30. Conduct due diligence

The bid evaluation only gets you to the point where you believe you have the best solution with the best value for money provider. At that stage of the process, it is important to remember that you still do not know whether the provider will be able perform as proposed in the bid for the agreed price, only that an offer has been put forward that you would like to accept.

Such uncertainty should be of key concern. Many believe that should performance not occur, it is merely a question of going to court to enforce the contract, and therefore choose not to invest in preventative measures. However, litigation can take years and the costs for court cases can be huge. Compounding the problem, the operational costs of unwinding deals gone badly can be one of the most expensive and disruptive exercises a client can experience.

It is in your best interest, with regard to risk management, to undertake comprehensive due diligence. The due diligence process involves investigating the provider's claim that:

- it is a sustainable entity,

- it what they have represented themselves to be in the bid is correct, and

- it can perform the services at the price and quality offered in the bids.

Because of the expense, due diligence is most commonly conducted after you have a preferred provider. This can be after a competitive tender process, or after a direct negotiation process. Certainly, when there has not been a competitive bidding process, due diligence becomes imperative.

Case: A medical company checks and stops

A medical services conglomerate, anxious to outsource its data centers, received an unsolicited bid from a leading provider. The provider's representative claimed that his firm could maintain KPIs and achieve 20% savings on a five-year contract, while a ten-year contract could achieve 30% cost savings. This claim was based on production and labor economies of scale, together with superior management practices inherent in a world-class provider. This was possible, according to the provider's representative, because they were higher up the learning and experience curve than the client, because they had superior management expertise than the client, and through the application of best practice that has been accumulated over many contracts.

A mere three hour investigation by the conglomerate of the claims against its actual performance revealed that it was large enough to achieve similar economies of scale itself, and that its management was actually very experienced. Moreover, when some of the superior management practices were described, it was clear that all of them could be replicated inhouse. Lastly, the conglomerate did not have many of the problems that the provider had assumed when it estimated the savings including high labor cost and expertise retention problems.

There are four different, but complementary, forms of due diligence:

- **Company/financial** - assesses the overall stability and long-term viability of the *contracting entity*.[94]

- **Contractual** - ensures that certain contractual obligations are evidenced to ensure no breaches exist at the time of signing.

- **Price** - assesses the viability of the price, underlying cost drivers, and the assumptions made.

- **Proposed Solution** - ensures that the proposed solution/s will work in your organization.

---

[94] Note that the term 'contracting entity' is used, for a specific purpose. Providers can operate under a number of separate entities, particularly global providers. The actual entity that will enter the contract (the *contracting entity*) may be a subsidiary, joint venture, or even a consortium (a number of entities). From a risk perspective, it is necessary to separate the contracting entity from the brand and parent/holding company that they are operating under. Many times the contracting entity does not carry the same insurances, has little financial strength, and has only a few employees and assets.

The first due diligence investigation is over the contracting entity as a whole. If the contracting entity is a joint venture, or a subsidiary of a larger company, then due diligence is also performed over the parent entity or entities. The next three investigations are over the proposed offer itself, having established that the contracting entity will be around and stable for at least the duration of the contract. These investigations assess whether the deal has any substantial risks that must be addressed prior to contract award.

In the next case, due diligence changed the client's entire sourcing strategy.

Case: Due diligence leads to radical solution change

A mining company had selected a provider based on their superior technical solution. Because the technology would be quite a strategic leap for the company, it decided to perform a solution due diligence as a prerequisite to signing the contract. It quickly discovered that the provider had not installed the technology in any geographic region in which the provider conducted its business and had no local experience in either implementation or management of the technology. In fact, the experience was all in one US city, and that team was fully booked for two years.

The client contacted the US and the team agreed to meet with them to discuss implementation and management. After a few meetings, the client was even further convinced of the benefits of the technology, but was completely unconvinced of the local arm's ability to deliver it. The contract was changed from an outsourcing contract to a straight technology/software and training purchase and the client created a team within its own staff to learn, implement and manage it rather than pay to have the provider's local staff trained up.

Due diligence has discovered major issues that required resolution to enable the client to award the contract. Just a few examples include discovering that:

- The provider entity, a joint venture (JV), did not actually exist. No work had been done to set up the JV and there was no agreement on how the JV would be operated or funded. The bidders intended to *"work all that out"* if they won.

- The winner had misinterpreted the client's information and as a result, it had grossly underestimated costs and did not have a viable price.

- The winner made a bidding error, leaving out a zero in the price.

- The winner had sold its factories during the tender process, and planned to subcontract offshore providers. The new business model, that of being a reseller of products manufactured in developing countries, was not mentioned in the bid and invalidated key parts of it.

You should rarely take the solutions of the bidder at face value, as presented in their bid. Unfortunately, many clients often overlook due diligence investigations into potential providers. The result is that significant issues are only discovered after the provider has begun the contract.

Building Block 6: Negotiate - Seal the Deal

"After the game, the king and pawn go into the same box"

Italian Proverb

ARCHITECT PHASE	ENGAGE PHASE	OPERATE PHASE	REGENERATE PHASE

BUILDING BLOCK 6
NEGOTIATE

So much emphasis has been on negotiation in outsourcing contracts that an inexperienced person could believe that it is the pinnacle of the lifecycle. If it does becomes the pinnacle, then something has gone wrong, or been badly designed, in the earlier processes. We warn you that if negotiations take more than a week (on even the biggest deals) then you are not in a good position. It is never a good idea to negotiate intent or critical matters under decreasing power conditions.

In following our building block approach, negotiation becomes one of refining the exact wording of the contractual documents. It is not a give and take of the intent of the arrangement. The contractual documents have already been developed in BB4 and the provider's exact preferred alternatives declared in BB5, the discovery/due diligence process for both parties has been conducted and concluded in BB5, and preparation for mobilization and contract management has occurred in BB3, and so on.

Nonetheless, some negotiations may need to take place and you need to be prepared for them.

There are many opinions as to the goal of negotiations and how to approach them, based on experience, culture, industry norms, as well as ideology, and in some cases, ego. The prime objective of successful negotiators is to reach sustainable solutions that work in the interests of both parties. It is not to win short-term arguments that may create more problems down the track. Reaching a mutually beneficial outcome (or one that does not harm either other party), marks the beginning of a relationship focused on problem solving, not one likely to be plagued with ongoing power fights.

We have found that successful negotiations occur when:

- the issues are known and analyzed in advance (Action 31),

- the negotiation teams from each party have clear roles and a mix of negotiation styles (Action 32), and

- there is a formal negotiation strategy and memorandum (Action 33).

Action 31. Analyze the issues

Make a prioritized list of all the issues you will want to address (including items made in the bid, but have not been included in the contract as yet)[95] and obtain a similar list from the other party. A simple category of high, medium, and low priority will suffice. You will want to focus on high priority issues and ensure successful results for these first.

This is different from a popular approach where the parties negotiate in order of the clause numbers, and each party raises the issues they have with regard to each clause in that order. While appearing outwardly systemic, the popular approach has the effect of mentally wearing out the negotiators before any serious issues arise and waste time and effort discussing immaterial items. You could negotiate

---

[95] Bidders make many representations in a bid. Often these can be promises to share global 'best practice', implement some form of knowledge sharing, communicate on the latest trends, and a plethora of other undertakings made under the "*as part of our services to you we will...*" banner. Failure to deliver promises appears regularly in our surveys as one of the most common failure factors.

20 items before the order of clauses hits anything of significance. Each issue is not of equal importance, does not require that everyone be present, does not require equal time, and you must get the high priority items solved first.

Then comes the analysis part, made up of five components:

- **Positions**. This involves stating what your preferred position is on each issue and what you believe the other party's preferred position will be. If you do not know what their position is, then you will need to generate possible positions.

- **Underlying drivers**. This is the most important step - to understand the drivers leading a party to that position, to answer the 'why?' question. If we do not know why, we cannot generate real solutions. There can be the same underlying driver for many issues, and if so, group the issues under that driver, because one solution may be able to solve all (or at least many) of these related issues. If you do not know why they have a position, then you will need to generate possible drivers.

- **BATNAs**. A BATNA (Best Alternative to a Negotiated Agreement), is otherwise known as 'plan B'. Parties tend to negotiate in accordance with their BATNAs, not their positions and so it is important to understand where each party might head if they do not get their way. If you do not know their BATNAs, then you will need to generate possible BATNAs.

- **Generate alternative solutions**. These must be based on the underlying drivers and not the positions. Fighting about positions rarely results in sustainable solutions.

- **Win/win scenarios**. Any combination of the alternative may yield an equally satisfactory result without harming the other - a win/win scenario.

This analysis is more involved than you might think. So it is best explained by walking through a single issue. Imagine that you have conducted a competitive tender and selected a preferred provider. The provider stated in their bid that they will meet the KPIs, but are proposing a bonus for beating them (which they call a "*partnering arrangement*"). You had, in the draft contract, financial recourse for failure to meet KPIs (which you called a "*performance rebate*").

Positions. Your position is to obtain financial recourse. The provider's position is the opposite, a bonus. Two opposing positions, this will not be easy.

Underlying drivers. You want a rebate because you are skeptical as to whether the provider will deliver. This is not due to experience with this particular provider, but because you have experienced others agreeing to KPIs, and yet constantly failing (with all of the attendant excuses). Your driver in this case is a lack of trust over providers in general.

Obviously, providers like bonuses to make more money, but we need to know why that is their position in this case. One common driver in such a scenario is that the provider's sales team, in their eagerness to get the sale (and their commission) bid a price that was below cost. However, the operations team has to make this deal profitable and they believe the bonuses can do that. In fact, operations cannot afford a rebate because then they will be making un-recoupable losses. So their driver is to make more money to turn a loss into a profit.

So, in this case, you have a trust issue and the provider has a profitability issue.

BATNAs. In our example, if you do not get the rebate, you may think that your BATNA is to go to the bidder, which you had rated second. The provider's BATNA may be to also walk away; withdraw because of the loss-making situation. If that is the case, there is a high probability of a lose/lose outcome, since both parties' alternative plan is to kill the deal. Both lose; you have to incur the additional time and cost of beginning again with a different provider, with no assurance that you will be in a better position; and the provider loses a customer.

In this case, both BATNAs are similar and extreme (walk away), and yet both seem reasonable when other ideas are lacking. Hence, the next step, to generate alternative solutions.

Alternative solutions.   We need to focus on solving each party's issues separately, then and creating a win/win outcome. To do this, we must reach a solution where both parties get their underlying drivers addressed without hurting the other party.

In the case of the client, there are many possible solutions to building trust that will not cost the provider money. Some of these include: speaking to the provider's current clients about whether the provider is meeting KPIs and what they do if the KPIs are not met (thus gaining and understanding of underlying processes); taking a tour of operations; speaking to the provider's staff (thus gaining credibility); and obtaining a performance guarantee from a parent entity.

Likewise, bonuses are not the only way to turn a loss-making contract into an acceptable profit. Scope could be adjusted where the provider's costs are higher than the yours, future work could be made available conditional upon achieving a period of good KPI performance (allowing a fixed cost base to spread over a greater volume of work), or a performance-based extension could be included (giving the provider a longer period in which to amortize costs).

Win/win scenario. Any combination of the alternatives may yield an equally satisfactory result. For example, you may be satisfied with having site visits, coupled with a performance guarantee to obtain a sense of confidence in the provider. This is a low cost solution from the provider's perspective and it does not put at risk funds it does not have. The provider may be satisfied with the assurance of future work based on good performance and a performance-based extension to gain a wider and longer revenue base in which to spread its fixed costs. You also save the time and effort of retendering.

This solution motivates the provider to do well without being punitive, while still giving you low cost access to recourse if things do not go well. When looking at this win/win scenario, both parties' original BATNAs of walking away seems extreme and ill-though out.

Action 32. Decide the right negotiation team, roles, and styles

Many books concerning negotiation focus on the individual negotiator, and on certain tactics that the authors believe to be the 'right way' to negotiate. We have not found the world of negotiation to be so clear-cut. But we have observed it is not a single individual, but the team (acting as a team), that makes a difference.

To get the right team dynamics, we found two critical factors, roles and styles, and their interrelation to be a determinant of efficient negotiations (when the parties are under relatively equal power positions). We will discuss roles first, and then introduce the concept of negotiation styles.

The key roles during a negotiation include:

- **The Chair** - the chair operates very similarly to a chairperson of a meeting. They keep things rolling smoothly and ensure negotiations keep to the agenda and timetable.

- **The Lead/s** - the one driving the negotiation of a particular issue. The lead negotiator does not have be the most senior person, or be the same person for every issue. It just needs to be the most appropriate person for the issue being negotiated. Each item being negotiated can have a different lead depending on the subject matter and negotiation style required.

- **The Trump** - the individual of last resort to whom issues are escalated if the negotiation teams cannot reach agreement. Ideally, the trumps from each party have already met and formed some sort of interpersonal relationship and have a long-term perspective on the deal.

- **Standby personnel** - people 'on-call' in the event something needs to be confirmed, better explained, or additional information provided. These people do not have to be at the negotiation, because you want to avoid a large cast where possible. They can merely ensure their phone is free for the period of negotiation.

- **Absent Approver** - in many negotiations, the people present are not the ones who must approve the results. It is very frustrating to be told after completing a negotiation, *"thanks, now we need to get it approved by New York"* when you had believed that the people there had decision-making power. To avoid appearing manipulative, approvers that are not present should be named and notified to the other party.

- **Minute-taker** - this individual should not be a participant in the negotiation, but is focused on capturing the exact dialog without interpreting any of it. Someone with a basic understanding of negotiation processes and contracts, with the ability to take copious notes quickly is ideal. Many use a (hired) paralegal for this activity.

The model that we have found the most useful when looking at individual negotiation styles, and their interaction within, and between, the parties is one developed back in 1977. Known as the TKI (Thomas Kilmann Instrument), this (and its plethora of variants that appear from time to time from various sources), contains five conflict resolution preferences as shown in Figure 7-6.[96] Let's discuss each, moving clockwise around Figure 7-6.

1. Collaborate. People with this style believe that conflict itself is neither good nor bad, but a sign of some underlying problem that needs to be fixed. They expect the parties to display creative problem-solving skills and capabilities that go beyond merely stating surface issues. For them, the journey as just as important as the destination. During negotiations, collaborators highly value the process by which the parties gain a better understand of one another, gain empathy

---

[96] Kilmann, R. and Thomas, K. (1977) "Developing a forced-choice measure of conflict-handling behavior: The 'mode' instrument", *Educational and Psychological Measurement*, 37(2) 309–325.

with each other's situations, and generate possible solutions. This style can, however, take a great deal of time.

Figure 7-6: Negotiation Styles

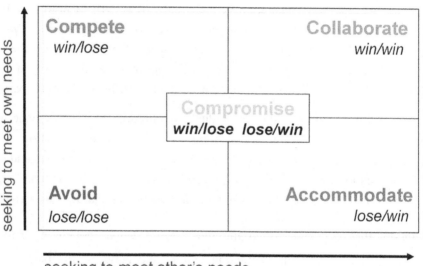

2. **Accommodate.** People with the accommodating style think that self-sacrifice, and placing the importance of continued relationship above one's own goals, is crucial for solving conflict. It is better to ignore or placate differences than to risk open combat and being judged as unreasonable, suspicious, or overly sensitive. Accommodating might take the form of generosity, obeying another person's orders when the preference would not be do so, or acquiescing to another's point of view. It can lend itself to the other party taking advantage of the accommodator's trusting, and in many cases, naive nature.

3. **Avoid.** For people with this style, conflict is seen as unpleasant and to be steered clear of. Avoiding might take the form of diplomatically sidestepping an issue, postponing the discussion with the hope it will go away, or simply withdrawing from discussion altogether. An avoider is more likely to hire external

help to lead negotiations, pass commercial concerns to legal for resolution, or get others in their organization to make and/or sign off on decisions.

4. Compete. People with this style places prime importance on getting one's way without concern for the relationship. He or she prefers to win, wants to establish dominance (which they may equate to status), and seeks a 'master-slave' orientation to commercial relationships where they are the one in charge and the other party would be wise to respect that. This is a power-oriented mode in where the means justifies the end, doing whatever it takes to win. Negotiation is viewed as a game to be played, not a forum for solutions to be developed.

5. Compromise. People with this style believe each party needs to 'win a little, lose a little' to reach acceptable outcomes. They try to find a resolution that partially satisfies both parties, often splitting the difference between two positions, exchanging concessions, or seeking a quick middle-ground solution. People with this style are known to keep an inner 'tally sheet' to keep track of what they perceive to have given and gotten. They can be suspicious when their tally is too far towards themselves (*"the provider is giving too much away, something is wrong"*), or overly focus on equaling the score if the tally is too skewed toward the other party.

The fact that a person prefers a given style does not mean he or she will not use other styles. Nevertheless, each person has a dominant style that reflects particular beliefs about conflict, preferences, and comfort zones.

While we would love to say that there is a right style for each role, we have not seen that to be the case. Avoiders have made great Chairs because they do not buy into any games being played, do not take things personally, and want to keep it as short as possible (thus keeping everyone to the timetable). Accommodators have made great Trumps because they saw the issue escalated to them as minutia in the big picture, and had no trouble at all agreeing with the other party. Collaborators as Leads have gotten great results in some areas, but took so much time many issues were not addressed.

We do know that certain roles require the person to be style independent or at least style compatible (e.g. the standby, approving, and minute taking roles), or the negotiations can get derailed. For example, we have observed cases where the approver was a Collaborator but the negotiation team consisted of Competers. She looked at the resultant agreement as so unduly harsh on the other party as to be unconscionable (her team thought it was "*the best ever*"). In another case, the Minute-taker was a Competer but the parties themselves were collaborating. The notes were deemed misrepresentative of the negotiations (did not reflect the spirit of the agreements made). And yet another case where the Standby was an Avoider and refused to provide an opinion on a technical matter, only that, "*I'm sure it'll be fine, whatever you guys agree.*"

However, once you know the issues (from Action 31) and the individuals (and their styles) who will be fulfilling the team roles, you can see if the combination makes sense. In many of our collaborative negotiations, both parties share this information with one another to determine if the inter-party combination also makes sense. When it does not, team changes, coaching, training, facilitation, etc. can be carried out prior to the negotiations to ensure things do not get a little crazy, which is what happened in the following case.

Case: A clash of styles

After months of discussions, an international accounting firm and global equipment company had agreed to a deal in principle. All that remained was to negotiate the details. The contract and SLA were moving along fine; however, the price negotiation was hitting major obstacles.

The provider's price negotiation team was led by the salesperson; the accounting firm's by the finance director. The salesperson wanted the deal done as quickly as possible and the finance director was not going to sign anything until the numbers were right and detailed. The salesperson tried every tactic he knew of to try to get the contract signed except deliver the prices in the breakout manner requested (avoiding traits). The finance director was growing increasingly frustrated to the point he refused further meetings until the price breakout would be presented (competing). When that meeting was convened, it was preceded by an hour-long presentation of the history of the relationship. The entire negotiation team of the firm by this time was visibly agitated. The firm required the removal of the salesperson from the negotiation table in order to proceed.

A more commercially astute and relationship-orientated state manager was substituted (collaborator). The deal was signed shortly thereafter, with not only the desired numbers in place, but exceeding the expectations of the client in many other areas. But negotiations took months rather than weeks, as originally expected.

Action 33. Prepare and execute the negotiation strategy

Reaching sustainable solutions is the true goal of successful negotiations, not to merely get the other party to agree to something that is not in their interests, which is a shortsighted tactical approach. To do this, some planning is in order. Winging it is a form of gambling with your organization's money. Wing it by all means - if the result, the contract, and the relationship are all immaterial. In every other case, however, you will need to put some structure around it. Figure 7-7 gives an example of this type of structure - a negotiation strategy that summarizes the work in the previous actions.

The negotiation strategy is not, however, what is sent to the other party. A very condensed version, called a **Negotiation Memorandum**, is provided which only includes the list of issues, timetable, each party's negotiation team (per issue) and the processes to be followed.

Figure 7-7: Negotiation Strategy Outline

---

1   Context

1.1 Background/recital

1.2 Scope

2   Overall Plan

2.1 Timetable

2.2 Negotiation team
- 2.2.1   Chair
- 2.2.2   Lead/s
- 2.2.3   Trump
- 2.2.4   Standby/s
- 2.2.5   Approver/s
- 2.2.6   Minute-taker

2.3 Processes to be followed
- 2.3.1   Logistics
- 2.3.2   Minutes
- 2.3.3   Redrafting and acceptance

2.4 Summary of Items to be negotiated

3   Items to be Negotiated

3.1 Item #1
- 3.1.1   Position of each party
- 3.1.2   Each party's BATNA (**best alternative to a negotiated agreement**) and WATNA (**worst alternative to a negotiated agreement**)
- 3.1.3   Underlying driver/s of each position
- 3.1.4   Alternative solutions based on the drivers
- 3.1.5   Win/win scenarios from the alternative solutions
- 3.1.6   Negotiation style required
- 3.1.7   Personnel required by each party (at the table, for consultation, for approval)

3.2 Item #2
- 3.2.1   Position of each party
- 3.2.2   Each party's BATNA and WATNA
- 3.2.3   Underlying driver/s of each position
- 3.2.4   Alternative solutions based on the drivers
- 3.2.5   Win/win scenarios from the alternative solutions
- 3.2.6   Negotiation style required
- 3.2.7   Personnel required by each party

Chapter 8   Manage for Results - the Operate Phase

The Operate Phase, where the deal is put in place, operationalized, and managed through its term, is comprised of these two building blocks:

- BB7 - Transition, and

- BB8 - Manage.

At this point, you generally face a monopolistic provider for the scope and duration of the contract (unless operating under a panel configuration designed specifically for continuous competition). From this point forward, if the deal is not working, you will rarely have any other option (pragmatic, economic, or political) other than to continue with the provider. Outsourcing deals can be prohibitively expensive to renegotiate, terminate and either backsource (bring back inhouse), or transfer to another provider.

It is in this phase that the benefits of the previous work done pay off (or not the problems accrue from not doing the work). The Operate Phase either proceeds smoothly as a result of the strategies, processes, documents, and relationship designed in the earlier building blocks, or the phase suffers, due to misinterpretations, ambiguities, disagreements, and disputes. At this stage, such problems can only be corrected through huge and tedious remedial efforts.

Building Block 7: Transition - Start Well

"It may be hard for an egg to turn into a bird: it would be a jolly sight harder for it to learn to fly while remaining an egg."

C.S. Lewis

ARCHITECT PHASE		ENGAGE PHASE	OPERATE PHASE	REGENERATE PHASE

BUILDING BLOCK 7
TRANSITION

A good jump out of the starting gate, hit the ground running, take the ball and run with it ... so many clichés for this phase of the lifecycle! But all true. The goal of this building block is get normal operations up and running as fast as possible.

These days we do not see as many tumultuous, and public, transitions as in the early days of outsourcing. Moving bits of an organization to a provider was novel and controversial twenty years ago. Now that outsourcing is such common practice, you may not read as much about it anymore. It is less newsworthy. But the challenges remain as they always have.

The biggest challenge continues to be the client organization underestimating the work involved, in particular the work the client has to do to in set-up, integration, transfers, and acceptance. The transition, or mobilization, is a project complete with its own contract schedule and clauses, its own payment structure, its own KPIs, and its own bi-party team (tri-party if the transition is to a new provider from an incumbent).

In theory, transition begins at contract commencement and ends on a specified date. In reality, it begins much earlier and ends much later. Indeed, if not properly managed, it may never end. However, you plan for this building block to end when the parties sign a transition acceptance certificate (which states that all transition-related work has been successfully executed). The actions involve:

- finalize the plans from BB3 (Action 34) - updating based on the results of the tendering and negotiation processes;

- get the transition teams in place (Action 35);

- manage staff that are staying, leaving, and transferring to the provider (Action 36);

- manage transfers to the provider of assets, third-party contracts, work-in-progress, and knowledge as appropriate (Action 37);

- re-engineer and integrate (Action 38) systems, process and procedures; and

- accept and close out the mobilization project (Action 39).

Action 34. Finalize and mobilize plans

All of the planning should have already taken place, so the transition is when the plans are updated and executed, allowing for the inevitable contingencies and adjustments needed when, as one CIO put it, "*the rubber hits the road.*"

This action should require only a refresh for any plans that may need some redesign, based on the results of the bid (in BB5) and negotiation (in BB6). Some of these could include the:

- **Transition-in strategy**. Your organization's initial strategy was designed in the early days of the outsourcing lifecycle in BB3 (Action 13), and you prepared the proposed mobilization schedule in BB4 (Action 22). Then in BB5, the provider bid its response. Now that you are in B7, make sure the current circumstances are reflected in this document.

- **Contract management and retained organization strategies.** Your organization's future needs were developed in BB2 (Action 9) as part of the profiles and both of these structures were designed in detail in BB3 (Action 14 and Action 15). An update would be prudent.

- **Communication strategy.** This was developed in BB3 (Action 16), which covers all the lifecycle phases. The transition-in component can be developed in more detail now.

Because of all the earlier work, transition is fundamentally the mobilization of human resources (training conducted, responsibilities reallocated, etc.), to get the teams and individuals prepared. Without the resources, a plan is irrelevant, as the following case highlights.

Case: A plan without resources

In this case, the provider was awarded a property management outsourcing contract in October and had specified a three-week transition period in its winning bid. However, the client made all but three staff redundant in June (to meet the budget requirements before the financial year-end of June 30). As there were no retained staff to speak of, there was no service delivery work performed since the staff were removed in June. When the provider came on board in October, there was a huge backlog and angry customers. Furthermore, as there was no retained organization, there was no one available to assist the transition. The actual transition took six months and the provider was never able to cleanse the inaccurate and incomplete client data inherited from the rushed process. Furthermore, since the client's entire process to outsource was rushed, it consequently had not extracted any of the strategic benefits from the deal, only the initial headcount reduction.

Action 35. Determine the transition team/s

The transition project may need many teams depending on the complexity of the change being introduced: changes in personnel, transfers of things to the provider (e.g. assets, work-in-progress, etc.), and the degree of integration and re-engineering required. The types of roles to consider for the transition projects are shown in Figure 8-1 and are described next.

Figure 8-1: Example Transition Team Structure

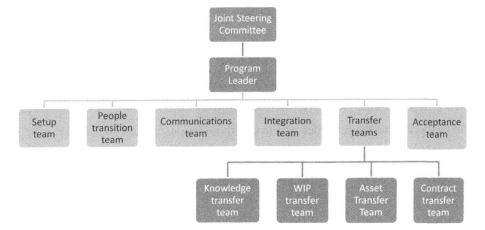

- **Steering committee or Joint reference panel** - guides the transition, provides strategic input and decision-making, and resolves issues.

- **Program leader** - manages all the transition activities to ensure consistency and reports to the steering committee.

- **Set-up team** - rapid-execution team that obtains space, issues access, conducts inductions, etc., so the provider can start working.

- **Communications team** - provides communication and change management, develops communications messages and media, and manages the feedback loop.

- **People transition team** - manages staff that are transferring, staying, and leaving (see Action 36) providing advice, support services, and assists setting up the contract management and retained organization.

- **Transfer teams** - carries out the transfers of assets and obligations from your organization to the provider (see Action 37).

- **Integration team** - conducts the systems/process re-engineering and integration between the two parties (see Action 38).

- **Acceptance team** - representatives from business, administration, and technical areas who conduct testing and work with the provider until the particular activity meets the standard that allows it to be accepted as complete (Action 39).

Whilst the function of all of these teams are important, we have found that the work of the communications team to be especially so. The amount of effort that will be required of this team should not be underestimated, as stakeholders may need to hear key messages several times and through different media. Setting the expectations of the customers or users of the service is particularly important if there will be changes to the KPIs or a new way of operating. It is important for you to work with the provider on the communications rollout so they have the full opportunity to 'sell' themselves, and the arrangement, and identify any expectation gaps. The following case gives an idea of how things can get out of hand.

Case: An insurance company leaves expectations wide open

After intensive negotiations concluding with an exhaustive marathon session over the weekend prior to the handover date, the final agreement was eventually signed. To reach the cost savings requirements of the customer, significant reductions in certain KPIs were negotiated to remove the cost of maintaining a mirrored environment and having experts on site. Each party believed that the other party would communicate the changes in operations to the client's stakeholders, thus neither gave it any thought. The provider thought that the customer would distribute the SLA and manage its own organization appropriately. The customer thought that the provider would put out some form of announcement. Each party had thought that reaching the agreement was the "*hard part*" and were just relieved that an agreement had been reached.

After a few months of operations, the buildup of dissatisfaction was becoming alarming. Both parties were spending an inordinate amount of time dealing with complaints and had thought that the users were just "*anti-outsourcing.*" After conducting a root cause analysis of the underlying nature of complaints, it was found that the users had issues with outsourcing; it was simply never communicated to them what they should expect.

Typically, the teams will be bi-party, that is, are comprised of staff from both parties. Thus, the transition is generally a co-sourced project, irrespective of what configuration has been design for the contract (refer Configuration Attribute #7: Commercial Relationship in Chapter 4).

As there are at least two parties that need to operate in conjunction with one another, a detailed responsibility matrix for transition is necessary to provide a clear description of the obligations of both parties in relation to the transition.

This becomes even more critical when the transition is a handover between two providers (the outgoing and the incoming), as case below highlights.

Case: Lawsuits threatened all around

A marine port picked the lowest bid, but the winning provider grossly under-scoped due to inexperience in the area and having misunderstood the requirements. When the systems began falling over in transition, the utility threatened to sue the new provider. The new provider then threatened to sue the former provider (it blame the state of affairs on the negligence of the old provider in the way it departed).

The former provider was able to prove that it left operations intact (by having photos, backup data, etc.). Rather than lose the contract (and face the possible lawsuit by the client), the new provider agreed to have the former provider reinstate the old environment and then subcontract the former (under very expensive rates) to run operations for no less than six months while it met certain transition milestones the client and the new provider agreed. Four years later, however, when this contract was retendered, the former provider won it back.

Action 36. Manage staff

The 'human side' of an outsourcing deal may be difficult to visualize at first, but it may not be long before it can become the biggest problem that you may face; especially if the fears and apprehensions of staff are not managed well. In some outsourcing deals, employees have not only refused to work, but have deliberately sabotaged the process itself. Not surprisingly then, some clients, as well as providers, have invested a lot of time and effort developing appropriate staff transition policies and practices.

The main issue we have observed here is that staff are anxious as to how the outsourcing arrangement will personally affect them. They are less interested in the benefits to your organization. To assist in recognizing the range of emotions that you may come across in your staff, below are examples of behaviors that are often displayed are given below, in a discussion of three fictional (but typical) individuals, Margaret, Albert, and Peter.

Firstly, there is **Margaret**. Margaret has worked for you for over 25 years and is vehemently opposed to outsourcing. Margaret will argue very publicly against it. A person like Margaret may never see the benefit of outsourcing. It is an inefficient use of your time to reason with, or use logic to sell the idea to, her. In the long term, Margaret will probably end up taking redeployment, early retirement, or a redundancy package rather than abide with the change. The challenge is not to let a Margaret-type attitude seep into other staff. One way is to take staff aside as a group, explain the strategy, and answer any questions they have. Give them the information needed to make an educated decision about the merit of outsourcing for them personally.

Secondly, there is **Albert**. He was a bit stunned about the announcement, and is in two minds as to whether this will personally be good or bad for him. People similar to Albert need to be as carefully managed as the 'Margarets' can sway such fence sitters. Albert's biggest concern is what he will have to do differently day-in and day-out. You may need to explain in the detail exactly how this change will affect him, preferable on a one-to-one basis, and effectively sell the personal benefits to him.

Lastly, there is **Peter**. He has previously wondered if he would have better career prospects with a provider. He is certain he would gain better training and a wider breadth of experience. He is anxious to get ready. Peter sees outsourcing as an opportunity, not a threat. The difficulty with Peter is keeping him focused on the current needs of the job, when he is keen to prepare his credentials and investigate opportunities with the potential provider. However, Peter can assist the outsourcing initiative substantially in a role as a positive opinion leader with the fence sitters like Albert, and giving them a counterpoint to Margaret's more negative perceptions.

While this may have sounded overly simplistic, the discussion is something we have found most clients readily identify with. It also highlights the three categories of staff transitions that may occur within the area to be outsourced:

- **Transferred staff** - become employees of the provider under either the 'negotiated transfer' approach (the recruitment process and the terms and conditions of employment are agreed between the parties), or the 'clean break' approach' (you are aware of, and fully support, that the provider will be making offers, but will have no direct involvement yourself).

- **Retained staff** - kept within the client, typically in a changed capacity. Some retained staff may develop what has become known as the 'survivor syndrome. These staff may experience a number of dysfunctional feelings about surviving the 'chopping block': they may feel guilty, may feel defensive, and may even feel aggressive towards management.

- **Redundant staff** - no longer required. Making staff redundant is one of the most difficult and unpleasant tasks a manager can do, and generally speaking, organizations have not shown themselves to be very good at it.

The future staff arrangements are not easy decisions, and can be surprising complex to execute. One thing we have observed far too often, however, is that particular areas of a client often act in conflict, albeit unknowingly, as the next case demonstrates.

Case: Teams acting in isolation kills a year

A telco's project team decided to use the clean break approach regarding staff employment when it outsourced. Past experience led management to believe that it was in the provider's best interest to let them have full control over the hiring decision, and in the employees' best interests to provide a severance package.

The provider had stated in their bid that they would require approximately 70% of the workforce to transfer and had detailed a solid recruitment process, thus the transition team was fully confident that the provider would obtain the necessary staff. Unbeknownst to the team, however, it was the company's policy under the clean break approach to preclude any employee that took a severance package from working for the provider (or the client) for two years.

Of the 300 people let go, only five took the offer from the provider (new employees for which the severance package offered little financial gain). The rest preferred to get the package and seek alternative employment. The provider was dependent on getting at least 200 of the staff to transfer to be able to perform the contract.

As this did not occur, a major recruiting drive was required. This delayed the handover by three months until a skeleton crew was assembled. During this time, neither party had any staff in which to conduct service delivery, thus the function was effectively abandoned. Furthermore, since the organizational knowledge also walked out the door (in the heads of the departing staff), normal operations were not in effect for another six months. In recognition of the difficult situation, the telco did not enforce the KPI during the first year of operations.

Irrespective of whether an individual will be staying, going elsewhere, or transferring to the provider, all personnel involved will be affected by outsourcing. Many managers fail to realize that outsourcing can be a tumultuous change on employees and that it will always have an emotional impact. To help staff come to terms with the impact (on their careers, financial positions, or even on their self-esteem), there are various techniques and services that organizations have used successfully. These include career counseling, outplacement, financial planning, and personal counseling described in Table 8-1.

Table 8-1: Staff Transfer Assistance Options

	Description
Career counseling	Many employees may require assistance in assessing their skills, goals, and career options. Providing career counseling helps them eliminate uncertainty regarding their capabilities in the market. The types of services offered may include skill assessments, goal formation and action plans, and job/skill matching.
Outplace-ment	Outplacement services assist staff in finding new employment; first by preparing individuals for the job seeking process (by assisting them prepare resumes, conducting mock interviews, and so on), and second, by finding them employment opportunities. The services offered may include preparing resumes, interview preparation, and placement services.

	Description
Financial planning	Financial planning specialists can be hired by your organization to assist staff in assessing and making provisions for their economic situation. The services that may be offered include superannuation/ pension planning, future salary needs and retirement planning, investment strategies, and redundancy payment options.
Personal counseling	To staff, outsourcing is an emotional issue. Personal counseling services can assist employees come to terms with the change in circumstances and move them through the stages of acceptance. The services to consider offering includes helping staff manage their emotional reactions, providing coping skills and techniques, and assisting them to manage the impact on their family/spousal relationships.

It does take effort and focus to support staff during the transition, which is why many clients do not do it (particularly if cost cutting is the driver for outsourcing). But when you do this well, the marginal cash outlay can quickly quash the needless cost of managing a highly distracted and unproductive workforce.

Case: An insurance company gets it right

An entire department of an insurance company was going to be outsourced. Needless to say, staff were in turmoil and work had nearly ground to a halt. The general manager was aware of this, but since all the people involved seemed to have different and unique concerns, she was not sure how to address all those issues. Furthermore, the general manager cared quite a bit about these staff and was concerned for them. After all, they had been working together, in some cases, for decades.

After speaking to the HR department, the general manager arranged a number of services to be provided to the staff. No one had to use these services; all were voluntary and would be paid for by the company. Staff were given four hours with a financial planner, four sessions with a personal counselor, and unlimited use of a recruitment firm for three months after being made redundant. For staff that were likely to be transferred to the provider, they were given two hours résumé and interview preparation. The 'FUD' factor (fear, uncertainty, and doubt) had turned into action, morale improved, and the general manager could sleep at night.

Action 37. Manage transfers (assets, third-party contracts, work-in-progress, etc.)

It is not just the transfer of data, assets, and work that is of paramount importance here, but also the transfer of intellect, knowledge, and political networks. Some of your organizations' people will have built up extensive knowledge crucial for service delivery (not just operational knowledge, but organizational as well). This knowledge is rarely encapsulated in an easily transferable medium; more often than not, it is carried in people's heads.

The main transfer tasks are shown in Table 8-2. In many cases, these transfers require dedicated teams made up of individuals from both parties, because these areas of the business were not designed to be easily transported from one organization to another.

Table 8-2: Transfer Tasks

Transfer Item	Transfer Tasks
Assets	• Audit inventory and condition of assets. • Finalize and agree ownership and separation issues. • Reconcile asset pre-payments and accrued liabilities at handover date. • Obtain copies of all asset related documentation.
Third Party Contracts	• Obtain copies of all third party contracts, licenses, agreements, etc. • Set date of novation/assignment. • Notify the third parties regarding novation or assignment. • Obtain all outstanding novation/assignment acceptances where required. • For any third party contracts unable to be novated/assigned, prepare contingency arrangements (let them run out, terminate, etc.).
Work in Progress	• Transfer current projects to provider along with all documentation. • Place order for approved projects that have not yet begun.
Knowledge	• Update procedure manuals, diagrams and other knowledge repositories. • Have provider shadow current operations (following and observing staff). • Conduct information-exchange workshops and process walkthroughs.

Action 38. Re-engineer and integrate practices

By virtue of outsourcing's radical shift in governance locus, new mechanisms are required to foster mutual understanding and trust, and manage potential goal divergence and opportunism, as well as the redistribution of authority and decision-making. When implementing the new way of operating that outsourcing represents, it is inevitable that the type of work, and how that work is accomplished, needs to be changed. Depending on the extent of outsourcing, your organization may need to make profound changes in its strategic and operational mechanisms.

The changes resulting from embarking on outsourcing are often significant and fundamentally affect the way your organization undertakes its business. The old ways of doing things are no longer appropriate. New workflows, communications, paper-flows, and signoffs are required to interact with the provider. New relationships need to be quickly formed. People accustomed to a certain way of operating need to start working in a completely different manner (or not, as the next case exemplifies).

Case: Outsourcing results in duplicate systems

A stockbroker outsourced all its IT operations as part of an automation, paperless office, initiative. No impact analysis took place regarding the need to re-engineer any work practices; it was assumed that once the technology was in place staff would merely disregard the old way of doing things and move right into the new. What happened, however, was that staff just added the new processes to the old rather than create new, more efficient processes ending up with two systems - one paper based and one electronic. This was discovered 18 months into the contract when internal audit was performing a review. They discovered that neither system functioned effectively, and that the hybrid system created was exceedingly time consuming.

An organization's business processes are usually fragmented into subprocesses and tasks that are carried out by several functional areas. Often, no one individual, or even function, is responsible for the overall performance of the entire process. Optimizing the performance of subprocesses, and taking full advantage of a provider's capabilities, cannot yield dramatic improvements if the process itself is fundamentally inefficient and outmoded. The required business process re-engineering triggered by outsourcing also offers your organization an opportunity to redesign the way work is done to better support and achieve improvements in critical performance measures, such as cost, quality, and speed.

For example, Kodak's landmark outsourcing of its IT to three providers in 1989 (which, as discussed in BB1, provided the impetus to outsource IT by the companies and governments across the world) was largely successful in reducing cost and enabling a core business focus at that time. But it was not the act of outsourcing that drove the successes, it was Kodak's five re-engineering studies and years of resultant re-engineering which occurred prior to outsourcing.

Action 39. Accept and closeout

Unfortunately, clients are often so eager to move out of transition, that transition closeout is one of the most neglected areas in this building block. Not only does organizational learning not occur, in some cases there has been significant incomplete work, failure to collect large payments for asset sales, and unproductive relationship behaviors taking hold.

The purpose of transition closeout is to assess the transition project and derive any lessons learned and best practices to be applied to the rest of the contract term as well as future transition projects (as you will undoubtedly go through similar events in the future). Transition closeout typically begins with a formal set of acceptance criteria (and acceptance certificate) that signifies that the transition has been successfully completed. This is particularly important where there is a separate mobilization fee (or milestone payments) are payable to the provider.

The following case, concerning a university, shows the need for clear acceptance criteria.

Case: A transition dispute

The parties to this outsourcing deal could not agree as to whether the transition was completed as there was no acceptance criteria on which to form an objective assessment. The university was withholding payment, as it believed the transition was not yet complete. The provider believed it was.

The parties had to hire an independent expert who reviewed the bid, the transition processes and the understandings (e.g. emails) exhibited during the transition. It was clear that the (poorly) specified tasks did in fact occur, but not to the university's satisfaction. Because the transition payment was specified as due when the list of tasks were complete and there was no mention of any acceptance criteria or process, the advisor resolved that the university could withhold payment only for items not delivered, as opposed to those that had been delivered but for which the quality was disputed.

Transition closeout concludes with a post-implementation review that solicits and acts on feedback from the transition teams (before they are disbanded) and stakeholders in both parties. In this sense, a transition closeout is no different than a project closeout. And like all project management models, the ability of an organization to learn from each project is a crucial sign of an organization's maturity and professionalism.

Building Block 8: Manage - Get the Results

"Strategy is a commodity, execution is an art."

Peter F. Drucker

| ARCHITECT PHASE | ENGAGE PHASE | OPERATE PHASE | REGENERATE PHASE |

BUILDING BLOCK 8
MANAGE

This is the longest of the building blocks, often lasting many years. All of the previous seven building blocks prepare your organization for this one. This is where the benefits of everything done before, and problems caused by things not done, appear. Even if everything has been well, many challenges remain, as you will see here.

Two decades of studies demonstrate that outsourcing cannot be contracted for and then not managed by the client.[97] Outsourcing is not divestiture. Overall, the academic evidence finds that outsourcing can deliver value to clients, but that it takes a tremendous amount of detailed management to realize expected benefits.[98]

---

[97] Starting with Cullen, S. (1994) *Information Technology Outsourcing Myths Exploded: Recommendations for Decision Makers*, Melbourne Business School to Willcocks, L.P., Cullen, S. and Craig, A. (2010) *The Outsourcing Enterprise: From cost management to collaborative innovation* (Technology, Work and Globalization), Palgrave, London, and many in between.

[98] Lacity, M., Solomon, S., Yan, A. and Willcocks, L. (2011) "Business Process Outsourcing Studies: A Critical Review and Research Directions," *Journal of Information Technology*, Vol. 26, 4 221-258.; Lacity, M., Khan, S., Yan, A. and Willcocks, L. (2010) "A Review of the IT Outsourcing Empirical Literature and Future Research Directions," *Journal of Information Technology*, Vol. 25, 4 395-433.

Outsourcing itself is not a panacea to your organization's challenges, but represents a different way of managing products and services. Much depends on experiential learning and sheer hard work by clients and providers alike on a daily basis. Our own work on management practice suggests that executives must climb a significant learning curve (see Figure 0-1 in the Introduction) and build key inhouse capabilities in order to successfully exploit outsourcing opportunities. They need to accept that outsourcing is not about giving up management, but rather managing in a different way.

Managers have to learn to manage outputs rather than inputs, use negotiation and relationship management in place of direct control, and rely on periodic planning and reviews to take the place of day-to-day oversight of operations. Specifications replace job descriptions. Control via contracts replaces control via employment. Invoices are paid, rather than salaries. These changes in management work are significant.

One way to look at this is through W. Edwards Deming's PDCA (plan, do, check, act) model, also known as the 'circle of quality'.[99] In Deming's work with quality management, he put forward the landmark continuous feedback loop model for successful business processes. We have modified his model in Figure 8-2, to show which party is accountable for what part of the circle when a client outsources.

As shown in Figure 8-2, your organization is no longer the 'doer' after it has outsourced; that becomes the provider's role. Your job is to <u>plan</u> the arrangement (and future generations of it), <u>check</u> that both parties are performing their obligations, and <u>act</u> on changes need to improve results or correct deficiencies. The cycle continues after the contract is in place with you continuously planning, checking, and acting, while the provider does the doing.

---

[99] See Deming, W. Edwards (1982) *Quality Productivity and Competitive Position*, MIT, Cambridge.

Figure 8-2: Deming's PDCA Model

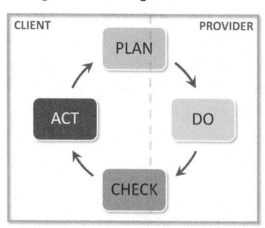

As a client increasingly move towards contracting, contract management is becomes one of the core activities. Furthermore, documents akin to contracts are also being increasingly used to manage internal service provision (e.g. the use SLAs or the award of inhouse bids), making the skills and strategies of contract management even more imperative. Our studies over the years have consistently shown that, on average, 6% of the annual value of an outsourcing contract is invested by the client in managing that contract.[100] Moreover, as outsourcing increases, that percent also rises.

Note that we refer to contract management as an investment, not a cost. It is an investment in getting the benefits that the deal was designed to achieve and minimize the risks over the years that it will be running. A contract only provides recourse in the event of breach - the document cannot manage itself. If there are not sufficient funds (i.e. resources) to manage it well, then it will be managed poorly, if for no other reason than scarcity of time, skills, and people. Therefore, if the plan was to manage the arrangement poorly, one has to wonder why people would bother to have a contract (or even outsource) in the first place.

---

[100] The range of investment is large in all our studies. But we observed averages around 6% for onshore outsourcing, and 12% for offshore, once we remove cases in crisis.

There are 12 key actions to manage a contract well, and these represent the action in this building block:

1. **Orchestrate the CM network** (Action 40) - of all the people that have dealings and contact with the provider so that they work within the contractual framework and not act in isolation from each other.

2. **Conduct compliance audits of both parties** (Action 41) - ensure adherence with the contractual documents.

3. **Continuously improve** (Action 42) - both parties and the interfaces.

4. **Control the finances** (Action 43) - accurate and timely billing and payment, total cost of contract, and financial trends.

5. **Ensure performance** (Action 44) - review and monitor inputs, process, output KPIs, and (potentially) outcomes.

6. **Forecast ongoing requirements** (Action 45) - demands for goods and/or services, provider capacity and capabilities, budgets, changes to the business, and the next generation.

7. **Invest in the relationship** (Action 46) - create strong interpersonal relationships at all levels, always balancing power versus partnering style behaviors.

8. **Keep informed** (Action 47) - of provider issues and situation, and of the market (technology, standards, prices, market conditions, and benchmarking).

9. **Manage issues and risks** (Action 48) - ongoing identification, prioritization, tracking, and resolution.

10. **Manage variations** (Action 49) - including written, verbal, and behavioral-based (estoppel) variations from both parties including requested, approved, and/or rejected variations.

11. **Manage disagreements and disputes** (Action 50) - prevent and treat occasions when the parties have differences.

12. **Record keep and report** (Action 51) - create and maintain documentation and audit trails, and reporting to stakeholders.

Action 40. Orchestrate the CM Network

Participation in the management of outsourcing arrangements is rarely the sole domain of one person. There is a network of individuals who are utilized as appropriate based on the particular nature of the arrangement and the skills present in the client. However, one of the concepts worth understanding at this stage is the concept of a CM network.

The CM network is the group of individuals who have dealings or contact with the provider after the contract is signed. This ranges significantly in each deal, but generally includes people from finance, business units, management, operations, and on occasion, legal representatives. It can include various head office functions (e.g. HR, IT, finance, etc.), end customers, internal audit, project teams, and many others depending on the nature and scope of the arrangement. The actual number of people involved can range from just a few to a few hundred.

Unfortunately, for many clients, not everyone in the network is familiar with contractual documents (or for that matter, has even read them). And most act according to their individual needs and wants, not in accordance with the agreement. For example, accounts payable may pay according to its own processes rather than in accordance with the contract (and thus put your organization in breach); business units may make demands and requests outside of the scope (and soar costs); and management may demand to be treated as VIPs (Very Important Person) who demand to be prioritized above other work (and crash the KPIs) ... the list goes on.

So rather than giving one person the title of a 'Contract Administrator' (for example), and assuming all will be well, it is important to have the CM network clearly defined, briefed on the deal, and trained up on the contract. The following case of a hospital shows what can happen when this did not take place.

Case: A hospital plans well, but drops the ball

The outsourcing contract was thoughtfully prepared with ongoing contract management requirements in mind. It had clear responsibilities and performance measures, specified a variety of regular meetings with respective attendees and agendas, and detailed a comprehensive reporting regime. After the contract was signed by the parties, management assigned it to an employee (who had no job specifications, training, or experience in contract management) with the instructions to "*administer this.*" She diligently rubber-stamped every invoice. Not one performance review took place, or meeting, and contractor reports were never opened, let alone reviewed, as she did not know what to review for. She was too busy with her real job of procurement, and had several dozen other contracts to 'administer' as well.

Figure 8-3 provides an example of an actual CM network for a defense logistics contract that worked very well for the client. There were 20 scope groupings and 10 business units. Each business unit could 'opt in' to any of the 20 services and had its own SLA (reflecting its particular needs) and representative. Each of the 20 services had a specialist (subject matter expert) who oversaw that particular service. This structure had a single contract manager who reported to a steering committee and was the liaison with head office functions. The contract manager had two direct reports, an SLA manager who managed the 10 business representatives, and a KPI manager that managed the 20 specialists.

Figure 8-3: Example Contract Management Network

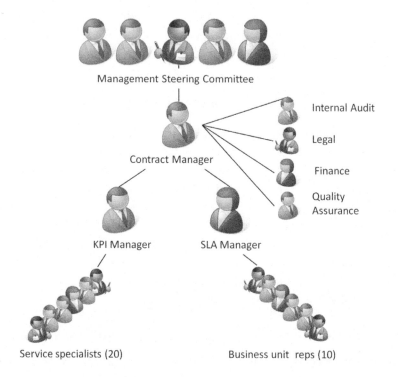

Management Steering Committee

Contract Manager

Internal Audit

Legal

Finance

Quality Assurance

KPI Manager

SLA Manager

Service specialists (20)

Business unit reps (10)

You will find many examples of CM networks and structures once you start looking. Be aware there is no 'best' structure for a CM network; each network is unique to each organization and each contract. Furthermore, organizations tend to have their own nomenclature for titles within such a network. The important thing is that the roles, and related accountabilities, are defined and the individuals act as a team.

In a complex environment, the contract management responsibilities might be spread amongst a dedicated group as opposed to residing with an individual. An example of a function of this type, from a bank, is shown in Figure 8-4. In this example, an 11-person contract management function managed the whole-of-organization contracts (contracts covering more than one business unit), while the business units managed the individual contracts that pertained solely to them (tending to be lower value, lower risk).

Figure 8-4: Example Contract Management Function

- **Strategic**
  - Strategic sourcing
  - Lifecycle standard operating procedures
  - BPR (business process re-engineering)
  - Education
  - Negotiation, dispute resolution, remediation
  - Vendor and panel portfolio management
- **Procurement**
  - Market pre-assessments
  - Specifications
  - Tendering, probity, and evaluation processes
  - Business case preparation
  - Contract set up and system entry
- **Financial**
  - Analytics, value for money and price sensitivity
  - Risk & liability determinations
  - Business case financials
  - Payments process
- **Audit**
  - KPI assessments
  - Contract compliance
  - Value for money
  - Business case validation
  - Risk
  - Benchmarking
- **Legal**
  - Legal portion of templates
  - Legal processes
  - Legal compliance audits
  - Legal advice
  - Regulatory compliance
- **Technical**
  - Service and Supply, Property, IT, HR

In this particular case, it took about a year to get the contract management function up and running, beginning from an effective capability starting place of zero. It had a 400% return on investment over its five years of operation and was the only function that survived a merger with a larger bank (and indeed, the head of the function was promoted to executive management of the merged entity).

Action 41. Audit compliance of both parties

Conducting audits of outsourcing deals is not something every organization focuses on. There are usually so many operational fires to be fought that review and compliance processes are often overlooked.

But making the practice of compliance audits a core part of contract management signals to everyone that the contract is not to be treated as 'set and forget' document and that compliance matters.

Your organization has likely made a significant investment in its contractual documents. But checks are not performed, the wisdom of making that investment is highly questionable. What gets checked, gets done. What does not get checked is apparently of such minor importance that it is not worth seeing if it has been carried out. It will usually be treated by the provider accordingly, as the following case demonstrates.

Case: Performance goes both ways

After four years into a five-year contract, the first compliance review was conducted by an independent audit firm that was paid for by the client, a large federal government department. The scope of the review was to determine the degree to which the provider was compliant with the contract.

The auditors found that the provider was only 40% compliant with the contract. Work totaling $200,000 a year had not been performed, many KPIs were not being reported, many reports were not being generated, and the list went on.

More interesting was the auditor's finding regarding the root cause of the provider's non-compliance - it was the client. The client did not follow up on missing work, unreported KPIs, missing reports, did not ask for performance reviews or planning forums, and so on. The key finding of the audit report was that the client did not install any governance over the contract, so the provider was allowed almost complete discretion in what it did. Yes, the provider was grossly non-compliant with the contract but the client was grossly negligent in its governance responsibilities. Because of this audit, the client put in place a seven-person contract management team, led by a senior contract manager along with contract management policies and procedures, and a detailed continuous review program.

Common reviews include, but are by no means limited to:

- compliance with the contractual documents,

- cost and service performance relative to the agreement and industry norms,

- source data and calculations of KPIs and any other data which one is party is relying on the other to accurately generate,

- improvement/innovation initiatives implemented,

- determination of ongoing value for money,

- the degree to which the arrangement will meet future needs and expectations,

- the provider's risk management and controls over service operations and costs,

- user and other stakeholder satisfaction,

- degree the business case has been realized,

- effectiveness of the contract management network, and

- efficient use of the provider's resources (e.g. use of peak times, expensive labor).

A common mistake many clients make is assuming (or hoping) that if an obligation has been stated in a contract, the provider will comply with it, and no further work needs to be done. However, astute clients do not assume compliance; they ensure it. The time to discover the provider has not done so is not when your organization is seeking to invoke a clause, as the next case illustrates.

Case: An applications contractor goes under

An application development and support contractor went bankrupt and discontinued operations. Under its standard outsourcing agreement signed with a number of customers, it was required to maintain source code and documentation in escrow (third party safekeeping). Furthermore, it was to ensure that its software licenses were transferable in the event of insolvency. It had done none of these things (nor had any client checked that it had). Customers were forced to run applications that could not be modified without unacceptable risk and had to replace the applications over time.

Audits of a provider can be complicated by the presence of the provider's other clients and the privacy and confidentiality rights of those clients. Additionally, if the necessary audit rights are not in the contractual documents, you may not be able to obtain access, conduct surprise audits, or may need to negotiate the degree of assistance the provider must provide (some being required to pay for such assistance). For this reason, the audits are conceptualized in the Contract Management Strategy (BB3, Action 14), and then the parties' obligations and rights specified in the Governance Charter (BB4, Action 21), to ensure you will have unfettered access and no surprise fees.

It is natural to concentrate on reviewing the provider in the first instance, since they are the ones you are paying to do the work. However, the success of a contract is the result of both parties performing, not only their contractual obligations, but also performing good governance. Merely looking at one party will not give you the full performance picture. A true review examines both parties' obligations, seeks root cause for adverse findings, and prevents recurrence. Shining a light into one room will not let you see the whole house.

In most outsourcing deals there are regular handoffs of responsibility between the parties. As you will find in most of your contracts, the effective (or otherwise) performance of one party has a considerable impact on the ability of the other to meet their responsibilities. So a better question is not, "*Who should be reviewed?*", but "*What obligations of each party will be reviewed?*"

No audit program can be accomplished without the right resources. A financial audit conducted by a technical person is unlikely be as efficient or get the same results as a financially skilled person. Likewise, a financial person reviewing compliance with the SLA is not as capable as a technical expert. There will be many different skill sets required in a typical audit program, and consequently many different resources must be used.

The timing of audits is also important. If an audit is done at the end of the contract, there will be little you can do in terms of corrective action that yields a good return on your audit investment.

Case: A homewares manufacturer leaves it too late

In this case, like most outsourcing arrangements, performance reports were to be supplied by the provider and the detailed reporting requirements were specified in the SLA. An end-of-contract audit found that the provider was only reporting two-thirds of what they had agreed to. Unfortunately, this reconciliation of actual practice to contractual requirements took place near the end of the contract and the data had never been collected by the provider, thus the information was unattainable. The provider agreed to report in full compliance for the remaining six months of the contract, a poor substitute for full compliance.

Failure to audit in a meaningful way is often due to poor planning - the client has not planned the activities, time, and resources required. By default, auditing becomes one of convenience (and luxury).

Action 42. Continuously improve

Most clients expect that their providers will continually improve, innovate, or carry out some form of 'value adding' as a normal part of a contract. Many are also then bitterly disappointed when it does not occur, feeling that the provider has misled them or let them down. Yet after you examine some of the typical clauses in this area, you can see that it can be difficult to understand what the client expects the provider to do and how the parties will work together to add value.

Let's take the following innovation clause that was contained within the 70 pages of general conditions (which also had 32 additional schedules) from a recent outsourcing agreement that we reviewed.

---

22. INNOVATION

22.1 With the view to be more efficient, to reduce unit costs incurred and overall costs incurred for the Services, the Customer seeks to encourage the Contractor to identify opportunities to introduce new technologies and/or processes. This may have the effect of improving services, reducing costs and may result in lower fees and charges for the Customer and lower outgoings for the Contractor.

22.2 Where the Contractor identifies such an opportunity that may produce a financial benefit for both parties, the Contractor will prepare and submit a business case to the Customer outlining the opportunity and how the financial benefit identified will be shared between the parties.

There are a number of observations that can be made after looking at this clause, to see if it will actually drive continuous improvement:

- This was the only clause devoted to the subject in all of the contract documents. From this, one could easily infer it was not important, or that it had just been thrown in as an afterthought.

- The client merely *"sought to encourage"* innovation, hardly an actual requirement.

- The innovation concept acts as a softener to the real objective; cut costs. But the provision is written almost to avoid the subject.

- If there was a financial benefit, it has to be shared in some way (to be worked out later). Sharing costs was not even contemplated, which infers the cost was to be borne by the provider unless they were able to get some money from the client.

If you were a provider, how much effort would you put into innovation, where it will reduce your revenue and the costs are all yours (but gains have to be shared), given that it appears unimportant to the client? The answer is what most clients actually get from such a clause. Zero.

In another example, shown in the next case, the price configuration (fixed lump sum) combined with an obligatory annual cost reduction, prevented any improvement at all.

Case: A deal motivating the provider not to improve

An insurance company found out that providers might not routinely put in a continuous improvement process, particularly when under a fixed price with little margin. In this case, by the end of a seven-year contract, the entire IT infrastructure and related practices were obsolete and effectively not supported anywhere in the industry (i.e. the desktop fleet had not been changed in the seven years). The contract had a 12.5% mandated annual cost reduction, capped profit, and capped labor; all driving the provider to retain obsolete technology and prevented any improvement.

We have seen many similar cases. Unlike many of the clients we have analyzed over the years, we do not define continuous improvement as equating to cost savings. It is an ongoing effort to improve products, services, or processes. These efforts can seek incremental improvement over time or breakthroughs all at once. In line with this concept, the staff of both parties can be expected to find ways to improve the performance of the activities they do, to keep the deal evolving.

Evolution, in the context of continuous improvement, actually encourages (productive) non-compliance with the contract. No contract is perfect. The contract was originally drafted under many constraints, namely the limited time, limited experience/skills, and various motivations of the people involved (some working at cross-purposes). Over time, the people from both parties working with the deal on the ground are likely to have developed better ways of doing business than the contract's authors had imagined. In such cases, the contract should be varied to reflect the better practices that have evolved, rather than assume the practice is wrong and the contract is right.

Good contract management allows the flexibility, opportunity, and scope for both parties to be smart and improve the way the work is done. Outsourcing contracts are just too long in duration to do otherwise.

Action 43. Control the finances

The accuracy of billing is where most clients begin in this area, comparing actual work to billed work, actual third-party invoices to claimed expenses, and so on. However, it is also useful to examine whether there are practices in place that create unnecessarily high costs. The following case is an example of both inaccurate billing and bad practices, which combined into much higher costs than should have occurred.

Case: An insurance company checks the bills

Just for assurance, a Contract Manager decided to use a re-deployed systems programmer, who had a bit of spare time on his hands, to review mainframe CPU processing consumption and related billing. The programmer obtained recent source data and discovered two very costly practices had been allowed to occur. First, the wrong times for peak and off peak usage were being used. Second, batch programs were being run at more expensive peak times if the provider had spare capacity during those times (rather than at the specified non-peak periods). How long this had been occurring was anyone's guess, as the old source data had been deleted long ago.

Another thing to review is the timing of billing. Contrary to the beliefs held in some quarters, clients really do want providers' invoices on time. Very few clients, and more pertinently, their accountants, are delighted to receive surprise invoices after the books have been closed on a project or for the reporting period.

Ensuring you pay on time is also important, not just to take advantage of available discounts and to avoid late payment interest charges, but so that you are not in breach of the contract. Many clients are notorious for late payments (intentional or just bureaucracy at work). Once you have this reputation, providers may feel it is necessary to hedge their prices higher to cater for the additional financing costs they are required to bear.

However, financial management does not end at billing. It involves the total cost of the contract. Even in a relatively simple deal, the total cost can be surprising, and is a key concept that needs to be well managed. When total costs are unknown and untracked, it can lead to suboptimal decision making ... or to idealistic, naive decision making, as described in the following case.

Case: A telco discovers cost is not always what it seems to be

A European telecommunications company was advised by its consultants to form a service delivery JV (joint venture), rather than a traditional outsourcing arrangement for all of its IT services, as it *"was the best way to ensure compatible goals."* So it did. While the telco had formed other JVs in the past, to enter new markets, this was the first in which the JV would be providing services back to the company. Management did not investigate how equity/service JV relationships work in practice and did not set up any form of retained competencies, contract management, or even JV oversight.

The telco was quite surprised to discover that its partner would sell labor and equipment to the JV at inflated cost to make an immediate profit rather than wait to split the profit from in the form of JV dividends. Management later put in a contract management team and an independent JV oversight board, but this was nearly two years after the JV had been operating; after significant cost escalation and inadequate service.

The total cost of contract represents the amounts your organization pays out to the provider plus your internal costs. This cost made up of at least the following:

- the provider's charges,

- retained costs that you cannot eliminate (e.g. leases or overheads),

- the cost of your organization's contract management (CM),[101]

- mobilization costs - the cost of getting the deal in place, and

- exit costs - the cost of unwinding the deal.

Some clients include the cost of getting to contract (BB1-BB6) as well, not just the costs after the agreement has been signed. There is no generally accepted practice here; the point is to consider the *full* cost, not just the money paid to the provider.

Table 8-3 is an example from a simple three-year equipment and support contract. The planned outlay to the provider is about $3 million, but the total cost of contract is over $4 million (comprising the full-time equivalents involved in mobilization, contract management, and exit, as well as the retained cost of old equipment leases that either have to continue or be paid out in full). If you only focused on the external payments, you would miss 30% of the cost of this contract (and probably where such focus could give you much greater results).

---

[101] Recall in Action 4 on testing stakeholder expectations, we discussed the average ongoing investment in contract management is 6% of the per annum value, double that for offshoring.

Table 8-3: Total Cost of Contract Example

Total Cost of Contract (in thousands)	Mobilization	Normal Contract Operations			Disengagement	Total
		Year 1	Year 2	Year 3		
Provider charges	250	825	852	881	125	2,933
Internal costs						
Mobilization costs	78					78
Retained costs		387	164	-		551
Contract Management	40	160	160	160	80	600
Disengagement costs					24	24
	118	547	324	160	104	1,253
TOTAL COST OF CONTRACT	368	1,372	1,176	1,041	229	$ 4,186

All figures are tax inclusive

Complex and long-term contracts require even more financial management, particularly if any of the following requirements were set up as part of the expected financial results (as defined in the Contract Scorecard, Action 17):

- **Historical** - keeping costs in line with previous periods or a baseline.

- **Budget/target** - keeping cost to a planned or targeted expenditure.

- **Market** - ensuring cost are close to current market rates.

- **TCO** (total cost of ownership) - reducing the entire supply chain, total asset, or total technology costs.

- **Subcontractor payments** - ensuring subcontractors are paid, especially in jurisdictions with laws that allow a subcontractor to seek compensation from the client if the (head) provider does not pay them.

To successfully manage the total cost of contract and obtain financial goals requires both parties to work together, sharing data and strategies. Accordingly, this action is so much more involved than merely checking invoices.

Action 44. Ensure performance

A more diligent client results in a more diligent provider, whereas a lax client tends to get lax providers. However, performance management is not just perusing the KPI reports submitted by the provider and then applying penalties or rewards, although that is what we observe as an all too common practice. That alone is insufficient, as KPIs never tell the complete story and can be easily manipulated, as illustrated in the following case.

Case: Staff get creative on recording KPIs

The outsourcing of a helpdesk had led to remarkable improvements in resolution times. However, unbeknown to the customer, as well as the provider's management, operators were not logging the calls into the system until the calls had been resolved. Rather, each operator was manually recording and tracking calls. When the call was resolved, it was then entered into the database; thus, resulting in the extraordinary resolution times.

This came about due to two factors: (1) to save the client money, an automated system had not been installed, thus proper recording was the responsibility of the operator and (2) the provider gave operators bonuses if they exceeded KPIs, primarily that of call resolution times. The operators quickly determined that these call resolution KPIs could be easily exceed by waiting to log the call, solving the problem, then recording the log date and resolution date. This was discovered a year after the contract was awarded when an astute auditor queried why the operators were so busy manually scribbling things down rather than keying data into a system, an unusual behavior in most helpdesks.

In the case above, the client was not willing to pay for an automated call logging system, preferring a manual one instead. So instead, there was a great deal of discretion and trust given to the operators. Once the operators were given financial incentives to meet performance targets, without a good recordkeeping systems (the client's decision) and without oversight (the provider's decision), the manipulation of data perhaps should not have been surprising.

To conclude the story, the client had little in the way of recourse. The provider did not breach any contractual obligation (there was no specification on the subject of KPI data collection techniques), the client could not prove any actual damages (financial losses) had occurred, and the client had imposed input restrictions to save money. Interestingly enough, when this client went to retender, the incumbent provider won. It was still the cheapest available.

Successful performance is comprised not only of the provider's outputs, but that of its inputs and processes as well. Although there are some who believe that getting involved in the provider's business makes one look like a 'control freak', this is a rather a naïve or idealistic view. Ensuring performance is a business requirement, not an ideological discussion. To ensure performance, we recommend periodic reviews of inputs, processes and outputs at a minimum, and then, where appropriate, outcomes. Each of these will now be explained.

Input reviews. Inputs are the resources (human and physical) used to carry out an outsourcing contract and have a significant bearing on the processes that are adopted and the outputs that are produced. A human resource review covers ensuring the right qualifications of staff, assessing their training and support, checking that individual performance reviews are aligned to the goals of the contract, productivity, and staff turnover trends and issues. Physical resource reviews cover the facility and technology platforms as articulated in the SLA. However, if the contract requires 'best' or 'industry' practice, this requires a benchmarking exercise to establish what is best or industry practice and compare to what is in place (see Action 47 for the discussion on benchmarking).

With input reviews, the goal is to make sure the provider is using the right resources as defined in the contract (typically the SLA). If input specifications have been left out, or ill-defined, this may present an unacceptable risk as in the next case.

Case: Getting the work done anyway possible

A power plant maintenance provider supplemented its dedicated workforce with temporary staff from a labor-hire company. Although the contract stated that only certified personnel were to work on certain items of equipment, the temporary labor had no such certifications. Due to the cost and time it would take to get the temporary workers certified, combined with the financial recourse available to the client if the provider fell behind schedule, the provider sought legal advice as to whether it would be in breach of the contract if the temporary workers performed a substantive part of the work.

The lawyer provided an opinion whereby the provider would not be in breach because the contract stated only the provider's employees needed to be certified and these were not employees as defined in the contract. However, the provider must use certified labor where it was required in law. That was all the provider needed to hear, and they proceeded to use the labor hire resources whenever and wherever needed to get the work done.

Process reviews. In outsourcing contracts, performance measures over the provider's processes will represent the bulk of the KPIs in the contract (e.g. turnaround times, response rates, delivery times, availability, etc.) Accordingly, reviewing KPI achievement and trends would be a normal part of any performance review and probably is what is being done in your organization now. In arrangements where the provider self-reports its performance, as is the case with most outsourcing contracts, no review is more crucial that the one that first checks whether the KPIs are actually measuring what you understand was the agreed performance. The case below highlights

Case: An accounting firm gets a guarantee but not performance

An international accounting firm had an equipment contract with a global provider. The firm knew that its members around the world depended on the computer equipment to arrive as quickly as possible. Otherwise, its staff would not be productive, or not even chargeable to its clients. Every day a staff member was without the equipment was one day lost in revenue.

It sought a KPI guarantee within the contract from the provider that the equipment *"would be delivered within 10 days of an order"*. After a bit of negotiation about which countries this guarantee would cover, the provider agreed. Satisfied, the firm announced this guarantee to their clients in those countries and told them to start placing their orders.

However, the firm's expectations were not in line with what the provider actually intended to measure. Because the equipment was being sold in each country through the provider's resellers and not the provider itself, the guarantee (in the provider's eyes) only covered the turnaround time from the factory to the delivery dock in each country, which always took less than 10 days. From that point, it was up to the resellers to get it to the client's offices. It was taking up to 30 days for the resellers to get it from the dock to the client's various offices in the countries. The KPI report, however, always showed that the provider was meeting, and in fact, beating the KPIs and was at no point in breach of the guarantee.

The client lived with this for three years until the contract expired and it was retendered. The incumbent lost after the client prepared a more explicit specification of the processes that would be used to achieve KPIs and specified exactly how they would be measured.

Output reviews. Outputs represent the quantity of the produced goods and/or services of the outsourcing arrangement, ideally geared towards the achievement of the desired outcomes. The review would examine current trends against historical trends to detect anomalies as well as patterns. An output review is not party specific. It looks at quantities, explanations, trends, and what both parties need to do to manage quantities better.

Outcome reviews. Outcomes are the end results you want from the inputs, processes, and outputs. For example, you may want a call centre to answer a lot of questions (outputs) in a very efficient and accurate manner (process), using qualified staff and current technologies (input). The end result you may be seeking is a satisfied caller, who then remains a loyal customer and does not switch to a competitor (outcome).

Outcomes, however, by their very nature, are never the result of a single organizational function, or the results of a single event; rather are shaped by numerous inter-related actions and events. Continuing with the example of a call centre, a customer's loyalty is achieved not only through a good (outsourced) call centre, but also through your organization's high quality goods and services, its accurate billing, its responsive management, etc. If an outsourcing arrangement covers the majority of input, processes, and outputs that create the desired outcome, then outcome measures may be possible. However, in the majority of outsourcing arrangements, the provider's contribution to outcomes is only part of the picture. The correlation between the provider's inputs, processes, and outputs with the desired end outcome may be too tenuous to be able to include outcomes in the performance management and reporting regime.

Action 45. Forecast ongoing requirements

Successful outsourcing cannot be guaranteed by contracts alone, as not all uncertainties can be specified at the time the contract is signed. Your business and organization will change, as will your providers' businesses. The longer the contract duration, the more things will change.

Planning is an ongoing part of contract management. Not only do you need to constantly be forecasting (in consultation with providers) your organization's demand for the provider's goods and/or services and its capacity requirements (and fluctuations), but also changes to its business that may affect the arrangement. It always surprises us how little attention is paid to regular forecasting of requirements and changes after an outsourcing contract has been signed (and the limited reconciliation of contracted requirements to the actual requirements that eventuated).

Case: Unmanaged 'scope creep'

As often happens in a major ERP implementation, a bank suffered enormous scope creep, driven by numerous requirement changes occurring on nearly a daily basis. Eventually, the ERP project blew out from $200 million to $800 million with only one module of the entire package implemented in a test site in New Zealand.

The bank called in an independent party to review how this had been allowed to occur. The bank's personnel did request the changes, formally and informally, and the provider put them into the project. Neither party acted as a devil's advocate, or set out a requirements updating process. Eventually the project was brought back inhouse and scaled down after much negative publicity and both parties filing lawsuits.

Action 46. Invest in the relationship

Outsourcing inevitably creates a strategic partnering relationship (albeit not in the legal sense), as your organization and its providers acknowledge greater levels of interdependence. Academics who study contracts have recognized that it is not the contract, or contract law that is really worth studying, but relational theories about people's behavior.[102] Many organizations know that a dysfunctional relationship commonly leads to increased costs and deteriorated service. Unfortunately, each

---

[102] See, for example Vincent-Jones, P. (2000) "Contractual Governance: Institutional and Organizational Analysis", *Oxford Journal of Legal Studies*, 20:3, 317-351; Collins, H. (1996) "Competing Norms of Contractual Behaviour" in D. Campbell and P. Vincent-Jones (eds) *Contract and Economic Organization: Sociolegal Initiatives*; and Campbell, D. (1997) "Socio-legal Analysis of Contracting" in P. Thomas (ed.) *Sociolegal Studies*. Dartmouth: Aldershot, 239-278.

party has a tendency to blame the other for its dysfunctions but rarely looks at their own contribution.

A relationship results from the interactions of the parties, hence the individuals in both parties need to exhibit constructive behaviors In this sense, analogies that liken the relationship to a marriage are appropriate, and, as many of us know, it takes two to have a good marriage and to make it work - or not, as in the next case.

Case: And the war begins

A telco's tendering team made a large investment in its relationship with the provider during the bidding and negotiation process. The client's contract managers, when they were handed the deal to run day-to-day, were traditionally adversarial and stayed that way; disputing all claims for out-of-scope work, disputing all bonus claims, disallowing any requests for excusable delays, etc. The provider quickly changed tack and set up its defenses. This included not performing work until a variation was signed off (a very long process in the telco), refusing to scale up KPIs that were being achieved with little effort and reporting only the minimum information that was explicitly defined in the contract, not the plethora of information available in the system (unless the client paid handsomely).

The contractual documents are important, but relatively superficial drivers of day-to-day behavior. Instead, it is the actions of both parties in interpreting and 'operationalizing' the contract that cause the arrangement to triumph or fail. As shown in Figure 8-5, the true behavior drivers are the underlying values held by the individual parties and the people involved in the agreement.

Figure 8-5: Getting Below the Surface

EASILY OBSERVABLE
MORE DIFFICULT TO OBSERVE
DAILY BEHAVIOUR
VALUES AND ATTITUDES
• Contractual documents
• Two separate enterprises
Superficial drivers of behaviour
• Communication orientation
• Conflict resolution orientation
• Relationship orientation
• Strategic orientation
• Values orientation
Deep drivers of behaviour

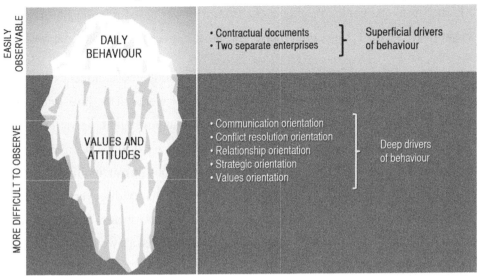

In most cases, the parties want to move from a power-based relationship that is reliant on the contract, to more of a partnering one, which is based on the underlying values, and attitudes of the key people in the parties (Figure 8-6).

Figure 8-6: Power versus Partnering-based Relationships

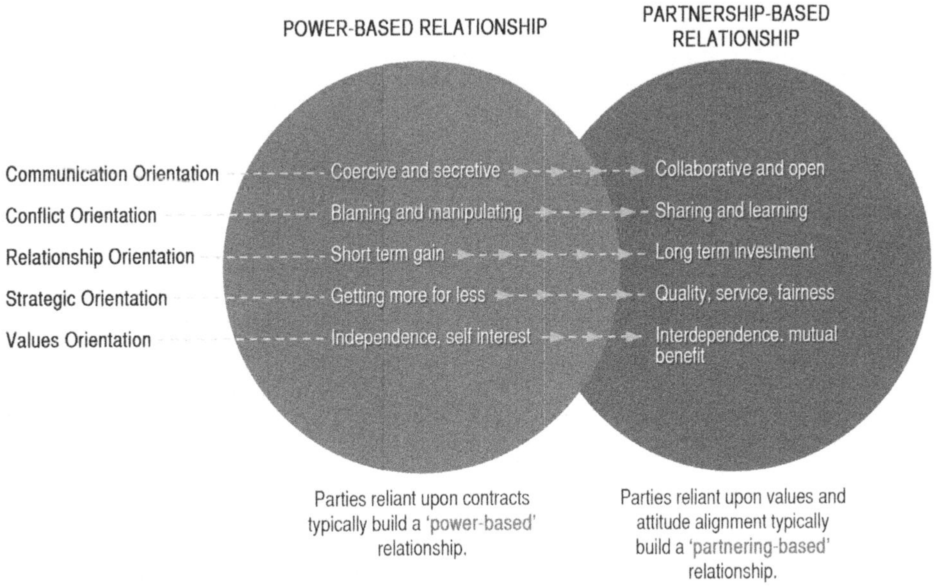

POWER-BASED RELATIONSHIP
PARTNERSHIP-BASED RELATIONSHIP
Communication Orientation
Conflict Orientation
Relationship Orientation
Strategic Orientation
Values Orientation
Coercive and secretive
Blaming and manipulating
Short term gain
Getting more for less
Independence, self interest
Collaborative and open
Sharing and learning
Long term investment
Quality, service, fairness
Interdependence, mutual benefit
Parties reliant upon contracts typically build a 'power-based' relationship.
Parties reliant upon values and attitude alignment typically build a 'partnering-based' relationship.

Partnering is a style of relationship, not a form of contract, with the behaviors in Figure 8-6 as the goal. Moving away from a power-based relationship does not mean there is a different contract, just a far greater investment in the relationship.

Most of the investment required comes after signing the contract, when true partnering behaviors are required to make the deal work. This investment is in addition to the normal contract management (covering oversight, operational issue resolution, variations, etc.) required in any outsourcing deal. The investment is geared towards ensuring strong interpersonal relationships at multiple levels in both parties, towards joint problem solving and opportunity discovery techniques, towards knowledge sharing and capturing solutions, and towards developing deep understanding of both parties' strengths and limitations as well as the political environments in which they operate.

When is this investment worthwhile? When there is a high degree of uncertainty in the contract (e.g. unpredictability of scope changes, uncertain resourcing requirements, or long duration). Only a partnering-style relationship can handle significant change and not treat the contract as a zero sum game where there is a winner and loser.

But the investment is not necessary with all providers. Clients use any number of providers; which have varying degrees of importance. In one of our global surveys, clients reported that 60% of providers were 'important/very important', and 40% 'somewhat important/not important at all' on average. [103] That 60/40 ratio applied even for those clients that were more dependent on their providers (e.g. as sole suppliers or prime contractors). It is important to recognize that only a portion of the providers will warrant the extra relationship management investment required; the rest are just not important enough.

---

[103] Cullen, S. (2006) "The Configuration Concept: Supplier Grouping", *Sourcing and Vendor Relationships Executive Update*, Vol 7 No 18. Cutter Consortium, Arlington.

Action 47.Keep informed

Your organization's evaluation of a provider could become obsolete very quickly in today's economic climate. Large global companies, as well as smaller local ones, can radically change during the life of a contract. The longer the contract, the more likely that the entity that signed the contract will not be the same entity at its end - it will grow or shrink, have new divisions and drop divisions, have new debt structures, change owners, buy other companies or get sold to one, get into financial difficulties (and hopefully out), etc. These changes can happen quite fast, and with no notice to your organization.

Case: A corporate takeover during mobilization

A contract was awarded to the 'best value for money' bid. It was a well-known provider, and thus the evaluation team did not think it necessary to conduct a company/financial due diligence. Shortly upon commencing mobilization, the provider was taken over by another company. This company had also bid, but was evaluated as the least preferred bidder in a race of five providers.

It was well known to both providers that this takeover was to occur, and to various industry watchers, but not to the client. The inevitable rationalization of the winning provider's staff commenced almost immediately, and key personnel from the original provider were replaced by the new organization. These new personnel had a very strict style of operating and interpreted the agreement differently than the predecessor. Scope debates and price variations became normal operations.

This warrants a reasonable ongoing awareness of what is happening with the providers you depend upon (as well as the key suppliers in the entire supply chain - the ones your providers depend upon) and not rely on an evaluation done years before.

Other changes will happen as well - technological, industry standards, regulations, price-performance ratios - that render your contract obsolete all too quickly. For this reason, benchmarking has become a highly desired practice by clients. But it is poorly executed when it is used as a negotiation tactic to squeeze providers, rather than to understand how the better performers achieved KPIs or reduced costs.

There are three fundamental approaches to benchmarking:

- independent consultant,
- partner organizations, and
- your organization's own 'database' of its providers.

First is the use of **independent consultants**. There are a number of benchmarking consultants where there are mature markets (many providers have been operating reasonably long with commoditized goods/services). The key to getting value for money from the exercise is to scope the consultant's data to a best-fit with your organization. Defining what you believe to be 'apples-to-apples' is the only way you can be assured of even getting something even fruit-related. The case below highlights this problem.

Case: Lack of meaningful benchmarks

A power company's CIO believed benchmarks were readily available and simple to apply; it was merely a matter of finding a consultant. He asked the consultants who were working at the company at the time if they had benchmarks and what it would cost. Happy with the answer, the CIO set the benchmarking project in motion. Upon receipt of the voluminous report, the CIO struggled to find any meaningful information. When he queried the attributes of the source data (age, industry, location, etc.) and the method of scope alignment between his organization and the data set, he was told all that was confidential. Having no way of knowing if the benchmarks represented current data, were in his industry, had comparable scope, and were from local or international sources, he threw the report out. But he still had to pay $100,000 for it. Here, the benchmarking yielded nothing but a strong desire not to go through it again.

Because consultants are typically the most expensive option (and possibly the least understandable), many choose a **few select organizations** that they 'partner' with. Your goal is to partner with other organizations from the same, or similar, industries as yours or with reasonably similar scale and scope of contract/s. While there will be less data points than a consultant's database, the data you collect is likely to be more meaningful to you. It allows you to do a detailed 'apples-to-apples' comparison, as well as investigate detailed explanations of differences and solutions.

Lastly, some clients create their **own database** using supplier panels or multiple providers for the same services. By having a reasonable number of providers compete on a regular basis for various contracts or 'work orders' over a defined period, you are in effect continuously benchmarking each contract.

Action 48. Manage issues and risks

Good issue and risk management in outsourcing is very similar to that for good project management. That is, there is a formal process for raising, recording, and resolving issues that arise and these are logged and tracked. It is not unusual to find at least 300 live issues on any given day in a reasonably complex outsourcing operations. Unresolved issues can be disputes waiting to happen if left to fester, thus sound issue management can make or break an outsourcing deal.

Issue management is focused first on prioritizing the issues so that high priorities are solved first. Otherwise, people can lean towards solving the easiest issues rather than the important ones. Secondly, the focus is on permanently solving the issue, rather than temporary workarounds. Third, the issue is assigned to an individual to solve it, not just a party. Individual accountability is crucial to getting it solved. Finally, the actual resolution is documented before the issue is closed out.

Having an issue management system is very beneficial, and not just to solve issues. It also creates a record of issues the parties faced throughout the entire life of the deal. This creates potential lessons and solutions for other contracts, as well as future generations of this contract. This history is also invaluable if key staff at either party leave and are replaced. New people can get quickly across the key issues - both past and current - by reading the issues log, resulting in handovers that are more efficient.

The question of 'what is an issue?' will often arise. It is good practice is to record something as an issue when:

- a party wants something solved, or a decision made, by the other party - an issue record provides a systematic way to raise concerns;

- a decision needs visibility - if you want evidence that some form of understanding, agreement, or resolution has occurred, and then raise an issue record. It does not matter whether something is solved in five minutes, only whether you want a record of it;

- something needs further investigation - issue management provides a tracking process for open items, otherwise it is to be forgotten until there is a crisis, which is what good issue management is designed to prevent; and

- someone raises a good idea - a way of improving something is also a good use of issue sheets; it does not just have to be about problems.

Action 49. Manage variations

Variations are a natural and, often frequent, occurrence. They can occur verbally (e.g. in meetings or over the telephone), in written form (e.g. email and other correspondence), as well as through the parties' behaviors (known as estoppel). Some variations will be 'official' (i.e. written and signed by both parties), however the bulk of variations will comprise countless incremental changes to scope, practices, personnel, procedures, etc that occur on a day-to-day basis.

Variation management is very similar to issue management. That is, there is a formal process for raising, recording, and resolving variations that arise, and these are logged and tracked using a documented form. The processes and forms that will be followed are specified in the Governance Charter (Action 21).

In addition to the normal operational changes that inevitably occur, major variations necessitating an effective rewrite of the deal often take place, typically around the two-year mark, for of any one of the following reasons:

- a change in systems - a rationalization, new platform/s, new enterprise software, formation of a standard operating environment, etc.;

- a change in KPIs - either appreciably upgrade or downgrade based on the providers' performance or the client's business requirements;

- the desire by your organization to backsource certain services - either because the provider has not been performing adequately and you do not believe it will improve , you wish to rebuild competence, or have (in hindsight) determined the work should performed internally;

- expected demand levels have changed - either to a much larger or smaller extent;

- incorporate further services - that were not foreseen, or are currently out-of-scope, but have been purchased repeated;

- to rectify defects or omissions - including accountability concerns (if actual operations have lead to resources or activities being duplicated or omitted), poor or ambiguous specifications, or inclusion of schedules to form part of the contract documents;

- to refresh the entirety of the agreement - either because there have been extensive variations or the agreement is not meeting the needs of either or both parties or to introduce good outsourcing practice deemed necessary (i.e. KPIS, incentives, etc.);

- to revise the pricing arrangement - to variabilize prices that were fixed but should not have been, to fix stable variable prices, clarify the reimbursables, meet new market prices, etc.; or

- a significant restructure of either party - merger, acquisition, divestment, reorganization, expansion, etc.; necessitating a contract overhaul.

At some point, you may want to consider releasing a new version of the contract if the number of variations becomes so great as to make the contract no longer understandable. Never be afraid to release a new version incorporating the variations into the agreement.

Case: Variations become unmanageable

A fourth generation maintenance contract had one binder for the contract and three binders for the agreed variations. The variations evidence included in those three binders included copies of emails, correspondence, and on occasion, a signed variation agreement. However, it was nearly impossible to know the current conditions of contract as many of the variations related to previous variations but none of the documents were cross-referenced. Inevitably, the parties agreed to rewrite the contract and re-sign it.

And most certainly incorporate them into the next contract if good solutions occurred that were not foreseen as being needed at the start. Otherwise, what tends to happen is the old obsolete contract, which did not work, is put back out to tender yet again.

Action 50. Manage disagreements and disputes

Think of disputes that occur in outsourcing deals as mushrooms. To grow and spawn they need an environment that is dark and full of 'fertilizer'. Your goal is to create an environment that is well lit and has little fertilizer for the mushrooms.

Disputes are not usually caused by a single particular issue, but are generally triggered after an accumulation of misunderstandings, disagreements, and adverse events that eventually lead the parties to start 'throwing mud at each other'. The case below shows how seemingly superficial events can create a 'fertilized' field ready for disputes.

Case: Disputes begin the first week

A state government department and a provider had just signed a 'partnering' BPO deal whereby the provider would not only maintain the facilities operated by the department, but also manage leases and other tenants as well.

On the first day of the contract, the provider's full-time account manager asked the client's director where his office would be. He had assumed that as it was a partnership, he and the director were to be colleagues, and he would have an office near the director. It was a reasonable assumption, since that was the arrangement in other deals with other clients.

This request came as a surprise to the client's director for a number of reasons. First, the provider's office was only a few blocks away so there was no logistical basis for the request. Second, he only expected to see the provider if his help was needed in resolving issues. Third, there was a shortage of space that was known to the provider.

However, the director was not going to be ungracious and refuse to provide an office. Due to the space shortage, he had difficulty locating one but did track one down. It was in the basement and not particularly welcoming. He felt he was being quite congenial first by not refusing and second by not charging the provider for rent.

However, the account manager took the gesture as an overt signal that the relationship was not going to be a 'partnership' at all. Quite clearly, the client intended a master-slave relationship and was going to try to take advantage of them. As a defensive move, he put the word out that the client was not to be trusted and the provider's staff were only to comply with the letter of the contract.

The first occasion to test the relationship happened in the first week, where something had to be done urgently, but was out of scope. The account manager refused until he had a signed purchase order from the client. He was not going to fall for the old trick of doing something without a PO, only to find out later that the client's accounts department would refuse to pay. When the director heard about this, his worse fears were confirmed. Partnering was just sales rhetoric; providers really do not implement it in practice. As his defensive move, he was going to make sure they complied with everything to the letter in the contract. It was the only way to manage providers.

Disputes soon percolated, raised by both parties regarding what the other was not doing in accordance with the contract. However, because of the original 'partnering' approach taken, not much effort went into the contract and it was full of ambiguities, conflict, and silent areas (where the contract said nothing). It was, in fact, a 'contract-light'. Since the contract was not of much help, it came down to who believed who said what during negotiations (for which minutes were not kept). Debates over who said what and mutual blaming kept going for a year until the provider sold its business to another organization and the client and the new provider negotiated a *"real contract."*

The most critical dispute management skill is the ability to stay out of disputes; not as an avoidance technique; but rather, as a careful cultivator who ensures that 'mushrooms' have no chance to grow. What is needed is the skill to prevent battles, not to fight them.

Too many contracts do not specify an internal inter-party escalation process, prior to getting third parties involved. With no agreed escalation, disputes can too quickly be dispatched to third parties. While most contracts will state that the parties have a duty to try to resolve a dispute prior to seeking alternative dispute resolution (discussed below), such contracts do not go far enough in specifying what that process should be.

Dispute management is very similar to that issue management. That is, there is a formal process for raising, recording, and resolving disputes that arise. Disagreements are normal, and must be treated as business as usual, rather allowed to fester and become personal. The processes and forms to be followed should be specified in the Governance Charter (see Action 21 - Draft the Governance Charter).

However, if the parties find that they cannot solve it themselves, there are three types of alternative dispute resolution, known as ADR, which are usually required to have been attempted before to a party can take the issue to court. These are:

- arbitration,
- mediation, and
- independent expert.

The history of these is quite interesting. Arbitration was originally created as an alternative to court, to save both parties (and courts) time and money. Nonetheless, these days it is rare that any organization goes to arbitration without their lawyers, so it does not save much money.

Mediation came next; and is arguably a cheaper form of ADR. A mediator does not make a decision, however. His/her role is to act as a facilitator who helps the parties reach an agreement without influencing the actual arrangement that may be agreed to. In fact, if any influence can be proven, the agreement could possibly be revoked and the mediator could lose their license to practice. This takes much longer than arbitration, but we have observed that it is the form of ADR that often begins to repair communications and thus the relationship.

Neither arbitrators nor mediators are likely to have a detailed understanding of either party's business. As a result, the 'independent expert' alternative is increasingly popular. This is where the parties agree on an expert in the area (e.g. an expert in facilities management) who bases a decision on industry norms and his/her own experience. Using an expert is usually the quickest form of ADR, since the expert is already a professional in the field and has seen this before. A key part of this process is that neither party brings their lawyers, as a practical solution is sought, not a legal 'win'.

However, once a dispute is resolved, the work is far from over. Many people, after believing that the other party might have 'won' a dispute (or feel that they 'lost'), prepare for the next dispute. They may set up better defenses or even seek revenge, *"They got me this time, but I'll get them back"*. Another truck of fertilizer has just been delivered!

If you cannot imagine ever saying you are sorry to the other party, you may not be able to recover from a dispute. If the parties still have to work together, baby steps are required. This involves just trying to do simple, non-controversial things together in an attempt to rebuild respect and, one day, trust. Parties that have recovered well often end up having a stronger relationship than they had before. New understandings are made, better ways of communicating are put in place, and more proactive problem solving techniques are utilized.

Alternatively, if both parties cannot put a dispute behind them, both will inevitably become expert mushroom growers.

Action 51. Record keep and report

One of the main functions of contract administration is to have a systematic repository and log of records and decisions. Maintaining diligent administration provides an efficient reference system and audit trail. This is invaluable if any aspect of the arrangement is questioned by either party or an external body (e.g. auditors, regulators). All too often, though, the paperwork side of things can be put to one side. It does take time, and may be perceived by some as even an unfriendly thing to do. But without documentation, you have no evidence of what has occurred, as the next case illustrates.

Case: KPIs are being met but dissatisfaction continues to grow

An international airline had outsourced its IT support services (LANs, desktop fleet management and help desk. In this case, stakeholder satisfaction surveys were yielding poor results and there was a general feeling of dissatisfaction with the provider. Yet, the KPIs were showing reasonable performance, certainly of a standard that did not warrant the animosity exhibited.

A root cause analysis determined that the major contributing factor was that both the provider's sales staff and its operational staff were making unwritten promises to various client personnel and not carrying them out or following them up. These promises included access to global research, technical briefings, facilitation of special interest groups, to name a few. Therefore, the client had immense expectations that were not articulated in the agreement, yet were the major source of dissatisfaction.

Neither party maintained records of the discussions nor had correspondence, thus an initiative was undertaken to gather all the unrecorded promises. Once this process was completed, the provider realized it could not meet these expectations and keep within its profit margins. The first step was to prioritize the promises and determine which the provider could perform at minimum cost. From among those it could not, the client was invited to choose those that it was willing to pay extra for. Lastly, to stop this problem from occurring again, the provider instituted a *"no promises unless supported with a variation"* procedure and instituted a minute keeping and review procedure for all meetings.

Documentation is critical in that it captures discussions, provides evidence of commitments and changes, and assists in resolution of disputes. It can be used as evidence during any legal proceedings, and captures the history of the arrangement.

Examples of the items requiring such diligent control include:

- agendas and minutes of meetings - particularly where decisions have been reached or implied agreements may have been made,
- all financial data - including bills and quotes,

- approvals and signoffs - as evidence it occurred,

- audit reports and findings - noting compliance, defects and proposed rectification,

- correspondence and discussions between the parties - particularly where decisions have been reached or implied agreements may have been made,

- customer satisfaction surveys - particularly to track history and provide information for improvement initiatives,

- changes to practices and understanding - as the primary source of the parties' understandings,

- issue logs - to track the history of issues and the resolutions (see Action 48),

- precursor documents (request for tenders, bids, etc.) - should the intent of aspects of the agreement need to be referred to, and

- reports - performance, progress, audit, etc.

Reports serve as analysis summary tools, evidencing the degree of success of the arrangement, providing KPI and operational indices, and identifying areas for improvement. There will be a number of reports that any client who has outsourced will require, and a number of stakeholders will want certain kinds of information. The design of the reporting framework is part of the Architect Phase, as your organization is in the best position to establish its reporting requirements before outsourcing occurs, and not afterwards.

Chapter 9   Better, Faster - the Regenerate Phase

All contracts end, either through early termination, or by reaching the natural end of the term.   The end of the current contract, in whatever manner it ends, represents the completion of the lifecycle of the current outsourcing initiative and the start of the next generation (or as we like to call it 'next gen').

The Regenerate Phase, where the next gen options are decided, consists of one building block:

- BB9- Refresh.

Most clients are in their second, third, and even fourth generation of outsourcing relationships. As contracts begin to mature, you need to decide what to do next. Should you renegotiate a contract with the incumbent provider? Switch providers? Backsource by bringing operations back inhouse? In this last phase of the current lifecycle, the past is assessed and the future is determined in order to go forward in an improved position; one that is faster, better, and cheaper.

Building Block 9: Refresh - Build the Next Generation

"Nothing endures but change"

Heraclitus of Ephesus

ARCHITECT PHASE	ENGAGE PHASE	OPERATE PHASE	REGENERATE PHASE

BUILDING BLOCK 9
REFRESH

If you have followed the suggested lifecycle, the next generation options have been considered and catered for in the Architect Phase (particularly Action 13 and Action 22 regarding the transition-out). Preparing for termination, handover to another provider, or bringing an activity back inhouse … all these seemed a very long way off when you were planning the current generation of a contract. Nevertheless, BB9 comes around much faster than most are prepared for (which is why the most common next gen decision is an extension of the current contract).

It is very important that you use the Architect Phase to plan the next gen options (and its implementation) to ensure all opportunities are facilitated; or, at the very least, not prohibited. If next gen options are not catered for in each generation, then your options may be limited, as the following case highlights.

Case: A law enforcement agency creates its very own monopoly

The helpdesk of a law enforcement agency was outsourced to a contract labor company under a one-year agreement. The duration configuration was short because management wanted to be able to competitively tender frequently to ensure low cost service delivery.

However, not considered by management at the time was how such retendering would actually work. The nature of the calls to the helpdesk was very specific to the force and required detailed organizational knowledge, not only of the systems, but also of the process of law enforcement. It took about six months to get the new helpdesk and the contractor's staff fully operational. Then, the client's staff were redeployed and the contractor took over full operations.

During the next round of tendering (after an emergency one year extension) the agency discovered it had created a private monopoly due the very specific nature of the knowledge the incumbent provider now had. No other bidder even came close to the incumbent in terms of knowledge and ability. The incumbent won at twice the original price because the agency had no genuine alternative.

Having the next gen planned in the Architect Phase, and then armed with the benefit of this generation's hindsight and experience, plus carefully carrying out this building block, allows each successive generation to yield a better solution than your organization had previously.

The actions in this building block, BB9, include the following:

- **Get the next gen capability** (Action 52) - ensure the team in charge of the next gen has expertise in the options (renewal, handover, and backsourcing) and related lifecycle processes (renegotiation, retenders, and exit).

- **Assess outcomes and lessons** (Action 53) - establish what worked, and did not work, to replicate successes and avoid repeat failures.

- **Make the next gen decision** (Action 54) - decide the option/s to be implemented.

- **Create the next gen roadmap through the lifecycle** (Action 55) - plan your route/s through the lifecycle for each of the options chosen.

Action 52. Get the next gen capability

Each generation, clients find themselves in a relatively new situation, having to learn anew. Configuration changes are likely (e.g. changing scope, moving from a sole-source configuration to a multiple provider one or vice versa, changing price models, etc.). The people involved in a particular generation may only have experience in the particular configuration of that generation's contract.

What is more, we have often observed that the team who conducted the previous lifecycle had moved on to other things, and that the contract management network experienced multiple replacements over the term. This results in a step backwards regarding organizational learning. The people charged with planning and executing the next generation may only be first generation themselves (with limited breath of experience with outsourcing and managing multiple generations). Some clients never get themselves out of a first generation capability - losing all organizational learning each generation.

It is not just the organizational learning that is required to make substantial improvements each generation; it is knowing how the lifecycle processes change dramatically in all generations after the first one. A retender is very different from a first generation tender, renegotiation with an incumbent is poles apart from the original negotiation, and backsourcing is nothing like outsourcing.

However, if each generation is carried out with the client having no more than a first generation capability, it would be rare to see much improvement. It would be more common to observe things actually taking a turn for the worst. The following case illustrates this pattern only too well.

Case: Knowledge shortfall leads to second-generation failure

The first responsibility of a new IT manager for a port logistics company was to conduct a retender for the network management services, as the current five-year contract was expiring shortly. Not knowing much about operations as yet, and knowing very little about outsourcing, he kept everything as it was and issued the same tender and contract as had been used five years ago (with a few date changes).

One of the bidders offered a price that was extraordinarily less than any other bid. The manager awarded the contract very quickly to lock in that price. He believed he had done a great job and got a great result, all for little effort.

However, the old contract he reissued was obsolete. It referred to the possible effects of potential legislation at the time, which had now had been in force for years, required compliance with organizational and government policies that no longer existed, and had clauses pertaining to the sale of assets sold five years ago, and so on. Even worse, the old specification he used was largely irrelevant to what was actually being provided. The specification was five years old and scope had changed significantly (largely undocumented and only known to the previous manager).

Lastly, he did not consider the need for any handover activities between the old and new provider to ensure a smooth transition. The handover consisted of the previous provider leaving on the day the contract expired and the new one walking in the next day. As an aside, the previous provider had prepared handover notes for the new provider. But since no handover was requested, the notes were just filed in the closeout file (a closeout was never performed as well).

Within a week, operations had stopped completely. The client could not assist the new provider in any guidance or instructions because he was as unfamiliar with operations as was the new provider. The previous provider was initially generous in responding to the many calls by the manager and the new provider, but within two days had to inform them staff had been redeployed and were no longer available. Within that first week, the new provider knew it was in over its head. The specification was grossly under-scoped (and thus under quoted), there was little available information on current operations, and most importantly and it did not have the required expertise.

After an initial round of threatened litigation (the client threatening the new provider, the new one threatening the old, and the old provider threatening both), the incumbent provider was subcontracted back at premium prices by the new provider and the client paid the extra (for what was in effect, the same provider performing the same work.

The capabilities your team should have to be able to make good next gen decisions, and carry out the next gen lifecycle competently, include the core expertise discussed in Action 2, plus the following additional competencies:

- **Re-tendering** - knowing when market conditions and/or scope changes warrant a retender, creating a level playing field for new entrants when there is an incumbent, approaching both markets (new entrants and incumbents).

- **Re-negotiating** - gauging the small increase in power that exists when a renewal is on the table, and being able to deploy collaborative forms of negotiation and mediation skills.

- **Disengaging** - unwinding a provider from your organization's systems, practices, and procedures; auditing, valuing, purchasing and disposing assets; intellectual property identification and collection; closeouts, post-termination operations, etc.

- **Handing over to new providers** - transitions in and out, tri-party project management, tri-party testing and acceptance, multi-party negotiations.

- **Backsourcing** - transferring knowledge, staff, assets (including intellectual property); rebuilding business functions, capabilities, and practices.

Action 53. Assess outcomes and lessons

The first point of call when assessing how successful a particular generation was (and why it was successful or why it was not), is to look at the original business case; and in particular, the strategic and tactical purposes the arrangement was designed to achieve. This is not always easy, as the following case reveals.

Case: No historical information limits assessment

Toward the end of a five-year contract, the Vice-Chancellor of a university directed a contract manager to assess whether the benefits sought by outsourcing were achieved. The results of this analysis were critical to the steering committee's planning for future outsourcing. However, no documentation had been maintained and none of the people involved in the outsourcing negotiations remained with the university. Furthermore, the current stakeholders all had differing opinions about the original objectives. These were cost savings; permitting the university to focus on its core activities; allow it to broaden its offerings; temporary or eventually backsource them to the university. The manager made a valiant effort, but he could not determine the intended benefits, let alone whether or not they had been achieved.

As a substitute, he enumerated actual achievements and how they had been accomplished. In other words, what had worked well.

The university gave the provider a greater span of control (that is, responsibility for a process or a function not just a task) which improved the provider's performance because the work could be measured by business outcomes via KPIs. It .then used rewards as well as recourse for these KPIs, which motivated the provider's behavior to do well better. He also found that conducting reference checks and using known approaches to provider integration led to the provider working well with other providers. Lastly, locking in explicit accountabilities in the contract reduced finger pointing between the parties.

Besides highlighting the benefits of keeping documentation pertaining to the Architect Phase to assist future generations, this case also highlights the benefits of a SWOT (Strengths, Weaknesses, Opportunities and Threats) to aid preparation for the next gen decisions (Figure 9-1).

Figure 9-1: SWOT

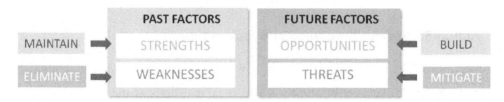

This involves assessing what the current deal has evolved to, what worked and did not work, and what can be learnt from the earlier generation, what needs to be addressed in the next gen and opportunities.

This analysis is designed to determine:

- **Strengths** - what worked well and you want to have continue to work well in the next gen.

- **Weaknesses** - defects that need to be corrected for the next gen.

- **Opportunities** - that could be taken up as part of the next gen.

- **Threats** - to be addressed and mitigated during the next gen.

Example questions we use to provoke SWOT thinking are provided in Table 9-1.

Table 9-1: Example SWOT Questions

Strengths	Opportunities
• What would your organization say were the successes of this generation? • What did the parties do well that should be incorporated in future generations? • Were there particular resources or skills that provided demonstrated benefits? • What would the incumbent view as your organization's strengths? What do you view as their strengths?	• Have there been any market innovations since the current deal was signed? • What is the current level of performance and prices compared to industry benchmarks? • Have better practices emerged in other organizations? What is considered leading practice in the market? • What are your competitors doing with their providers and supply/value chains?
Weaknesses	**Threats**
• What did not work well? What did either party do poorly and could improve upon? • What risks actually materialized in the current deal and can they be prevented next time? • Did either party make any mistakes that should be prevented in the future? • Were there resource or skills gaps? • What obstacles did either party face? • What does the provider view as your weaknesses; and you as theirs?	• Have there been changes to the market, regulation, taxation, sourcing practices, etc., which may concern either party? • Are there any adverse events in the market (e.g. labor or materials shortage)? • Will there be a change of government in the locations covered within the scope? • Are there any uncertainties surrounding your organization in the foreseeable future (e.g. business/structural changes, market exits, etc.)?

The experiences of the next two cases highlight how easy, and how important a SWOT is.

Case: A Story of Two Cases

A federal government department went to retender and selected a provider that was priced well below the incumbent bid. The incumbent had been quite flexible in its approach, allowing the client to exceed capacity restrictions without extra charges, allowing scope creep in certain areas, but maintaining the same fixed price, etc. The new provider was well known in the market as a vigorous 'out-of-scope' hunter, typically bidding low then aggressively making profits from minimalist interpretations of scope and charging for additional work. The client hadn't considered performing a SWOT because it assumed that all providers behave the same. The client then behaved with the new provider as it had with the old one (e.g. exceeding capacity, changing scope, etc. The client quickly learnt that the new game was different; it was all about managing scope variations and cost escalations. The client was now aware of its own weaknesses, as well as the previous provider's strengths.

Contrast this to a utility company that had conducted a detailed SWOT. It believed this was necessary because it had amalgamated three geographic regions comprising five contracts into a two regions. It was planning to conduct a tender for one region and then backsource the other region to a wholly-owned subsidiary in order to regain the operational competence it had lost from nearly 15 years of outsourcing (this was the third generation). But it was concerned that having a related entity as a provider would throw out its very successful governance and relationship management processes.

Based on the SWOT, the key areas of strength were a comprehensive and 'reader-friendly' contract, diligent contract management, monthly detailed performance reviews, retained inhouse management of core operational systems and ongoing benchmarking between the parties. Weaknesses surrounded a fixed price contract when the client needed to be able to chop and change services. The company signed substantially the same agreement with the subsidiary as it did with the independent provider and put in the same governance. After some initial politicking, the subsidiary 'fell into line as an arms-length provider' and was soon delivering the market equivalent standard of service.

Of course, you do not need to wait until the end of a contract to perform a SWOT. Diligent contract management will make it part of the regular process of review and continuous improvement. Thus, when entering the final phase, the client is better prepared and can act quicker.

Some clients have used the SWOT to assess the entire contract portfolio, which can be hundreds of contracts. In this manner, systematic weakness (e.g. late payments) can be identified and mitigation strategies put in place, good practice via the identified strengths (e.g. strong interpersonal relationships) can be cross-pollinated to other deals, opportunities generated across contracts (e.g. aggregating demand), and threats (e.g. new regulations) addressed across your entire organization, as opposed to only individual instances.

Action 54. Make the next gen decision

There are three fundamental options with regard to the decisions for the next generation (each for all or part of the scope):

- Retain the incumbent provider - by renewing or renegotiating,

- Backsource - bring inhouse, or

- Seek new provider/s - via competitive negotiation or retender.

One study showed that clients that renewed contracts reported high levels of product, service, and relationship, as well as low switching costs. Clients that switched providers reported high product and service quality, but low relationship quality and high switching costs. Clients that backsourced reported low levels on all four variables.[104] But this does not mean that you should automatically keep the incumbent or never backsource. The decision must be made carefully, each generation, always considering all three options (or combinations thereof).

Consider retaining the incumbent provider, if:

- there is little change to scope and expectations,

- the incumbent has performed at or better than the specified KPIs,

- the incumbent will provide the services at or below market prices,

- desired changes to the contract can be agreed without undue tension,

- both parties save significant time and effort by not retendering, and

- both parties wish to continue the relationship.

---

[104] Whitten, D. and Leidner, D. (2006) "Bringing IT Back: An Analysis of the Decision to Backsource or Switch Vendors," *Decision Sciences,* 37, 4, 605 – 621.

Consider backsourcing, if your organization:

- wishes to rebuild its competence in the area, and/or
- believes the scope is more effectively or efficiently provided internally.

Consider switching providers, if:

- market prices, technology, or practices have changed significantly,
- scope has changed significantly and your organization believes other providers may have greater expertise or offer better approaches, and
- the handover to a successor can be effectively conducted.

Note that we do not recommend retendering unless you have a genuine intent to switch providers. Far too many are conducted for no reason other than bureaucratic compliance, or just fishing to see if there is a provider willing to 'buy the contract', or to gather ammunition to renegotiate with the incumbent.

For these reasons, providers have a healthy skepticism regarding retenders. Most providers, in their 'bid/no bid' process, put the existence of an incumbent in the 'no bid' category unless the client has a demonstrated a genuine commitment to switching providers. This is because the new bidders know that the switching costs can be massive (comprising your costs to disengage the incumbent and transition to the new provider, as well as the new provider's startup costs). This cost can be so high as to preclude any cost effective solution other than to keep the incumbent. So it is not worth putting in much effort in a retender exercise that has no likely return, which favors the incumbent yet again.

It is difficult to break this cycle. Once you have chosen an incumbent again, your ability to convince new entrants to bid further erodes. Some clients have had to go to extremes to break this cycle including barring the incumbent from bidding and paying bidders to bid. If yours is a situation that has a long-standing incumbent, with no compelling reason to switch, without proven investment in working with the new entrants, and without substantial evidence that you have made necessary switching preparations, you will be investing far too much in an exercise that will end up retaining the incumbent for many more years.

When the Regenerate Phase is conducted prudently, all options usually take place in a single contract. Some services are backsourced, some the incumbent provider continues to supply, and some a new provider supplies. To what extent this occurs varies widely, but the next case illustrates this situation.

Case: Assessing options

A gas utility had been outsourcing its maintenance function under five contracts for many years. It took two years to align the contracts so that each had the same termination date and that the next generation options were catered for (both contractually and operationally). Following are the eight options that the utility identified:

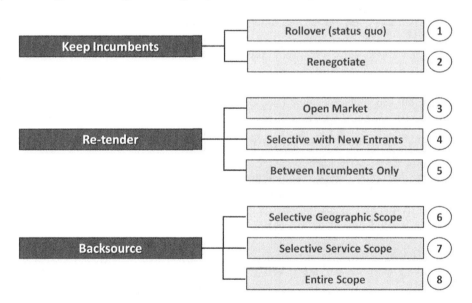

Those eight options became a shortlist of three after an analysis was performed regarding the strategic fit (expected benefits including innovation, flexibility, operational improvement, and cost saving) and the risks (disruption, integration, ability of the client to implement and manage). This is shown in the next diagram.

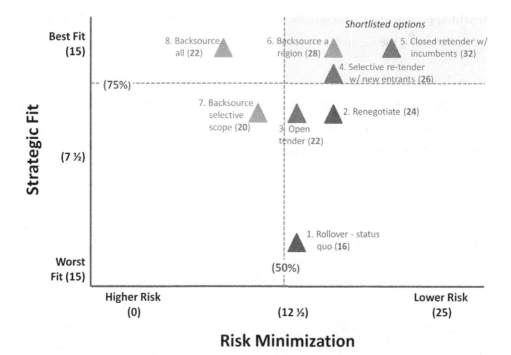

Strategic Fit

Best Fit (15)

Shortlisted options

8. Backsource all (22)

6. Backsource a region (28)

5. Closed retender w/ incumbents (32)

4. Selective re-tender w/ new entrants (26)

(75%)

7. Backsource selective scope (20)

3. Open tender (22)

2. Renegotiate (24)

(7 ½)

1. Rollover - status quo (16)

Worst Fit (15)

(50%)

Higher Risk (0)   (12 ½)   Lower Risk (25)

Risk Minimization

The solution was to reconfigure from five contracts covering three regions into two regional, full-scope contracts and backsource one region. Two contracts went to retender and were won by two of the five incumbents; the new entrants' bids all rated poorly. The third region was given to a newly formed wholly owned subsidiary under a nearly identical arms-length agreement. The entire next gen process took three years to move from a *"working, but low benefit"* second-generation situation to a very successful third generation. The third generation was so successful in terms of the benefits that actually accrued, that the next generation decision was to keep the solution in place.

Action 55. Create the next gen roadmap through the lifecycle

Depending what next gen options your organization chooses, you will take a different path through the lifecycle (see Figure 9-2), and quite possibly all the paths simultaneously if all options are taken. All paths begin with the Architect Phase and end with the Regenerate Phase.

Figure 9-2: The Next Gen Lifecycle

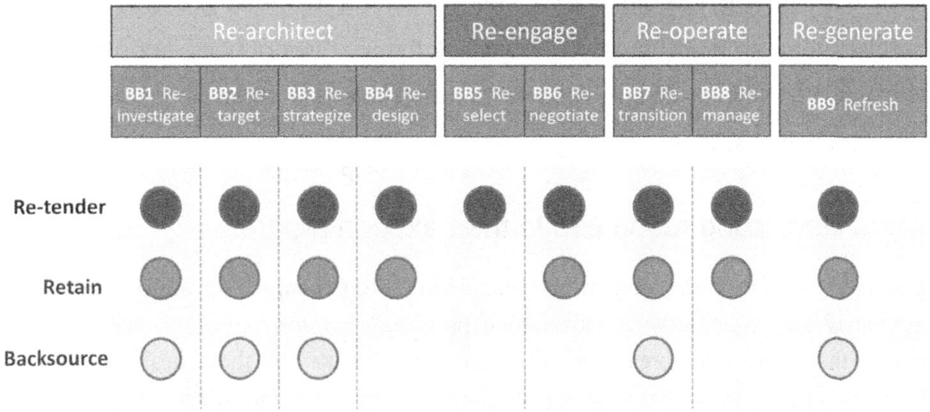

Re-architect				Re-engage		Re-operate		Re-generate
BB1 Re-investigate	BB2 Re-target	BB3 Re-strategize	BB4 Re-design	BB5 Re-select	BB6 Re-negotiate	BB7 Re-transition	BB8 Re-manage	BB9 Refresh

Re-tender ● ● ● ● ● ● ● ● ●

Retain ○ ○ ○ ○ ○ ○ ○ ○

Backsource ○ ○ ○ ○ ○

If the contract is to be retendered, then it is a full lifecycle again, albeit quite different from a first generation lifecycle. For example, BB1: Investigate focuses on harvesting insights from those that have retendered and switched providers, testing switching expectations with stakeholders and updating intelligence on the state of the market (expansions or contractions, new price/performance ratios, new supply chains, etc.).

If the work is brought inhouse, or backsourced, you need to gain acumen on how difficult backsourcing is (BB1) and what it will take (particularly the profiles in BB2). The need for the BB3 transition-in to insourcing is obvious, but the transition-out leaving the next gen option of a return to outsourcing in some form is possibly less so. We have observed so many instances of a next gen backsourcing inevitably leading back out again in due course, that it is wise to plan for it. Negotiating transfers and transition assistance with the provider (BB6), and then executing the transition (BB7) wind up this generation, until BB9 hits again.

If the incumbent is retained, the contract is typically renegotiated (BB6) after re-architecting the deal to reflect changes in the market (BB1), your organization's changed requirements (BB2), and improved practices and contractual documents (BB3 and BB4).

The effort required for executing BB9 decisions appears to surprise many clients, particularly first generation ones. For this reason, the next gen planning is not merely limited to make decisions regarding the next gen options, but planning the next gen lifecycle in detail. Underestimating this is a common problem, as the next case demonstrates.

Case: Dedicating resources to the next gen program

A federal government department was retendering a BPO contract for the HR function. It previously had a single source deal (one provider), but for its second generation had broken the scope into three areas. In order to execute the three deals with limited resources, it adopted a phased rollout approach, disengaging incumbents as the contracts were awarded to other providers. It required a full-time program manager to keep all three projects, the interdependencies, and the teams on track, as well as ensuring lessons were captured from one to the other. This role was not foreseen at the time the rollout was determined, and was not provided for in the budget until the first two deadlines were missed due to poor project management. The role became the heart of the three projects, and the project manager was the only individual with comprehensive knowledge on all three deals, status, decisions, stakeholders, etc.

We have found next generations to be the most exciting for buyers and sellers alike. Very few of the truly innovative and breakthrough outsourcing we have observed over the past quarter of a century occurred in the first generation. Nonetheless, we do know that success is achievable, in every deal and every generation. It takes no more overall effort than managing failure; but puts the effort into the right places at the right time, each generation.

But it appears that clients have to go through a period of hard-earned maturity when it comes to outsourcing, and the lifecycle, to be able to harness real and significant benefits and escape idealized (and often counterproductive) notions. One of our profound frustrations has been to watch clients repeat mistakes that others have made in every phase, in every building block, generation after generation. The next chapter offers seven journeys and lessons, so that you may gain your own insights … and possibly skip a generation of learning.

Chapter 10 Seven Cases - Journeys and Lessons

This chapter relates the lifecycle stories of seven case studies from five different industries. While all the cases were in the IT arena, there is insight to be gained from their stories, no matter what you are thinking of outsourcing.

In each case, the study focused on the single largest contract. Financially, the contracts represented $261 million in total annual spend, with an average value of $37 million per annum. The contracts represented 15% to 80% of each organization's total IT spend. The duration of the contracts was between one and nine years. Scope ranged from the ongoing supply of hundreds of body-shop application coders, to whole-of-IT deals. The geographic coverage ranged from state-based deals to global operations.

Senior managers from each organization were asked to score their organization's performance in each of the lifecycle building blocks on a 5-point Likert scale (1 = conducted very poorly to 5 = conducted very well). They all believed they had performed between the '3' level (conducted adequately) and the '4' level (conducted well). BB9 was the exception, however, in which all case believed they had performed, at best, poorly. Very few even considered or planned for the next generation until it was upon them.

Each case followed a different lifecycle journey. What they all had in common though, was that every individual interviewed would not have undertaken the lifecycle the same way again "*had they only known*" the implication of their choices. Those planning their next generation of contracts planned to do so in a very different way than the first generation. Only one case could be described as a success (in that what was achieved met or exceeded expectations). Accordingly, this chapter presents experiential insight that may help you skip a generation of learning, potentially saving your organization years of avoidable issues.

Case 1 (MAN1)

MAN1 is a national diversified manufacturer of packing products with nearly 8,000 staff. It is one of the world's largest packaging companies, with annual sales of around US$7 billion and over 200 plants in 40 countries. Many manufacturing companies outsourced sub-assembly and finished products long ago, leaving design, branding and marketing inside the client. Thus, outsourcing the entire shop to one provider made sense to MAN1, to enable it to focus on its core business. It never considered alternatives to total outsourcing. After a competitive tendering process, a contract was awarded to a single provider, for which MAN1 was its first local client.

MAN1 had the worst outcomes amongst the seven cases, and terminated two years into the agreement. The causes of the problems experienced by MAN1 was that they picked a new entrant provider without the necessary experience (BB5) "*it was the first deal for them in the country*", did not have an effective contract (BB4) "*it was an ambiguous contract with too many silent areas.*"[105] Nor did MAN1 put in place requisite governance and safeguards (BB3 and BB8). Within 15 months, both parties were in a crisis. The lack of a facilitative relationship (BB8), meant that the deal had deteriorated too far before the parties began being honest with one another. "*Disputes dragged on for 12 months, big and small. We pushed back too late. No resolution process or internal escalation.*"

What is interesting about this case is that the client did not score the process execution poorly in most respects. For instance, they gave themselves a score of 3.5 (between adequate and well) for BB1: Investigate. But they did not know the risks common with an untested provider; particularly when the price was based on theoretical economies of scale from potential new clients, let alone how to mitigate such risks. "*We must take responsibility for the failure factors. We didn't know*

---

[105] The term 'silent areas' refers to issues that should've been addressed in the contract, but are missing.

the risk of the supplier not getting additional clients and the sustainability of their business." Even though MAN1 hired lawyers and consultants to tender, evaluate and write up the deal, the lawyers were inexperienced with outsourcing arrangements and the consultants were "*too driven by methodology.*"

Another example of the apparent incongruity of the perceived conduct of the process was in BB5: Select. Again, a score of 3.4 suggests that the managers thought the process was better than adequate. Yet, the CIO stated, "*Manufacturing organizations are control freaks. We were concerned about having a 'Tier 1' supplier as we would be medium-sized therefore of medium-range priority. We were 50% of our supplier's revenue[106] and we overestimated the value to them of that. You don't have to be a big fish in a little pond to get good service as we've learned with the next round.*" However, they did recognize that the due diligence process (BB5) was done poorly, and this is the stage where the provider's financial viability, amongst other things, should have been assessed.

The only building block that MAN1 scored itself poorly on was BB8: Manage. But this score appears to be predominately based on the provider's behaviors rather than the client's. "*For 15 months it was good, but we did have to talk around potholes. After the supplier hit the first financial year, the consequences of viability hit. They removed all key personnel involved in the initial deal, went to the start of the deal, and reinterpreted everything, making claims from inception. We tried - I was not the CIO for 9 months, 3 days and 4 hours while this dragged on. At that fourth hour, we brought in our MD and CEO to talk to the supplier. From that point on it was negotiating the settlement.*" The contract manager further stated, "*We hit the penalties hard and they hurt. They found that doing MACs[107] in three days was too expensive; and found it cheaper to miss the KPIs.*"

---

[106] Note: The other 50% was from the provider's inhouse operations and not an external client.

[107] MACs are *moves*, *adds*, and *changes* of equipment and services.

From this case, it is apparent that clients may not always understand what a good process is, and why one would want to conduct certain activities. With MAN1's limited exposure to the outsourcing lifecycle, they had no reason to believe that what and how they were doing was in any way high-risk. Furthermore, the technical and legal advisors, in which MAN1 vested a great deal of decision-making capacity, were not adequately experienced. One must be as careful choosing one's advisors as one is in choosing the actual provider/s!

Case 2 (SERV1)

SERV1 is a government-owned business enterprise of 35,000 staff, providing logistic, retailing, and financial services. It outsourced 35% of its total ICT spend. The particular contract in this case was for applications development, implementation, and support functions comprising 43% of the outsourcing spend. It always adopted a multiple-provider approach to outsourcing. This deal was no different in that two providers were given the work. Basically, the CIO made a *"take it or leave it"* offer to two of its 28 incumbent application developers. *"Give me as much labor as I need for a fixed hourly rate of 10% more than what it costs me now inhouse."* They both grabbed it.

SERV1 had a simple process and the CIO's rating for the conduct of the process was the highest of all the cases. There was no competitive tender for the applications work, just the 'take it or leave it' offer. SERV1 had good outcomes across the board according to the CIO, who was the sole person who designed and implemented the deal.

However, although the CIO believed the process was exemplary and the outcomes good across the board, things were not quite as rosy from the staff, provider, and business units' perspectives. Staff and the provider noted that the deal had large problems predominately centered on identifying who was responsible for what. The provider's labor force understood that they were there to develop applications under the direction of the client. The client's staff believed the provider was there to perform the management function, as well as provide applications development methodology. The CIO was aware of this, but blamed the team for *"trying to pawn off their responsibilities."* Furthermore, the business units, accustomed to playing any of the 28 previously engaged providers off against each other for each application, were forced to use the two mandated by the CIO. They looked upon this as IT trying to run the business, and where possible, subverted the agreements and used other providers. Due to this and other factors, the CIO was terminated from the company.

The root cause of the problems can be traced to the Architect Phase - in the CIO's words as being, *"both process and people issues"*. The most significant area of failure was in communication to, and obtaining buy-in from, the senior business executives (BB3). The CIO's perception that IT was a *"colleague to business, business units are not customers"* was not shared by the business units, who viewed IT as supporting the business. The business units were forced to use the contracts against their will, *"giving up control to IT, no longer able to divide and conquer suppliers themselves."* The business units had the providers they preferred, and were forced to change to ones they did not.

The pervasive ambiguity in the deal was the result of an oversimplified process coupled with the client's lack of enough experience with applications development and maintenance activities (BB1). *"You need direct management experience in what you are outsourcing."* Also contributing significantly to the current problems was the incomplete profiling (BB2), which resulted in the incomplete allocation of responsibilities between the parties (BB4). The CIO's hindsight was to *"understand what you are doing in some depth, know the end-to-end processes and technology - and continue to know it."* Clear roles and accountabilities had still not been settled four years after the agreements were signed.

From this case, it was apparent that a quick process and rapid agreement does not necessarily equate to sustainable solutions; and a singular focus on cost can result in insufficient consideration to other important needs by the stakeholders.

Case 3 (MIN1)

MIN1 is the world's largest diversified resources company with some 35,000 employees working in more than 100 mining operations in approximately 20 countries. The Board of this major global resources company issued a directive to all management, *"Get out of anything not core business, and get cash sales for LOBs (lines of business)"*. The Board instructed MIN1 to solicit invitation-only bids from a limited number of large providers, and sold their wholly owned IT subsidiary to the successful provider. In return for a good offer on the purchase, the provider received a long-term deal for all IT services across the globe.

Initial successes were attributed to managing the LOBs' CIOs (BB3) *"outsourcing was not done to them, it was with them,"* eventually getting the right contract management in place *"too late, but one month before signing,"* and dedicating a transition manager to the transition process (BB7). Transition took 3-6 months, but 18-24 months to settle down, prompting the contract manager to recommend to other clients *"Manage the hell out of transition - be ready on day one and start as you intend to go."*

The major difficulty MIN1 encountered was in managing its own efforts. First the contract lost executive sponsorship after the deal was signed as *"the executives believed their job was done"*, highlighting the common belief that the major effort centers around getting signatures on the contract as opposed to managing the arrangement (BB8). MIN1 did not plan the contract management function or retained organization (BB3), replacing the entire IT department over the three years after signing the agreement. *"We recruited new skills rather than train old staff. No worker bees any more. We focus on strategy, business analysis, architecture, and relationship management."* Furthermore, out in the business units, they *"trained LOB IT managers but did not change them"*. In addition, MIN1 had left too much detail out of the contract, in particular the SLA (BB4). The agreement was being renegotiated every day, somewhere in the world. *"Renegotiation is constant. Didn't expect it. Everything needs fixing. We have master terms and 50 contracts."*

In addition, in having the contract covering the globe, the relationship management aspect has made MIN1 much more sensitive to how the provider was assessed (BB8) in different cultures. For example, in South America, *"we give good ratings but bitch about them. We don't want to embarrass them."* In Australia, it is *"a bit of a mate thing, if they like the staff."*

MIN1 rated the Architect Phase as poor to adequate, and this was the worst of the cases. Nonetheless, MIN1 believed that the defects in the early phases of the lifecycle were in the process of being overcome through diligent contract management. The contract management/retained organization (BB8) were *"viewed originally as administration. Immediately became a hub. We now have contract management handbooks, monthly get-togethers, and forums globally. All monthlies are open and transparent."*

Their key lesson involved people and lifecycle, *"different phases need different people and skills,"* and in the future they will *"get the people who will manage the deal in at least six months before and manage stakeholders constantly."* MIN1 believed that the lack of thinking beyond negotiation (BB6) and thus not planning for the later stages caused many of the issues they faced. They were already beginning to fix this lack of forward thinking by beginning the Refresh Phase (BB9) two years before the contract term ends.

Case 4 (GOV1)

GOV1 is responsible for delivery of one of the state's most important services and has 51,000 employees. The Department has been outsourcing for some time, often using multiple providers based on regional capabilities. It typically has 30 contracts in place at any given time covering approximately 60% of its IT budget, but has 120 providers and 300 technicians *"on the books"* from which to choose. Worth noting, in this case, is that the CIO came from a senior role in a major provider. His experience led to the underlying principle that *"you should never outsource knowledge as it is the bridge between business and technology...if you outsource that, the connection is broken."* Accordingly, GOV1 brings in best-of-breed expertise as required, but has a focus with regard to outsourcing on as out-tasking - *"doers only."*

This contract for the installation and support of 40,000 notebooks achieved everything it had set out to do. GOV1 received excellent value for money, although ongoing cost reductions eluded them. Operationally, it was superior to anything they had before. The key to success, they believed, was conducting a competitive tender (BB5) as their price and service expectations were far short of market capabilities (due to lack of BB1 work). Further, the CIO stated that the contract (BB3) was *"well written and fair, user friendly, with no silent areas,"* which is not a something typically said about government contracts. Lastly, success was largely attributed to the hard work of the project team through the Architect and Engage Phases. Moreover, unlike some of the other cases, they picked the right provider who delivered to expectation and to the contract.

The difficulty occurred in the Operate Phase. The users did not know how to utilize the notebooks. Many went unused and most under-utilized. Thus, GOV1 realized the importance of facilitating user efficacy. The 'field of dreams (build it, they will come) did not work in this case. GOV1 attributes this to their own shortcomings in planning and managing the initiative as a whole. As a result, IT people were being used to support the technology adoption process, and not the strategic activities they had hoped.

The biggest surprise happened in year three when the notebooks began needing replacement. The provider's definition of the allowable *"fair wear and tear"* resulted in a $1 million unplanned expenditure which wiped out the entire cost savings achieved in prior years. The comment from the CIO? *"Finances are a rubber band, they snap back on you."* They now plan to fully understand the entire lifecycle regarding what they are outsourcing (BB1). Furthermore, they learnt that they must plan the retained organization function better (BB3), in that it is the client that drives getting outcomes from the deal, not the provider.

Case 5 (GOV2)

GOV 2 is one of a large State department. It employs over 12,000 people directly and over 80,000 people indirectly through a range of largely autonomous organizations responsible for the actual service delivery. GOV2 outsources only 10% of its IT shop and has 225 contracts in place covering applications development and support, as well as systems integration, strategic planning and training. It outsources only where it does not have the capability or the resources. GOV2 chose to create panels of pre-qualified providers and set in place a rule that all providers must be chosen from those panels.

The particular project studied in this case was for the development of new technology to enable the analysis of lab results and fast recall of food and products. It was a one-year deal.

This was a very successful applications development initiative. Success was firstly attributed to the *"gun developers"* at the provider. This is an interesting case in that the client did not look at the price until it picked the best provider (BB5). While most clients would be horrified by this idea, in this case it worked. Hourly rates were agreed with the 132 developers via two panel arrangements that were at least three years in duration (BB3). Thus, GOV2 effectively created its own benchmarking database of market rates for a substantial number of providers (BB1).

What really made this contract work, however, was that the provider was willing to take a significant loss on this project to ingratiate itself with the client. As a result, they became one of GOV2's most preferred developers. Secondly, it was attributed to the attitude of the client (BB8) *"we were proactive; we wanted the supplier to succeed."* Because of this shared objective, the provider's staff were co-located at the client's facilities, creating a seamless project. This then led to direct and open communications as well as frequent meetings being the norm

GOV2 did learn a few lessons from this contract. First, they needed to develop better specifications (BB4). The fixed price/lump sum contract had vague specifications that caused significant scope variations (BB4). While in this case, the provider swallowed the substantial cost overruns, another provider may well not have. Accordingly, project management was slated to be instilled as a core competency within the client (BB3). Second, a large part of this problem was attributed to the contract manager having no IT expertise. Thus choosing the right manager for each contract was another key lesson (BB3). Nonetheless, the contract manager led the way for the client in demonstrating how to develop, and maintain relationships through adversity (BB8), and resulted in the most successful relationship the client has had with a provider.

Case 6 (CON1)

CON1 operates with 10,000 staff in the health industry. CON1 frequently buys and sells businesses. Three years before the this study was conducted; it had three providers providing similar services to three of its major businesses. It believed this was uneconomical and selected the most "*culturally aligned*" incumbent since it wanted a value-add commercial relationship. Most importantly, CON1 wanted consolidation and stability; hence, it chose a large-scope, sole supplier configuration. It went with a six-year deal to get the *"right financial outcome"* (lowest price offered).

CON1, like SERV1, scored the lifecycle as well-conducted (overall score of 3.9). It was worth noting, however, that the results may have also suffered from partial bias because the CIO interviewed was the key decision maker at the onset of the lifecycle. The lifecycle effectively began at BB6: Negotiate, because this was the core skill of the team at the time, "*the team had negotiated many deals, and knew the game.*"

CON1 chose, as the only qualitative criterion (BB5), the most "*culturally aligned*" incumbent since it wanted a value-added commercial relationship. The CIO believed that the poor strategic outcomes, a key area that CON1 had "*wanted to hit goals*," were due to the selection criteria. The problem was attributed to choosing the provider only against their relationship needs, not CON1's technical needs. Hence, they had to "*train the supplier into being good at operations*." Also contributing to the choice not to have a competitive tender was that fact that the CIO had worked with the provider before in other capacities, and liked their disciplined approach. He expected the same behavior, but did not investigate whether this would be the case (BB1); or specify that was what he wanted (BB4). The expected discipline was not evident within the provider's outsourcing business. The technical areas were run as independent silos and did not share accountabilities or integrate processes well. Nonetheless, the CIO believed "*I am better with them than without them*."

The CIO did not go to tender (BB5), although when interviewed, he said he "*would always advise it, but it was cheaper at the time to choose an incumben*t". With the help of its commercial negotiator, CON1 knew market prices outside of current contracts (BB1), and locked in its financial goal of a 25% reduction.

CON1 achieved all of its financial and operational goals, which were the first priority of the deal. The CIO believed CON1 "*may have over-killed KPIs and reporting, but it was necessary at the time to upfront to fully understand the environment*" (BB4). However, it was not easy. Four months into the agreement, major renegotiations started taking place with the provider "*crying poor, crying bad deal*." CON1 had to exercise the rights it had in the contract and force the provider to be more diligent in assessing and auditing, "*teaching them to deal with us in fair manner and that we will hold them to the contract - it's not a club, it's a contract*". As a result, the provider's account manager had to be replaced with one more financially diligent and an additional position created to bridge the provider's gap between its sales and its operations areas.

In addition to the provider lacking the necessary financial skills, the partnering approach that was good in sales and senior management was not translated to operations (BB8). CON1's move from a best-of-breed to a sole provider did enable consistency and stability; however, CON1 was forced to train the sole provider in service operations for months after it became apparent that the provider did not have the required expertise. It had effectively foregone expertise in the scope because of the focus on the value-added relationship it desired.

The saving aspect was that CON1 later employed very experienced people to manage the contract and thorough processes were put in place (BB8). These included thorough reviews of the monthly report, full customer and stakeholder satisfaction assessments with daily polling, and formally structuring the relationship (BB4), *"relationships are temporal, and we wanted better structure."*

The root cause to their problems was in the process. They chose an untested provider for their specific needs without going to market (BB5), did not set up the necessary governance (BB4), and did little operational thinking (BB2) before signing the deal, *"The service provider has gotten us better than where we were, but not where we need to be in the future."*

"Would I do it again? Yes." What they plan to do next time, according to the CIO, is a competitive tender *"taking a careful look at service scope and ensure the right match of scope to the market"* and have shorter duration contracts. Although CON1 went with a six-year deal to get the right financial outcome, the CIO *"would always advise shorter-term contracts even though we needed a six-year term to get the right deal."* Both the CIO and the contract manager emphasized what they learnt most significantly was that it was their people (BB3) and their governance over the deal (BB8) that made the difference.

Case 7 (CON2)

CON2 employs 10,000 people in 40 countries, operating four distinct manufacturing businesses. The push for outsourcing was to sell off non-core businesses, and IT was considered non-core. All the data center resources were sold and contracted back. Like MIN1, configuration was designed to obtain the highest selling price. Accordingly, it was configured as a sole supplier, full scope deal, with all the resources transferred to the provider.

Only one final offer was received for the sale, although many offers came in to provide the services. But it came with a high service fee. This was the provider's first client in the country (hence the offer for the data center as the provider needed the infrastructure). Given the short-term goal of getting cash for the data centre, CON2 went with the offer. Unfortunately for CON2, they never received payment for the data center (the point of the deal). The client was so distracted trying to manage the massive transition exercise (Activity 37), that the payment was forgotten. To finally obtain their payment, CON2 had to sign up for an extension.

Like MAN1, CON2 was also the provider's first commercial client (not a related party) and it was also its largest client. The provider was chosen because the preferred provider ended up not being able to buy the data center, thus the selection criteria were effectively thrown out (BB5). Furthermore, not only was the transition the first for CON2, it was the first for the provider and involved the full transfer of asset, facilities, and staff.

Because of the sole-supplier, large-scope configuration of the deal, according to CON2, "*the supplier behaved as a monopoly, for five years because we had no alternative and they milked us for out of scope work.*" Then, when it came time to make its payment for the data center, the provider forced CON2 to sign up for a two-year extension. When the new CIO and contract manager joined CON2, it was their intention not to renew (BB9). However, they discovered that the extension had already been signed up. To try to get the costs aligned to market prices, they exercised CON2's benchmarking rights in the contract. The study determined that the market rates were 20-35% less. The parties could not resolve their issues and ended up in mediation.

At the end of the extension period, the provider was not successful. Of all its goals, CON2 had only been able to reduce staff numbers during the first generation deal. However, its second generation has been very successful. CON2 executed all the activities in BB9: Refresh very thoroughly as well as BB1 to BB7 of the second-generation lifecycle. In doing so, it realized a 70% cost savings and there were no service issues.

Discussion

In all of these cases the success and failure was attributed to the choices of the decision makers and their depth, or absence, of requisite lifecycle knowledge.

MAN1 initially put the blame on the inexperience of its advisors and the provider, but then ultimately on their own inexperience. The knowledge MAN1 gained in its first generation gave them the necessary ability to hire better advisors and to execute the Regenerate Phase and subsequent lifecycle, with very good results.

SERV1's CIO was very experienced and did the deals quickly, but did not involve other organizational stakeholders. The CIO did not believe business units should be given any choices in the early part of the lifecycle, and this inevitably led to the business units' revolt during BB8. She also saw no need to plan any part of the lifecycle beyond BB6: Negotiate. This case highlights that one person should not act unilaterally when the entire organization is affected, and not assume a deal will be inherently manageable despite no effort to make it so.

MIN1 attributed its positive outcomes to the contract management team that overcame the shortsighted decisions made by others earlier in the lifecycle. Senior management had designed the deal to obtain a large immediate cash injection from selling the IT shop and then contract it back. The contract management team had to redesign and renegotiate the deal every day to make it work.

GOV1's management attributed their problems to their own shortcomings in understanding the full scope of the initiative, as well as the full lifecycle of the assets involved. GOV1 had little understanding of the support the users required and the impact of retiring assets. Thus, they under-scoped and under-staffed the exercise. Substantial unforeseen charges were incurred when old assets had to be replaced, eroding all financial gains and making it a very expensive lesson.

GOV2 put the credit for success on the teams in both parties, both very experienced in different ways, and sharing an inter-party team attitude missing in SERV1. GOV2 was the only case that recognized it did not perform most of BB1: Investigate, in *any* fashion, even with the vast experience it had in managing 225 contracts. It is currently addressing this issue through program management. Its goal is to facilitate institutionalized organizational learning, as opposed to the isolated individual learning that had previously taken place.

CON1 blamed itself for choosing a provider they felt comfortable with, rather than a provider that had proven it could do the job. CON1 gave itself quite high scores for the Architect Phase, implying that management believed they were quite knowledgeable before selecting the provider, and yet they had barely perceptible benefits. Their decision to perform limited architecture work and select a relationship-orientated as opposed to a performance-orientated provider resulted in most of the architecture work being performed after the contract was signed (in BB8). Interestingly, they also scored themselves a perfect score of '5' in every activity in BB8, due to their ability to overcome the resultant issues. However, it was a '5' for *crisis* management, not contract management.

CON2 blamed its failures on the inexperience of the management teams. CON2 did not understand the connect between a high prices for asset sales and the resulting high service cost (tender team), failed to receive payment for the assets sold asset sales payments (transition team) and then signing up to a high-cost extension to obtain the payment (contract management team). This highlights how devastating the lack of management capability can be. But senior management believed the lifecycle ended effectively after BB6: Negotiate and just assumed all would be well. CON2 could only make significant progress in the Regenerate Phase, taking two years to extract itself from the first generation.

PART 3: EMERGING AREAS

A diverse and interesting body of work has emerged over the last few years. In Part 3 of this book, we highlight what we believe will be of greatest interest to organizations that buy and sell outsourcing services.

In Chapter 11, we offer a very personal look at the various personalities of individuals involved with, or managing, contracts. In this chapter, we discuss our research into the personality types (we call them *'contract management styles'*) and what they mean for you, your team, and your organization. There is also the opportunity for you to discover your style through an online instrument.

Chapter 12 focuses on the debate between sole supplier arrangements and using multiple providers in a trend we call *bundling*. Bundling is amassing sizable collections of different, but complementary, scope into larger deals and outsourcing to a single provider.

Innovation has been difficult to achieve with outsourcing. In Chapter 13, we explain why this is so, but more importantly shows how it can be achieved.

Offshoring trends and tales make up Chapter 14. Offshoring is *the* trend in outsourcing. While the cost savings from offshoring can be immense, it is surprisingly difficult to choose which country, which operating model, and which practices to adopt.

Chapter 15 explores a number of current trends we have observed and researched ranging from new organization structures sparked off by outsourcing, to technologies in the spotlight, as well as looking at some fascinating rising markets.

Chapter 11 The Human Side - Contract Management Styles

"I have never in my life learnt anything from any man who agreed with me."

Dudley Field Malone

Why do some people in the parties to a deal, the client and the provider, not get along? We can have a good deal, a fair contract... and yet conflict arises. This conflict can become quite personal at times. Such conflict is not limited to just relations between the two parties, for it can also exist between the individuals within a party as well.

A functioning relationship is an amorphous, ambiguous, but all-encompassing critical factor in the success, or otherwise, of any outsourcing contract. Although many business writers talk about the value of relationships between organizations, it is common knowledge (and commonsense), that relationships are between people and not entities. Nonetheless, there continues to be an almost ideological belief that a contract is simply a transaction that involves negotiating an agreement between organizations, and once signed, all the hard work has been done.

However, contracts are seldom as simple as one might wish; nor are they just a single transaction. They are complex strategies for managing the delivery of organizational needs through external parties; parties comprised of people who are just as likely to have goals that conflict, as they are to have objectives in common.

This research investigates the different values and behaviors (what we call *'styles'*) held and exhibited by the people that develop and manage contracts, based on a study of 1460 participants who completed an online profiling instrument during a two-year period from 2011 to 2013, to explain why some of the conflict exists and offer solutions.

The identification and definition of these styles were developed in response to our think tank session with the London School of Economics some 10 years ago as an explanation as to why clients with similar contracts with similar providers can have radically different approaches, degrees of satisfaction, and results. A taxonomy of six distinct styles emerged from the observed values and behaviors exhibited by the people that develop and manage contracts with our immense case base. The styles model was then refined and tested over the years, cumulating with the development of an online profiling instrument in 2011.

An initial study was conducted at that time with the Chartered Institute of Purchasing and Supply (CIPS) with nearly 700 of its members.[108] Over 750 non-CIPS profiles have since been completed as at the end of 2013, including various operating divisions of banks, defence, city governments, and police organizations.

The bulk of participants were from the client/purchaser (86%), with the remaining 14% being providers. Of those representing the 'buy side', it was fairly evenly split between those working in the government sector (53%) and those in the commercial sector (47%).

Participants ranged from new trainees to managing directors and everything in between, with the greater part being low to middle management (shown to be critical in outsourcing in Chapter 3).

---

[108] Cullen, S. (2012) *A study of contract management styles in Australia 2011-12: The different values and behaviours exhibited by the people who develop and manage contracts*, Chartered Institute of Purchasing and Supply, Melbourne.

11.1 About the Styles

Each of the six styles (Figure 11-1) will now be described. Before we begin, however, it is crucial to understand that the point of distinguishing these styles is not to say one is bad and another good. Each style is useful in different circumstances and in different contracts. The principal aspect of these styles is that, irrespective of what a person's official job is within an organization, that person is more likely to naturally behave in his/her preferred style, without being instructed to do so.

Figure 11-1: The Six Contract Management Styles

All six styles are useful in different ways, and one style is not necessarily better than another. Deals are unlikely to fall apart because one of these styles is missing from your organization, or from that of the other party.

Nonetheless, if your people hold a certain set of values, but their colleagues in the other party have a different set altogether, then misunderstandings are inevitable. Left unresolved, these differences can fester. Conflicts are the common result. Such style conflicts consume scarce time and resources, because everyone is right. The relationship should be good, problems should be solved, records should be kept, things should consistently improve, information should drive decisions, and risks should be mitigated.

But no one person can exhibit all of these styles all of the time. Most people strongly favor one or a few styles. A balanced portfolio of styles in the teams of both parties will yield outcomes that are more productive for both in the long term, and greater satisfaction between the parties as a whole.

Relationship Developer

The *Relationship Developer* values and facilitates trust, respect, and interpersonal relationships. Their core belief is that interpersonal relations, not contracts, make or break deals. A good relationship yields returns for Relationship Developers in the form of the ability to discuss matters in an open and candid way.

Relationship Developers tend to be known for concentrating more on what other styles might consider social activities (lunches, going for coffee, and the like) with stakeholders in both parties, other third parties, and indeed any party involved in the contract. It is not unknown for Relationship Developers to make friends within the other party; friendships that often outlast the contract.

Amongst our participant group, this was the strongest style, both on average and as a lead style. It was valued nearly equally by both parties (but to a lesser extent in the government sector). However, only a third of individuals had this as their lead style, which is why all contracts are not (what other styles may view) a 'hug fest'.

Problem Solver

Problem Solvers make things happen and fix problems. They view issues as 'hiccups' not obstructions, and like to break down barriers that get in the way of what they believe are real results. This individual rarely cares who is to blame for something going wrong; they just want to get it fixed. They often have a natural team approach, rather than an 'us versus them' outlook in their desire to have things working as smoothly as possible.

On average, this style was preferred slightly less than Relationship Developer. However, providers tended to have twice the rate of Problem Solvers than do clients. Thus, providers are likely to exhibit greater, in what a client might interpret as reactive (if not frantic) conduct while they 'put out the fires' that inevitably occur during contracts. Meanwhile, providers can be equally frustrated with clients that make every issue the provider's' problem to solve despite the client often being part of the problem as well as part of the solution.

Organizer

Organizers maintain better records, audit trails, controls, plans, and processes than the other styles. This individual often keeps detailed records of any meetings they go to, commonly has a daily diary in which they record conversations (or 'file notes'), and frequently keeps hard copies of emails as well as electronic backup. They believe in good processes, systems and documentation, which is important in contract administration. However, this can be almost to a fault, holding up matters until the proper paperwork has been completed. Organizers spend a fair bit of time developing and/or getting administrative systems working and strongly wish that everyone were more compliant with it.

Organizer was a moderate style (not strong or weak). It was the third preferred style on average, and the lead style of nearly a quarter of participants (mostly on the client side).

Clients (particularly in the government sector) had three times the extent of Organizer type behaviors and beliefs than did providers. Organizers are likely to exhibit greater, in what a provider might interpret as, possibly controlling or overly administrative conduct when they try to impose order and controls over the chaos that Organizers often find (not only with providers, but within their own organizations).

Entrepreneur

Entrepreneurs seek innovation, better ways of doing things, and long-term potential out of the relationship. This individual is a natural disruptor; always querying why, *"why can't we do x?"'* and *"why not try y?"* An Entrepreneur would rarely, if ever, accept a justification of *"that's how we've always done it"* as a reason to continue to do something a certain way. Without an Entrepreneur pushing for change, you may find that your deals, and how they work in practice, becoming quite stagnant.

This was a moderate style, on average. But clients tended to have 1.5 times the preference for this as a lead style compared to providers. At the clients' senior levels, this was more acute with over 35% having Entrepreneur as their lead style (while the managers and front line had only 15%).

If you are a provider, it is worthwhile to understand your clients may be expecting greater degrees of innovation, and certainly continuous improvement, at a minimum. Because it is a *value*, the client may not have made those expectations explicit in the contract. And the more senior the person at the client, the more this becomes important, which is why we discuss our research into effective leadership pairing in Chapter 13.2 on collaborative innovation.

Scanner

Scanners are well networked/connected, natural explorers, who may know many details of other agreements and relationships. They are driven by their desire to be as informed as possible. People might be surprised as to what this individual knows, as the Scanner seems to be familiar with a lot about, say, the personal circumstances of people. To non-Scanners, this might be gossip, but to Scanners it is all part of the knowledge base.

They are characterized either by a keen use of the internet, mostly in their own time, and/or by having a large number of acquaintances from which they source and share information.

Because they are natural information seekers, they are natural bench-markers. In fact, they may already have done so informally. So you may hear the Scanner on your team saying things like, *"did you know that the other outfit paying $x and we're paying $y?"*, or *"how come our competitor has ten people managing their contract and we have only two?"*

This was one of the lesser styles present in both clients and providers. Providers tended to have 1.5 times the preference for Scanning, as you might expect due to a greater desire to be aware of what the competition is up to, what is happening with their clients, what trends are in the market, and so on .

Monitor Protector

Monitor Protectors believe that their organization must be protected from the other party. They focus on what risks the other party brings to the deal and whether the other party is conforming to the contract. If responsible for drafting the contract, they may prepare a biased agreement in favor of the party they represent. If in charge of the contract, they prefer to focus on the other party's performance and non-compliance, rather than that of their own organization.

Occasionally, a Monitor Protector's behavior may resemble that of a bully; being close to recriminations and threats. However, more commonly, the behavior will be a firm and unyielding position. The other party's concerns and issues will generally be considered as being "*their problem, not ours.*"

Monitor Protector was least preferred style for both parties on average and was the style of last resort for over 40% of people involved in contracts.

Still, clients had over three times the degree of lead Monitor Protector type behaviors and beliefs than did providers. Clients are more likely to exhibit adversarial conduct in the eyes of providers. As you might expect, clients can be a bit suspicious of providers, wondering just how much money is being 'made off' them and how. They may feel a need to protect themselves from what they believe is a real risk of opportunistic behavior. Providers may find it more constructive to understand, and possibly empathize, with Monitor Protector behaviors and not take it as a reflection on the provider itself.

Research Results

Overall, there is a clear pattern that emerged amongst the 1460 participants that work with contracts, as shown in Figure 11-2.

Figure 11-2: Average Style

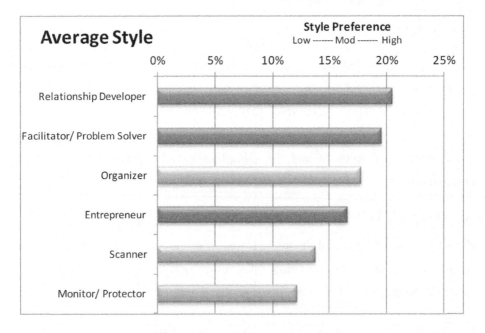

The two most common styles among the survey participants were, on average, that of Relationship Developer and Problem Solver. These two styles often work hand-in-hand to create sustainable relationships and solutions.

The next set of styles - the moderate styles of Organizer and Entrepreneur - do not work so well hand-in-hand. Entrepreneurial behaviors can disrupt the systems that Organizers so highly value. And if you want to see an Entrepreneur get angry, just say, "*We do that because that's the system.*"

The least prevalent styles were the Scanner and Monitor Protector styles. This means behaviors regarding the seeking of external information and trying to protect one's own organization from the other party were the least common. In fact, as the next discussion reveals, very few people use these as their lead style, while they generally tend to be the last style a person would choose to adopt.

An individual's lead style reflects the set of behaviors and values that are the most dominant. It is likely that the lead style would not only be employed first, but also more often than the other styles.

While the vast majority of people (80%) had only one lead style, one in five had two equally lead styles. Three lead styles were present in only 2%.

As shown in Figure 11-3, the most popular lead style was that of *Relationship Developer*. Over a third of people manage their contracts, first and foremost, from the perspective of the relationship. In fact, it was the only style preferred by 2% to the exclusion of nearly every other style.

Figure 11-3: Lead Styles

A bit over a fifth of people involved with contracts want things done systematically, and with good records; these are the Organizers. But since the majority of other people value such things to a lesser degree, this undoubtedly leaves a lot of administrative work for the Organizers.

Problem Solver was next most popular style. Generally, people with this as their lead style want issues resolved quickly. They are likely to become annoyed with other's slow reactions, even aversion, to problem solving.

The Scanner and Monitor Protector styles were rare as lead styles. People working with contracts are unlikely to be interested in information (Scanner) or risk and protection (Monitor Protector), in the first instance. In fact, those two styles were the least exhibited by either party (Figure 11-4) and Monitor Protector was the only style almost completely absent from some people (representing 6%).

Figure 11-4: Least Preferred Styles

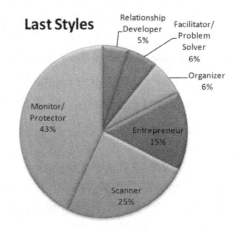

The style that is last on most people's list (Figure 11-4) is the Monitor Protector. Over 40% of people indicated they would use the Monitor Protector style as a measure of last resort. Of least concern is how much the organization is protected against possible adverse acts of the other party or transferring risk to the other party. Ensuring the relationship is okay, problems are solved, things are organized, benchmarks show good results, and improvements are achieved are all of greater importance.

The other least common last style was Scanner, but to far lesser degree to that of Monitor Protector. External information was of least importance to one in four people working with contracts, who would rarely seek benchmarks, outside data, independent facts, and the like.

11.2 Comparing the Styles between Organizations

We now compare different groups: the first being an exploration of the differences between clients/purchasers and providers, the second delving into the differences between the two client sectors: commercial and government.

Between the Parties

Both parties led most often with the Relationship Developer style that promotes rapport between them. In theory then, there should be no reason why parties should not get along well. Unfortunately, that is where the similarities end.

The differences between client/purchasers and providers became apparent when we looked at what styles the parties might first exhibit; their lead styles (Figure 11-5).

Some of the possible tensions between the parties can be explained by the style that tends to be exhibited first or most. What is striking in Figure 11-5 is that providers with Problem Solver as their lead style and clients with Organizer as their lead style outnumber the other party by 2:1.

Figure 11-5: Lead Styles of the Parties

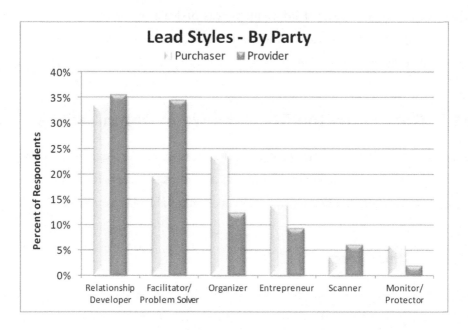

Because of differing values, both parties may initially display what the other sees as undesirable behavior. If the provider is focused on solving today's problems, a request from the client's Organizers to complete a report, finish entering data into a system, or even produce an invoice ASAP would not be welcome at best, and exasperating at worst. But, the client may just want things done systematically, with good records; things that Organizers see as a basic capability, and the lack of doing so a form of incompetence.

Meanwhile, providers, as the Problem Solvers, are far too busy solving the problems. The constant problems and frantic solutions can make providers look chaotic and out of control to the 'control and order' Organizer.

Furthermore, clients may want continuous innovation while exposing the provider to higher risk; a situation resulting from the combination of greater lead Entrepreneurs and Monitor Protectors. This can be commercially unviable for many providers.

Between Purchasing Sectors

Client/purchasers were comprised of two sectors: the commercial/ private sector (47%) and the government/public sector (53%).

Figure 11-6 shows their lead styles. What stands out immediately is how much the commercial sector contains Relationship Developers relative to the government sector (and providers). The relative lower level or interest in relationship development, coupled with greater perceived bureaucratic requirements, explains why some providers avoid government tenders and contracts. It represents a different value system, and a way of doing things that some providers cannot, or do not want to, work with.

The government sector is not wrong, of course, just different. There is, in most government entities, an obligation to not appear to favor any particular provider in addition to maintaining evidence of how it spends the taxpayers' money. This requires provider relations to be at arm's-length (but not necessarily unfriendly) and requires extensive recordkeeping and reporting.

Figure 11-6: Sector Lead Styles

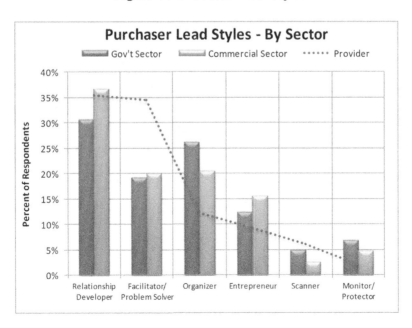

11.3 What this Means for You, Your Team, and Your Organization

For You

Each person that completes the online profile[109] receives a 16-page report discussing the effect of each style in depth and compares his/her profile to that of clients and providers. However, even without completing a profile, you can still gain valuable insights from this discussion of styles by becoming aware of them and appreciating their differences.

For example, you may be able to guess what your lead style is just from reading this chapter. You may also be able to speculate the style of others. Most importantly, you may now be able to recognize possible sources of conflict with other people, within your organization and within the other party.

It may not be a simple personality clash. It could just be that your opposite number holds very different values to yours, when it comes to managing contracts. You may be expecting the other person to behave in accordance with your values, and not his or her own (and likewise they with you)

Here are just a few examples:

- If you are primarily a **Relationship Developer** and your counterpart is a **Monitor Protecto**r, you may never get along. Your offers to lunch will be rebuked; which to you might feel as a personal rejection but to them is merely good policy. Work within their rules; they are quite willing to act professionally, and even be friendly, but they do not want to be your friend.

---

[109] If you would like to complete a profile (for a nominal fee), see www.contractmanagementstyle.com

- If you are a **Monitor Protector** and your counterpart is an **Entrepreneur**, all their great ideas will be met with skepticism. You probably would prefer if they just did the job they are supposed to do and forgot about all the attempts add 'adding value' (or, as you see it, 'increasing risk'). But some of that value just might be real and the risks perhaps only possible, not probable. Spend some time listening to their proposals; some of them just might work.

- If you are primarily an **Entrepreneur** but your counterpart is an **Organizer**, you may be frustrated by their lack of innovation, feel they cannot see the big picture, being too focused on minutiae, and are a burden to a progressive deal. But they can help you see systems issues with your new ideas; a good thing if you want them implemented well.

- If you are primarily an **Organizer** and your counterpart is a **Problem Solver**, you may be constantly frustrated by how sloppy and disorganized they are, seemly running frantically around slapping bandages on everything. However, they are fixing things, and you may not be.

- If you are primarily a **Problem Solver** and your counterpart is a **Scanner**, you might wonder why they seem to spend so much time getting seemingly useless information when there is so much to be done on this deal ... now. Just what is it they do all day? Probably finding out things you do not know. Channel that energy to things that would be useful to know.

For Your Team

A team's style depends on the styles of its members, especially those of its formal leader and any other members who are particularly influential.

Teams with different styles tend to operate with very different behaviors and have quite different atmospheres. For example, Monitor Protector teams are more likely to exhibit many asserting/ defending interactions with others and to have an intense and 'edgy' feel. In Entrepreneur teams, in contrast, people tend to build on one another's ideas, with an atmosphere that is more exploratory and open-minded (and higher risk).

Having dominance in a few styles is very common, because managers often hire people with similar beliefs and behaviors like themselves. Any norm or pattern, however, should not be inferred as being 'correct'. It is ideally a style chosen as a strategy, not one that has just been allowed to occur.

When faced with a wide range of lead and least preferred styles, it is important not to let the dominant styles dictate how the team functions. This can cause personality conflicts in which team members can misunderstand, even resent, teammates with styles different then their own. Conflict between styles can become personalized when people focus their energy on what is wrong with each other, rather than appreciate the different ways to view a situation.

Studies of unsuccessful business decisions have shown that they all had something in common.[110] It was stifling dissenting views and dismissing evidence when things were not working as they were 'supposed to'. Accordingly, the people in your team who may be able to learn the most from each other are the opposites. Utilize the diversities within the team, not the similarities.

A person in charge of others needs to be aware that his/her lead style may different from the people they manage; and may in fact be the least preferred style of the team. That is not a bad thing; in fact, is probably quite the reverse. Leaders can learn as much from their staff as vice versa. And each style offers much in the way of contribution to a team.

---

[110] See for example, Finklestein, S. (2003) *Why Smart Executives Fail*. New York: Portfolio.

For example:

- It is important to have a **Relationship Developer** in your team who can gain the trust and personal respect of individuals in the other party. This is the 'schmoozer' in your team, whose building of relationship capital will help to overcome inevitable bumps along the life of a contract.

- All organizations benefit by having the solutions designed by a **Problem Solver** incorporated into future contracts. Doing so makes for constructive contracts, not just documents used solely for disputes and possible court action.

- **Organizer** is an important style for someone in your team to have. Many try to assign the record-keeping role to a team member, but if they are not naturally meticulous with a history of unswerving dedication to the audit trail, then records are more likely to be haphazard despite the best of intentions.

- An **Entrepreneur** sees the most potential in a commercial relationship and is the driver for continuous improvement. It is rare to find a deal that does not need, or will not benefit, from continuous improvement. Yesterday's solutions rarely will work for all time.

- Because **Scanners** are natural information seekers, curious about many aspects of any particular deal, they are natural benchmarkers (for practices, costs, risk, contract clauses, people, etc.).

- A **Monitor Protector** is a useful part of the team and you would not want to enter into a contract without someone having this as a key style to ensure your organization is not unnecessarily exposed to risk.

For Your Organization

Some organizations have a preferred style, and explicitly so. With others, it may not be as unequivocal, but it soon becomes apparent to all that work there, and to those who work with it.

It is important for your organization to consider whether it wishes to have a preferred style (or set of preferred styles). One could argue that any organization requires all six styles without any one being dominant. This might be true if it has many different types of contracts, with many diverse parties, facing many different situations, across a wide range of industries. However, given the particular kind of contracts, parties, and circumstances your organization is managing, it may be more sensible to have certain lead styles over others.

Each style has different 'tools of the trade'. With 'style as a strategy', your organization can put in place efficient and appropriate techniques, frameworks, templates, and training. Letting individuals 'go native' on his/her particular part they play in the lifecycle, based on their personal preferences, leaves too much to chance. Clear direction, coupled with useful tools, offers a much higher prospect that your organization's goals will be accomplished. Moreover, it also enables you organization to select providers that are a better fit to the way your organization wishes to engage and work with provider markets.

More importantly, it allows alignment amongst the various 'silos' in your organization. Many organizations employ a 'silo approach' to manage the contract lifecycle, where different people or groups handoff a deal to another as a contract progresses from 'womb to tomb'. For example, in a client, this could be management deciding what it wants to go to market for, the legal team drafting the contract, procurement running a tender process, and finally, operations managing the contract. In a provider, the handoff is often from pre-sales (which develops relationships and solutions), to sales (which quotes), to the operations team (which delivers).

As the styles can be quite different between these various groups, the deliverables produced by one area and handed over to another may be of little perceived use or value, with possible adverse consequences.

For example, consider the situation that arises when an Organizer forces a (usually) ill-fitting suite of template processes and documents onto Problem Solvers and Entrepreneurs. They may comply initially, and then get on with the 'real business' of making things work and surreptitiously introduce creative approaches (both large and small) after the Organizer's influence has diminished. The templates are treated as a burden one must bear, not something that creates value.

At the very least, there needs to be a strong alignment of styles between the people involved during the lifecycle or the return on the investment made by your organization in getting to contract and then getting results from those contracts is likely to be much lower than you had expected. Discarding the investment made by people upstream by those downstream is far too common. But upstream people have not created anything that meets the needs of anyone downstream.

Contracts, for example, can reflect the styles of the majority of people who then have to work within the parameters of these contracts.

The need of all Relationship Developers is to have good communication, a solid working relationship, and to build interpersonal trust. Organizations that recognize the importance of relationships have adopted the Governance Charter (a contract schedule specifying the inter-party management arrangement) and the Contract Scorecard, which measures the health of the relationship (do not confuse this with a satisfaction survey).

Problem Solvers require 'reality-based contracts'; ones reflecting common sense and realistic solutions to frequently occurring issues. Unfortunately, existing contracts and templates are rarely updated to reflect the successful solutions put in practice. Even more unfortunate, future contracts are often based on old contracts or templates that did not work so well before and will not start to work well now. Reasonable and pragmatic contractual solutions that work for both parties can certainly become the norm in all your organization's contracts once a solution-orientated approach is introduced rather than a fear driven approach.

And let us not forget the Entrepreneurs. Continuous improvement and innovation is much more than current contracts emphasize, let alone articulate, in a practicable way. This certainly does not need to be the case, as there are relatively simple ways to specify innovation as a contract requirement, and effective ways to measure it as an outcome.

Chapter 12 To Bundle or Not to Bundle?

"It is better to debate a question without settling it than to settle a question without debating it."

Joseph Joubert

12.1 Introduction

Choosing the appropriate sourcing model is a critical component in the planning of outsourcing. Multi-sourcing, or best-of-breed sourcing, is a strategy in which a client engages multiple providers. Best-of-breed sourcing recognizes that providers have different strengths and weaknesses and carves out work best suited for each of them. All outsourcing markets continue to grow through multi-sourcing (which for over 20 years has always been the dominant practice) but now bundling work into a sole-source agreement is an important and rising trend.

We have previously discussed these two options, Sole Supplier and Multiple Supplier arrangements, in the Configuration chapter (see Attribute #2: Supplier Grouping), as well as other forms of how providers are grouped and ungrouped. We are expanding the discussion in an entire chapter here because the debate about whether to use a few wide-scope providers or many specialists has existed since outsourcing began. This debate will never be settled because there are equal pros and cons for either option. In this chapter, we explore what leads clients to choose one over the other, and why some clients go even further by packaging up scope across previously disparate 'silos' so it can be done by a single provider.

While multi-sourcing helps clients access best-of-breed providers and mitigate the risks of reliance on a single provider, it also means increased transaction costs as clients manage more providers. Multi-sourcing also means that *providers* incur more transaction costs. Providers must bid more frequently because contracts are shorter, providers face more competition because smaller-sized deals means that more providers qualify to bid, and providers need to attract more customers in order to meet growth targets.

Enter bundling. This is a technique for reducing the number of providers by aggregating scope into a single contract with a 'one-stop-shop' provider. The provider does not subcontract any scope nor manage any subcontractors.

It involves defining an optimal mix of services purchased from the same provider where synergies and efficiencies are sought in end-to-end processing, governance, relationship management, cost, and performance. On this definition, taking IT as an example, there can be bundling *within IT* (e.g. the same provider for infrastructure, applications, and development). Likewise with business services, there can be bundling *within BPO* (e.g. training, development, and payroll in the HR function), or *across ITO and BPO services* (e.g. procurement, IT applications, and selected HR activities). It is not limited to merely service scope, of course. Regions (geographic scope) can be bundled and multiple business units (recipient scope) can be packaged up as well.[111]

As you can see, the possible choices for bundling are considerable - making these complex decisions with important cost and operational consequences. Moreover, there are question marks about whether providers have developed sufficient capability to take on large-scale bundled deals. And how can a manager understand the economic payoffs of sole-source bundling versus multi-sourcing?

---

[111] See the Configuration chapter, Attribute #1: Scope Grouping, for a discussion on the three types of scope: service, geographical and recipient.

Therefore, the key sourcing issue before all clients is, "*How do we make the optimal sourcing decision, given the range of options now available internally and in the marketplace?*" We think we have found an informed answer to this perennial management riddle.[112]

We studied over 1850 outsourcing contracts, and carried out interviews with 69 leading clients and providers in ITO and BPO services. At the macro level we found IT, infrastructure, and applications bundling accounting for over 70% of bundling activity, followed by bundled BPO, (e.g. billing, finance and accounting) representing some 15% of bundling activity. As yet, we found few clients who outsourced both their main IT together with BPO to the same provider.

We uncover the key role that 20 drivers play when considering bundled or unbundled services. These drivers are grouped into the following five areas that form the basis of our decision-making matrix:

1. client factors,
2. relational factors,
3. provider market,
4. capabilities factors, and
5. cost effectiveness characteristics.

From the research, we also distilled five client profiles of those clients more, or less, likely to buy bundled services. These are:

- Strategic Explorer,

- Conservative,

---

[112] A detailed discussion of our latest findings on bundling appears in Lacity, M. and Willcocks, L. (2012) *Advanced Outsourcing: From ITO to BPO and Cloud Services*, chapter 6, Palgrave, London. The research was carried out by Leslie Willcocks of LSE, Ilan Oshri of Loughborough University and John Hindle of Accenture, who sponsored the research.

- Operational Exploiter,

- Experimenter, and

- Multisourcer.

We will examine these client profiles later in this chapter. Let's first look at the trade-offs managers typically have to make when looking at the options, and then report what we have discovered when multi-sourcing or sole-source bundling is the optimal decision. There are some worrying findings in here, but there is an answer, and, indeed, a summary matrix to help you make the right choice.

12.2 Assessing the Trade-Offs - Myths and Reality

What are the common trade-offs clients consider and how far are these based in reality? The major concerns are:

- Control - does multi-sourcing or bundling give you more control? How?

- Risk - is going with one provider more risky or less risky?

- Incremental or big bang - should you grow into bundled outsourcing or can it be done in one deal?

- Tidy then outsource - should you straighten out our technology and processes first, or does bundling obviate this need?

- Cost and operational gains - is there a big difference in the costs of management for bundling versus multi-provider and sole-sourcing? Does a primary contractor model solve the problem?

On control, multi-sourcing may give a client more power and more control over each provider, with less dependence on each. However, increased control comes at a price in terms of increased management cost, time, effort, and measurement. At the same time, an argument can be made that bundling makes a client larger and more important to a provider, thus making the provider more responsive.

In multi-provider environments, the management capability needed to manage outsourcing regularly costs between 4-10% of annual contract value. Our recent analysis finds these management costs for offshoring to be even higher - to be between 12-15% of annual contract value. Wherever multi-sourcing governance moves up the outsourcing agenda, we are seeing these costs also rise further.

On risk, there is more risk in depending on a single provider; much depends on the provider's capabilities and financial strength, for example. However, with multi-sourcing the risks move into other areas, including service cracks between providers, security issues, hidden costs with continued monitoring and renewal of contracts, and possible replacement of providers. One must also ask how big the risks are with bundling or not bundling relative to the other risks a business will take in its main line of operations. In other words, a client will often impose - inconsistently - a higher standard of risk for a back office deal than even for a strategic business initiative.

On incremental bundling (aggregating scope over time to a single provider), we found many organizations taking this route over time, but we also found several organizations gaining from making a major one-off bundling deal, though this was a relative rarity when it came to complex arrangements. Much depends on the ability of both the client and provider to manage such arrangements. Such capabilities are not yet commonly held.

A related approach that we have seen in clients is where they have straightened out their own processes first, sometimes through a shared services route, and then sought a bundled outsourcing arrangement. This is a more tactical route that mitigates some of the risk of outsourcing inefficient services and processes. However, the risk may well be worth taking, if it saves time and cost, as we saw in some cases. On cost, the cost gains of bundling two or more business functions (e.g. IT and HR, or procurement and HR), rather than outsourcing them separately to different providers can be of the order of 10-15%. This may well be where a provider can bring in a more standardized management and measurement process, and can truly implement standardized processes and services.

A head contractor model can be a halfway house. But it is unlikely to achieve significant cost savings, or process standardization or innovation over a bundled outsourcing arrangement. The head contractor model also runs its share of risks and has not always had a happy history. Our own research points to cases where management costs were not noticeably lower than other models and best practices were not shared between the different providers. In fact, one of our global studies involving 877 contracts ranging in value from $US200,0000 to $1 billion per annum showed that the head (or prime) contractor model, has the least client satisfaction of all the possible supplier grouping options (Figure 12-1).[113] This study also showed that unbundled contracts, using multiple providers and panels, yielded greater satisfaction than bundled contracts using sole providers or primes.

Figure 12-1: Supplier Grouping Satisfaction

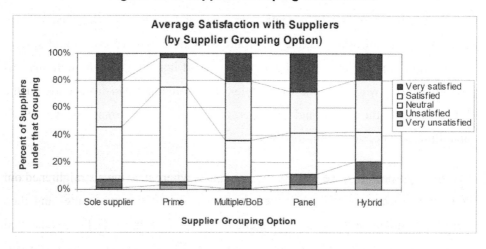

So when does bundled outsourcing make operational sense?

---

[113] Cullen, S. (2006) "The Configuration Concept: Supplier Grouping", *Sourcing & Vendor Relationships Executive Update*, Cutter Consortium, Vol 7: No 18.

The major advantages experienced with bundling include:

- Simplify governance process and points of contact, thus reducing duplicate management layers, processes, and costs.

- Reduce operating risk by limiting points of failure.

- Standardize and simplify operations.

- Achieve operational synergies across business processes and between a business process and technology infrastructures.

- Reduce provider costs/prices through simplified management and scale economies.

- Support the pre-existing standardizing technology and process trajectory.

- Ability to drive larger holistic back-office change.

However, this does not make bundled outsourcing a 'no-brainer', far from it. These gains are possible, but a great deal really depends on the maturity and capabilities of both client and provider to deliver on the promises inherent in the bundling deal they go for.

12.3 Is Bundling the Answer?

Our research provides some key insights on this question, foremost being whether the parties have the maturity required. The maturity of the client to manage innovation and providers has a big influence on their ability to contemplate bundled services. This was the case with a major oil company and a telecom multinational, both mature and with their inhouse capability sorted, and both willing to bundle services as they felt necessary going forward. Secure in their ability to manage and implement sourcing strategy, they had high propensity to buy bundled services if they could find the right provider and right risk/reward structure. Mature clients will look at bundling if they can get innovation (i.e. they have high ambition in these sort of deals) *and* if they can shift risk to, or share it with, their providers.

More mature clients all emphasize the relationship. If you know them well and the track record is okay to good, you are more likely to go for bundled services. Good relationships and track records lead to incremental buying of further services.

However, we are finding that clients do not know how to evaluate getting value from bundled services. This is quite an important, if worrying finding. We would suggest that this inhibits their ability to identify the value of the bundled proposition and pushes them into uncoupling services. Clients need some way to identify, in detail, the synergies from bundled services. In interviewing one European and one Indian-based major provider, we found that they also struggled to identify the financial advantages accruing from both technical synergies (production costs) and from common management arrangements (transaction costs); although they could point to how such financial advantages could arise.

As a result, with bundled services, a client will tend to take an even more political than economic approach to decision-making. In other words, lack of reliable economically-based reasons means decisions will be based on individual judgment and political influences. Thus, bundling often occurs where there is peer pressure, or a strong and large-scale change agenda, or a belief that it will be cheaper.

Some clients did bundle, as start-ups or to achieve a fast change, but were immature in their ability to manage outsourcing. They subsequently had poor experiences. One consequence was a move to multi-provider sourcing in their second and third generation outsourcing arrangements. Some of these organizations are now rethinking the extent of their multiple-provider sourcing.

A bundled service proposition really does need a Board member from the client to drive it. One clear, ancillary finding was that relationship factors received strong independent endorsement but that relationships needed to be 'many-to-many' between client and provider with lots of touch points and 'glue'.

12.4 Drivers of Bundling/Unbundling Decisions

In what follows, we pinpoint the 20 key drivers that determine whether a bundled or unbundled decision is the optimal route for a client. From this, and as a way of consolidating the research lessons, we provide a weighted 20-factor framework to enable clients make more effective decisions in this important area. Finally, we detail from our research base five client profiles, distilling the alternative routes organizations have been pursuing into bundled services.[114]

In Figure 12-2, we grouped the key factors shaping bundling and unbundling decisions into five major areas. Let us look at each of these factors in more detail.

Figure 12-2: Main Factors in Bundled/Unbundled Outsourcing Decisions

---

[114] A note on the research. We analyzed the literature and our own research work. We placed a model in front of outsourcing specialists to gain feedback. From this, we arrived at a provisional list of *factors*. For each factor, we established rationale as to why each factor would influence buying behavior from prior research. From our database of outsourcing arrangements, we selected 300 deals with sufficient data to draw conclusions on all 20 factors. Each factor was weighted in importance in that deal. For the 300-deal sample, we then found the median for each factor. We tested the factors against 69 interviewees and finalized the framework. We found many cases where certain factors outweighed others in different ways than the ones expressed here, so the median was more robust than the mean in the presence of outlying values.

12.4.1   Client Characteristics

There are eight factors comprising Client Characteristics. Their combined weight of 40% is because client factors were found to be the most influential of the five groupings shown in Figure 12-2.

The first factor is whether the **decision-making process** is centralized or decentralized. A more centralized process favors a bundled service decision. It is interesting to note that organizations that multi-source wrestle continually with the issue of needing to simplify and coordinate governance and decision-making, but while decision-making processes remain more fragmented, bundled service decisions, especially across ITO and BPO, are unlikely.

Who the main decision-makers and influencers are in the sourcing decision, and their preferences, have a considerable role to play in what decisions are made. Is procurement in charge? What is the influence of advisers and their solution 'recipes'? How do CEO, CFO, CIO and COO knowledge and preferences play out? These are difficult to predict and need close attention to understand. But key influencer preferences are important in shaping a '**dominant coalition**' in favor or against a degree of bundling services.

The **maturity** of a client's ability to develop sourcing strategy and manage providers, its history of success, learning, and of requisite capabilities built. These all influence bundling decisions. Mature clients are in a better position to undertake a bundled services option. But a strong preference for competitiveness amongst providers, and question marks on provider capabilities can also lead mature clients to adopt a best-of-breed strategy. On the other hand, we have examples of clients with limited resources or weak learning capabilities also going for single source contracting.

Organizational and technological factors also have a bearing on bundling decisions. These relate to size, infrastructure, interdependence of activity, degree of reliability, transparency of information needed. Large size, high complexity, high interdependence of activities, and high reliability needs will favor longer-term bundled service contracts. Organizations needing technological integration and seamless information and technical service will prefer to go for bundled services, where available.

Business profile, and the existence of a 'burning platform' (an extremely urgent or compelling situation), may well work in favor of a bundled decision. A business doing badly, or needing to do something different, may well see bundled services as a cost-driven, low management solution. But we also found also large, well performing organizations tending to buy bundled services, where other factors were favorable. A burning platform (e.g. cost reduction, a new CEO/CFO/CIO, a change in business strategy, or in acquisition policy) may well favor a bundling decision.

Heavy users and **high spenders** on outsourcing will tend to consider bundled services. A further factor we identified related to **risk attitude.** Organizations with a high-risk perception concerning IT or back-office back up, security, complexity tend to favor bundled services.

12.4.2 Relational Factors

We identified three sets of relational factors, scoring them a combined weighting of 12%. **Culture** (whether clients were transaction-orientated or relationship orientated) had a role to play here. For example, the USA and UK tend to be more transaction-orientated than South Korea and Scandinavian countries. Other things being equal, relationship-oriented cultures will favor service bundling. **Prior relations** between client and provider, especially where the provider has had good communications with a client's dominant coalition, can influence client's propensity to contract for bundled services. However, relationships were more influential where developed as an **incumbent provider.** Strong relationships as an incumbent, when combined with a good track record of service delivery, incline a client to outsource more services to the incumbent provider.[115]

12.4.3   Client Market Forces and Characteristics

We gave a combined weighting of 10% to four factors under this heading. In a highly regulated environment, the strong requirement for **regulatory compliance** will usually favor bundled decisions. Bundled services will lower complexity, especially if the provider offers assistance with regulatory mandates. **Geography** can have an effect. Bundled service options are more likely to be taken up in the lead markets of the USA and UK, cancelling out their transaction-orientated cultures. More relationship-orientated cultures, outside the USA and UK, are starting to take up bundling at an increased pace. We found a strong propensity for it amongst large companies in Norway and Netherlands, and also in South Korea.

Additionally, bundling is favored by organizations requiring a higher level of **innovation** from a provider. Here, bundling is the quid pro quo to the provider for its innovation investment and its provision of more integrated services. There is also **sector influence.** For example, the telecoms, manufacturing and utilities sectors take the lead on bundling, especially where an organization is based in a single region and is large buyer. Some sectors prefer industry verticals (e.g. UK military logistics in 1990s). Thus, certain sectors are to be found creating a momentum in favor of, or against, bundling.

---

[115] From a 2007 Everest Research Institute private analysis - *Scope Aggregation in Outsourcing: Why the Strong Get Stronger.*

12.4.4   Supplier and Outsourcing Market Characteristics

Here we identified four factors, with a combined weighting of 18%. **Initial choices and incumbent providers** shape future bundling. Incumbency, and the capability to do other services, encourages a client to give a provider bundled services. This goes beyond the relationship effect mentioned above. Incumbents with additional capability shape bundled services strategy and stand to gain from these. Reinforcing this finding, a 2007 Everest Research Institute survey of BPO scope aggregation found that if a buyer initially selected a generalist provider, 40% of the time the buyer would select the same provider for other functions.[116]

Part of this incumbent advantage relates to demonstrable additional capabilities. Indeed **provider capabilities** are a bigger influence than mere incumbency. Here clients look for a provider that is widely capable across different services and able to use IT in each, offers a wide scope of service geographically, and can deal with large contract size. The few providers that can service large scope bundled deals will be prioritized, but there is a caveat. A limited number of provider options may also inhibit bundled service decisions.

We identified two lesser factors under this heading. Where a provider offering is of **interdependent services** then a 'lock-in' effect can occur where the client is more likely to buy the combined service, already integrated, as bundled services. Finally, media attention given to bundled services can create a **bandwagon effect**, increasing a client's propensity to look for bundled services. However, this effect can be short-lived if performance does not improve and providers fail to develop dependencies between bundled services, and deliver on their promises.

---

[116] Clearly, the first outsourcing decisions and who the incumbent providers are can have considerable affect on subsequent bundling patterns. From a 2007 Everest Research Institute private report *Scope Aggregation in Outsourcing: Why the Strong Get Stronger.* Everest calls this the 'penetrate and radiate' model.

12.4.5   Cost Effectiveness Characteristics

The area of cost is weighted 20%. Cost is a constant key concern. Two types of cost savings emerged from the study, namely **management and integrated services efficiencies**. As we discussed above, management and transaction costs should be demonstrably lower, and integrated service efficiencies much more achievable with bundling of services.

From a client perspective, the transaction cost saving from a bundled purchase is large, but hidden. They typically include:

- risk reduction,

- less governance and lower relationship management costs,

- less management time getting to contract, simpler contracting, and cheaper legal costs, and

- ability to move to standardized practices with synergies across services and processes.

The transaction cost savings between a single and multiple provider route may be substantial enough to offset where a single provider might offer a less attractive deal on production costs. But it is likely, if the provider is instituting the practices listed below, that these will also be lower anyway.

Most large providers are now reducing their internal transaction costs (the costs of doing business within themselves) and their production costs by focusing on standardizing as a shared service across all processes - the customer contact they run for a client, and likewise for its administrative back-end (e.g. reporting). This leaves the middle sections which tend to be more domain-specific (e.g. procurement) or sub-components (e.g. within HR: recruitment, training remuneration). Here the idea is to standardize for the client globally on the relevant process and charge for departures from that standardized process.

This then enables the provider to provide a standard contract for all standardized shared services (but not necessarily the domain specific ones). Obviously the reduction in both transaction and production costs is large if this can be achieved across a client's several activities. The size of this gain as passed on to the client will be one attractive aspect of a bundled purchase.

12.5 Action Point - Making the Optimal Decision

'There is a surprising thing in mathematics. In a multi-variate problem, the optimal result is often reached with none of the variables at its maximum value."

Simon Sammons of Accenture

This observation applies equally well to decisions on bundled/unbundled services. Clients will continue to adopt multi-sourcing and best-of-breed strategies and will find plenty of good reasons for doing so. However, the market has moved on, technologies have developed, client and provider capabilities have grown apace, and new possibilities have opened up. One important growing trend, containing several mini-trends within it, has been the bundling of services.

Under what circumstances can a client take business advantage of this rising set of capabilities? What sort of client is likely to gain from bundling rather than unbundling? And what sort of client is better suited to multi-sourcing approaches? In Table 12-1, we provide a decision matrix for client use.

Table 12-1: To Bundle or Not -The Decision Matrix

		Tend to Bundle	Tend NOT to Bundle
1. Client Factors	1. **Decision-making process** (3)	Centralized	Decentralized
	2. **Dominant coalition preferences** (12) e.g. procurement, C-levels, advisors	Possible	Possible
	3. **Outsourcing maturity** (5) history of success, learning, building capabilities	Yes	Best-of-Breed if desire for competition
	4. **Organizational and technological factors** (6)		
	• Size	Large	Small
	• Complexity and interdependence	High	Low
	• Reliability needs	High	Low
	• Technological integration	High	Low
	• Seamless service	High	Low
	5. **Burning platform** (4)		
	• Cost crisis	Yes	No
	• New CEO or CIO	Possibly	Possibly
	• Acquisition/merger	Likely	Possibly
	• New consolidation strategy	Yes	Unlikely
	6. **Business profile** (4)		
	• Business doing badly/ need to do something different	Yes	Unlikely
	• Large, well performing firm	Likely	Possible
	7. **Heavy users and high spenders on outsourcing** (3)	Yes	No
	8. **Risk attitude to back-up, security, complexity** (3)	Perception of high risk	Perception of low risk
2. Relational Factors	9. **Culture (2)**		
	• Transaction-orientated e.g. UK	Less likely	Probably
	• Relationship-orientated e.g. South Korea	Very likely	Less likely
	10. **Prior relational aspects** (4) strong relations between the parties' executives	Very likely	Less likely
	11. **Relationships/performance as incumbent provider** (6)	Strong relationships and record of service delivery	Weak, poor record
3. Client Market Forces & Characteristics	12. **Strong regulatory compliance needs** (2)	Reduce complexity with provider assistance	No complexity reduction, no provider help
	13. **Geography - advanced market** (3) e.g. USA and UK	More likely	More likely
	14. **Level of innovation required** (2)	More provider investment, more integrated services	Low innovation required, low integration
	15. **Sector influence** (3)		
	• telecoms and utilities	Likely	Possible
	• retail	Possible	Likely
	• high preference for industry verticals	Likely	Possible
	• high competition intensity	Likely	Possible
4. Provider & Market Characteristics	16. **Initial choices and incumbent providers** (4)	Incumbent with additional capabilities	Poor record, no strong additional capabilities
	17. **Provider capabilities** (10)		
	• Widely capable across services	Yes	Concern over too few providers
	• Able to use IT in each geographic scope	Yes	
	• Can deal with large contract size	Yes	
	18. **'Lock-in'** (2) Provider offerings as interdependent services	More likely	Less likely
	19. **External media and bandwagon effect** (2) - high media attention on bundled services	Likely	Likely - if no improvements and no dependencies between bundled services
5. Cost	20. **Management and services efficiencies**		
	• Management and transaction costs (10)	If demonstrably lower	Possible
	• Integrated service efficiencies (10)	Yes	Unlikely

How to Use the Decision Matrix

You base your evaluation on the five sets of factors listed below. Each set is weighted, with the sets combined forming a total possible score of 100.

- Client   40%
- Relational   12%
- Client market forces & characteristics   10%
- Supplier & outsourcing market characteristics   18%
- Cost effectiveness   20%

                                        TOTAL   100%

Step 1. The unit of analysis is a group of services that a client is wishing to outsource. For example, this could be HR payroll, related IT applications and HR training and development. Should these be bundled and outsourced to one provider, or left unbundled and outsourced to several providers?

Each factor has an individual weighting. Score each factor from a 'Tend to Bundle' perspective. Thus for factor 1 from Table 12-1, if the decision-making process is highly centralized score three. If, however, factor 1 is very decentralized, score zero or one. As another example, under Relational factors if the culture is very transaction related, score zero or one, but if it is very relationship-orientated, favoring bundling, score two Under Client Market Forces & Characteristics, if the level of innovation required is high, then a bundled decision is more likely so score it a two. If innovation needs are low, or very low, then score this factor one or zero. Under Provider & Outsourcing Market Characteristics, provider capabilities (factor 17 from Table 12-1) are a key issue. If a provider really can support bundling, then score it nine or ten; otherwise make a judgment as to what the provider can support, and score it to suit. Under Cost Effectiveness Characteristics, does bundling lead to demonstrably lower management and transaction costs? If so, score this factor between seven and ten. If not, score it lower than this to suit.

Step 2. Having scored each factor, total the scores to make a single score.

Step 3. Use Figure 12-3 to interpret your organization's score. A score between 66 - 100 means that the client is past the tipping point for bundling, and should make a bundled decision for the services under consideration. A score between zero and 33 is past the tipping point for unbundling and means that an unbundled decision is the right one.

Scores between 34 - 65 need much further analysis. A score between 34 - 50 suggests unbundling is the right way to go; but you need to assess which factors need to be leveraged to make this a good decision, and perform a risk assessment of the consequences of leveraging these factors. Alternatively, a score between 51 - 65 suggests bundling is a better decision; but only after further assessment, leveraging salient factors, and ensuring that the risk profile of the consequent decision is sensible.

Figure 12-3: Sourcing Factor Analysis

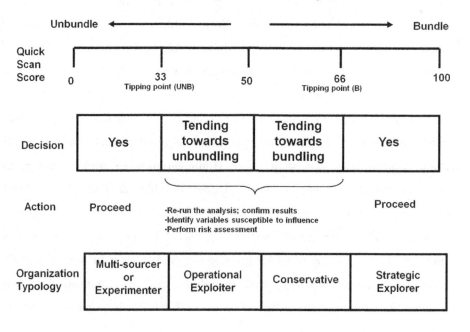

12.6 Emerging Client Types

While the last analysis was at the level of several services, we also found five types of clients that tending to be making bundled or unbundled decisions. Our analysis included generating a typology of the clients more, or less, likely to buy bundled services. These are:

- The Strategic Explorer type,

- The Conservative type,

- The Operational Exploiter type,

- The Multisourcer type, and

- The Experimenter type.

1. The Strategic Explorer Type.   The Strategic Explorer possesses highly developed outsourcing capabilities in most areas critical for successful outsourcing projects such as provider selection, relationship management, provider management, domain expertise, learning capabilities; all developed through scale and advanced management systems. The Strategic Explorer (which outsources both low-value and high value activities and which experiments with both single and multi-provider settings) is confident in its ability to enter a large bundled-services contract because of its strong retained organization and highly developed domain experience. This type will expect innovations and the ability to realize synergies between the different services outsourced. The Strategic Explorer will be able to assess the degree to which synergies between the different services have been realized and will aspire to systematically measure these outcomes. Its approach to bundled services is '*My vendor and I can improve my value proposition only when we innovate across my end-to-end services*'.

In our sample, we found that none of the clients had developed a full-blown Strategic Explorer profile. Some, though, are thinking strategically about bundled services. However, they may fail to design and implement a system that leverages the potential value across the range of services.

2. The Conservative Type: The Conservative type has been outsourcing for a while; however, the client tends to work with one provider or a very small number of providers. Its learning and outsourcing management capabilities, which tend to be limited and in most cases focus on low value activities, have been developed mainly based on the long-term relationships it has had with one or a very small number of providers. For this reason, bundling services seems like another step in the outsourcing activities that the Conservative type has pursued. Its approach to bundled services is, '*It only makes sense to outsource another service to my current provider*'. In other words the Conservative moves further into bundling services through an incremental 'add-on' strategy, as it builds its capability to manage only a few providers, strengthens relationships with incumbent providers, and satisfies itself that provider capabilities merit extending both the contract duration and the service scope.

A Conservative buyer will have a dominant coalition within its ranks that favor provider consolidation, and will recognize that its size, complexity, and interdependence of operation continually point towards the need for reliability, technological integration, and seamless service. A Conservative buyer will also be looking to outsource more in the future, though it may not be too clear on the cost advantages of bundling rather than unbundling specific services. A Conservative type will come to be worried about becoming more strategic in its approach to the market and aligning its sourcing approach with business strategy. Quite a few of the cases we have studied fell into this category.

3. The Operational Exploiter Type: The Operational Exploiter has likely developed good outsourcing management capabilities that focus on the daily operational aspects of managing individual outsourcing contracts through SLAs, but less so on the long-term, strategic, innovative and relational aspects. They very likely have limited learning capabilities developed around synergies between the various outsourced services, though will have developed routines and practices to ensure the delivery of value from each single outsourced service. The

Operational Exploiter tends to outsource mainly low value but also some high value activities and has experimented with both single and multi-provider settings.

Bundling outsourced services would become an option when more and more services are outsourced and where potential operational efficiencies start becoming evident. The Operational Exploiter will be aware of the synergies between the outsourced services. However, it will be able to extract little value from these synergies. This is mainly because of the way its outsourcing management capabilities have been developed, focusing on extracting value and efficiencies from a single contract. Its approach to bundled services is '*I should outsource another service because there are cost advantages and efficiencies in bundling this service with the others*'.

Some of the organizations we studied have focused on developing operational excellence around the management of outsourcing and therefore their selection of provider. In such cases, the services to be outsourced and managed have been geared towards what we have titled here as operational exploiter.

4. The Multisourcer Type: Typically, the Multisourcer type has built a strong capability to manage multiple providers, and is into its third generation of outsourcing contracts. Its dominant coalition favors both outsourcing, which it does extensively, and also a best-of-breed strategy, which it manages tightly, in an aligned way with business strategy, and with strong governance mechanisms in place.

The Multisourcer tends to outsource in ways that keeps the switching costs low in and out of different providers, while retaining advantages from keeping providers in competition for work. They will readily incur the management and transaction costs required to maintain this multi-provider strategy, though they work hard to continually reduce these costs.

The client may well be large and in parts complex, but does not have high needs for reliability, interdependence, seamless service and technological integration, or manages these aspects itself, or is willing to manage the gaps between provider service and what is required on these aspects. Where they achieve integrated service cost efficiencies, it will be because they manage and run these themselves. A Multisourcer tends to look to itself for innovation rather than through relationships with a provider, though more recently they have been looking for closer relationships with, and more value from, their longer-serving providers.

5. The Experimenter Type: The Experimenter type has just got on the outsourcing learning curve; therefore, its management capabilities and knowledge are underdeveloped. Its learning has been based on sporadic experimentation with various sourcing models and settings that addressed some specific needs. In most cases, these are small-scale contracts covering low value, stable services. At the same time, the lack of experience can result in the Experimenter making sometimes quite serious mistakes in outsourcing risky, or critical areas, to the wrong provider/s on poor contracts.

The Experimenter type tends to switch between providers, and configurations, in a continuous search for superior performance. A bundled service is just another value proposition in this regard. As the Experimenting type's approach is neither strategic nor operational, its philosophy is "*this could be gold.*" The issue for the Experimenter is its under-developed internal management capabilities, making it unable to manage large-scale contracts, form strong relationships with providers, or assess the economics of different outsourcing models. This may well be combined with an understandable orientation amongst decisions makers and influencers towards risk mitigation through multi-sourcing, shorter-term contracts, and a 'best-of-breed' approach to providers.

Experimenters were much more frequent in the period 1992-2003. More recently, only a small number of organizations followed this profile of behavior.

12.7 Building Client Capabilities for Managing Bundled Services

Our analysis demonstrates that many clients have not developed their outsourcing management capabilities to realize the synergies and efficiencies offered by bundled services.   Most of the clients have developed their outsourcing management capabilities to correspond with the Operational Exploiter or Conservative type. At the same time, the Multisourcers in our sample revealed a strategic sourcing approach that worked for them, based on their assessment of the limited capabilities providers were offering in the marketplace.   They also recognized the need to engender competition amongst providers, and the advantages of retaining considerable internal capability, as well as their own specific needs might not be served by bundling certain services.

For clients that would consider pursuing bundled services as a strategic approach, we offer the framework shown in Figure 12-4. [117] For those clients that wish, and have strong rationales for, retaining a Multisourcer stance, we still recommend that they improve their management and strategic sourcing capabilities.

Looking at Figure 12-4, there are two areas needing development within the client in order to capitalize of the promises of bundled services. One is the strategic sourcing capabilities developed inhouse, mainly focusing on aligning sourcing strategy with dynamic business strategy over a five-year period, as well as creating the conditions for partnership with the various providers. The second area is sourcing management capabilities. This should focus on extracting efficiencies, building management capabilities, and developing tools and methodologies to realize the potential in forming strategic relationships with providers.

---

[117] The typology was developed jointly with Professor Ilan Oshri and Dr. John Hindle. See Lacity, M. and Willcocks, L. (2012) *Advanced Outsourcing: From ITO to BPO and Cloud Services*, chapter 6, Palgrave, London.

Figure 12-4: Developing Bundled Services Client Capabilities

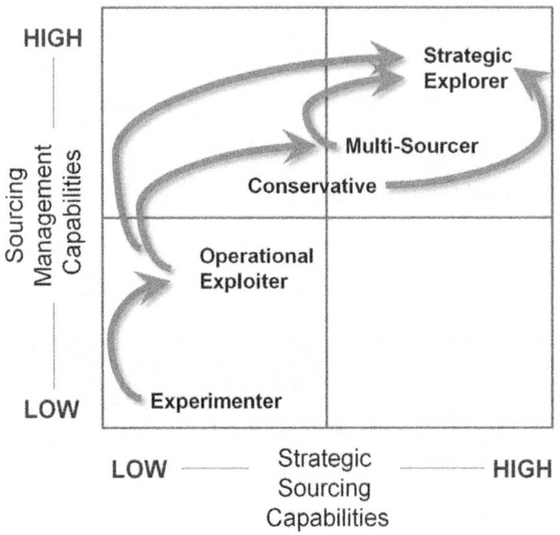

On our analysis, most of the clients identified as Operational Exploiters were well positioned to improve the benefits from bundled services by further investing in relational capabilities and provider development. Clients identified as Conservatives were even more inclined toward bundling and will be even more willing to make the necessary investment in strategic sourcing and sourcing management capabilities. But Experimenters require massive investment in both areas, and therefore should first assess whether bundled services is a strategic direction that they need to take.

In Figure 12-4, we mapped the development path emerging from our research. The Experimenter tends to move towards being an Operational Exploiter. Its hard-won experience leads it to take a multi-provider route, outsourcing relatively stable, mature activities on 3-5 year contracts. It has learned to mitigate operational risk with outsourcing, and will look to build up its sourcing management capability but will not focus strongly on building strategic sourcing capability. The Operational Exploiter tends to develop that strategic sourcing capability based on its heritage in multi-provider outsourcing and tends to evolve into a Multisourcer. On the other hand, a Conservative has a different heritage and more strategic understanding. Improvement lies in evolving towards the Strategic Explorer profile.

Finally, Multisourcers have a huge learning and capability investment in a multi-provider approach. However, because they have strategic sourcing insight, they may well see the advantages of bundling some services after they have identified providers with the requisite capability, when the technology has developed to support integration of services, when they can see a strong economic rationale, and after they feel confident that rationalizing providers will result in a loss of control over their sourcing arrangements.

12.8 Conclusion

The maturity of the client to manage innovation and providers has a big influence on their ability to contemplate bundled services. Clients lack clarity on how to assess getting value, especially cost efficiencies, from bundled services. As result, they tend to evaluate based on function or silo. Lack of reliable, economically based reasons push decisions towards individual judgment, logic, and political influences. Organizations mature in their sourcing strategy and management capability are attracted to bundling where they can get innovation and if they can offset risk to, or share risk with the provider.

More mature clients emphasize that if the relationship with a provider is strong, and it has performed, and then go for bundled services. Relationships need to be 'many-to-many' between the parties with lots of touch points and 'glue'. Some clients bundle as start-ups or to achieve fast change. If they are immature, in outsourcing management terms, and have poor experiences as a result, then they move to multi-provider sourcing in their second and third generation outsourcing arrangements. Some of these clients then eventually look for provider consolidation.

Bundling occurs often where there is a strong and large-scale change agenda, through peer pressure, or in a belief that, in a recession, with limited resources available, it will be cheaper. A bundled service proposition of any scale needs a client Board member driving it. Some organizations reach a tipping point where the client is likely to pursue an add-on strategy, gradually bundling services over time, until they decide to go for a more comprehensive bundling strategy.

The perennial bundle or not-to-bundle challenge presents a key strategic decision point for clients, with long-term consequences whose risks need to be mitigated. It is important to make the right decision based on your strategy and capabilities. The 20-factor framework supports this decision-making process. It is also important to have a sourcing strategy going forward. The client profiling and evolution map offers a starting point for planning the trajectory of sourcing strategy, capabilities, and practices.

Chapter 13 Innovation

"We cannot solve a problem by using the same kind of thinking we used when we created them."

Albert Einstein

There is an increasing need for outsourcing arrangements to provide innovation as well as just cost savings. Innovations can be changes in operations, in business processes or in products and services offered, or in the business model of how the organization competes. The need for innovation comes about because of changing business requirements, economic swings, and the globalization and technolization of markets.

To survive and thrive requires sustainable change. A focus on cost cutting alone, or even cost efficiency, may solve a short-term problem, but at the expense of building the future business.

The challenge of achieving innovation requires many more clients to make a step-change to collaborative leadership. Our recent research suggests that innovation using the external services market is increasingly realistic, but it does require that both parties are mature in their ability to go beyond traditional relationships, and build the collaborative arrangements necessary for innovating.[118]

---

[118] Throughout 2010-2012, we researched 26 outsourcing arrangements where significant innovation had occurred. See Willcocks, L. and Lacity, M. (2012) *The Emerging IT Outsourcing Landscape: From Innovation to Cloud Services.* Palgrave, London. Fellow researchers were Dr. Edgar Whitley and Andrew Craig of the LSE Outsourcing Unit. Also Willcocks, L. Cullen, S. and Craig, A. (2011) *The Outsourcing Enterprise: From Cost Management to Innovation.* Palgrave, London.

How do they do this? In this chapter, we first identify the characteristics of collaboration and innovation, and how they mutually support effective outsourcing. We then provide details of the processes and practices that make dynamic 'collaborative innovation' successful. Our findings suggest that an effective process with four interrelated components is needed. These are: leadership, contracting, organizing, and performing.

The outsourcing industry can no longer ignore the potential for innovation, and value, buried in and overlooked by its more traditional modes of operation. The practices we document in this chapter require a change in a mind-set and behavior of all parties determined to meet the innovation challenge.

13.1 Understanding Innovation and Collaboration

13.1.1   Innovation

What does innovation mean to the organizations we studied and what sort of innovation they care about? Some of their comments are given below"

> *"Innovation is twofold. One is the ability to wake up one morning and realize there is a different and better way of doing something. Secondly, combining that with an ability to deliver. My job is to get into suppliers and make sure that my company has a higher percentage of their innovators' and decision-makers' time than other companies."* An energy company.

> *"Innovation to me is really simple. It doesn't have to be a product or a new service. It's doing things differently for the better, that's innovation."* Spring Global Mail.

> *"Although it might be the 20th time that we implement some sort of system or product or whatever, for our client, it's usually the first time, a one-off. For them it might be really innovative, while for us, it's just business as usual."* A Supplier innovation executive at a manufacturing company.

From these statements from senior executives, it can be seen that innovation is the introduction of something new that creates value for the organization that adopts it.[119]

This aligns with insights from the literature on innovation. This literature talks of product, process, and organizational innovations. It refers to new products (or services), new ways of doing things and new ways of organizing and managing people. Innovations are also characterized as incremental (small series of changes), radical (large, transformative change) or revolutionary (game changing).[120]

For our purposes, we adapt Weeks and Feeny's definitions on the three types of innovation: [121]

1. **Operational innovations** are technology, work and personnel changes that do not impact organizational-specific business processes (e.g. in the case of IT operational innovations they might include new email platforms, new operating systems, infrastructure remodeling and new staffing arrangements). These could lead to better business use of IT, for example, at one insurance company introducing agile systems development led to IT being in place quicker to support the business.

2. **Business process innovations** change the way the business operates in some important way. For example, in one bank we found fundamental changes to business processes and relationships with customers through CRM

---

[119] The definition was developed for use at Intel. See Westerman G. and Curley M. (2008) "Building IT-enabled capabilities at Intel", *MIS Quarterly Executive* 7(1) 33-48.

[120] See, for example, Davenport T., et al. (2006) *Strategic management in the innovation economy,* Wiley, New York; Westland J. (2008) *Global innovation management,* Palgrave, London; McKeown M. (2008) *The truth about innovation,* Pearson, London.

[121] Weeks, M. R. and Feeny, D. (2008) "Outsourcing From Cost Management to Innovation and Business Value," *California Management Review* (50:4) 127-146.

implementation. In an aerospace company, IT enabled changes in project management systems that changed the basis on which parties would design, develop, and deliver big projects. In a water utility, billing system innovations created new linkages between accounting, maintenance, service fulfillment, and customer reporting.

3. **Strategic innovations** significantly enhance the organization's offerings for existing customers, or enabled it to enter new markets. For example, in Asia Pacific we found a casino introducing technology to automate (and thus speed up) roulette and so increase revenues from high rollers. Similarly, a car parts distribution company, with the aid of providers, introduced remote computerized car monitoring to pre-empt mechanical breakdown, and provide positive response in terms of spares and repair.

Given these definitions, our research points to a new agenda for outsourcing practitioners to aim at over the next five years. Essentially, superior performance through innovation is now feasible in a maturing industry, but requires a step-change in focus. The messages of our findings are presented in Figure 13-1.

Figure 13-1: The New Performance Agenda

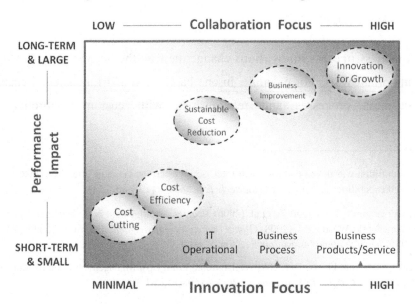

Without an **innovation focus** (the lower axis in Figure 13-1), outsourcing usually achieves cost cutting as of a once-off event, or at best, a cost efficiency (similar service at lower cost). But focusing on innovations in IT operations can and does achieve larger, sustainable cost reductions.

The real **performance impacts** (the left axis) over time come from business process and business product/service innovations. Business process innovations create sustainable business improvements in areas much bigger than IT operations alone; a bigger target, a more impactful innovation. Business product/service innovations can, and do, support organizations' revenue and profit growth targets.

In outsourcing, the **collaboration focus** (the top axis) and capabilities of all parties determine the type and degree of innovation possible. Only a high collaboration focus makes large business process and strategic innovations feasible. Collaborative innovation finds ways of sharing and offsetting risk. It also galvanizes behavior towards lessening risk and achieving shared goals. Collaborative innovation supports superior performance more realistically than more traditional outsourcing relationships.

13.1.2   Collaboration

Collaboration is a cooperative arrangement in which two or more parties work jointly in a common enterprise towards a shared goal. In the context of business relationships, the word collaboration signals close partnering behaviors developed over, and for, the long term. These behaviors are distinguished by the high trust, flexibility, risk sharing, and investment of resources and time that is essential if high-performance goals are to be achieved.[122]

---

[122] Our definition but backed by a significant literature in the strategy, but not the outsourcing literature. See also Kern, T. and Willcocks, L. (2000) *The relationship advantage: Information technologies, sourcing and management.* Oxford University Press, Oxford.

All outsourcing requires a relationship to succeed. But what kind of relationship works? This depends on the activities being outsourced. Commodity services such as accounts payable processing, or specialized repeatable processes like credit checks can be accomplished with relatively hands-off, contract-based relationships between a client and its provider/s. But a deeper, more trust-based relationship is required if external parties are to be used for more sophisticated, risk bearing, and critical services including large-scale projects and innovations.

This comment, from a senior executive in an Asia Pacific-based insurance company, speaks volumes about the change required in the parties' behaviors, *'The standard behavior in an organization is everybody does their job, they deliver it and then somebody else goes and creates the same thing over and over again. But, with collaboration comes leverage. In collaboration, you will be welcoming an advance from me to be able to find out how you did it and to share it with me. Partnering is an ongoing relationship where you are leveraging the skills that your partner has and learn from them. Leadership is key in making progress in collaboration."*

Collaboration also has to stretch across providers, as the director of innovation at Netherlands-based KPN makes clear, *"What we need is collaboration from our providers. If they are competitive then we have a very special meeting and say this behavior is unacceptable; you have to work together. Collaboration only happens if there is a higher-level goal for everyone. We put in the necessary incentives for them to put their best people on it and they can't succeed without the help of the other providers."*

Thus, collaboration requires a different mindset towards other parties, underpinned by different forms of contracting and behaviors.

13.2 Putting it Together - The Process of Collaborative Innovation

Many people talk about the need for collaborative innovation, but how is it effectively delivered? Our research points to a fourfold process (see Figure 13-2).

Figure 13-2: The Collaborative Innovation Process

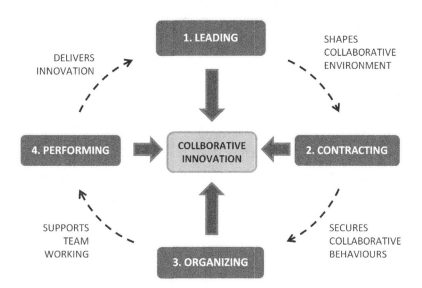

Let's walk through the process, looking at each part in detail.

13.2.1   Leading

Whilst leadership is important for all forms of outsourcing, leadership also creates the environment for innovation. In earlier ITO deals, especially the long-term 'strategic alliances' signed in the 1990s (e.g. EDS and Xerox, IBM and Lend Lease, BAE and CSC, UBS and Perot Systems) innovation was cited as something the clients expected and which the 'world class' provider could and would deliver. Study after study, however, has failed to find such innovation forthcoming.

One response to this problem has been to create special 'innovation funds' that providers can bid for. However, research has found that even large innovation funds have rarely produced lasting, important innovations.

The same applies to many joint venture and equity share initiatives (see Configuration Attribute #7: Commercial Relationship in Chapter 4) designed partly to stimulate innovation. They invariably disappointed because they were mere add-ons in mainly arms-length deals where, in practice, both parties prioritized service and cost issues above innovation issues. Thus, whilst they may espouse innovation, in practice they tend to encourage low levels of sustainable development and performance transformation.

In order to understand how leadership shapes the environment for collaborative innovation in outsourcing, it is helpful to draw on the work of Ronald Heifetz.[123] He distinguishes between technical and adaptive challenges. According to Heifetz technical challenges are rarely trivial but what makes them technical is that the solution, in the form of specialist know-how, techniques and routine processes, already exists within the client's, or the provider's, repertoire. Consequently, managers can delegate such work to specialists and monitor the outcomes.

In contrast, leadership deals with adaptive challenges. In fact, Heifetz defines leadership as, "*shaping and mobilizing adaptive work,*" that is, engaging people to make progress on the adaptive problems they face. For him, the hardest and most valuable task of leadership is advancing goals and designing strategy that promote adaptive work. An adaptive challenge is a particular problem, often difficult to specify precisely, where the gap between values and aspirations on the one hand and circumstances on the other cannot be closed by the application of current technical know-how and routine behavior. Adaptive challenges require experiments, discoveries, and adjustments from many parts of an organization.

---

[123] Heifetz, R. and Linsky, M. (2002) *Leadership on the line.* Harvard Business Press, Cambridge, MA.

Modern outsourcing is full of adaptive challenges, and work that cries out for leadership strategies. In our research into 26 outsourcing deals experiencing innovation, we identified one common strand: the CEO and senior executives addressed the adaptive challenges of outsourcing by shaping its context.

Across the cases, we identified the following practices:

- Formulating and monitoring a sourcing strategy that fits with changing strategic and operational business needs over the next five years.

- Ensuring the client can buy in an informed way by understanding the external services market, provider strategies, capabilities, and weaknesses, and what a good deal with each provider would look like.

- Shaping relationships and putting in place a process for managing outsourcing across the lifecycle.

- Shaping the conditions for a contract that delivers what is expected and needed without sustaining hidden or switching costs.

- Developing and sustaining a contract management capability that retains control while leveraging provider capabilities and performance.

- Facilitating the maturing of business managers' ability to manage and own IT as a strategic resource, including stepping up to roles as sponsors and champions of major IT-enabled business projects.

Innovation is also essentially an adaptive challenge. We found our 26 case studies saturated with leadership challenges over and above those found in mainstream outsourcing arrangements. As one executive told us, "*You establish trust through delivery but when it goes wrong you have to show leadership. Taking responsibility is the beginning of leadership. If you keep telling people what to do they will never become leaders.*" The payoff from leadership was indicated by Andrew Wolstenholme, the Heathrow Terminal 5 construction director, "*We set up an environment within which innovation could flourish; I didn't come up with all the clever ideas. We created a place where people could innovate and that's the act of good leadership; making it safe for people to stick their necks out.*"

To illustrate the role of leadership in shaping the context for outsourcing contracts, Figure 13-3, presents four options demonstrating that collaborative innovation only occurs if leadership creates an environment that is conducive to both high performance transformation and sustainable development.

Figure 13-3: Innovation Potential Matrix

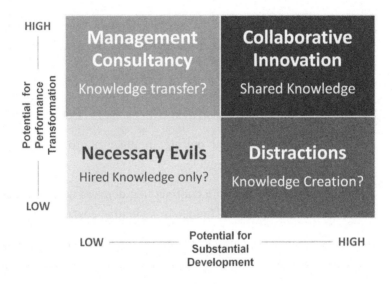

Do-It-Yourself approaches score highly for sustainable development because control and value are within the client. But to succeed it requires both funding and skills that may be lacking in the client. It is also the option most likely to encounter internal resistance if senior management does not lead with clear signals of its importance.

The **Management Consultancy** route brings in external energy, gives a clear signal of commitment to major change by bringing in outsiders, and reduces political resistance. The most significant risks are cost escalation, lack of sustainability and limited knowledge transfer.

Fee-For-Service Outsourcing can see limited, usually 'one-off', innovations through reforming inherited back office management practices, streamlining business processes, and fresh investment in new technology. However, even where these are forthcoming, the research record shows that the innovation zeal is rarely sustained and delivered on.

Our work on suggests the following new rules for leadership:

- Leadership begins in the boardroom, with the top management team demonstrating beliefs by their own behaviors and suffusing leadership at every level in the organizations.

- Outsourcing and innovation are essentially adaptive challenges.

- Keep the stress levels within a tolerable range for doing adaptive work.

- Focus attention on ripening issues, not stress-reducing distractions.

- Give the work back to the people, but at a rate they can stand.

- Protect voices of leadership without authority.

In our 2013 research on high performing BPO relationships, we found that a pair of extraordinary people led the innovation agenda - one leader from each party.[124] The leaders were strong as individuals; were experienced, capable, and had high levels of credibility, clout, and power within their own organizations. Effective leadership pairs enjoyed working together, described as *"chemistry."*

Effective leadership pairs displayed these behaviors and held these attitudes:

- **Focus on the future.** The leadership pair focused on where they wanted the relationship to go, not where the relationship was.

- **Spirit of togetherness.** The pair presented a united front to stakeholders in their respective organizations.

- **Transparency.** The pair was open and honest about all operational issues.

---

[124] See Lacity, M. And Willcocks, L. (2013) "Outsourcing Business Processes for Innovation" *MIT Sloan Management Review,* 54, 3, 62-69.

- **Problem solving.** The pair sought to diagnose and fix problems; they did not seek to assign blame.

- **Outcomes first.** The pair always did what was best for the client and then settled a fair agreement.

- **Action-oriented.** The pair was not afraid to use their powers - they acted swiftly to remove, or workaround, obstructions to innovation stemming from people, processes, or contracts.

- **Trust.** Perhaps because of these previous behaviors, the leadership pair felt secure and confident in the other person's good will, intentions, and competency.[125]

This list mirrors what we often see in the relationship quadrant of Contract Scorecards (see Action 17 in Building Block 4), reflecting the expected (and measured) behaviors not only of leaders, but all key people in both parties.

However, in several cases, we found client-provider pairs who were both experienced leaders, but the combination simply did not work. Changing one or even both leaders can improve performance.[126] For example, at one now high-performing BPO relationship based in Europe, the client leader requested a different provider account manager because he could not collaborate effectively with the initial person assigned. The provider granted his request. The client leader contrasted the two provider leads, *"The provider appointed a delivery account manager, and through the initial sort of bloody period, the relationship did not work. I don't know whether it was chemistry or what. He was a more*

---

[125] Bidault and Castello found that very low levels of trust and very high levels of trust are detrimental to innovation - the optimal level of trust is somewhere in between. See Bidault, F. and Castello, A. (2010) 'Why Too Much Trust is Death to Innovation," *Sloan Management Review*, Vol. 51, 4 33-38.

[126] Two researchers, Davis and Eisenhardt, also found that rotating leadership produced more innovation in inter-organizational relationships. See: J. Davis and K. Eisenhardt (2011) "Rotating Leadership and Collaborative Innovation: Recombination Processes in Symbiotic Relationships", *Administrative Science Quarterly,* Vol. 56, 2 159-201.

senior guy with the attitude, 'Well, I've done it, I've got the t-shirt, I know what I'm doing, I don't know why you're panicking, leave me alone to get on with it.' He may have been a very good bloke but I couldn't work with him. The provider bravely and ultimately was correct to say, 'okay, if that's the case, we'll pull him out.' They put somebody else in who was actually more junior but was somebody with whom we could work."

This 'chemistry' issue is something we observed over the decades, and explained early in Chapter 11 on the human side of contracts. Innovation leaders tend to have the **Entrepreneur** set of values and behaviors above all other styles (and tend to be unlike others in their organizations). The chemistry works, particularly concerning innovation, when the individuals who need to create it as colleagues have shared styles, in addition to shared goals.

13.2.2 Contracting

Several of our case respondents pointed explicitly to the real dangers in contracts that led to becoming overly reliant on the provider for technical and business innovation. This was most dramatically observed in examples of transformation outsourcing. The problem here is when transformation is treated largely as the provider's responsibility.

Transformation, as the word suggests, is rarely just a technical matter. It invariably involves behavioral, organizational, social, and political issues. Nor is it easy to define in advance precisely the outcomes and responsibilities of the transformation. This means transformation is about learning, experimentation and bringing many different forms of know-how together to deal with adaptive challenges. This immediately means it requires primary leadership and learning by the client, something our more innovatory case respondents understood and practiced.

In contrast, some of our interviewees were able to point to contracts structured around cost/service issues. These contracts did not encourage the provider to innovate. Supporting findings elsewhere, there was often an over-reliance on the provider to innovate in business areas where innovation should be primarily an inhouse concern. The provider became focused on selling extra services to make further margins and also became imbedded in solving today's pressing crises and operational problems. The client failed to develop or employ sufficient people capable of innovating. Often the client lost interest in joint boards and admitted to downplaying the inhouse responsibility to leverage the relationship further.

A major issue recognized by respondents who achieved innovation was the need to contract in a way that incentivized knowledge and best practice sharing across all parties involved. To overcome this problem, our case research shows a step-change in contracting is required. The greater the innovation ambition, then the more it is likely that there is a distinctive risk/reward component in the contracting arrangement. In fact, across the cases examined, we identified three key contracting practices that supported collaborative innovation. These contracts:

- shared risk and reward, and offset risks,

- focused on the business imperatives (the 'what') but allowed for adaptiveness in how these are achieved (the 'how'), and

- were designed to encourage innovation, flexibility, collaboration, and high performance to achieve common goals.

13.2.3 Organizing

Where management is providing leadership to shape a collaborative environment, and this is supported by contracting practices that share risks and encourage collaboration, there are still significant organizational challenges that must be addressed. Technical work requiring the application of existing specialist know-how and techniques can be outsourced relatively safely, assuming competent specialists can be hired. The more that work becomes adaptive, then the more that multiple stakeholders need to be engaged with defining the problem and working together on arriving at, and implementing, a solution.

As previously mentioned, adaptive challenges represent situations where problems and solutions are unclear, a multi-functional team is needed, learning is vital, innovation is necessary, and a general business goal (rather than precise metrics) point the way forward. The organizing of collaborative behaviors needs to maintain direction and shape the context and process by which all this can happen. Moreover, the more radical and business focused the innovation required, the more that leadership should be primarily by the client.

In practice, inhouse leadership is vital to large-scale innovation and transformation because these inherently comprise adaptive challenges. But, as described above, even fee-for-service outsourcing has some adaptive challenges and these are often mistaken for technical challenges. For example, tried and tested technology introduced into a new client environment will have an impact on existing technical and social systems and hence presents adaptive challenges. The specialist will need to work in a selectively participatory way with business users and inhouse people to meet these challenges. Teaming across organizational boundaries and functional silos is vital for adaptive-innovative work (see Table 13-1).

Table 13-1: Technical, Adaptive, and Innovative Work in Outsourcing

Aspect	Technical	Techno-Adaptive	Adaptive-Innovative
Problem definition	Clear	Clear	Unclear, requires learning
Solution and implementation	Clear	Requires learning	Requires much all-party learning
Locus of primary responsibility	Specialists	Specialists and user; participatory	User with specialists; Multi-functional teams
Type of problem solving	Technical	Technical-adaptive	Adaptive-innovative
Type of contract	Outsource	Time and materials; resource-based	Shared risk-reward; outcomes-based
Objective	Efficient use of existing technical know-how	Effective implement-ation of existing solution in new setting	Effective business solution
Primary leadership	Specialist	Selectively participatory	Collaborative, driven by client sponsor and champion

All our respondent organizations looking for innovation understood this and were actively putting it into practice. As the project director involved in building Heathrow Terminal 5 argued, "W*e got sufficient leverage and sufficient buy-in and understanding from all the senior executives in the supply chain to say, we are prepared to sign up to this. This is about behaviors. This is about how we work together in this unit that we call integrated teams and it appears that you are going to take off our shoulders the traditional commercial risk that we'd otherwise be carrying. In response to that, we need to give you our best people and we need to make sure their reputation is high. This is a very different sort of commercial leverage.*"

Several senior managers also pointed to the difficulties they experienced when mistaking techno-adaptive for specialist work. The result was insufficient collaboration and misuse of the provider as illustrated by the following comment from a senior executive in an energy company, "*It was a new use of existing software, but frankly, throwing the job over the wall to the supplier didn't really work, because it was a different context and use, and we really had to learn to work together to get it running. We took that learning forward and have become much better at identifying where innovation is needed, and how to do it.*"

Across these cases, we identified the following organizing practices that supported collaborative innovation:

- More co-managed governance structures and greater multi-functional teaming. These must extend across the parties and people responsible for delivering results.
- Teaming requires the ability to collaborate within a client, between client and provider, and between providers.

13.2.4   Performing

Leadership, creative contracting, organizing, and teaming in new ways build the fundamental performance changes needed to undertake collaborative innovation. At the heart of performance is behavior.

In Building Block 8 (Action 46 - investing in the relationship), we discussed the difference between power-based and partnering-based relationships and the behaviors exhibited. We replicated a key figure here (Figure 13-4) to focus again the behaviors exhibited, but now in terms of its effect on innovation.

Figure 13-4: Power versus Partnering Relationship

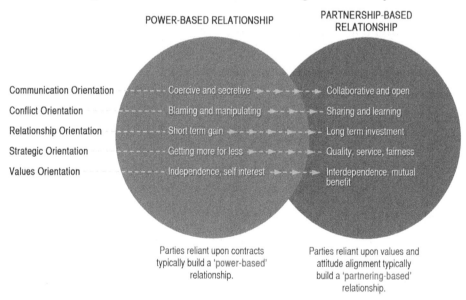

The power-based behaviors, represented on the left side of the figure, are limiting in terms of what can be achieved by either party. And unfortunately, the sort of recessionary conditions being experienced in the last few years has put pressure on the parties to regress to this default position. But a crisis may be a terrible thing to waste. The best way to deal with a recession may be to innovate your way out of it; something we found nearly all our case organizations focusing on. Behavior change can come about because of a crisis, but lasting collaborative innovation draws on the previous insights into leadership, contracting and organizing, which create rising levels of trust, teaming, and performance.

As Andrew Wolstenholme noted of the T5 project, "*There was a mindset change at the centre of T5. It was not a perfect project, but one where people woke up in the morning thinking, I know what the directives are and I'm part of a single team and I'm going to make this work. I think we'd worked with each other for sufficiently long enough that we had a level of trust. We actually had to spend a lot of time and investment in people and in understanding relationships.*"

Behaving as trusted partners is a key component for collaborative innovation. Although studies have noted there is no such thing as instant trust in outsourcing it can be built over time through demonstrable performance.

Finally, organizations do not deliver collaboration and innovation, people do. The importance of the behavior change exhibited in Figure 13-4 becoming part of the 'DNA' of individual actions is captured well by an IT provider for an oil company, "*Being a strategic partner, as a supplier, means that if I tell you to come and visit me because I've got a problem, you will come and visit me. I always make sure I get more of the time of both decision makers and the innovators in those supplier organizations. It's only the people in that company that can be innovative and innovative (as opposed to inventive) people back up words with actions.*" In Statoil Hydro, senior manager Rune Aase remarked, "*Innovation comes from a supplier that surprises me! I always say to my people, and suppliers, 'surprise me!' I want them to be pro-active. They do it before you ask them.*"

Our work suggests, then, the following lessons on performing:

- Leading, contracting, and organizing in new ways shape new behaviors.

- Collaborative innovation is most effective when it generates high personal, competence-based, and motivational trust between the parties. **Personal trust** is the confidence one has that another person will work for the good of the relationship based on their integrity and adherence to moral norms. **Competence-based trust** exists when one party has confidence that the other will deliver successfully on their tasks and responsibilities. **Motivational trust** is where both parties believe their 'pain and gain' is geared towards achieving joint goals - a 'win-win' situation. Ultimately, all three trust types have to be present.

- Deep trust is a key component and shaper of the collaborative, open, learning, adaptive, flexible and interdependent behaviors required.

13.3 Encouraging Innovation

As we saw previously on contracting, providers need incentives to focus on innovations that improve the *client's* performance, rather than on innovations that solely increase the *provider's* revenue or margin. Both clients and providers in our 2013 study identified mandatory productivity targets, innovation days, and gainsharing at the project level as the most effective incentives for innovation. The threat of competition (according to providers) and special governance for innovation (according to clients) were also reported to encourage innovation effectively. Figure 13-5 shows, what we found to be the least and most effective.

Figure 13-5: Effect Collaborative Innovation

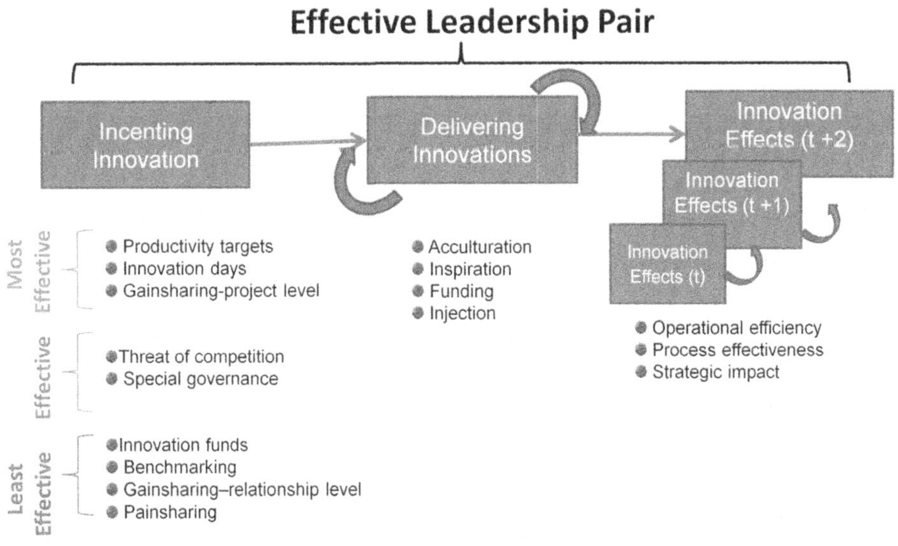

Effective Leadership Pair

Incenting Innovation → Delivering Innovations → Innovation Effects (t +2) → Innovation Effects (t +1) → Innovation Effects (t)

Most Effective
- Productivity targets
- Innovation days
- Gainsharing-project level

Effective
- Threat of competition
- Special governance

Least Effective
- Innovation funds
- Benchmarking
- Gainsharing–relationship level
- Painsharing

Delivering Innovations:
- Acculturation
- Inspiration
- Funding
- Injection

Innovation Effects:
- Operational efficiency
- Process effectiveness
- Strategic impact

We now discuss only the most effective incentives.

Mandate productivity improvements.   Many outsourcing contracts are still priced based on resource inputs, such as labor.   Clients like the simplicity and predictability of labor rates, but they also realize that input-based pricing discourages the provider from implementing innovations that would reduce inputs (e.g. labor), because the provider's revenues would decrease.   To overcome this disincentive, many clients necessitate innovation by mandating productivity improvement requirements in the contract that require the provider to improve the client's productivity, most typically by 4% to 5% per year.

Both clients and providers reported positive results from mandatory productivity targets.   For example, the provider of one HRO deal implemented a number of innovations, including new dashboards for better reporting and a new employee referral recruitment program to attract highly skilled talent such as engineers.   The client was delighted with the innovations.   Of the dashboard, the client said, "*I'd say one of the recent innovations that we began to push for and the provider responded to beautifully was more fact-based analysis.   If a measure of client satisfaction was off the key service indicator, they don't just report the score.   We could actually dive down and see what part of the business it was coming from. We could analyze hiring patterns…It was not part of the original relationship, but they really brought that to the table.*"

The provider for this client confirmed that the innovation was prompted by the productivity requirement, "*The dashboard is an innovation that we have implemented in the last year at no additional cost to the client.   It is a part of our ongoing continuous improvement.*"

Dedicate time each year to drive the innovation agenda. Innovation objectives can quickly slide down the list of priorities if everyone's attention is focused on operations.   In high-performing relationships, the parties don't let operational issues stall innovation; they contractually dedicate time each year to drive the innovation agenda.   These contractual clauses are called a number of things, including innovation days, invest days, or innovation forums. They work slightly differently in each contract, but the essential commonality is collaboratively defining the innovation agenda for the coming year.

One provider's account manager explains how it works on her client, *"We have, in every major service line, what is called an innovation forum at least once a quarter. We bring what we see in the market and the client brings what they are seeing in their market. We'll look at this, combine it together, and figure out what our continuous improvement agenda needs to be collectively over the next quarter."*

Another provider explains how the innovation agenda is set on his client, *"Between ourselves and the client, we ask, 'what additional value in innovation can we bring in any given year?' We have our basic operational plan for any given year. What sits on top of that is that is an innovation plan that we try to focus on at least four to six key value innovations in any given year."*

From this process, the parties developed an innovation agenda that included moving 40% of the training courses online, including mobile learning capabilities through Smartphones.

Gainshare the benefits from specific innovation projects. Among all the ways to encourage innovation, gainsharing packs the most punch because it promises to increase the provider's revenue as well as the client's performance. On our 2013 innovation survey, 79% of clients, 77% of providers, and 78% of advisors indicated that gainsharing on innovation benefits was the best way to encourage innovation. However, in a follow-up question, clients indicated that only 40% of innovations delivered on their accounts used gainsharing.

Our paired interviews also found less than half the clients had gainsharing clauses. Even when gainsharing was in the contract, only half of these clients availed the gainsharing option. On the other hand, a quarter of clients reported that gainsharing was prompting powerful innovations on their accounts.

What distinguished successful from unsuccessful gainsharing? Gainsharing was most effective when used at the project level. Clients and providers who built a business case for each innovation project and agreed in advance how the financial compensation would be allocated, reported great results with gainsharing. In contrast, clients who contracted for a yearly gainshare or painshare based on overall provider performance reported poor or mixed results, which we discuss further below.

One of the best examples of project-level gainsharing comes from Microsoft.[127] Microsoft has a global contract for financial and accounting services with Accenture. The parties agree to the gainshare allocation for each innovation project in advance. Specifically, the parties agree upfront how much Microsoft's bill will be reduced and how much Accenture's profit margin will increase. As Microsoft's senior director of financial operations explains, *"If I run a project together with Accenture that takes a person away, then Accenture loses the revenue of say $100 and a profit of $10. That would be stupid of Accenture to do. So what we then did was looked at those projects to make sure we have a split of the gainshare to make it attractive for both of us to do this."*

Under this scenario, Microsoft might encourage Accenture by agreeing to pay $20 after the transformation, allowing Accenture to double its profit while reducing Microsoft's bill by $80. The overall effect is the creation of strong incentives for Accenture, as described by the provider executive for the Microsoft relationship, *"My client recognizes that I need to meet my financial commitments as the service provider. That may sound strange but there is a realization that, fundamentally, I have to be incentivized to do some of the things I need to do. The key message is a spirit of partnership that I don't think exists in the other engagements that I've come across."*

---

[127] See Lacity, M and Willcocks, L. (2012) *"Mastering High-Performance: The Case of Microsoft's OneFinance"*. Available at www.accenture.com/Microsites/highperfbpo/Pages/who-got-it-right.aspx

The threat of competition incents some providers. Several providers in our study felt highly pressured to deliver innovations to clients because of the ubiquitous threat of competition. For example, one provider said, *"There is nothing in our contract that says we have to innovate at all. In my mind, if we don't innovate, at the time of contract renewal, the client will take this business somewhere else if we can't prove that we are delivering value beyond transactions."*

On another client, the provider sees innovations as a way to differentiate their services in a highly-competitive market, *"I think it is part of the valued added that we bring. We are constantly challenging ourselves to step up our game to improve all the time and adding value to the client's business. In doing so, we are also creating some offerings within our BPO space that are very different than conventional BPO"*.

Special governance for innovation incents some clients. Large outsourcing relationships are typically governed by operating committees focused on day-to-day operations, management committees focused on monthly invoices and service level reports, and steering committees comprised of the senior most executives, but who only meet annually (unless there is an escalated dispute).

The majority (60%) of the clients responding to our innovation survey indicated that innovation needs special governance outside the constraints of these existing committees. However, only 42% of providers agreed. In our paired interviews, we found that the people selected to lead, the *Leadership Pairs*, are more important than the structures erected to govern.

The least effective incentives, at the relationship level, were innovation funds, benchmarking, and gainsharing/painsharing. An innovation fund is a separate account set aside to fund future innovation projects. On our survey, innovation funds were recommended by 38% of clients, 30% of providers, and 33% of advisors. These lower percentages may be due to the fact that such funds are often too small to excite and motivate parties.[128]

Third-party benchmarking of best-in-breed prices and service levels are often intended to incent providers to increase performance in step with competitors. In reality, external benchmarks often trigger more disputes than innovations. For example, when an external benchmark found that the provider's unit price was well above best-in-breed price, the client wanted the price reduced. The provider claimed the comparison was unfair because the provider was maintaining the client's old technology. Newer technology, the provider argued, would be more efficient and thus have a lower price. We recommend that benchmarking be used to keep abreast of practices and prices, and identify new ways of doing things, but not be used as a win-lose negotiation tactic (see Action 47 in Building Block 8).

Clients who defined gainsharing or painsharing at the relationship level claimed that the annual performance targets were set too low. One client explained, "*The standards were a bit one-sided and not difficult to meet. It ensured that each year there was a good bit of gain, and the gain went to the provider. We lose the notion of pain/gain. To me, you should really challenge yourself to be accurate on your projections of cost as humanly possible. Your metrics should be at a high level and your performance should be at a high, agreed-upon level. You should be truly delivering something fairly extraordinary to benefit from gainsharing. That wasn't necessarily the case.*"

---

[128] See Weeks, M. (2004) *Information Technology Outsourcing and Business Innovation: An Exploratory Study of a Conceptual Framework*, (Oxford, Oxford University, Ph.D. thesis; Lacity, M. and Willcocks, L. (2011) "Part 1: What Suppliers Say About Clients: Establishing the Outsourcing Arrangement," *Cutter Consortium Sourcing & Vendor Relationships Executive Report*, Vol. 12, 2.

13.4 Delivering Innovation

Our new research provided fresh insight into the **organizing** and **performing** practices for achieving innovation. While the parties may encourage innovation by including productivity targets, allocating innovation days, and agreeing to gainshare on innovation projects, innovation still won't happen unless both parties implement a process we describe as AIFI—Acculturating (across parties at all levels), Inspiring (joint, provider and client generated ideas), Funding (in general proposers fund innovations) and Injecting (strong change management to transition individuals, teams and organizational units from the present to future state).

Acculturation: Merge cultures to foster innovation. BPO relationships don't just operate in two organizations (the client and provider), but in four or more groups within these organizations, each with its own culture:

1. the client's centralized business services area that 'owns' the relationship, known as the contract owner;

2. the client's decentralized business units that receive the services from the provider, known as the recipients;

3. the provider's centralized organization that sells the services and allocates resources to accounts; and

4. the provider's regionally dispersed service delivery centers (which may operate in several countries for example India, China, and the Philippines).

Each group typically wants different things from the relationship. The client's contract owner often wants tight cost controls, high productivity, and process standardization. The client's service recipients are bothered by controls, procedures, and standards. Instead, they want responsive, flexible, and customized services. The provider's sales area will likely value aggressive growth. The provider's delivery teams want to please both their supervisors and customers, which can leave them caught between conflicting cultures.

The leadership pair is tasked with acculturation, the process by which two or more cultures merge to form a cohesive culture. In the context of dynamic innovation, the resulting culture must be transparent so that even remotely located provider employees understand how their work contributes to the client's performance. As one provider explained, *"When someone is sitting in a place miles away, it is really important for that person to understand the impact of what he or she is doing to the client organization. As soon as you are able, get that culture in offshore delivery locations, or even onshore delivery locations, so they can relate to what kind of impact they are bringing to the client. I think it makes a huge difference in performance."*

The culture must also encourage, welcome, and reward innovation ideas.

Inspiration: Find innovation ideas. We asked respondents of the innovation survey to identify who was the primary source for innovation ideas. Clients, providers, and advisors agreed that the majority of innovation ideas were either jointly created between the parties (as described by the innovation days practice above, and in our previous work on collaborative innovation[129]) or the providers generated innovation ideas on their own.

In high-performing BPO relationships, the leadership pair actively encourages all levels in the provider organization to challenge the status quo, to question assumptions; in short, to find innovations that will improve the client's performance.

---

[129] Whitley, E. and Willcocks, L. (2011), "Achieving Step-Change in Outsourcing Maturity: Toward Collaborative Innovation," *MIS Quarterly Executive*, Vol. 10, 3, 95-107.

For example, a client executive and his remotely-located provider employees have monthly meetings to encourage, to recognize[130], and to financially reward, continuous improvement and innovation. He explained, *"We absolutely encourage – and I've done this face-to-face sitting there in India – to challenge us. We know we are complex, we know that we create some of our own problems; we are our own worst enemies in some areas. We absolutely want you to point some of those things out and point out some ideas. We have tried to make that positive. It's generated lots of good ideas that we've been able to put into practice."* The provider employees know that their ideas will be heard, vetted, and recognized.[131]

Providers are well poised to propose innovations, if encouraged to do so, because of their breadth and depth of expertise. In contrast to clients, providers focus intensely on their service category, execute services frequently, cross-fertilize ideas across a global client network, and spot trends quickly. The evidence for the provider-driven innovation is most convincing when presented by clients we interviewed.

For example, one electronic design automation client was quite pleased with his procurement provider's ability to innovate based on their expertise. Of the provider account delivery manager, he said, *"He's constantly thinking about procurement savings, category expertise, supply chain management and so on. That's what you get by having someone focus on one area specifically."* This client also said that providers can attract and retain top talent better than a client's inhouse function.

---

[130] Researchers have found that people innovate more when incentives are based on recognition and status rather than monetary rewards. See J. Birkinshaw, C. Bouquet, and J. Barsoux (2011) "The 5 Myths of Innovation," *Sloan Management Review*, Vol. 52, 2, 43-50.

[131] For on innovation funnels to find the best ideas from employees regardless of where they are based, see M. Reitzig (2011) "Is Your Company Choosing the Best Innovation Ideas?" *Sloan Management Review*, Vol. 52, 4 47-52.

Funding: Pay for innovation projects. As we learned from the gainsharing incentive, innovations are best funded as projects, each with a sound business case. But who pays for innovation under an outsourcing contract - the client or the provider? We ask respondents of the innovation survey to answer that question. In alignment with the primary source for innovation ideas, 44% of innovations were jointly funded, 36% were provider funded, and 20% were funded by the client.

Taking advisors out of the data, we mapped funding responses to the source of the idea responses (Table 13-2) and found that the party who proposed innovations also helped fund innovations. People may be only pitch innovation ideas if they themselves would benefit, and thus are willing to finance the innovation project in whole or in part.

Table 13-2: Source of Innovation Ideas and Funding

	Provider's idea	Client's idea	Joint idea	Total
Provider-funded	35	4	16	55 (36%)
Client-funded	13	12	5	30 (20%)
Jointly-funded	14	14	39	67 (44%)
Total	62 (41%)	30 (20%)	60 (39%)	151 (100%)

Injection: Manage the change. Clients from high-performing BPO relationships understand that they cannot be passive recipients of innovation. Evidence shows that clients must aggressively manage the change that innovation brings to their organization. In other words, the provider incentives lay the foundation, but the execution of dynamic innovation requires strong change management to transition individuals, teams, and organizational units from the current state to the desired future state. Innovations have to also be accepted by the two groups within clients: the contract owner and the service recipients.

Sometimes, it is the client leaders that decide against an innovation idea because they lack the energy or resources to lead the change management effort an innovation idea requires, or other activities may have priority. One client said, *"For some of the provider's ideas they've brought to us we've said, 'thanks for telling us', but actually we're not prepared to make the change."*

The risk here is that the provider will stop investing their time and resources in identifying innovations if clients continually reject ideas. If the client leaders are excited about innovation and if those leaders are respected within their own organizations, then they are usually successful in their change management efforts. One provider on a high-performing BPO relationship said of his client lead, *"He knows the business very well. He knows how relationships work and he's very politically savvy. So I think it's very important that your relationship person is respected within the client, has weight with them, and is a very strong political operator."*

Chapter 14 Offshoring - Tales from the Front Lines

"Your bottom line begins with your front line."

Jacques Phillippe Villeré

Introduction

Note: This chapter is based on excerpts from: Lacity, M. and Rottman, J. (2009) "Effects of Offshore Outsourcing of Information Technology Work on Client Project Management," *Strategic Outsourcing: An International Journal*, Vol. 2, 1, 4-26; Lacity, M. and Rottman, J. (2008) *Offshore Outsourcing of IT Work*, Palgrave, UK; Lacity, M. and Willcocks, L. (2013) *The Rise of Legal Services Outsourcing*, Bloomsbury, London

In Chapter 1, we introduced the topic of location decisions; decisions about where staff and operations are best located. This chapter more deeply focuses on *offshoring* decisions. Offshoring decisions include captive centers (a wholly-owned offshore subsidiary that provides products or services back to the parent company) and offshore outsourcing (contracting with a provider with offshore facilities and staff). Senior executives from Western-based countries, like the US and UK, choose offshoring when they wish to reduce production costs, access an abundance of overseas labor, and/or create 'follow-the-sun' operations. Our research found that many of these expected benefits from offshoring are realized, if senior leaders dedicate enough resources and support to ensure success.[132]

While strategic outsourcing decisions should be crafted by senior executives as we discussed in Chapter 2, those decisions are executed by middle managers and other staff who may not share the vision or enthusiasm of their senior leadership team. Research has found that senior executives often have an overly optimistic view of their strategic sourcing decisions because their direct reports significantly filter information. Consider the following quote from our research by an IT Architect in charge of executing an offshore outsourcing decision made by his senior leadership team, *"You didn't want to tell senior management the bad news about offshoring too much because this was their baby and you didn't want to say, 'You have a terribly ugly baby!"*

In order for executives to ensure their offshoring decisions are successful, they need a deeper understanding of the expectations, perceptions, and behaviors of the managers they assign to execute their vision. In this chapter, we focus on the role of the onshore PM (PM). Among the many stakeholders affected by offshoring, the onshore PMs were most responsible for integrating providers into project teams and for delivering projects on time, on budget, and with the required quality and functionality. Based on interviews with onshore PMs responsible for IT and legal work, we found that the changes to their roles are vast and profound.

---

[132] We began studying offshore ITO in 2004. Between 2004 and 2007, Rottman and Lacity interviewed 232 people from 68 organizations in clients, providers and advisors (middlemen). The focus of much of this chapter is on the 67 stakeholders collectively labeled as 'onshore project managers'. In reality, these participants held various titles such as Project Manager, Team Lead, Team Architect, Senior Software Engineer and Process Lead. Their common role was integrating offshore providers into their internally-managed teams. These project managers worked in 24 US-based organizations and one UK-based organization, representing many industries. We use pseudonyms to protect the identity of organizations. In 2012-2013, Lacity and Willcocks also studied global sourcing of BPO and LSO services, including offshore outsourcing to providers located in India, the Philippines, China, Northern Ireland, South Africa, and Slovakia.

Offshoring is harder than domestic sourcing because of time zone and cultural differences, increased efforts in knowledge coordination and boundary spanning, the need for more controls, and difficulties in managing dispersed teams. IT and legal work are more difficult than other domains such as call centers and low-end transaction processing because requirements are often less certain and the work requires extensive domain knowledge.

In this intense context of offshoring knowledge work, onshore PMs had to learn to manage differently compared to projects sourced with internal employees or with domestic contract workers. They had to learn new ways to coordinate work and new practices to transfer, protect, and renew knowledge. By first understanding their views on the benefits of offshoring as well as an overview of country location decisions and operating model choices, we discuss their challenges and experiences as front-line managers. For executives, we conclude the chapter with suggested practices to empower onshore PMs.

14.1 Benefits of Offshoring

Senior executives and project managers report the same benefits of offshoring, although the magnitude of benefits reported did very, particularly for cost savings. These benefits included:

- modest cost savings,

- quicker staffing of many projects,

- accesses to skills,

- faster development,

- improved onshore processes, and

- on a personal level for the onshore PM - good staff attitudes and a career boost.

*1. **Modest cost savings.*** According to onshore PMs, offshoring cost savings ranged between 15% and 30% in most organizations we studied. These cost savings consider total costs and occurred only *after* learning curves had been climbed and after best practices were in place. These overall cost savings are modest compared to some of the expectations executives hoped to achieve with offshoring.

Executives often were seduced by offshoring by comparing only the labor rates between onshore and offshore staff. They saw figures such as these:

- an IT programmer based in New York City costs $120 per hour compared to $35 an hour in Bangalore, and

- a lawyer in the US charges $250 per hour compared to $22.50 an hour in Gurgaon India.

Such simple labor comparisons excite executives who quickly calculate a 300% or more cost savings, but the total costs of offshoring include considerable search, investment, transition, and transaction costs.

Realistic costing was rarely found in companies we studied. In our research, the most common cost savings metric was calculated by multiplying the costs of the offshore hours and comparing this number with what it would have cost the client had domestic contractors been assigned the work. The number, however, does not consider transaction costs, productivity, or quality. An hour of programmer time offshore is not likely equal to the amount and quality of work for an hour of programmer time onshore—the same goes for other knowledge workers.

Some US clients used comparative cost measures that did include transaction costs and overhead costs. One telecommunication company, for example, calculates net savings as equal to the Employee Loaded Rate less Vendor Steady State less Transition Costs less Overhead. But again, this measure does not factor in productivity or quality. Because no metric is perfect, companies need a balanced scorecard approach that provides an overall indication of the value of the offshoring in terms of cost, quality, productivity, and cooperation.

2. Quicker staffing of many projects.   Many onshore managers welcomed offshoring because their projects were staffed quickly. A provider's deep bench of available talent was certainly a positive attribute from the onshore PM's perspective. One participant from a retail company told us, *"Our supplier is great at finding people. Before them, I would be scrambling within [retail] trying to find more people. Nobody had anybody available. So, I can just go to [the provider] and say send me three people and they are here."*

3. Access to skills.   Many onshore managers were delighted to have access to the offshore provider's scarce technical skills. At one US financial services firm, for example, onshore PMs used the offshore providers to meet critical skill shortages in Java, Perl, and web-based development. The provider staffed 250 people in all. As one participant from this company said, *"Our take on cost savings with offshore, even if it's a wash on cost savings, I'd have a hard time finding and bringing in 250 employees here at headquarters."*

4. Faster development when time zone differences were coordinated.   One of the unique promised benefits of offshoring is the ability to offer 'follow-the-sun' or 'sunrise-to-sunrise' development, provided that onshore managers effectively coordinate work across time zones. Some onshore managers said that their projects were indeed completed more quickly because of the offshore provider.

For example, one participant from a retail company said his large system was built in three months with the help of an offshore provider instead of the estimated six months for onshore development. He synchronized work so that the Indian employees were working on the project while US workers slept, and vice versa. Although there were more errors with offshore than inhouse development, the delays caused by fixing more errors were still offset by an overall shortened development cycle. On this project, 'follow-the-sun' development was possible because of good project management.

In a book called, *I'm Working While They're Sleeping*, Carmel and Espinosa discuss strategies for coordinating teams based in different time zones.[133]   The authors call 'timeshifting' (moving one team's work hours to accommodate another team's normal working hours) the 'mother of all solutions'.   In India, for example, millions of call center, ITO, and BPO employees work at night to service customers based in Western Europe or North America.   While timeshifting accommodates the team on the other side of the world, it can wreak havoc on the timeshifters and their families, as was documented in a video by Thomas Friedman called *The Other Side of Outsourcing.*

Carmel and Espinosa also discuss 'scattertime' as the main strategy used by onshore PMs.   Scattertime is a mode of work in which knowledge workers spread out their work into scattered chunks of time broken up by home and personal activities.   For example, US project managers may get up very early for conference calls to India or China, and then get their children ready for school before doing more work.

5. Improved onshore processes.   Outsourcing is increasingly enabled by standards defined by such groups as the International Standards Organization (ISO), the Supply Chain Council, the American Productivity and Quality Center (APQC), and the Software Engineering Institute (SEI).   Business process standards help organizations reduce costs, increase quality, transform many processes into commodities, facilitate communication, and enable smooth hand-offs of work. Business process standards also make it easier to evaluate inhouse costs versus outsourcing costs and to compare providers.[134]

---

[133] Carmel, E. and Espinosa, A. (2011) *I'm Working While They're Sleeping*, Nedder Stream Press, US.

[134] Davenport, T. (2005) "The coming commoditization of processes", *Harvard Business Review*, Vol. 83, 6, 101-8.

Onshore PMs said their offshore providers have more mature processes that helped to improve the client's onshore processes. For example, one participant from a transportation company said, *"A real problem we had was our 'process maturity level 1.5' guys talking to the vendor's 'process maturity level 5' guys. So together, we have worked out a plan with our vendor to help bring our levels up. When we do, it will be a benefit to both of us; our specifications will be better and so they can use them more efficiently."*

6. Personal benefits. In addition to the five common organizational benefits mentioned above, onshore PMs mentioned some personal benefits.

Some onshore PMs said they enjoyed working with offshore employees because ***they are bright and eager to please.*** Even though there are significant cultural differences to understand between Western-based clients and offshore providers, nearly all onshore PMs noted that offshore employees are intelligent, pleasant, have good senses of humor, and are keen to do well.

Onshore PMs felt offshore outsourcing ***helped their careers.*** The ability to manage provider relationships and the ability to manage globally dispersed teams are valued and relatively scarce skills.[135] A few project managers in our study said that serving as managers on offshore projects enhanced their careers. For example, one project manager from a financial services company was quickly promoted from managing offshore IT projects to the Program Management Office (PMO) that managed both ITO and BPO providers. After two years in that position, he was recruited by a top global provider. Another project manager was promoted at another financial services company after a merger, *"Well, after the merger and the renewed interest in offshore, my path was clear. I was the only one with any offshore experience, and so I was fast tracked and ended up running*

---

[135] Zwieg, P., et al. (2006) "The information technology workforce trends and implications 2005-2008", *MIS Quarterly Executive*, Vol. 5, 2, 47-54.

the PMO and now we have over 200 active projects. I was in the right place at the very right time!"

Despite these benefits of offshoring, there are more risks to be mitigated compared to domestic sourcing. When companies choose to source operations outside the country that uses the products or services, additional practices are needed to coordinate work, to transfer knowledge, to manage time zone differences, and to deal with cultural differences. Executives have to select among many countries, operating models, and business practices to ensure their offshoring decisions deliver on its promises.

Next, we discuss country location decisions in more detail.

14.2 Which Country?

Executives have two general approaches to selecting offshore destinations: they (1) can hire an advisory firm to find the best location or (2) offshore to locations where the organization wants to have presence for strategic reasons.

Advisory firms have country data for all sorts of operations, including IT, legal services, manufacturing, business process services, etc. For example, Vashistha and Vashistha of NEO Advisory consider government support, labor pool, infrastructure, educational system, cost advantage, and quality factors.[136] They identified "*leaders*", "*up and comers*" and "*late starters*" as shown in Table 14-1.

Table 14-1 also shows how A.T. Kearney ranked the top ten countries for global services, based on financial attractiveness, people skills and availability, and business environment. For UK organizations, OMC Partners compared offshore locations for legal services by considering the number of qualified lawyers,

[136] Vashistha, A. and Vashistha, A. (2006) *The Offshore Nation: Strategies for Success in Global Outsourcing and Offshoring*, McGraw Hill, New York.

paralegals and law graduates, English language skills, salaries, social costs, taxes, infrastructure and other factors. Table 14-1 lists their ranking based on number of qualified lawyers.

Table 14-1: Offshore Country Rankings

Vashistha and Vashistha (2006)	A.T. Kearney (2009)	OMC Partners (2011)	Willcocks et al. (2013)
Top locations for global services	Top locations for global services	by # of qualified lawyers	by skills
Leaders	1. India	1. India	1. India & Philippines
1. India	2. China	2. Philippines	
2. Philippines	3. Malaysia	3. South Africa	2. Northern Ireland & Poland
3. Russia	4. Thailand	4. Scotland	
4. China	5. Indonesia	5. Ireland	
5. Canada	6. Egypt		3. South Africa
6. Ireland	7. Philippines		
Up and Comers	8. Chile		4. Malaysia & Egypt
1. Czech Republic	9. Jordan		
2. Poland	10. Vietnam		5. Sri Lanka
3. Hungary			
4. Mexico			6. Kenya and Morocco
5. Malaysia			
Late Starters			
1. Vietnam			
2. Singapore			
3. Central America/			
4. Caribbean			
5. Brazil/South America			
6. Israel			
7. South Africa			

We, ourselves, have also done a number of location attractiveness studies.[137] For example, we surveyed and interviewed 30 senior global sourcing analysts working in client, provider, consultancy, market analysis, and research organizations to assess the relative attractiveness of nine countries providing ITO and BPO services. The assessments included cost, skills, infrastructure, environment, risks,

---

[137] See: Willcocks, L., Lacity, M. and Craig, A. (2013) "Compass Points: Assessing Countries," *Professional Outsourcing*, Issue 13, 22-31; Willcocks, L., Griffiths, C. and Kotlarsky, J. (2009) *Beyond BRIC: offshoring in non-BRIC countries: Egypt – a new growth market: an LSE Outsourcing Unit report,* London School of Economics and Political Science, London, UK.

and market potential factors. The skills assessment in Table 14-1 provides an example of one of our country rankings (in the far right column).

The skills assessment also considered the size of the labor pool with required skills, including technical and business knowledge, management skills, languages, the ability to learn new concepts and innovate, as well as the size of the local sector providing the outsourcing and related services. But location attractiveness factors, such as cost drivers and risk factors, can rapidly shift, entrapping some organizations to locations that no longer meet their needs.

A second approach calls for executives to consider a broader set of business criteria by considering the company's strategic objectives and overall commitment to certain destinations. A good question to answer is, *"Does my company have or want to have a significant presence in this country?"*

As mentioned in Chapter 1, one aerospace company selected Malaysia as their IT offshore destination because they hope to sell planes in that country. Another hardware company selected China because they hope to sell computers there. One U.S. client chose Canada because it wants providers in close physical proximity to their end customers for rapid deployment. Other participants selected offshore locations where they have existing manufacturing or R&D facilities to serve as launch pad, with current employees serving as guides to the country, providers, and culture.

14.3 Which Operating Model?

Executives also need to consider which operating model is best; a captive center, a build-operate-transfer model, a joint venture, or offshore outsourcing. Each model has a different risk profile (see Table 14-2). The most common model used to be captive centers, but with the explosion of viable providers world-wide, offshore outsourcing is becoming more widespread.

Table 14-2: Offshore Operating Models

Model	Description	Setup costs & Financial risk	Operational Control
Captive Center	A wholly-owned offshore subsidiary providing products or services back to the parent company.	Highest	Highest
Build-Operate-Transfer (BOT)	A provider owns, builds and operates an offshore facility on behalf of a client and then transfers ownership to the client after operations have stabilized.	Medium	High
Joint Venture	Both parties have equity ownership in an offshore operation.	High	Medium
Offshore Outsourcing	A client signs a contract for specified products or services in exchange for paying the provider a fee.	Lowest	Lowest

Captive Centers. With the captive center model, the parent company builds, owns, staffs, and operates its own offshore facilities. To be successful, senior executives must be willing to invest their own resources in human, social, intellectual, technical, and physical capital. Such investment is only warranted if senior executives make strong commitments to offshoring in terms of a large volume of work over a long period of time.

Among our client companies, a UK-based financial information services company made the most extensive use of captive centers. This company erected seven captive centers on four continents to significantly reduce costs, improve service, and tighten controls.

Captive centers are also justified when control over the work is vital, such as when the work content is secretive or sensitive, or because customers demand it. One example of the latter is a captive center built in India by IBM Global Services to reduce IT costs for one of its large customers, AT&T. At the time, AT&T had a seven-year contract with IBM worth nearly $1 billion and AT&T's CIO pushed IBM to create a captive center.

Build-Operate-Transfer (BOT).[138] Companies use this model as an interim step on the road to owning a captive center. With the BOT model, the offshore provider builds, owns, and operates the facility on behalf of the client, then transfers ownership to the client after completion. Rather than try to traverse the quagmire of local laws and customs on their own, the client hires a provider with local presence to build the captive center on their behalf. The provider runs the operation until stability has been achieved, at which time ownership transfers to the client.

Amazon provides a good example of the rationale behind the selection of a BOT model (see the case below). However, according to the CEO of one consulting firm we interviewed, of his 75 US clients he helped to offshore outsource, none of them actually went through with the transfer phase of the BOT model. By then, his clients were comfortable with the provider and did not want to take over the facilities. One informant quipped the reason he backed out of the transfer was, *"I don't know who to call when the lights go out, and they do!"*

Case: Amazon use of a BOT for offshore call center

As a retailer, Amazon's busiest season is Christmas. Amazon wanted to locate its next call center for customer support in the southern hemisphere to ensure that employees could get to work easily because it's summertime there in December. Amazon's other customer contact centers are predominantly located in the northern hemisphere and sometimes employees cannot commute in severe winter weather. Amazon chose South Africa as its next location. The Senior Site Leader for Amazon said, "*South Africa is aligned with European time zones. That makes it easy for us to provide service during their same hours*

---

[138] The BOT model is also known as a BOOT (Build, Own, Operate, Transfer) model in Canada, Australia, New Zealand, and Nepal.

of the day. Then it also enables us to have a site to provide overnight support for our North American businesses." In addition, Amazon deemed that South Africa has a language diversity that is difficult to find in other locations.

Amazon had compelling reasons for establishing call center capabilities in South Africa, but it did not have the resources or time to build a 1,000 plus seat center from scratch in its first year of call center operation. Amazon engaged the South African-based BPO provider, Full Circle, in 2010 using a BOT model. Full Circle helps international businesses, like Amazon, build service delivery capabilities in South Africa with its version of a BOT model it calls the *"Model Office"* solution. The Model Office is a facility that allows clients to experience customer service delivery from South Africa for a trial period prior to making any long-term investment or commitment with regard to location or specific operating model. For those clients wanting to move beyond the Model Office, Full Circle help clients transition work to a client's own captive center or even to other providers.[139] The CEO of Full Circle explained, *"We offered them the Model Office as an option which meant that they could literally be up and running within two months, with the connectivity and the staff trained, out of Cape Town...So we literally helped them with the entire transition into our Model Office where they grew to approximately 220 seats."*

While Amazon was providing customer services from the Model Office, Full Circle introduced Amazon to all the South African providers that would become its long-term associates, including recruitment partners, connectivity partners, and IT partners. By 2013, Amazon's captive center for customer services had about 1,100 employees. The center provides a range of phone, email, and live chat services, including inbound customer service for the US, UK, and German retail businesses, 'how to' assistance and more technical support for Amazon's Kindle e-reader, and support for the Amazon's US digital businesses, including Amazon Instant Video, the MP3 store, Cloud Drive and Cloud Player.[140]

Joint Ventures. With joint ventures, the client and provider both have ownership in the offshore facilities. Clients such as CSC and Perot Systems chose this model because they were willing to sacrifice some control in exchange for the provider's local expertise. Among the companies we researched, several large ones partnered with smaller Indian firms. The initial use of the joint ventures was to provide

---

[139] See www.fullcirclesa.com/docs/brochure.pdf

[140] Ovum Group (2012) "Amazon Case Study".

services back to the client investor. Clients liked this model because it required less investment and less risk than a captive center. The Indian providers liked this model because they could to use the client's stature to grow their business organically.

Many companies use **blended approaches**. For example, Ilan Oshri discusses the notion of a 'hybrid captive' in his book, *Offshoring Strategies.*[141] With a hybrid captive, a parent company owns an offshore facility that both services the parent company as well as outsources some work to local, external providers. Hybrid captives are thus a mix between a captive center and offshore outsourcing. According to Oshri, the hybrid captive allows the parent company to perform higher-value work themselves while outsourcing lower valued work to providers.

It is also not unusual to see organizations switching models. They may initially start with a captive center, and then sell it later, as in the case below. Alternatively, companies may enter a country with offshore outsourcing and later erect a captive center. One of our informants from a financial services company, for example, began with a fee-for-service, offshore outsourcing model. But as volume of work increased to 3,000 full time equivalents, the client moved to a captive center to capture the Indian provider's 30% profit margin.

Case: Alpha switches from a captive center to offshore outsourcing

Alpha is a pseudonym for a large global firm with about 300 employees in its enterprise legal department. In 2007, Alpha sought to reduce its legal spend. It decided to erect a captive center in a low cost destination because a captive center would serve to reduce legal costs while still retaining a high level of control. Alpha chose India in 2008 because of its low costs and large legal labor pool. At its peak, the Indian captive center employed 25 people, including lawyers, paralegals, and administrators. They performed tasks, ranging from simple contract reviews and regulatory filings, to administrative tasks like creating presentation materials.

---

[141] Oshri, I. (2011) *Offshoring Strategies: Evolving Captive Center Models*, MIT Press, Boston.

To manage the interface between the enterprise legal function and the captive center, Alpha assigned an expatriate manager to launch and manage the center. Expatriates are expensive and difficult to recruit, and when the first one was reassigned, a local manager took over. Soon after, the viability of the captive center came into question because the turnover rate was 40% and the captive center needed a significant financial investment in tools and technologies to better manage workflow; money Alpha did not want to spend.

Alpha decided to look for a Legal Service Outsourcing (LSO) provider to buy the captive center. Alpha's General Counsel assembled a team to manage the tendering process, which was guided significantly by Alpha's procurement department to ensure compliance around policies like ethical sourcing. The team narrowed the selection to two LSO providers. Alpha selected their LSO provider ultimately because of its strengths in people, processes, and technologies and because of its experience with serving large Western-based clients. In addition, Alpha's General Counsel said, *"They were flexible on the terms and conditions and their pricing was keen as well. They had a creative lead...I think he was impressive."*

Overall, Alpha reports that the LSO provider is meeting expectations because the cost savings are significant and because the General Counsel has been able to keep internal headcount flat, despite increased workload.

14.4 Challenges on the Front line

Thus far, we have focused on the positive benefits of offshoring, country location decisions, and operating model choices. We now turn to execution.

Our research found that enacting strategic offshoring plans is extremely difficult and front-line managers reported that offshoring created 20 significant operating *challenges*. 'Challenge' is our benign term for what onshore PMs actually called problems, headaches, or even crises.

Table 14-3 categorizes the 20 challenges of offshoring into six areas of concern: organizational support, project planning, knowledge transfer, process standardization, managing work, and managing people. The effect of is then discussed in more detail.

Table 14-3: The 20 Offshoring Challenges

Effect Category	Description	Challenge number	Chapter reference
Organizational support	Challenges arising from a lack of organizational support from the parent/client.	1-3	14.4.1
Project planning	Challenges arising from project estimation and scheduling.	4-7	14.4.2
Knowledge transfer	Challenges arising from transferring knowledge from onshore to offshore staff.	8-12	14.4.3
Process standardization	Challenges arising from different work processes between onshore and offshore employees.	13-14	14.4.4
Managing work	Challenges arising monitoring and delivering work to project schedules and estimates.	15-17	14.4.5
Managing people	Challenges arising from working with people from different cultures.	18-20	14.4.6

14.4.1 Organizational Support Challenges

Ideally, project managers should not be assigned to lead projects with offshore providers unless they have strong organizational support in the form of a robust Program Management Office (PMO) and extensive training on how to manage offshore providers. Researchers have shown that unstable organizational support can adversely affect an offshoring program.[142]

In the 25 organizations we studied, no organization initially provided the ideal level of support for onshore PMs. PMOs were typically understaffed. Most clients did hire outside firms to conduct cultural awareness training, but few

---

[142] Kotlarsky, J., Oshri, I. and Van Fenema, P. (2008) *Knowledge Processes in Globally Distributed Contexts*, Palgrave, London.

project managers received training on how to actually manage offshore providers. The level of organizational support adversely affected project managers in three ways:

Challenge 1. Onshore PMs had to fill many of the roles that should have been performed by the Program Management Office.

Challenge 2. Onshore PMs needed specialized training the first time they managed a project with offshore resources.

Challenge 3. Some onshore PMs felt offshoring hurt their careers.

1. Onshore PMs had to fill many of the roles that should have been performed by the PMO. Roughly a third of project managers mentioned that the launch of their offshore projects was delayed by internal structural issues they had assumed the Program Management Office had previously addressed.

The most frequent issues that caused delays were the inability to:

- quickly obtain visas (average time to obtain an H1b visa for the US was six months),[143]

- provide offshore personnel secure access to client systems and remote data (some project managers had to coordinate the build of shadow systems on provider sites, replicate testing data, etc.), and

- set up logon IDs (such as lack of social security numbers, requirements that a logon ID be assigned to a specific provider employee and not a generic job title).

According to the PMO Director of a biotechnology company, "*It really took us a long time to figure out how to make the on boarding process run smoothly. Since the suppliers needed access to systems from various business units and IT sectors, we had to cross organizational boundaries and create new protocols and rights*

---

[143] http://en.wikipedia.org/wiki/H-1B_visa.

profiles. However, without these processes, the suppliers sit idle waiting for us. We should have had all these processes in place much earlier than we did."

2. Onshore PMs needed specialized training the first time they managed a project with offshore resources. Researchers have found that project managers need specific training to successfully manage global projects.[144]

In our study, nearly every client provided project managers with rudimentary offshore outsourcing training. Typically, training was offered by an offshore advisory firm and focused on high-level cultural issues. However, over half the project managers said their training was too generic. These training sessions frequently only covered a country's economy, culture, music, and educational institutions. Particular attention was paid to the differences between cultural norms, but little attention was paid to managing offshore projects. Project managers needed a better understanding of how to package and transfer work to/from providers, how providers assign work to teams, and how providers monitor and report on project status.

A participant from a financial services company relayed the fatal results of having inexperienced onshore PMs working with inexperienced provider employees, *"There was a project that had gone amuck. I thought my manager had enough training to work with an [offshore] supplier and we had a supplier employee that I thought had enough training. Well, the supplier employee ended up facing off against my own inexperienced project manager. And so the two of them together, both inexperienced project managers, facing off against each other, led the project amuck."*

3. Some onshore PMs felt offshoring hurt their careers. For all the extra work offshoring poses to onshore PMs, several project managers felt offshoring hurt

---

[144] Tractinsky, N. and Jarvenpaa, S. (1995) "Information systems design decisions in a global versus domestic context," *MIS Quarterly*, Vol. 20, 12, 507-34.

their careers. Much of the project's success is outside of the project manager's control, yet they are held accountable for outcomes. Two project managers at one company we studied did everything possible to avoid managing more offshore outsourcing projects. They were worried that the difficulties related to project cost overruns and missed deadlines would follow them throughout their career. One project manager worried about the 'offshore stigma'. The other project manager said, *"I can't wait to move off of this [offshore] project! And, I am not alone, I know other project managers who are actively avoiding any projects with an offshore component. I don't want unsuccessful projects to follow me."*

14.4.2   Project Planning Challenges

Although project plans are often negotiated with business sponsors, capital budgeting committees, planning committees, and providers, onshore PMs are responsible for delivering those projects on time, on budget, with promised functionality. On the positive side, project staffing was much easier because of access to the providers' large staff according to participants. However, the inclusion of offshore providers, particularly for the first time, challenged many onshore PMs to deliver projects on time and on budget. Project plans were often unrealistic. False assumptions about costs and schedules were not uncovered until the project was already under the onshore PM's control.

The inclusion of offshore providers adversely affected project planning in the following ways:

Challenge 4. Onshore PMs needed to thoroughly verify offshore provider's work estimates, which tended to be optimistic.

Challenge 5. Onshore PMs experienced higher transaction costs.

Challenge 6. Onshore PMs experienced more project delays because of cultural differences.

Challenge 7. Onshore PMs experienced more project delays because of time zone differences.

4. Onshore PMs needed to thoroughly verify offshore provider's work estimates, which tended to be optimistic. More than half the PMs said that their offshore provider's work estimates were too low. For example, one onshore PM at a biotechnology company said he estimated internally that a project would cost about US$80,000 and take about six to nine months to complete. The provider's bid was $40,000 and they estimated it would take four months. The provider ended up spending an additional six months and the onshore team ended up fixing the product and doing the testing themselves.

At a retail company, underestimated bids were so pervasive that the CIO assigned an offshore task force to investigate the reasons. The task force identified three reasons, being that the offshore providers underestimated work because: (1) they did not fully understand what the client needed; (2) they were unfamiliar with complexities of retail's technical environment; (3) they are inherently optimistic or wanted to please the client. To counter-balance this tendency to underestimate, some PMs had frank discussions with their offshore provider managers and said, "*this estimate is too low.*" They had to reinforce that they wanted the 'most likely' forecast, not the 'most optimistic'. Some PMs simply added a buffer by increasing time estimates 30% to 50%.

5. Onshore PMs experienced higher transaction costs. Much research has identified the higher transaction costs associated with offshore outsourcing compared to domestic outsourcing.[145] These higher costs include search costs, travel costs, monitoring costs, and coordination costs. According to a study by the Meta Group, Gartner Group, and Renedis, transaction costs of offshore sourcing range from 15.2% to 57% of contract value for provider selection, transitioning the

---

[145] See for example: Qu, Z. and Brocklehurst, M. (2003) "What will it take for China to become a competitive force in offshore outsourcing? An analysis of the role of transaction costs in supplier selection", *Journal of Information Technology*, Vol. 18, 53-67; Dibbern, J., et al. (2008) "Explaining variations in client extra costs between software projects offshored to India", *MIS Quarterly*, Vol. 32, 2, 333-66.

work, layoffs and retention, lost productivity due to cultural issues, improving development processes, and managing the contract.[146]   In contrast, transaction costs of domestic outsourcing range between 4% and 10% of contract value.[147]

More than half the onshore PMs we interviewed discussed transaction costs. We note, however, that project managers frequently called transaction costs 'hidden costs'. The project managers from a retail company offered two examples of higher infrastructure costs. Several project managers said additional software license fees were not included in their budgets. On large projects with 50 people offshore, software licenses proved to be quite costly. The onshore PMs had assumed the providers held licenses for most products, but providers did not, *"I'm buying licenses for my offshore team and I'm buying licenses for my onshore team because both teams have to be able to troubleshoot and test the same piece of code. Seems like they should foot the bill for this but their expectation was that we would pay for those licenses."*

Onshore PMs also had to unexpectedly replicate the testing environment. The offshore providers could not effectively use the testing environment at the retail company's headquarters because it was too slow.   So a shadow testing environment had to be built offshore. In addition, the testing data had to be frequently updated, shipped to India, and synchronized with the US. All this contributed to cost escalation.

6. Onshore PMs experienced more project delays because of cultural differences. In addition to unidentified costs, more than half the onshore PMs also experienced project delays. Some PMs experienced project delays because of the lack of *onshore-side* readiness, such as obtaining visas, logon IDs, etc. Some

---

[146] Amrosio, J. "Experts reveal hidden costs of offshore IT outsourcing", *CIO Magazine*, available at: searchcio.techtarget.com/tip.

[147] Lacity, M. and Willcocks, L. (2001) *Global Information Technology Outsourcing: In Search of Business Advantage*, Wiley, Chichester.

projects were delayed because of lack of provider-side readiness. For example, an IT Lead at a biotechnology company said, *"[The small providers] would take forever to find resources with the skills and levels of experience we needed. The small vendors did not seem to be able to attract and retain good people. That really hurt our projects. It took longer to ramp up and if there was unplanned turnover, we were dead."*

The most frequent reason, however, for projects delays was the consequence of Challenge 4. Providers underestimated the amount of time it would take to complete work. Assigning more staff did not accelerate project completion (a phenomenon in IT known as the 'mythical man-month').[148] Some PMs identified the offshore provider's holidays and personal events as sources of project delays. Personal events (e.g. weddings and births) and national events (e.g. elections and holidays) often take much longer in Eastern cultures than Western ones. For example, weddings in India are frequently weeklong events.

7. Onshore PMs experienced more project delays because of time zone differences. Onshore PMs found that time zone differences hindered their projects. When the timing was not well coordinated, employees in India remained idle for an entire day while waiting for the US team to respond to a query or to review work. One PM, from a financial services company, said the client's onshore database administrator *"leaves at 5:00 every day even it means my team in India will be idle for a day waiting for him to add the schema."* Time-zone challenges are so pervasive that many clients pursue nearshoring to source to providers with significant time zone overlap.[149]

---

[148] The mythical man-month phenomenon shows that adding more resources to a late software project delays it even further; first described in Brooks, F. (1975) *The Mythical Man Month: Essays in Software Engineering*, Addison-Wesley, Reading, MA.

[149] Carmel, E. and Abbott, P. (2007) "Why nearshore means that distance matters", *Communications of the ACM*, Vol. 50 No. 10, 40-6.

14.4.3   Knowledge Transfer Challenges

Knowledge transfer to providers (whether domestic or offshore) has long been recognized as a ubiquitous outsourcing challenge. Knowledge transfer is one of six critical outsourcing success factors identified by Koh, et al. in their 2004 study of the psychological contract (one's beliefs about each party' obligations) in outsourcing relationships.[150]

Our study found that onshore PMs often had difficulty transferring knowledge to offshore providers. Many clients initially ignored, or drastically underestimated, knowledge transfer requirements. The provider needs deep knowledge on the client's business requirements, technical platforms, and internal practices and procedures before they could be assigned actual work.

A financial services firm noted that offshore providers have generic knowledge about banking, but this firm needed the provider to understand how the firm processes credit cards for particular business customers. In comparison to transferring knowledge to new internal employees or to domestic contractors, project managers had to learn new ways to transfer, test, and renew knowledge to/from offshore providers.

Specifically, project managers described five challenges on knowledge transfer:

Challenge 8.   Onshore PMs had to do more knowledge transfer upfront.

Challenge 9.   Onshore PMs were forced to shortcut the knowledge transfer process because of deadlines set by senior leaders.

Challenge 10.   Onshore PMs had to ensure that knowledge transfer was successful by testing/verifying the provider employee's knowledge.

Challenge 11.   Onshore PMs had to ensure knowledge renewal.

---

[150] Koh, C., Ang, S. and Straub, D. (2004) ''IT outsourcing success: a psychological contract perspective'', *Information Systems Research*, Vol. 15, 4, 356-73.

Challenge 12. Onshore PMs had to ensure that provider's knowledge about the new applications or technologies was transferred to the client.

8. Onshore PMs had to do more knowledge transfer upfront. When team members comprised only internal staff and domestic contractors, project managers said they transferred knowledge incrementally. However, when a project included offshore employees, knowledge transfer occurred in a more concentrated timeframe. Some members of the offshore delivery team were only on site for a few weeks, so the project managers planned for intensive knowledge transfer. A participant from a retail company said, *"When you have an internal person, you give them a little bit because you know they are around. They can come up and ask you a question. When you bring in someone offshore, knowledge transfer is more structured. We have to invest more time. When you know they are going back offshore, you need to take advantage of those three to four months and give them as much information as you can."*

Similarly, a development manager in a financial services company reported the need for knowledge transfer, *"When a large project was delivered, we ran into problems with bad code. I got the distinct impression the supplier had placed novice programmers on the job. In fact, I think just a few of the nine developers had received any knowledge transfer from the more experienced members of the team. This caused us to see all résumés for all developers and take a more diligent approach to knowledge transfer."* This effect was quite common, and mentioned by nearly three quarters of project managers.

9. Onshore PMs were forced to shortcut the knowledge transfer process because of deadlines set by senior leaders. This effect was only mentioned by two project managers, but it is quite interesting. In one telecommunications company, senior leaders told the project managers that they only had eight weeks to transfer knowledge before turning control over to the offshore provider. The project managers said they needed four to six months. Senior leadership enforced the mandate. After eight weeks, the work was outsourced to the offshore provider and client-side project managers were reassigned or terminated. Quality deteriorated. The provider kept trying to track down the reassigned project managers to ask for help. Two months later, a substantial system bug made it through the provider's testing phase, causing the telecommunications company financial losses and loss of goodwill with their external customers.

10. Onshore PMs had to ensure that knowledge transfer was successful by testing/verifying the provider employee's knowledge. We heard from many project managers that Indian employees often do not express lack of understanding. An onshore PM's superficial question *"Do you understand?"* prompted superficial provider responses such as *"Yes."* To the offshore provider, a *"yes"* to that question meant, *"Yes, I hear what you are saying to me"* and not *"Yes, I understand your requirements."* To ensure knowledge transfer has truly occurred, many onshore PMs orally quizzed their offshore providers.

A participant from a retail company said, *"During the knowledge transfer portion, the project manager actually gave them oral tests every Monday based on what they learned. She quizzed them to see what they learned so she could tell 'Are they really picking up the knowledge?' And she'd say, 'yeah, they did well!"* Of course, 'quizzes' were not official tests, but rather frequent and detailed conversations to ensure that offshore employees understood the business requirements.

11. Onshore PMs had to ensure knowledge renewal. According to the majority of participants, unexpected provider turnover threatened to erode the client's initial upfront investment in knowledge transfer. High staff turnover in low cost countries has been a major problem for providers. In India, LSO turnover rates in Gurgaon can be as high as 30% because the proliferation of providers makes it easy for workers to find alternative employment. Clients and providers understand that turnover will occur. The General Counsel for a UK based company that outsources legal services to India said, *"Turnover is a reality of outsourcing. So,* *you need to have good systems in place on their part so that capturing knowledge and sharing that knowledge is within team."*

Onshore PMs reported a number of strategies to protect the knowledge investment by requiring the provider to implement knowledge renewal practices. A retail company ensured knowledge renewal by including a contractual clause that required the provider to have replacements shadow incumbent employees for a period of two to four weeks, depending on the nature of the work. The problem was that the onshore PMs often had no good way of verifying the work shadowing actually occurred because workers were located offshore. A few project managers suspected that new hires were assigned to projects and billed to clients before the required shadowing period took place.

A manufacturing company had one of the most formalized approaches to knowledge renewal. This company's project managers spent a considerable amount of time initially training the provider's IT leads that had been brought onshore for knowledge transfer. Once this initial training was done, the client project managers never planned to do any more provider training. Instead, the provider was responsible for additional knowledge renewal and transfer to other provider employees. Before the client-trained provider leads returned to India, they were required to train their replacements through onsite work shadowing for a few months. The provider welcomed this practice, *"The overlap allows us to help ease the transition. We can share the stories, and the history at a personal level. For example, there are 'inside jokes' that only the delivery teams would understand. We can transfer that 'soft knowledge' along with technical lessons learned about the creation of embedded software."* Once the provider leads then went back to India, they went on to train the offshore provider employees. This practice has worked quite well for the manufacturing company since 2004.

12. Onshore PMs had to ensure that provider's knowledge about the new applications or technologies was transferred to the client. In addition to transferring knowledge to offshore providers, some project managers also discussed the issues of transferring knowledge <u>from</u> offshore providers. With domestic contractors, knowledge transfer from the provider to client was frequently informal. Client staff literally looked over a domestic contractor's shoulder or sat by their side to learn about the domestic contractor's deep technical expertise and to understand the systems they were building for clients. In contrast, offshore contractors were located remotely from client staff, thus informal knowledge transfer did not take place.

For one retail company, this issue meant that the retailer's onshore PMs could not always support the applications built by offshore teams. After years of a good outsourcing relationship with their large Indian provider, the retailer began to assign them more strategic work. One particular application determines the type and volume of products to stock in retail stores. The retailer's onshore PMs were very pleased with the provider's work. However, one negative consequence of the project was that the retailer's internal team did not learn enough about the application to support it in production. The offshore provider was given the maintenance contract. As the Development Director said, *"If something happens to [the offshore provider], God forbid, we'd be at a complete standstill."*

14.4.4   Process Standardization Challenges

Outsourcing is increasingly enabled by process standards. In the context of software development, different cultures rely on different development processes.[151] Many offshore providers rely on their advanced levels of SEI's CMM (Capability Maturity Model) and CMMI (Capability Maturity Model Integrated) to develop applications for clients. CMM/CMMI has five levels of process maturity; level 1 being the least mature and level 5 being the most mature

---

[151] Iivari, J. and Huisman, M. (2007) "The relationship between organizational culture and the deployment of systems development methodologies", *MIS Quarterly*, Vol. 31, 1, 3-58.

(see Figure 14-1). As process maturity increases, so does quality and productivity.[152]

Figure 14-1: Process Maturity in Software Development

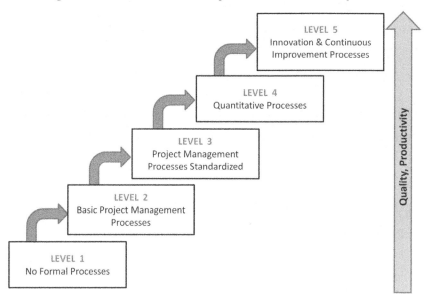

In addition to improving software quality and productivity, CMM/CMMI are designed to facilitate communication and enable smooth trade-offs between clients and providers. This assumes, however, that clients and providers have similar maturity levels.

In our research, the majority of the 25 US and UK-based clients had lower CMM capabilities compared to their offshore providers. This posed real problems for the transfer of work to/from offshore providers. Our participants are not unique in this regard, *"Having standardized processes can help keep costs down, but there may*

---

[152] These sources all examined the effects of process standardization on product quality: Adler, P., et al. (2005) "Enabling process discipline: lessons from the journey to CMM level 5", *MIS Quarterly Executive*, Vol. 4, 1, 215-27; Ramasubbu, N., et al. (2008) "Work dispersion, process based learning, and offshore software development performance", *MIS Quarterly*, Vol. 32, 2, 437-58; Harter, D., et al. (2000) "Effects of process maturity on quality, cycle time, and effort in software product development", *Management Science*, Vol. 46, 4, 451-67.

not be much of an advantage for a company at a CMM Level 2 to hire a software company at a Level 5. The client company doesn't have the internal discipline to take advantage of the Level 5 provider's standardized routines. They will pay a higher price and not be able to take advantage of all the provider can offer them. 'It's like being a car salesman in Alaska touting a car's great air conditioning. It may be great, but you can't take advantage of it' says Bill Peterson, program director for software engineering process management at the SEI."[153]

A second issue that emerged from our study was the extent to which providers were truly committed to CMM/CMMI processes. Because CMM/CMMI levels are only assessed once, a provider may lay claim to their CMM/CMMI capability for life. Some onshore PMs claimed that providers did not always follow their own CMM/CMMI processes. However, project managers noted one positive effect - providers helped the client improve their own internal processes.

The two challenges of process standards on the role of the onshore PM are:

Challenge 13. Onshore PMs had to provide greater detail in requirement definitions because of process standardization.

Challenge 14. Onshore PMs had to ensure the provider's employees were fully trained in process standards as promised by providers.

13. Onshore PMs had to provide greater detail in requirement definitions because of process standardization. One consequence of the fact that clients had lower process maturity levels than their offshore providers was that onshore PMs had to provide much greater detail in their requirement definitions. In many clients, requirements definition had traditionally been more informal. Close physical proximity between project managers and users allowed them to iteratively define requirements during systems development.

---

[153] King, J. (2003) "The pros & cons of CMM", *Computerworld*, Vol. 37,49, p. 50.

At a biotechnology company, for example, requirements definition is still an informal process when done onshore. Project managers speak frequently with users who are usually located on campus headquarters. The user feedback cycle is quick. In contrast, project managers working on the offshore pilots had to engage in many formal and planned communications with providers and users to create the provider's required documents. One participant said, "*the overhead costs of documenting some of the projects exceeded the value of the deliverables.*"

We heard many other stories on the level of details required with offshore outsourcing. One project manager from an insurance company said he was surprised when a financial statement came back with the dollar fields left justified. According to him, the provider responded, "*You didn't say you wanted them right justified.*" The project manager at a financial services company noted, "*You ask for one button to be moved and the supplier has to first do a twenty page impact analysis - we are paying for all this documentation we don't need.*"

One participant from a retail company said she was surprised about how much she needed to define requirements, "*It's been a real shift for us to have to deal in the level of detail that this offshore model requires. I'm used to delegating something to very knowledgeable people who could fill in details. With offshore, you first have a high-level design called a use-case. My folks [at Retail] can take that use-case and run with it. [With offshore] you have to turn use-cases into detailed requirements.*" Whereas these onshore projects managers felt burdened by the provider's commitment to process standards, other project managers actually complained that providers failed to follow their own processes.

14. Onshore PMs had to ensure the provider's employees were fully trained in process standards as promised by providers. At a retail company, one onshore PM said that the offshore provider bragged about its process maturity during sales and negotiations, but the provider employees assigned to her team were slow to respond when she asked to see their code reviews, inspections, and test cases. After a significant delay, she would be handed something that was of inferior quality. After much probing, she found out that the provider assigned new hires to her contract before they completed their advertised *"intensive process training."* What annoyed this project manager most was that the new provider people were not introduced as new. They were introduced as fully trained. It wasn't until the project was underway that she discovered their low level of experience, *"We expected to get someone pretty experienced. They should be able to read a dump. And they should know what a soft seven is, that kind of stuff. On average, two were fine, but one couldn't answer very basic questions."*

The final quote in this section is from a project manager at a manufacturing company. He said it took nearly four years to figure out how to effectively engage offshore providers. Improving their internal processes was a key enabler of success, *"We have come a long way in four years. The first time we did this (utilize offshore development teams), we thought we could 'throw the requirements over the ocean' and good code would come back. It was a terrible mistake and looking back, we really didn't understand our own processes. We had to rethink our entire development process and analyze how we train our own people, how we manage the development process, and how we actually develop code. Our second attempt is moving along much better."*

14.4.5   Managing Work Challenges

Research has shown that the geographic dispersion of teams often caused by offshore outsourcing creates significant barriers for project managers and requires specialized mechanisms to overcome those barriers.[154] The changes to the onshore PM's role were particularly evident in our study for turnkey projects (projects

---

[154] Maloney, M. and Zellmer-Bruhn, M. (2006) "Building bridges, windows and cultures: mediating mechanisms between team heterogeneity and performance in global teams", *Management International Review*, Vol. 46., 6, 697-720; Maznevski, M. and Athanassiou, N. (2006) "Guest editors' introduction to the focused issue: a new direction for global teams research", *Management International Review*, Vol. 46, 6.

where the offshore provider is responsible for the management and delivery of a predefined project).

On turnkey projects, onshore PMs had to manage the provider's work *products* rather than the provider's *staff.* Many onshore PMs said this was difficult because offshore providers uniformly did not report when they were going to miss a deadline. This made it difficult for onshore PMs to trust the provider to independently complete work. In order for the onshore PM to manage the provider's work products, they created more frequent milestones, required more detailed status reports, and requested more frequent work meetings.

These three challenges were pervasive and mentioned by more than half the participants:

> Challenge 15. Onshore PMs needed to set more frequent milestones.
> Challenge 16. Onshore PMs needed more frequent and detailed status reports.
> Challenge 17. Onshore PMs needed more frequent meetings to prevent client-caused bottlenecks.

15. Onshore PMs needed to set more frequent milestones. To help onshore PMs manage work (not people) many project managers required more frequent milestones for work packets. For example, onshore PMs at a manufacturing company segmented work into small, well-defined tasks. These tasks were typically five to seven business day activities that had clearly defined objectives and requirements. Onshore PMs at a retail company created intermediate milestones and more frequent 'code drops' so that project managers could better track progress. For domestic contractors, the retailer typically has two or three milestones for an eight-month project. For offshore providers, some project managers went to weekly milestones.

16. Onshore PMs needed more frequent and more detailed status reports. At several client companies, onshore PMs requested more frequent and more detailed status reports from offshore providers than from domestic providers. At one US bank, the project manager required daily status reports using a form with very targeted and specific questions for the offshore team lead. She said that it was easier for the offshore team lead to report delays in written form. At a retailer, several project managers went from weekly status reports to daily updates. One participant said, *"When they first came, we were meeting weekly with them. We do it daily now. Every single day, on both projects, we spend an hour with them going over what they're doing. Every single thing."*

17. Onshore PMs needed more frequent meetings to prevent client-caused bottlenecks. On development projects, many onshore PMs said that offshore providers halted work when they needed the client to answer a question, approve a deliverable, enable the infrastructure, or test the provider's work. These are quite legitimate reasons to halt work, so onshore PMs had to find ways to avoid the bottlenecks. The project manager at a financial services firm had to appeal to senior leadership to *"light a fire"* under the client's infrastructure staff.

At a retail company, project managers created two daily meetings during the requirements analysis phase for large-scale development. Project managers met with the offshore provider engagement managers every day from 4:30 to 5:30 pm. During this meeting, onshore PMs gathered unresolved issues from the offshore provider and provided answers from users to yesterday's queries. Every morning, onshore PMs met with users to seek answers to the provider's questions in time for the 4:30 meeting. A participant from the retail company said, *"When there are 50 people offshore and everybody has a very specific thing to do and they are stuck, they need a quick turnaround."*

14.4.6   Managing People Challenges

While onshore PMs must learn to manage work interfaces with offshoring providers (rather than micro-managing the provider's offshore staff), onshore PMs could not fully escape managing offshore people. For example, onshore PMs needed to fully understand the work of each provider employee to verify provider invoices on staff augmentation engagements. In particular, onshore PMs had to manage the provider's onsite engagement managers and staff. Besides welcoming and integrating onsite provider employees, the main issue that arose from our research was the need for onshore PMs to manage the user-provider interface.

The people challenges were:

Challenge 18. Onshore PMs had to motivate the provider to share bad news.
Challenge 19. Onshore PMs needed to accompany offshore providers to client-facing meetings.
Challenge 20. Onshore PMs had to spend time to make offshore providers feel welcome and comfortable.

18. Onshore PMs had to motivate the provider to share bad news. One uniform complaint we heard is that the Indian providers did not like to report when they were going to miss a deadline. Researchers have called this the offshoring 'mum effect'.[155] This makes it difficult for onshore PMs to trust the provider to independently complete work. A participant from a retail company said, *"They don't like to tell you that they're going to miss a deadline. I think they think they can make up for it and hustle and get there, but they can't. So you find out very shortly before the deadlines that they are going to be missed."*

Several participants from a biotechnology company mentioned this as well. The Offshore Project Coordinator said, *"When the project was going so far off course, they never really told us that they were behind on deadlines. They always said everything was going well."* One IT Lead summed it up by saying, *"The place could be on fire and they would say, 'Oh it's great, a little warm, but it is great!'"*

[155] Ramingwong, S. and Sajeev, A. (2007) "Offshore outsourcing: the risk of keeping mum", *Communications of the ACM*, Vol. 50, 8, 101-3.

To motivate the provider to deliver bad news, one development director had a very frank discussion with the provider. She said she needed advanced notice when a deadline might be missed. She would work with the provider to determine the best way to address the issue. She said it was in his best interest to forewarn her because then she could not accuse him of being late because he made a decision without her. With advanced notice, the decision was made together. Furthermore, she said the provider was losing money by pouring resources in, working the weekends, working nights, when some of this could be avoided if the provider provided realistic status updates.

19. Onshore PMs needed to accompany offshore providers to client-facing meetings. By accompanying onsite engagement managers to client-facing meetings, project managers (or their representatives) served important social boundary-spanning roles. The client project manager prevented scope creep, ensured understanding, and fostered the user-offshore employee relationship.

Concerning scope creep, one PM from a retail company said, *"Scope creep? It was scope explosion!"* If the client wanted it, then the provider said yes and created a new project. She continued, *"Because they're so willing to do things and so willing to please, that's their culture, we were finding they were doing things that we couldn't afford. Now even though they may go to user meetings, there's always an IT person there."*

Another onshore PM from a manufacturing company said in their first attempt at offshore outsourcing, the only people who saw the scope creep were the accounts payable people on the client's side and the accounts receivable people at the provider's side. Now, each task has an owner and projects are watched from both functional and accounting perspectives. By using this strategy, the manufacturer is seeing much less rework and the quality has improved considerably.

Besides controlling scope, a second reason for accompanying providers to client-facing meetings was to foster the user-offshore employee relationship. Without the onshore PM's presence, some users complained about having to speak directly to the offshore staff. According to the Director of Development in a retail company, *"There were a couple of occasions where Provider A went directly to the person that had the issue and there was a language thing there. Why is this man calling me? I don't know what he is asking. I don't know his name."*

20. Onshore PMs had to make offshore providers feel welcome and comfortable. Offshore provider employees need to develop a rapport with the client's team members. Nearly all the onshore PMs in our study appreciated that it was difficult for foreign workers to come to a strange country for extended periods of time. The managers welcomed them by including them in social events at work and by being considerate of cultural differences.

For example, one PM said she made sure every work-related event included vegetarian meals when offshore employees were invited to attend. By including them in social events, the rapport between the parties strengthened, and some even developed lasting friendships. One manager from a manufacturing company said, *"They got to be friends with and got to know all of the people here and the people here got to know them. So when they go back to India they're not some nameless face that's just working on software. They're friends of the people who are here."*

14.5 Executive Practices

Executives must enact practices that will better help their front line managers deliver on their strategic outsourcing decisions. From our research, we found that executives that used the following four practices had better outcomes in terms of aligning and empowering their employees and achieving expected business benefits from offshoring:

1. Provide enough resources to implement the sourcing strategy.
2. Be willing to change internal work practices.
3. Build social capital with key provider executives.
4. Seek independent assessment of sourcing strategy effectiveness.

1. Provide enough resources to implement the sourcing strategy. According to onshore PMs, senior executives need to invest enough resources to make sure they can execute their duties. These resources include:

- top internal talent to manage the offshoring program,

- top onshore PMs to lead project teams,

- outside consultants to help select destinations, investigate providers, and negotiate contracts,

- training for internal staff that will be assuming new roles,

- investments in knowledge transfer, knowledge protection, and knowledge renewal, including training, work shadowing and mentoring for provider staff,

- onsite provider managers (who cost more than provider staff located offshore), and

- sufficient funds for travel, infrastructure, etc.

Simply stated, it takes money to save money. At one financial services firm, the CFO invested $13.5 million upfront in order to achieve the expected benefits. In contrast, one of the biggest causes of offshore outsourcing failure in our case companies was insufficient internal resources. In fact, we were shocked that so many Program Management Offices (PMO), for example, were understaffed considering all the roles they were expected to fulfill. Lack of funding for a properly resourced PMO pushed its functions onto the already burdened onshore PMs.

Insufficient resources were primarily found in companies using offshore outsourcing primarily to reduce total costs. Senior executives were legitimately afraid to invest too many resources because they knew these additional costs would erode much of the expected savings.

However, total cost savings cannot be generated unless the executives commit enough of these internal resources. For example, a provider employee will only be productive and produce high quality work after a significant investment in knowledge transfer. The solution is that the outsourcing program has to be large enough to generate overall savings, *given the required investment* in these resources.

2. Be willing to change internal work practices. While senior executives often hold the view that offshore providers need to adapt to the client's work practices, clients had more success with outsourcing when they formalized their internal processes to match better provider process capability. Providers adopt best-in-class work practices and follow process standards more closely than clients. To us, it makes sense for clients to increase formality given the empirical evidence that process maturity increases quality and reduces development time and effort. In the long term, process standardization facilitates communication, enables smooth hand-offs, and makes it easier for clients to compare providers.

3. Build social capital with key provider executives. While executives from large clients are not involved directly with project work involving providers, it is important that executives establish relationships with the provider's senior management. A close relationship with provider executives increases the provider's commitment to the client, provides a conduit to access the provider's best resources, and establishes the clout to quickly remedy problems. Onshore PMs cannot successfully navigate through big issues, such as excessive provider employee turnover or crises in the provider organization.

For example, one CIO spoke many times with the offshore provider's CEO and operating officers about the nuclear tensions between India and Pakistan, *"I had their chief officers calling me at least monthly to update me on the political situation and their planned responses. They were positioning resources in Canada to be able to pick up operations and provide business continuity outside of India."*

Most importantly, social capital must be viewed as a business asset. While friendships among client and provider employees are pleasant, the real purpose of social capital is to add business value. Social capital enables knowledge and resource exchanges that add value in terms of increased efficiency, better quality, and more innovation. Because work is done through people, these relationships matter.

4. Seek independent assessment of sourcing strategy effectiveness. Senior executives should occasionally engage an independent third party to assess the effectiveness of their sourcing strategy. Although it was common among our cases for executives to assign this task to internal teams or the PMO, we found that lower-level employees are less likely to honestly report on sourcing issues. Many onshore PMs simply did not feel they could complain to senior leaders (which is why they may have complained anonymously to us during our research).

At one company, for example, the PMO reported each month to executives that offshore outsourcing was successful in meeting cost objectives, yet our own interviews with the company's onshore PMs found mixed results and that success varied widely across projects. Many team leads and project managers did not report significant issues to their superiors because the message was *"offshoring had to succeed."*

While an executive's strong commitment to success is a key enabler, the commitment cannot come at the price of lost learning. Independent assessments of a sourcing initiative will objectively gather learning across projects without compromising the staff's confidentiality.

14.6 Conclusion: Successful Offshoring

Successful offshoring requires a deep understanding of the expectations, perceptions, and roles of all the stakeholders from both parties. In this chapter, we have provided a deep understanding on one of those stakeholder groups, the onshore PMs responsible for the daily operations of offshore engagements.

Offshoring can produce significant business benefits, including lower costs, quicker staffing of projects, access to skills, faster development, and improved onshore processes. But achieving these benefits requires senior executives who are will to invest enough resources in offshoring, and onshore PMs capable of facing the challenges related to organizational support, project planning, knowledge transfer, process standardization, and the management of work and people.

It is important to understand the challenge perceptions discussed in this chapter are the reality for the people who hold these views. Whether some of these onshore PMs were 'wrong' or merely whiners and complainers is irrelevant. The bigger issue is that these are their perceptions, and understanding their perceptions is a first step in helping improve relationships.

By understanding the effects of offshoring on the project managers onshore, senior executives can better understand the evolving roles and responsibilities of global project managers and increase project success by empowering their management team with the organizational support, training, and resources needed to successfully engage offshore providers.

Chapter 15 Ideas Whose Time have Come

"All the forces in the world are not so powerful as an idea whose time has come."

Victor Hugo

Much of this book has covered the fundamentals of successful sourcing. Indeed, the first nine chapters provided 'all you need to know' about the essentials of sourcing, in general, and of outsourcing, in particular. Mastery of these essentials is required before tackling more advanced practices, such as bundling (Chapter 12), innovation through outsourcing (Chapter 13) and offshoring (Chapter 14).

In this final chapter, we present ideas that are not widely disseminated, but have proven to boost outsourcing performance in our recent case study research. These ideas are advanced practices whose time has come.

The first three concepts are about redesigning back offices and integrating the provider more meaningfully into the client:

- Goodbye Pyramids, Hello Diamonds (section 15.1),
- Go For Big Picture KPIs (15.2), and
- Refocus: From Conflict to Resolution (15.3).

The next five focus on the technologies, in our Technology Spotlight:

- Self-service portals (15.4.1),

- Automation (15.4.2),

- Workflow and governance tools (15.4.3),

- Analytics (15.4.4), and

- Cloud computing (15.4.5).

Finally, there are a number of niche markets warranting consideration in our Rising Market section, including:

- Rural sourcing (15.5.1),

- LSO - Legal services outsourcing (15.5.2),

- Crowdsourcing (15.5.3), and

- Impact sourcing (15.5.4).

15.1 Goodbye Pyramids, Hello Diamonds

Let's face it. In many large companies, back office functions (e.g. IT, HR, financial and accounting services, indirect procurement, and legal functions) are still neglected and messy. These have been cobbled together through decades of mergers and acquisitions or just been starved of investment and senior management attention. Low-performing back offices are characterized by under-investment, low employee morale, inefficient and non-standardized processes, and by outdated, redundant, and non-integrated technology.

Even in 2014, we find plenty of these around - especially in areas that have not traditionally been under the threat of outsourcing. In contrast to the low-performers, high-performing back offices are characterized by lower and more variable costs, service excellence, business enablement, innovation, scalability, flexibility, and compliance.

How can low-performing back office functions become high-performing? The five main transformation levers we discovered amongst high performers are centralization, standardization, optimization (e.g., reducing errors, redesigning processes), technology enablement, and labor relocation to lower cost areas. We also see organizations transforming the shape of their back office functions from 'pyramids' to 'diamonds' (Figure 15-1).

Figure 15-1: Pyramids to Diamonds[156]

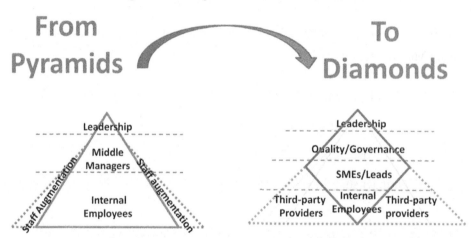

Pyramids are heavily populated with employees, most of who are at the bottom of the pile. The benefit of the pyramid design is that employees continually build valuable, organization-specific experience as they move higher up the pyramid. The pyramid is strong on retained knowledge, but it is also costly.

Managers recruiting university graduates to fill the lower ranks must compete with providers who court these recruits with richer career paths and the opportunity to work with many more of their peers. When recruiting fails, or 'head count' restrictions are imposed, the pyramid then tends to fill in skill and resource gaps with expensive local contract workers (staff augmentation in Figure 15-1).

---

[156] Adapted from Jim Lammers, Express Scripts and from Sandy Ogg, Unilver.

Diamond-shaped organizations replace the heavy bottom of the pyramid with outsourcing providers. Transactional activities that were performed by employees are instead performed by providers, typically in a low-cost location.

Diamonds need more quality assurance and governance skills to coordinate services with providers. So rather than having middle managers, there are subject matter experts (SMEs) and project leads.

The benefits of the diamond-shaped design include lower costs, access to providers with best-of-breed skills, and greater flexibility because providers can more easily adapt to increases or decreases in volumes. The challenge of the diamonds is providing a rich enough pool of people to groom for mid-career positions.

Companies like Unilever, BP, Microsoft, Samsung, Canon, Bank of Ireland, and Express Scripts have moved, or are moving to, diamond-shaped organizations. The diamond is an idea whose time has come. But the new structure requires high-performing outsourcing relationships. The next set of ideas shows the way.

15.2 Go For Big Picture KPIs

In Building Block 4 - Design, (Action 19), we discussed the importance of a good SLA. This document is the part of the outsourcing contract that formally defines the 'who, what, where, and when' of the services to be performed. SLAs draw clear lines of responsibility and accountability between parties.

Managing SLAs are certainly a vital outsourcing fundamental, but mature clients also work with providers to manage processes end-to-end, and help with the client's internal KPIs, along with the on the provider's SLA-based KPIs (Figure 15-2).

Figure 15-2: End-to-End Performance Measurement

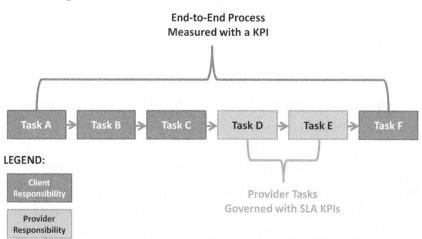

Consider, for example, invoice processing. The client usually cares about the total time and cost it takes to process invoices, whereas a provider's SLA might only consider the number of days it takes the provider to process an invoice once it has completed the relevant work. Getting providers to process invoices fast is certainly valuable, but not as valuable as working with providers to reduce errors, to increase the speed of the entire procure-to-pay cycle, and to reduce costs anywhere in that cycle.

On one financial and accounting outsourcing (FAO) arrangement, the parties focus on the end-to-end metrics rather than just spotlight whether the provider's KPIs within the end-to-end process are *"green"*[157] or not. For example, the parties aim to hit an end-to-end metric of 95% of the journal entries on the client's balance sheet being less than three months old. They now report the end-to-end metric to the financial controllers, not just the provider's performance.

The client explains it like this, *"You could go to a Financial Controller in a country and show them a sea of green in the provider's SLAs while the end-to-end*

---

[157] "Green" indicates that the provider is meeting the contractual obligation for performance.

process was actually pretty poorly performing. Now, combining the provider metrics and the end-to-end metrics, we can show that the end-to-end is working fine or not working fine, and the provider piece inside of that is performing well or not performing well."

Managing a process from end-to-end requires full transparency, and this is where providers can add value. Describing the value of transparency in an end-to-end process reported on by a provider, the provider's account delivery manager said, *"Clients praise our ability to map the processes and report on all the exceptions. They praise the visibility they have within that process that shows how many exceptions and how many workarounds are slowing down the process."* The parties recognize that jointly focusing on the end-to-end process creates more value to the client's organization than the more traditional 'you do your job, and I'll do mine' approach.

15.3 Refocus: From Conflict to Resolution

Throughout this book, we have written much about 'great' outsourcing relationships. By 'great', we mean relationships that deliver cost savings and business benefits, meet or exceed KPIs, satisfy client stakeholders, improve the client's performance each year, AND generate a good profit margin for the provider. This last part is key. It is in the client's best interest to actively care about and protect a provider's profit margin. Why? Because our research shows that when providers do not make their target profit margins, client service suffers (see Building Block 5, regarding the Iron Triangle and the Winners' Curse).

But here is the really interesting insight: great performing relationships are not conflict-free, but rather the parties resolve conflicts in a healthy and systemic manner.

A conflict is a circumstance that adversely affects the interests of one of the parties. Disputes in outsourcing arise from events that cause a commercial loss to one of the parties, or from a series of minor events that accumulate to eventually create a significantly negative consequence. The primary sources of disputes stem from payment claims, pricing, scope of services, and performance.

Our research is finding that high-performing outsourcing relationships are not free of conflicts, but rather recognize them as normal, and have an agreed process to resolve disputes without the use of third parties and most importantly, resolve conflict collaboratively. [158]

Collaborative conflict resolution approaches are characterized by close relationships through which parties listen to the commercial and political implications of each side, seek and negotiate the win-win solution, and then present a united front to sell the resolution to their respective organizations. The most common outcome is that conflicts are resolved with the relationship strengthened.

In contrast to the collaborative approach to conflict resolution in high-performing relationships, we found all too many clients and providers still taking the aggressive stance characterized in poor performing relationships known as the 'compete' style of negotiation (see Building Block 6 for our discussion on the various negotiation styles people display).

The 'Compete' conflict resolution style is typified by a party's aggressive defense of their own interests, without consideration of the effect on the other party's interests. The other party normally reacts in a similar aggressive manner. At best, this approach results in resolutions that weaken the relationship, and at worst, with the dissolution of the agreement.

Consider the next two contrasting cases.

------

[158] Lacity, M. and Willcocks, L. (2012) *Mastering High Performance BPO: Resolving Conflicts In BPO Relationships*, LSE Outsourcing Unit /Accenture, London.

Case: Collaboratively dealing with conflict in an FAO arrangement

In one global FAO contract spanning over 90 countries, the client claimed that there had never been a significant conflict. He said, *"I'm not sure that we've had a significant conflict. We've always kind of sat down and found a common ground or common financial outcome."*

Do the partners argue? Of course, particularly when a change has significant commercial implications. When record processes were added to the scope of the FAO deal, the original transaction-based pricing did not fit. After back and-forth debates, the parties agreed that they had to find a common sense solution rather than rely on the letter of the contract.

What they learnt going forward was that a contract model does not produce a 'fact' but instead produces a starting point for a conversation. They agreed that the top two leaders from each side would meet quarterly for two days away from the office. The idea was to vet issues before they escalated to the formal twenty-person governance meetings. *"So every quarter, the three, four of us go spend two days together, work through all these things and ensure that nothing ever comes to the boil,"* said one of those executives.

Case: A dispute leading to dissolution of outsourced procurement

In another company, the parties escalated the fight over gainshare allocations to a formal dispute. The context was a procurement deal in which the provider would get a percentage of any discount from a third-party vendor's list price for any new products the provider bought on the client's behalf. The dispute centered on the interpretation of the word 'new'.

The provider renewed a hardware vendor contract on behalf of the client that was 55% lower than the hardware vendor's list price. The provider calculated a multi-million dollar gainshare, claiming the contract was for new products as evidenced by new material codes. The client refused to pay, claiming the previous contract with the hardware vendor already had a 50% discount and the client was purchasing the same material, it was just that the vendor's newer models used different codes. The provider described the dispute as, *"We took it to the point where our legal teams were involved, interpreting that savings definition to the letter in that contract. And it was a very heated discussion around how we saw it and how they saw it. And there was some tempers that flared."*

The client allocated about 150 hours on inhouse legal counsel to the dispute, and brought in the advisory firm that helped negotiate the original contract back into the deliberations. The client put so much energy, time, and resources to the dispute, that in the end the client reported, *"the provider gave up."* Although the parties did resolve the conflict, the relationship was weakened. According to the client, *"It went all the way to dispute process and it left an incredibly bitter taste with our executive team."* Eventually, the client switched providers and negotiated a better gainsharing mechanism with the new provider.

Both of these cases are about conflicts with serious financial consequences. The client and provider on the FAO deal collaboratively resolved the conflict and strengthened the relationship. The client and provider on the procurement deal assumed a competing approach that hurt the relationship, ending with the client switching providers.

15.4 Technology Spotlight

From our research, we found many clients commending their providers' deployment of technology to enable lower costs, better service, and tighter controls. Six common technologies whose time has come are listed in Table 15-1. [159]

Before we describe these technologies in more detail, we must underscore the fact that technology, in itself, is never a silver bullet. The data that feeds any technology must be standard, accurate, and timely. Technologies that are broadly disseminated, like self-service portals, require large numbers of users to be trained and, moreover, are not welcome by more change-resistant users.

One client at a major aerospace defence company for example, said, *"The portal is great, but we've also had people who just can't get the hang of using the technology."* More profoundly, effective technology deployment for analytics, forecasting, workflow, and governance requires clients and providers to commit to a high-level of transparency and collaboration. With that caveat, we can now describe how these technologies are enabling better client outcomes.

---

[159] Lacity, M. and Willcocks, L. (2012) *Mastering High-Performance: Technology as Enabler*, LSE Outsourcing Unit /Accenture, London.

Table 15-1: Technology Spotlights

Technology	Reduces costs	Speeds deployment	Speeds delivery	Improves quality/ reduces errors	Better Compliance	Adds business value
	Benefits					
1. Self-service portals	✓		✓			
2. Automation	✓		✓	✓		
3. Workflow tools					✓	
4. Governance tools					✓	✓
5. Business & predictive analytics			✓	✓	✓	✓
6. Cloud computing	✓	✓				

15.4.1   Self-service portals

Since the advent of personal computers, more and more tasks are performed by knowledge workers, rather than by support staff. First, we had fewer secretaries as more knowledge workers began to type their own memos, emails, and reports. Now, user-friendly, web-enabled, self-service portals allow end-users to perform tasks that require more business process expertise (e.g. travel and expense reimbursement or supply orders). Self-service portals reduce direct costs by reducing staff support, and speed service access and delivery. In our case studies, we have several examples of how self-service portals in HR functions reduced costs and improved service. On one HR outsourcing contract, the provider implemented eHR, a portal that enabled client users to manage their own benefits, training, travel, and expenses. It is also used for recruiting. According to the client, *"We had a lot of very good feedback. The technology is great."*

15.4.2   Automation

Automation reduces costs, speeds delivery, and reduces errors. Invoice automation is one example from our case studies. On one BPO contract for FAO services, the provider had already reached 100% on their KPIs for processing invoices and had reduced costs through labor arbitrage and process standardization. The provider's account delivery manager began to think about how to further reduce the costs per invoice. The provider identified electronic invoicing as the best way to reduce costs, *"We proposed to implement an optical character recognition (OCR) system and an electronic invoicing solution to make invoicing automated and paperless. This change was driven through because we agreed to focus on the business outcome of reducing cost per invoice."* Electronic invoicing will reduce the provider's headcount, and thus their revenue, but the provider is encouraged to do so through gainsharing. Beyond the gainshare on a particular innovation, the provider believes that doing the right thing for the client brings long-term rewards (e.g. scope expansion and contract extensions).

15.4.3   Workflow and Governance tools

Workflow tools help control the sequence of tasks required to produce a product or service. High-performing outsourcing relationships increasingly rely on technologies that enable better controls and compliance. These operational tools, used by both parties, facilitate complete transparency in the day-to-day operations of the relationship.

One of the best examples is the *Controller Workspace*, a centralized tool used to manage the FAO relationship between Microsoft (the client) and Accenture (the provider). The tool is a central repository that may be accessed by employees located around the globe to get accurate, timely, and reliable data. In the *Record-to-Report* function, for example, all the tasks needed to be closed out each day are listed, including the person responsible, and the current status of each task. Microsoft's finance controllers and staff as well as Accenture's service delivery personnel all have one shared window into the daily operation. In 2011, the tools used in this relationship won the Global Excellence in Outsourcing Award (GEO) for Innovation, sponsored by the International Association of Outsourcing Professionals.[160]

Governance tools help to manage an outsourcing relationship, including the management of SLAs, performance reporting, and billing. Like workflow tools, good governance tools provide a shared view of timely and accurate information. Governance tools also facilitate complete transparency among the senior levels managing the outsourcing relationship, such as C-suite executives, global, regional, and divisional functional leaders, commercial directors, and contract managers. Again, one of the best examples is the *Governance Workspace,* a centralized tool used to manage the FAO relationship between Microsoft and Accenture at the strategic level. In addition to KPI and performance reporting, the Governance Workspace also incorporates a planning and control tool which helps eliminate unnecessary and unwanted surprises by showing, in real time, the status of service and by providing an efficient reporting tool for SLAs, measurements, transactions, and deadlines.

15.4.4   Business and Predictive Analytics

Note: This section is based on excerpts from Lacity, M. and Willcocks, L. (2012) *Mastering High Performance BPO: Domain Expertise and Analytics.* LSE Outsourcing Unit /Accenture, London.

Business analytics are tools that enable organizations to continuously analyze past business performance to gain insight and to identify ways to improve performance. While business analytics examines past business performance, predictive analytics forecast the probabilities of possible future outcomes and plans accordingly.

---

[160] See IAOP's Global Excellence in Outsourcing 2011 award winners: www.iaop.org/Content/19/165/3131.

Clients want both analytic capabilities. However, doing it on their own can cost a million dollars or more. An immense effort is needed to collect data from multiple internal and external sources. The data must be extracted, transformed, and loaded into a central repository called a data warehouse. From there, more tools are needed to analyze the stored data to produce reports in a consumable fashion (think colorful dashboards) to explain 'what happened'. Sophisticated statistical and modeling tools help predict 'what will likely happen next' (Figure 15-3 provides a simple schematic on how this works).

Figure 15-3: Business & Predictive Analytics Flowchart

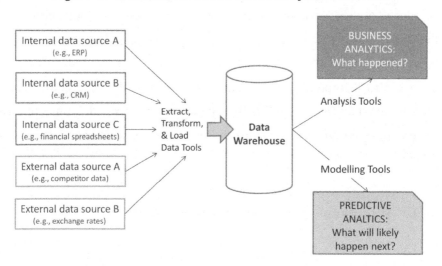

In a 2011 survey of the Society for Information Management (SIM) members, Luftman and Ben-Zvi found that Business Intelligence (BI) remained the top application/technology development, having been in the top three since 2003.

While a lot of excellent work has been done examining how organizations implement BI themselves, there is very little on the role of BI in outsourcing relationships. In recent research, we have examined how providers deploy BI to help improve a client's operational, tactical, and even strategic performance.

Increasingly, clients are turning to their providers to help deploy analytics. Providers are increasingly using business analytic tools to report on KPIs that are standard within an industry. As one client said, *"[The provider] provides us with a lot more reporting on what's going on in these areas than we ever had before. They can tell us things about our process that we never knew before, like how much time to post an invoice, the average time banks are holding onto our money, the percentage of decline to direct debits per country, and so on and so on and so on. They have a whole set of metrics that they sort of bring along as standard."*

Another powerful benefit of KPI standardization is the provider's ability to aggregate and disseminate learning across clients. More clients are expecting providers to infuse new ideas and innovations based on business analytics of standard KPIs across clients and industries.

In high-performing outsourcing relationships, analytics is increasingly the most critical driver of innovation after other transformation levers such as labor relocation, centralization, and process standardization have been deployed. One provider in a high-performing BPO deal explained, *"Whoever you select as a provider, within a relatively short period of time the service levels will become green. That is bound to happen. In many cases, the business cases are based on labor arbitrage and fixed headcount reduction driven through by continuous improvement activities. As time progresses, the question that will quickly come to the fore is, 'How can additional value be delivered over and above what has already been committed?' The key ways to drive out additional value will be through analytics and significant improvements by looking at the processes end-to-end."*

Clients in high-performing BPO relationships increasingly rely on the provider's technology-enabled predictive capabilities. In one BPO contract for a large, multi-state healthcare organization, the BPO provider examines healthcare claims and predicts whether the claim will require rework. By auditing just 1% of the total claims population, the provider identified and corrected more than 50% of the preventable financial rework. Predictive analytics saves between $25 to $50 in administrative costs per overpaid claim, and between $6 to $12 per underpaid claim.

In another BPO manufacturing company, the provider deployed a better forecasting tool for supplies and proposed a new KPI: delivery date fulfillment. These innovations helped the client improve the customer order fill rates for new parts from 60% to 85% and the turnaround time for delivering parts to grounded aircraft from 21 hours to 17 hours.

How do clients as diverse as a multi-state healthcare organization and a manufacturing company get such great results from their providers' analytics capabilities? Our research found that the providers applied their domain expertise to deploy a rigorous analytics process that measured the right KPIs, deployed tools to measure and report on KPIs and deployed algorithms, models, and sophisticated statistics to identify weaknesses and opportunities, and then redesigned processes to deliver measurable business outcomes (see Figure 15-4). As more data was collected and analyzed, domain expertise increased. The iterative domain expertise and analytics processes produced high performance results in the clients we interviewed.

Figure 15-4: Domain Expertise, Analytics, and Outsourcing Performance

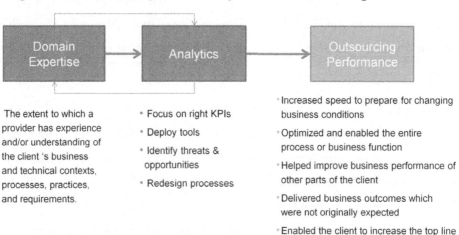

Domain Expertise	Analytics	Outsourcing Performance

The extent to which a provider has experience and/or understanding of the client 's business and technical contexts, processes, practices, and requirements.

* Focus on right KPIs
* Deploy tools
* Identify threats & opportunities
* Redesign processes

* Increased speed to prepare for changing business conditions
* Optimized and enabled the entire process or business function
* Helped improve business performance of other parts of the client
* Delivered business outcomes which were not originally expected
* Enabled the client to increase the top line

15.4.5   Cloud Computing

Cloud computing is defined by the National Institute of Standards and Technology as *"a model for enabling ubiquitous, convenient, on-demand network access to a shared pool of configurable computing resources (e.g., networks, servers, storage, applications and services) that can be rapidly provisioned and released with minimal management effort or provider interaction."*[161]

Cloud computing is an important technology that will continue to help drive innovations in future generations of outsourcing relationships.   Providers are increasingly working on offering software as a service (SaaS), platform as a service (PaaS), infrastructure as a service (IaaS) and hosted services.   Integrating some of these can achieve business process as a service (BPaaS), reflecting the focus on business-specific services.[162]   Clients, however, will need to assess the cost-risk-benefit profile of private, public, and hybrid options and the capabilities of competing providers.   Our research also points to client concerns around security and legal risks, contact and relationship challenges, lock-in and management issues.[163]   However, it is already clear that cloud computing can, if managed carefully, be harnessed to business purpose.   As one executive told us, *"Cloud computing in its best form lowers the barrier to actually getting the business what they want."*

As one of the many examples of this trend, Australia-based Qantas has moved its massive frequent flyer program to a cloud-based computing platform in order to keep up with growing demand.   Its 22-year-old Fortran-based system has been replaced by an Oracle on Demand service, incorporating a scalable architecture

---

[161]NIST Cloud Computing Definition Published 25 October 2011.

[162] For detail on these options see Willcocks, L., Venters, W. and Whitley, E. (2011) *Cloud and The Future Of Business 1 – The Promise.* LSE/Accenture, London. See www.outsourcingunit.org.

[163] See Willcocks, L., Venters, W. and Whitley, E. (2011) *Cloud and The Future Of Business 2– The Challenges.* LSE/Accenture, London. See www.outsourcingunit.org.

designed to cope with changes in demand. Using Oracle's Siebel Loyalty and On Demand offerings, the system can provide consistent service to more than seven million members, while also dealing with rapidly growing member activities. Qantas also sees the new platform as providing the opportunity to target loyalty promotions and extend its loyalty program by introducing new partners - something that would have been difficult with the older system.[164]

We are already seeing providers adding value by moving some of their client's services to the cloud. On one procurement deal for an electronic design automation client, the provider moved the client's procurement platform to the cloud to lower the client's costs and to speed-up their access to upgrades. Updates can be made to the software, and new configurations and capabilities can be implemented through the cloud configuration. The provider explains, *"One of the biggest innovations was moving the client to this on-demand platform. And as a result, they now see regular innovation because, given that it's in the Cloud, updates are made to that software and new configurations and capabilities are implemented through that Cloud configuration. The client would have had to pay a consultant to come in and hardwire their CD version. So that's certainly helping them innovate from a technology standpoint."*

Although these examples show the promise of the cloud, we are skeptical of over-optimistic estimates of the rapidity of adoption and size of market. The reality today is that the cloud cannot achieve the plug-and-play simplicity of electricity. But we would challenge practitioners to think about what the cloud could mean in the long term. The real potential strength of the cloud is that it can be a catalyst for more innovation. In fact, as cloud computing continues to become cheaper and more ubiquitous, the opportunities for combinatorial innovation will only grow.

---

[164] For details of the research see Willcocks, L., Venters, W. and Whitley, E. (2014) *Moving To The Cloud Corporation*. Palgrave, London. See www.outsourcingunit.org.

The distinctive features of cloud computing offer many opportunities for business innovation, particularly given its service (and service quality) focus, coupled with the flexibility that new technology delivery mechanisms provide. These features serve to change the risk profile of business innovations to the extent that it is now increasingly possible to specify new business processes and their associated required KPIs, to experiment with them for a short time and either disband them if they are unsuccessful, or rapidly scale those that have potential.

We are finding that retained capability identified earlier in Chapter 3 with a cloud expertise spin, are vital to managing and leveraging cloud effectively. We have also found that the hype surrounding the cloud suggests it can be introduced seamlessly and fast, but this does not do justice to the lengthy process of diffusion that we observed taking place in many clients during 2013/2014. Clients are also seeking to fit cloud with their existing technology trajectories and business plans, rather than treat it as the panacea and game-changer presented in all too many discussions on the subject. The more giddy proponents are all too ready to ignore the drag effects of recessionary times on any major new project.

15.5 Rising Markets

Rural sourcing, legal services outsourcing, crowdsourcing, and impact sourcing are the rising markets we explore in this section.

15.5.1   Rural Sourcing

Note: This section is based on excerpts from Lacity, M., Rottman, J. and Carmel, E. (2012) "Emerging ITO and BPO Markets: Rural Sourcing and Impact Sourcing", *IEEE Readynotes*, IEEE.

Providers are constantly struggling to attract, train, and retain a qualified workforce. Most providers locate their operations in urban centers like Dallas, New York, Bangalore, Hyderabad, Dalian, Beijing, and Tel Aviv, where a large labor pool exists. But the downsides of these urban locations are high salaries and turnover. Some providers are pursuing a rural location strategy by building delivery centers in rural areas, away from the major cities currently serving as their centers. The main idea of rural sourcing is to locate centers in low cost areas so that employees can be paid lower wages, allowing providers to pass cost savings to clients in the form of lower prices.

The US providers with delivery centers in remote, non-urban, low-cost areas include small-but-fast-growing entrepreneurial organizations like CrossUSA and Rural Sourcing, Inc. (RSI) with ITO delivery centers in Eveleth, Minnesota (population 3,865) and Jonesboro, Arkansas (population 55,515) and others listed in Table 15-2. Large global providers, like IBM and Dell/Perot Systems, have built delivery centers in rural areas like Columbia, Missouri (population 100,733) and Twin Falls, Idaho (population 40,380).

Table 15-2: Examples of US Pure-Play Rural Sourcers

Rural Sourcer	Founded	Primary Service	Location(s)	Population
Cross USA	1998	ITO	Eveleth, Minnesota Sebeka, Minnesota	3,865 710
Onshore Outsourcing	2005	ITO	Macon, Missouri Joplin, Missouri	5,538 50,208
RSI (Rural Sourcing Inc.)	2003	ITO	Augusta, Georgia; Jonesboro, Arkansas	136,381 55.515

We estimated that the US ITO 'pure-play' rural outsourcing market to be about $200 million in 2011. This estimate was based on the identification of about 20 entrepreneurial rural ITO providers in the US, with average revenues of $10 million per organization. We have no good way to estimate the value of all the work performed in rural-based delivery centers that are operated by larger providers like IBM or Dell/Perot Systems. It is quite possible that the US rural outsourcing market is worth $1 billion if the value of work from all non-urban delivery centers were included.

Rural sourcing as a location strategy is a global phenomenon. Providers in many countries are locating delivery centers away from the metropolises currently serving as outsourcing hubs.[165] We studied providers in India, China, and Israel building delivery centers in rural locations.

Consider India: despite the global economic recession, global demand for Indian services is still very strong. Consequently, Indian providers are still experiencing 14% to 22% turnover in urban areas.[166] By building delivery centers in 'Tier 3' cities, Indian providers lower costs and attrition rates. Chinese providers also cited lower costs, but not necessarily lower attrition rates, by locating in Tier 3 cities. Specifically, they reported that labor costs are up to 50% lower and real estate costs are 70% to 90% lower in Tier 3 cities compared to Tier 1 cities. Because the term 'rural' means very different things in different countries (and can even be considered a pejorative term in some cultures), we called this practice remote domestic locations (RDL) when discussing non-US based providers.

Based on our US client interviews, rural outsourcing clients can be generally classified into three groups: (1) clients seeking an alternative to expensive domestic models (i.e., hiring part-time contractors or engaging urban-based providers), (2) clients seeking an alternative to frustrating relationships with offshore providers, and (3) clients pressured to perform work onshore.

In general, the value proposition of rural outsourcing is that clients pay lower prices for services compared to services based in urban areas; and clients receive a better service experience compared to offshore outsourcing.

---

[165] Parakala, K. (2011) "Rural BPOs in India: Are they Over-Hyped?", www.globalservicesmedia.com; Zouhali-Worrall, M. (2009) "An Internet for Rural India," posted on money.cnn.com/2009/07/08/smallbusiness/internet_for_india.fsb.

[166] Everest Research Institute (2011) *The Risky Side of Offshore Growth.*

Price-wise, rural outsourcing offers prices that are 25% to 50% less expensive per hour than urban rates in cities such as New York City, Los Angeles, and Chicago. Compared to offshore outsourcing, hourly rates are more expensive with rural outsourcing. For IT work, rural outsourcers charge blended rates between $40 and $65 per hour for software developers, but the transaction costs are significantly lower compared to offshore outsourcing. Compared to offshore outsourcing, rural outsourcing clients spend less money on travel, coordination, rework, knowledge transfer, and onsite liaisons.

Concerning service quality, rural outsourcing promises to offer superior services when compared to offshore outsourcing because of better domain knowledge, greater cultural compatibility, and time zone advantages. Furthermore, the high retention rates in rural outsourcing firms protect knowledge transfer investments. We also heard from clients who wanted to send work offshore because they are satisfied with the prices and service quality, but regulations or end-client preferences/restrictions prevent them from doing so. For example, a Healthcare company manages benefits for low-income families supported largely by government programs like Medicare. Their IT manager said, *"We work for state governments. It's important for them to know where the work is happening. It's a very different conversation to say that work is going to go to St. Louis or rural Missouri than it is to say that work is going to go offshore."*

For clients, the main downside of rural sourcing is scalability. US rural providers point to the fact that of the 300 million people living in the United States, about 60 million live in non-urban areas, and thus rural sourcing is highly scalable. In reality, scalability can only be achieved by building many rural delivery centers.

15.5.2   Legal Services Outsourcing (LSO)[167]

While many back office functions like IT, financial and accounting services, indirect procurement, and HR have long since outsourced at least some processes, up until recently inhouse legal functions have been largely immune to outsourcing. Now, nearly all legal firms and inhouse counsels consider the opportunities and risks afforded by Legal Services Outsourcing (LSO), the practice of procuring legal services from an external provider.

LSO is growing because of larger market forces driving enterprise legal functions to transform into leaner organizations.[168] Inhouse counsels are no longer exempt from the cost cutting and streamlining imposed on all other support functions. Enterprise legal functions are seeking ways to reduce costs by erecting captive centers in low cost areas, by pressuring major law firms to reduce fees and to be more efficient by offshoring, and by engaging LSO providers directly.

Some sources estimate that the global LSO market was worth $2.4 billion in 2012[169] and will exceed $3 billion by the end of 2013. Growth rates estimates vary considerably from 26% annually[170] up to 60%.[171] Some sources even suggest

---

[167] This section is based on excerpts from Lacity, M., Willcocks, P., and Burgess, A. (2013) *The Rise of Legal Services Outsourcing*, Bloomsbury Publishing, London.

[168] Wood, L. (2011) "Research and Markets: The Global LPO Market is Expected to be Worth $2.4 billion in 2012," *Business Wire*, March 11; see also, the *Black Book of Outsourcing: 2010 Leading Providers of Legal Process Outsourcing*. See Susskind, R. (2008), *The End of Lawyers? Rethinking the Nature of Legal Services,* Oxford University Press, Oxford; Gulian, C. (2012) "Tightened Client Budgets Fuel Need for Outsourcing", *Rochester Business Journal*, Vol. 28.

[169] Wood, L. (2011) "Research and Markets: The Global LPO Market is Expected to be Worth $2.4 billion in 2012," *Business Wire*, March 11; see also, the *Black Book of Outsourcing: 2010 Leading Providers of Legal Process Outsourcing*.

[170] "Research and Markets: The LPO Market in India to Grow at a CAGR of 27.5%," *Business Wire*, March 08, 2012; Deloitte, *The Resurgence of Corporate Legal Processing: Leveraging a New and Improved Legal Support Business Model*, 2011, available online.

[171] Source: Wikipedia.

that LPO growth stalled in 2011 as law firms reduced fees through their own captive centers.[172]

Regardless of its present size, the *potential* global LSO market is enormous. Just considering the US market, the legal services industry is worth about $245 billion, of which 80% of the dollars is generated from law firms and 20% from inhouse counsel. According to First Research, the US market is **highly fragmented** and includes about 180,000 law offices, **with** 50 of the largest firms generating only about 15% of revenue.[173] Competition is fierce in fragmented markets and increasingly clients are pushing back against large legal bills, for which prices have increased by 75% (compared to 20% for non-legal business services) in the past decade.[174] In 2011, a survey of inhouse counsel heads found that more than half of all respondents use or would consider using offshore legal process outsourcing.[175] LSO is a proven way to reduce costs, which is thus one of the main drivers of LSO market growth.

Presently, the LSO provider landscape is varied and includes specialty LSO providers like CPA Global, UnitedLex, Integreon, Mindcrest, Pangea3, and Quislex, and, to a lesser extent, large, global providers like WNS, Infosys, TCS, and Wipro. Indian-based providers are the leaders in the offshore LSO space, with more than one million lawyers and 128 LSO providers exporting legal services worth $640 million in 2010.[176] Indian's LSO market may grow to $4 billion by 2015. The Philippines, often considered the second largest LSO offshore

---

[172] Griffins, C. (2012) "LPOver and Out?" *The Lawyer*, October 22, p. 16.

[173] First Research, Legal Services Industry Profile, 2012, see www.firstresearch.com/industry-research/Legal-Services.html

[174] Harris, M. (2012) "Why More Law Firms Will Go the Way of Dewey & LeBoeuf," *Forbes*, May 8, www.forbes.com.

[175] "Law Department Operations Survey Results," *PR Newswire*, Jan 19, 2012.

[176] Wood, L. (2010) "Research and Markets: Indian Legal Process Outsourcing Market," *Business Wire*, October 7.

destination after India, has 40,000 lawyers.[177] But the LSO provider landscape is changing swiftly, with mergers, acquisitions, and divestitures. New model organizations like Axiom are emerging that are blending the traditional law firm model with rural and offshore delivery models.

LSO providers perform a variety of services such as researching, drafting, and managing documents, preparing matters, performing legal and commercial analyses, providing legal advice, taking legal action, and managing legal and non-legal services. Services are quite diverse and require a range of skills from secretarial to advanced legal skills (see Figure 15-5).

Figure 15-5: LSO Services

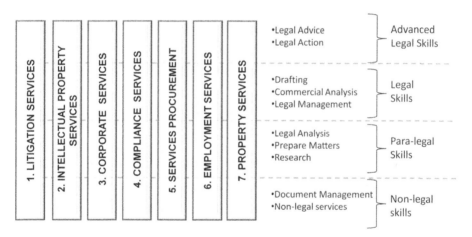

Like all outsourcing, managers from inhouse legal functions will have to learn how to manage legal services differently after outsourcing. Our LSO research, comprising case studies of early adopters as well as detailed data on 26 LSO providers, uncovered the same cultural issues found in our other outsourcing

---

[177] "Legal Process Outsourcing is as Much About Efficiency as Cost-Cutting." *Layer2B*, 2011, Vol. 7.

research.[178] For example, many Indians did not ask for instructions to be clarified if they didn't fully understand the client (see Chapter 14 on offshoring). Instead, Indian teams often 'took their best shot' and then found out they completely misunderstood the client's requirements.

Although this is the first time the clients in this study outsourced legal services, it is not the first time their organizations have outsourced business services. Seasoned client executives from other support functions like IT, HR, and Finance had already conquered the outsourcing learning curve of packaging work, designing process interfaces, and bridging cultural differences. In hindsight, some of the clients we interviewed wished they had sought the advice from other functional areas. For example, one client said, *"I wish we could have spent a little more time working with somebody in our business group that was familiar with outsourcing."* The lesson here is that fundamentals of outsourcing are known and apply to new functional areas considering outsourcing for the first time, if someone would just ask their colleagues.

15.5.3   Crowdsourcing

Six years on from the term first being coined by Jeff Howe in 2006 in a *Wired* column[179], the increased use of crowdsourcing now presents a challenge to traditional outsourcing. The difference between crowdsourcing and traditional outsourcing is that a task is outsourced to an undefined public (the crowd) through an open call via a web-based business model rather than a defined entity. This has spawned a new breed of crowdsourcing technology platforms (e.g. Mechanical

---

[178] See Carmel, E. and Tjia, P. (2005) *Offshoring Information Technology: Sourcing and Outsourcing to a Global Workforce*, Cambridge University Press, Cambridge; Krishna, S., et al. (2004) "Managing Cross-Cultural Issues in Global Software Outsourcing," *Communications of the ACM*, Vol. 47, 4, 62-66; Lacity, M. and Rottman, J. (2008) *Offshore Outsourcing of IT Work*, Palgrave, UK.

[179] Howe, J. (2006) "The Rise of Crowdsourcing" *Wired* 14.06, www.wired.com/wired/archive/14.06/crowds.html.

Turk, Crowdspring, Kickstarter), providers (e.g. Kaggle, CrowdFlower, InnoCentive), as well as the 'crowdworker' (individuals who partake in crowdsourcing initiatives for a living).

In traditional outsourcing, the 'winner' is chosen from a few bids and then is paid to do the work. In crowdsourcing, the crowd does the work first and the individual or team with the best solution is then awarded a monetary award, or 'prize money'.

Not all crowdsourcing has prize money, however. Non-profit (no monetary reward) crowdsourcing is used as a problem-solving mechanism for government, academic, and non-profit organizations. A famous example of this is the June 2012 public release by the UK Police of thousands of CCTV images (on a *Facewatch* app) to help find those suspected of committing crimes. The most famous of all non-profit crowdsourced projects is, of course, *Wikipedia,* the online encyclopedia written almost entirely by over 100,000 unpaid volunteers.

One of the most influential considerations in any business case is cost, and even more so when it comes to outsourcing decisions. Providers of traditional outsourcing, in particular offshoring to lower wage countries such as India, can usually provide a lower cost to a client than performing work inhouse. Crowdsourcing can be much lower still. It is entirely up to the client as to how much prize money it wishes to offer, if any. For many crowdworkers, it's not just the money, but also the prestige of winning that drives them.

However, the overheads to the client can be just as high as traditional outsourcing, even though dramatically different in nature. Crowdsourcing can be initially cheaper than outsourcing because there is no need to write a detailed specification and contract, run a competitive tender, and manage the contract. Rather, the client must only disseminate the problem to be solved (along with any 'big data' required), or a brief on the design to be created, or just a question to be answered.

The overhead cost of crowdsourcing occurs in the evaluation of the solutions. Rather than evaluate a few bid responses to choose the winning provider, the client must evaluate the many and varied solutions. Thus, the cost of crowdsourcing is not necessarily cheaper, it just occurs later in the process. The evaluation of the solutions can be quite costly depending on the complexity and number of solutions provided.

At this stage, there has not been much in the way of research into the client-borne costs associated with crowdsourcing. We do know from a number of global studies that, on average, outsourcing costs approximately 6% of the value of a contract to manage that contract. However, the quantitative financial data on the cost of crowdsourcing has nowhere near the degree of robust information and we have little equivalent data. Nonetheless, some academics have put forward hypotheses that crowdsourcing's net cost to a client is substantially lower than inhouse, and lower than traditional outsourcing as well.[180]

15.5.4   Impact Sourcing

Note: This section is based on excerpts from Carmel, E., Lacity, M. and Doty, A. (2013) "The Impact of Impact Sourcing: Framing a Research Agenda," *4th International Conference on the Outsourcing of Information Services*, Mannheim, Germany and Lacity, M., Rottman, J., and Carmel, E. (2012) Emerging ITO and BPO Markets: Rural Sourcing and Impact Sourcing, *IEEE Readynotes*, IEEE.

Impact sourcing is a sourcing model that aims to transform marginalized people's lives, families, and communities through meaningful employment in the ITO, BPO, and digitally-enabled microwork sectors. Marginalized people are individuals relegated or confined to a lower or outer limit or edge of social standing.

---

[180] See for example: Li, Z. and Hongjuan, Z. (2011) "Research of Crowdsourcing Model Based on Case Study", *Service Systems and Service Management (ICSSSM), 2011 8th International Conference*, pp. 1-5 and Felstiner, A. (2011) "Working the Crowd: Employment and Labor Law in the Crowdsourcing Industry", *Berkeley J. Emp. & Lab. L.*, vol. 32, no. 1.

Poverty is a primary attribute of many marginalized individuals, but individuals might be marginalized because of race, religion, gender, sexual orientation, disability, education, or other criteria. Examples of marginalized populations include Native American tribe members, war veterans, prisoners, women in ultra-religious cultures, and high-school dropouts.

Globally, impact sourcing may employ as many as 561,000 people and may generate as much as $20 billion world-wide by 2015.[181] Despite the importance of impact sourcing on improving the lives of people world-wide, too few clients consider the role impact sourcing could have in their global sourcing portfolio. Impact sourcing is an idea whose time has come.

Impact sourcing comprises an ecosystem of different stakeholders, including the impact sourcing providers (**impact sourcers**) and their employees, their clients, and the communities where those employees reside.[182] Impact sourcers are the entrepreneurial companies hiring, training, and employing marginalized populations in delivery centers around the world.

Table 15-3 provides some examples of impact sourcers. These providers perform a wide spectrum of work complexity, ranging from microwork (e.g. data entry and oral transcription) to complex tasks (e.g. developing software). For companies like Cayuse Technologies (the case after Table 15-3), their state-of-the-art delivery center in Oregon employs 250 people and provides BPO and ITO services.

---

[181] See two reports sponsored by the Rockefeller Foundation: (1) *Incentives& Opportunities for Scaling the "Impact Sourcing" Sector*, 2012. Corporate report by Avasant consultancy www.rockefellerfoundation.org/news/publications/incentives-opportunities-scaling; and (2) *Job creation through building the field of impact sourcing*. Corporate Report by Monitor Consultancy.

[182] See Accenture (2012) "Exploring the Value Proposition from Impact Sourcing: The Buyer's Perspective," available at www.accenture.com/us-en/Pages/insight-exploring-value-proposition-impact-sourcing.aspx.

Why should a Western-based client hire an impact sourcer? For clients, the overall value proposition of impact outsourcing is favorable pricing, good services, and meeting corporate social responsibility (CSR) objectives.[183] First and foremost, impact sourcers do not preach their social missions to clients; they sell clients good services at a good price. Meeting CSR objectives, such as buying a certain amount of services each year from minority-owned businesses, is a bonus; Accenture (2012) notes that CSR contributions are superseded by a client's business reasons for outsourcing. Costs, quality, freeing up strategic company resources and global expansion priorities come before CSR objectives.

Table 15-3: Examples of Impact Sourcers

Impact Sourcer	Founded	Marginalized Targets	Primary Services	Location
Cayuse Technologies	2006	Native Americans	ITO ~35% BPO ~65%	Oregon - Reservation of the Confederated Tribe of the Umatilla Indians
Digital Divide Data	2001	Unemployed high school graduates ready for work/ study	BPO	Cambodia, Laos, Kenya
Maharishi Institute	2008	Disadvantaged populations with high school diplomas	BPO	Johannesburg, South Africa
Matrix Global	2004	Ultraorthodox 'haredi' Jewish women	ITO	Modi'in Israel
Rural-Shores	2008	Disadvantaged populations	BPO	Multiple centers in rural India
Sama-source	2008	Bottom of the pyramid	BPO (microwork)	Headquarters in San Francisco; 16 delivery centers with partners in Haiti, Kenya, India, Zambia, Cameroon, Uganda
Techno-Brain	1997	Poor and vulnerable populations	ITO, BPO	Nairobi, Kenya, Uganda, India
TxtEagle (now Jana)	2009	Urban workers with high school educations	BPO (microwork)	China, India, Latin America, SE Asia, Africa

---

[183] For more information on CSR criteria in global sourcing, see Babin, R. and Nicholson, B. (2012) *Sustainable Global Outsourcing: Achieving Social and Environmental Responsibility in Global IT and Business Process Outsourcing*, Palgrave, London.

Case: Cayuse Technologies employing Native Americans

In North America, the term 'Native American' is used to describe indigenous populations of tribes that preceded European immigration. There are roughly 1.4 million Native Americans, including Alaskan Natives, American Indians, and Aleuts. About half live on 300+ reservations located in remote areas, and all but two have populations of under 10,000. Income, employment, and graduation rates on reservations are considerably lower than the US average.[184] Gaming and gambling are the main sources of income after Congress passed the Indian Gaming Regulatory Act of 1988, recognized the right of Native American tribes to establish gambling facilities on their reservations.

Impact sourcing promises to offer much better employment opportunities. Cayuse Technologies (CT), for example, was founded in 2006 and is owned by the Confederated Tribes of the Umatilla Indian Reservation in Oregon. The idea for the company came from Randy Willis, an Accenture executive and Lakota tribe member. Willis knew that the reservation, with 17% unemployment[185], needed prospects beyond the casino.

CT"s main client is Accenture. Where appropriate, Accenture subcontracts to partners like CT to provide good work that costs less than urban-based alternatives. CT has to compete for work along with Accenture's other delivery options. In subcontracting engagements, an Accenture serves as the interface between CT and Accenture's client. The clients do not typically engage directly with CT employees, except for customer contact center work. One of CT"s largest subcontracts with Accenture is for a 60 seat, Tier 1 call center support with a Fortune 500 company. The client found that insourcing the call center was too expensive, but that outsourcing to Asia was not a good cultural fit for this work. CT was selected because call center rates were less than inhouse rates and because the quality was expected to be better than Asian-based providers. Compared to offshore rates, CT is about $15 an hour more expensive than a call center based in India.

The Accenture Client Lead for the call center subcontract was most pleased with the quality of service. He said, *"We are exceeding all customer satisfaction metrics with Cayuse. I just had a meeting with my Vice President and two Executive Directors and I love showing our satisfaction numbers. The call center handles 12,000 calls a month and our numbers are off the chart. Most responses rate the Cayuse service as 8.5/9.0. That is unheard of in a call center. They go the extra steps to follow up with clients and make sure the problems are resolved. I don't tell them to do that, but I am very happy they do!"*

---

[184] en.wikipedia.org/wiki/Reservation_poverty

[185] Accenture (2012) claims the unemployment rate was even higher (35% before Cayuse) and dropped to 15% by 2011.

CONCLUSION

The last chapter of this book focused on emerging developments in back office redesign, high performance practices, technology enablement, and niche, growing markets. It points to the fact that outsourcing continues to grow and morph while, as a set of practices, it globalizes. This chapter completes a very important part of your journey.

You are now completely up to date, as at beginning of 2014, with what the best research and practitioner experience knows about outsourcing effectively to achieve high performance. You will have learned that outsourcing is a tool and that its management (i.e. what you use it for, and how you and your colleagues design and execute outsourcing makes the critical difference).

What follows is a short 'A to Z' of some key principles you will have learnt that address Machiavelli's concern that outsourcing "*reduces a principalities power*" that we met in our Introduction.

- **Accountability**. The client's ultimate accountability for the success of the outsourced activity can *never* be abdicated to a provider. And strategic flaws cannot be displaced or sold off.

- **Contracts**. There is no standard contract, only headings. Go through the issues in meticulous detail. Ensure the contract is usable at a commercial and operational level, not just legally 'safe'.

- **Cost**. The lowest price may turn out to be the highest cost. There is also no such thing as a fixed price. Outsourcing is not an auction. Get the best price with a superior provider with sustainable solutions under a fair contract.

- **Employee relations**. Believe it! Outsourcing is emotional. Manage from the very beginning the FUD factor (fear, uncertainty and doubt).

- **Negotiations**. Post tender negotiation should only be on exact wording, never on intent or design of the arrangement. Calculate, and then negotiate.

- **Ongoing management**. Outsourcing is not about less effort, but another way of managing.

- **Outcomes**. Outsourcing has been claimed to be able to achieve many things (the honeymoon) and is regularly blamed for many things as well (the backlash). Realize that these claims are not inherent in the act of outsourcing itself, but how the lifecycle is managed.

- **Partnering**. Requires significant investment. It is not an opportunity for shortcuts, or abandoning responsibility to the provider.

- **Performance**. People, and providers, manage according to what they are measured and incentivized by. A contract alone will not ensure performance.

- **Planning**. Ignorance is not bliss. What you don't know and have not planned for will hurt you.

- **Strategy**. Outsourcing is a strategy, not an economy. Do not try to obtain perceived advantages with a poorly thought out strategy. Risk *is* inherent in outsourcing. For each advantage it provides there is a disadvantage, and vice versa. Identify and manage both.

- **Win-win**. Not just a good idea, but the heart of effective outsourcing. The result of thorough preparation, shared information, engaged skilled management on both sides, and respect for each other's objectives.

You are now in a great position. As you go forward practicing outsourcing effectively, you can further access updates to our knowledge base as they become available. This will be on a regular basis. Outsourcing is still maturing, our research is ongoing, and, as we have discovered over the last 25 years, ever-new twists and way of operating emerge. Go well, and we will be ensuring that your journey will be guided by all you need to know.

ABOUT THE AUTHORS

Dr. Sara Cullen is the Managing Director of The Cullen Group, a boutique firm offering consulting, training, and methodologies regarding commercial agreements, and a former National Partner at Deloitte in Australia. Sara specializes in the design and management of commercial agreements. She has consulted to over 135 commercial and government sector organizations, spanning 51 countries, in over 175 contracts worth $16 billion.

Dr. Cullen is a widely published author. Her 115+ publications include *The Outsourcing Enterprise, The Contract Scorecard*, and *Intelligent IT Outsourcing*, in addition to research with various universities since 1994 including the London School of Economics and Melbourne. Her expertise is globally recognized and she performs peer reviews regarding outsourcing research for the *Harvard Business Review, California Management Review*, and *the European Conference on Information Systems*. Dr. Cullen has lectured at many universities including Melbourne, Monash, Swinburne, Queensland University of Technology, and the Royal Melbourne University of Technology. She is also a Chartered Accountant (US) and a Certified Mediator.

Contact: scullen@cullengroup.com.au

 **Dr Mary Lacity** is Dr. Mary Lacity is Curators' Professor of Information Systems and an International Business Fellow at the University of Missouri-St. Louis. She is also Visiting Professor at the London School of Economics, a Certified Outsourcing Professional ®, Co-Chair of the IAOP Midwest Chapter, Industry Advisor for the Outsourcing Angels, Co-editor of the Palgrave Series: *Work, Technology, and Globalization*, and on the Editorial Boards for *Journal of Information Technology*, *MIS Quarterly Executive, Journal of Strategic Information Systems,* and *Strategic Outsourcing: An International Journal.* She was the recipient of the 2008 Gateway to Innovation Award sponsored by the IT Coalition, Society for Information Management, and St. Louis RCGA and the 2000 World Outsourcing Achievement Award sponsored by PricewaterhouseCoopers and Michael Corbett and Associates.

She has published 16 books, most recently *The Rise of Legal Services Outsourcing* (Bloomsbury Press, London, 2013, coauthors Leslie Willcocks and Andrew Burgess) and *Advanced Outsourcing Practice: Rethinking ITO, BPO, and Cloud Services* (Palgrave, 2012; co-author Leslie Willcocks). Her publications have appeared in the *Harvard Business Review, Sloan Management Review, MIS Quarterly, IEEE Computer, Communications of the ACM,* and many other academic and practitioner outlets.

Contact: Mary.Lacity@umsl.edu

Dr. Leslie Willcocks is Professor of Technology Work and Globalization at the London School of Economics and Political Science and director of The Outsourcing Unit there. He is internationally known for his work on global sourcing, information management, IT evaluation, e-business, organizational transformation as well as for his practitioner contributions to many corporations and government agencies worldwide. He is an Associate Fellow at Green-Templeton College, University of Oxford. He has been Joint Editor-in-Chief of the *Journal of Information Technology* for the last 25 years, is Editor of *JIT Teaching Cases,* and is joint series editor, with Mary Lacity, of the Palgrave book series *Technology Work and Globalization.*

He has co-authored 39 books, including most recently *Advanced Outsourcing: Rethinking ITO, BPO and Cloud Services* (Palgrave, London 2012), *The Rise of Legal Services Outsourcing* (Bloomsbury Press, London, 2013), and *Global Business Management Foundations* (Steve Brookes Publishing, Stratford, 2014). He has published over 230 refereed papers in journals such as *Harvard Business Review, Sloan Management Review, MIS Quarterly, MISQ Executive, Journal of Management Studies, Communications of The ACM, and Journal of Strategic Information Systems.* He is a frequent keynote speaker at international practitioner and academic conferences and is regularly retained as adviser and expert witness by major corporations and government institutions.

Contact: l.p.willcocks@lse.ac.uk

APPENDIX - RESEARCH BASE AND PUBLICATIONS

The Research Base

This book is based on original research conducted by the authors, and many contributors, over the years. Since 1989, we have interviewed over 2,500 clients and providers in North America, Europe, Australia, Asia, and Africa. We have also conducted ten large-scale sample surveys. Our primary co-authors, in alphabetical order, have been Andrew Craig, David Feeny, Guy Fitzgerald, John Hindle, Rudy Hirschheim, Thomas Kern, Julia Kotlarsky, Ilan Oshri, Joseph Rottman, Peter Seddon, Eric Van Heck, Will Venters, and Edgar Whitley. We have researched and published with many others and gratefully acknowledge their help and support. Their names appear on the publications we list later.

The Research Journey

We draw upon rich case and survey research conducted between 1988 and 2013, a period that saw the dramatic rise of outsourcing to a global phenomenon. We, along with our co-authors, have examined every aspect of outsourcing, and most twists and turns in the market and practice, from both client and provider perspectives. Academic research methods are extremely well equipped to explore and diagnose contemporary organizations. One fundamental aim that we have shared has been to improve practice by disseminating the behaviors, arrangements, and lessons that differentiated successful from failed sourcing outcomes.

Our work forms a 1600+ case research base held by the researchers at the London School of Economics Outsourcing Unit, the Universities of Melbourne and

Missouri, St Louis Information Systems departments, and the Cullen Group. Our survey work research base by 2013 represented data from 4000+ organizations and a further 1450+ individuals. The research base covers all major economic and government sectors, including financial services, energy and utilities, defence/aerospace, retail, telecoms and IT, oil, transportation, central, state and local government, health care, industrial products and chemicals, and is drawn from medium, large and multinational organizations based in Europe, USA, Africa, and Asia Pacific. Most importantly, we have been able to track many of our cases over the life of their outsourcing contracts, and indeed, into their second and third generation, thus providing us with unique insights into clients' and providers' *a priori* expectations juxtaposed to actual outcomes.

Our work so far has consisted of 12 major research streams with many sub-projects, which we now describe.

ITO

Our initial research projects focused on the major market at the time, namely ITO. The first research base we draw upon for this book consists of 112 sourcing case histories (mainly in the area of IT) studied longitudinally from 1990 to 2001. These are described in Lacity, M. and Willcocks, L. (2001) *Global IT Outsourcing: In Search Of Business Advantage*, but the cases are being continually updated through further research; see Willcocks and Lacity (2009, 2012) and Lacity and Willcocks (2009, 2012). The second is a study of relationships through seven case histories. This appears in Kern, T. and Willcocks, L. (2001) *The Relationship Advantage*.

A third research stream, by Sara Cullen, crossed into BPO and assessed 107 ITO/BPO initiatives of a variety of business functions during the decade from 1994 to 2003 to determine what worked and what did not work, what drove the various degrees of success and failure, and the emerging lessons. The research is represented in Cullen, S. and Willcocks, L. (2003) *Intelligent IT Outsourcing* and Cullen, S. (2009) *Toward Reframing Outsourcing: A study of choices regarding processes, structures, and success*. This research also instigated Cullen's work on measuring success, resulting in *The Contract Scorecard (Cullen, 2009)*.

BPO

The fourth research stream is a 2000-2005 longitudinal study of BPO practices, with a particular focus on four cases in aerospace and insurance. In 2000, Lacity, Feeny, and Willcocks began to study BPO based on 70 interviews. We studied companies that outsourced business processes from HR, policy administration, claims settlement, and indirect procurement (see Lacity et al. 2003; Feeny et al. 2005; Willcocks, L. and Lacity M. 2006).

We also draw upon a fifth research stream consisting of ten cases of application service provision, published in Kern, T., Lacity, M. and Willcocks, L. (2002) *Netsourcing*. A sixth research stream analyzed provider capabilities and is represented in Feeny, D., Lacity, M. and Willcocks, L. (2005) "Taking the Measure of Outsourcing Providers". This focus on BPO continued into a more recent seventh research stream looking at high performance BPO. From 2010 to 2013, Lacity and Willcocks conducted research into high performing BPO arrangements, using the evidence from a 263-organization survey produced by Everest, and carrying out in-depth interviews with client-provider executive pairs in 20 organizations. Meanwhile, Willcocks, Craig, and Whitley carried out parallel research into 26 organizations identified as high performers in collaborative innovation (see Willcocks, Cullen, and Craig, 2011).

Offshoring and Outsourcing

Our eighth research stream has been offshoring and outsourcing. In 2003, we began studying offshore outsourcing, primarily to Asian providers. Rottman and Lacity interviewed 238 people, including 53 provider employees in India and 34 in China (Lacity and Rottman, 2008). Oshri, Kotlarsky, and Willcocks also began a large research project on offshore outsourcing. They interviewed some 110 executives in Mumbai, Gurgaon, Bangalore, Amsterdam, San Paulo, Zurich, and

Luxemburg. This work was extended to include knowledge, social capital, and innovation issues related to global outsourcing (Oshri, et al. 2007; 2008). Meanwhile Lacity, Willcocks, and Zheng (2009) published a book that focused on their combined research, with colleagues, on China as an emerging offshore and outsourcing market. Willcocks, Kotlarsky, and Griffiths (2009) then studied location attractiveness of 14 countries, and carried out an in-depth study of Egypt. Subsequently, Willcocks, Lacity, and Craig (2012) compared ten competitive offshore locations in a major study of South Africa.

Newer Trends Researched

Our ninth research stream has been rural and impact outsourcing by Lacity, Rottman, and Carmel (2012). Rural sourcing is the practice of locating outsourcing delivery centers in low-cost, non-urban areas. Impact sourcing is the practice of hiring and training marginalized people in services that normally would have few opportunities for good employment. Rural sourcing and impact sourcing intersect when marginalized people in rural areas are hired, trained, and employed in outsourcing businesses. Based on 62 interviews with providers and clients in the US, Israel, India, and China, we discussed the challenges, best practices and lessons for providers seeking to build capabilities in remote areas or with unique populations and for clients seeking to buy their services.

A tenth research stream has been cloud computing. Between 2010 and 2013, Willcocks, Whitley, and Venters completed a large cloud-computing project, sponsored by Accenture. This involved completing over 56 interviews. In 2013, they re-engaged with the subject on a new Accenture sponsored project with colleagues Peter Reynolds, Mary Lacity, Alan Thorogood, and Daniel Schlagwein, and carried out multiple interviews and two surveys focused on cloud computing. One product has been Willcocks, Venters, and Whitley (2014) *Moving To The Cloud Corporation* (Palgrave, London).

An eleventh research stream is Legal Services Outsourcing (LSO). Lacity, Willcocks, and Burgess (2013) studied 27 LSO providers and conducted five case studies in global clients that engage LSO providers. This work examines key practices used by clients, providers, and advisors to realize value from LSO services. The practices address the transformation of legal work, LSO strategy, provider selection, contractual governance, stakeholder buy-in, transition, and coordination of work, provider turnover, and relational governance.

The twelfth research stream is the study of individuals, as opposed to organizations. In 2011, Cullen developed on online profiling instrument (based on ten years of empirical observation) to assess the values and behaviors of people who design, manage or otherwise influence contractual relationships between clients and providers. The patterns of the 1450+ participants show distinct characteristics between countries, between industries, but also between client and provider organizations. These distinctions can give rise to conflict between parties and individuals when the differences are considered to be defects, but can also yield synergies when the differences are recognized and embraced.

Throughout our research we have also drawn upon ten outsourcing surveys carried out in USA, Europe, and Australasia in 1993, 1997, 2000, 2001, 2002, 2007, 2010, 2011 and 2013 covering multiple sectors and over 2000 organizations.

Methods

In our research, we have always sought to understand sourcing from the perspective of multiple client and provider stakeholders. What did each stakeholder expect from outsourcing? What roles did they play in the decisions and implementation of outsourcing? What practices were used to manage the relationship? How do they perceive the outcomes?

We often used field interviews to explore these questions for several reasons. Why? First, field interviews allow new ideas to emerge from the research process.

Second, many people would likely perceive outsourcing as a sensitive subject, thus we selected an interview method because it allows researchers to clearly communicate the purpose of the research, to ensure confidentiality, and to build trust during a personal interview. Third, we believed that busy professionals would be more likely to respond to a personal interview than to an anonymous survey. We often selected semi-structured interviews because we wanted to leave the method fluid enough to let ideas emerge, but rigid enough to compare responses across participants.

We have also carried out multiple case studies. Case studies comprise extensive field interviewing and include document collection, site visits, and participant observations. Although case studies are time consuming, they offer rich contextual understanding of sourcing practices and help to answer 'how' and 'why' research questions.

We chose this method to study critical and innovative cases, such as Kodak and Enron back in 1989 because they were among the first large-scale adopters of ITO. We chose DuPont as a case study because it had one of the largest global deals that operated in 22 countries. We chose Lloyds of London and BAE Systems because of their innovative partnership model with Xchanging. We chose to study start up providers like Host Analytics, Onshore Outsourcings and Cayuse Technologies, as well as some of the largest providers like EDS (now HP). We chose case studies in the government sector to understand how sourcing issues compare and contrast with the commercial sector, including Inland Revenue, Internal Revenue Service, Westchester County, the government of South Australia, and the State of Missouri. We validate our case studies using a number of positivist and interpretive validity checks such as participant review, embedding direct quotations in the text, and providing a logical chain of evidence from data collection to coding and analysis. Publishing much of our research in peer-reviewed journals has provided further valuable validity checks.

In order to gain an understanding of patterns, trends and gain large amounts of data on particular issues, we have also used surveys throughout our research journey. We have found combining case studies with survey work particularly apposite for understanding the outsourcing phenomenon.

In addition to our own empirical work, we have done two large-scale meta-analyses of all the academic literature on ITO and BPO (see Lacity, et al. 2010; 2011). We gained 1356 BPO and ITO findings from 254 academic research studies identified as robust. We coded the empirical findings from the 167 ITO articles and from 87 BPO articles. In total, we coded all the empirical academic findings on the determinants of outsourcing decisions and outcomes, of which 741 findings pertain to ITO and 615 findings pertain to BPO.

Improving Practice

We have utilized this collective and rich research output in many ways. One way has been to disseminate the results academically. As at December 2013, we had between us co-authored or written over 45 books (and contributed chapters and cases to over 50 other books), nearly 90 refereed journal papers, and a considerable number conference papers on the subject of outsourcing. We have also over 90 publications in practitioner journals, newspaper articles, and for trade magazines. We have contributed to numerous best practice publications since 1994 - writing, editing, or contributing to guides for federal, state, and local governments as well as various institutes and individual organizations.

These outputs express our desire not just to explore and understand outsourcing and its dynamics globally, but also to try to distil key issues and progress outsourcing practices. This has come together in the considerable number of advisory engagements and keynote presentations we have carried out from the beginning of the 1990s through to the present day. Most recently, these multiple objectives have come together in the founding of the Outsourcing Unit at the London School of Economics and Political Science. The Outsourcing Unit represents a global network dedicated to research and its dissemination, education on sourcing, and improvement of practice (see www.outsourcingunit.org). A further development has been The Global Sourcing website to bring together research, news, workshops conferences and education initiatives (see www.globalsourcing.org.uk). The Cullen Group also publishes a series of practitioner guides, templates, and examples (www.outsourcingtoolset.com).

Publications

Books

Cullen, S. (1994) Information Technology Outsourcing Myths Exploded: Recommendations for Decision Makers. Melbourne Business School, Melbourne.

Cullen, S. (2005) *Relationship Design and Management.* The Cullen Group, Melbourne.

Cullen, S. (2005) *Staff Transitions.* The Cullen Group, Melbourne.

Cullen, S. (2006) Going to Market and Request for Proposal (2nd edition). The Cullen Group, Melbourne.

Cullen, S. (2007) Contracting for the Outsourcing Lifecycle: A Practical Guide. Cutter Information LLC, Arlington.

Cullen, S. (2009) *Configuration Strategy (2nd edition).* The Cullen Group, Melbourne.

Cullen, S. (2009) *Contract Scorecard (2nd edition).* The Cullen Group, Melbourne.

Cullen, S. (2009) *Governance Charter (2nd edition).* The Cullen Group, Melbourne.

Cullen, S. (2009) *Managing the Outsourcing Lifecycle: 56 Key Activities for Success*. Cutter Information LLC, Arlington.

Cullen, S. (2009) *Outsourcing Lifecycle (2nd edition)*. The Cullen Group, Melbourne.

Cullen, S. (2009) Pricing Options and Financial Schedule (2nd edition). The Cullen Group, Melbourne.

Cullen, S. (2009) The Contract Scorecard - Successful outsourcing by design. Gower, London.

Cullen, S. (2009) Toward Reframing Outsourcing: A study of choices regarding processes, structures, and success. Lambert Academic Publishing, Germany.

Cullen, S. (2010) *Provider Evaluation and Selection (2nd edition)*. The Cullen Group, Melbourne.

Cullen, S. (2011) *Due Diligence (2nd edition)*. The Cullen Group, Melbourne.

Cullen, S. (2011) *Service Level Agreements(2nd edition)*. The Cullen Group, Melbourne.

Cullen, S. and Willcocks, L. (2003) *Intelligent IT Outsourcing: Eight Building Blocks for Success.* Butterworth-Heinemann, Oxford. Korean version (2007), Elsevier.

Currie, W. and Willcocks, L. (1998) New Strategies in IT Outsourcing: Major Trends and Global Best Practices. Business Intelligence, London.

Finnegan, D. and Willcocks, L. (2007) *Implementing CRM – From Technology to Knowledge.* Wiley, Chichester.

Kern, T. and Willcocks, L. (2001) The Relationship Advantage: Information Technologies, Sourcing and Management. Oxford University Press, Oxford.

Kern, T. Willcocks, L. and Lacity, M. (2002) *Netsourcing*. Prentice Hall, New York.

Kotlarsky, J., Oshri, I. and Willcocks, L. (eds) (2012) *The Dynamics of Global Sourcing.* Springer, North Holland.

Kotlarsky, J., Willcocks, L. and Oshri, I. (eds) (2012) *New Studies in Global IT and Business Service Outsourcing.* Springer, North Holland.

Lacity, M. Willcocks, L. and Burgess, A. (2014) *The Rise of Legal Process Outsourcing.* Bloomsbury Press, London.

Lacity, M. and Rottman, J. (2008) *Offshore Outsourcing of IT Work.* Palgrave, UK.

Lacity, M. and Willcocks, L. (2009) Information Systems and Outsourcing: Studies in Theory and Practice. Palgrave, London.

Lacity, M. and Willcocks, L. (2001) *Global IT Outsourcing: Search For Business Advantage.* Wiley, Chichester.

Lacity, M. and Willcocks, L. (2006) *Global Sourcing Of Business and IT Services* Palgrave, London.

Lacity, M. and Willcocks, L. (2012) Advanced Outsourcing: Rethinking ITO, BPO and Cloud Services. Palgrave, London.

Lacity, M., and Hirschheim, R. (1993) Information Systems Outsourcing: Myths, Metaphors and Realities. Wiley, Chichester.

Lacity, M., and Hirschheim, R. (1995) Beyond the Information Systems Outsourcing Bandwagon: The Insourcing Response. Wiley, Chichester.

Lacity, M., Rottman, J., and Carmel, E. (2012) *Emerging ITO and BPO Markets: Rural Sourcing and Impact Sourcing.* IEEE Readynotes, IEEE Computer Society.

Lacity, M., Willcocks, L. and Zheng, Y. (eds) (2010) *China's Emerging Outsourcing Capabilities.* Palgrave, London.

Oshri I., Kotlarsky J. and L. Willcocks (eds) (2008) *Outsourcing Global Services: Knowledge, Innovation and Social Capital.* Palgrave, London.

Oshri, I., Kotlarsky, J. and Willcocks, L. (2012) The Handbook of Global Outsourcing and Offshoring (2nd edition). Palgrave, London.

Willcocks, L. (2012) *Global Business Management Foundations.* Brookes Publishing. Stratford (kindle and Lulu.com). Includes two chapters on global sourcing.

Willcocks, L. and Fitzgerald, G. (1994) *A Business Guide to Outsourcing Information Technology: A Study of European Best Practice in the Selection, Management and Use of External IT Services.* Business Intelligence: London.

Willcocks, L. and Lacity, M. (2009) *The Practice of Outsourcing: From Information Systems to BPO and Offshoring.* Palgrave, London.

Willcocks, L. and Lacity, M. (2012) *The New IT Outsourcing Landscape: From Innovation to Cloud Services.* Palgrave, London.

Willcocks, L. and Lacity, M. (eds) (1998) *Strategic Sourcing of Information Systems.* Wiley, Chichester.

Willcocks, L. and Lacity, M. (eds) (2009) *Outsourcing Information Systems: Perspectives, Practices, Globalization.* Sage, London.

Willcocks, L. and Lester, S. (eds) (1999) *Beyond the IT Productivity Paradox: Assessment Issues.* Wiley, Chichester. Includes a chapter on outsourcing evaluation.

Willcocks, L. and Sauer, C. (eds) (2000) *Moving To E-Business*. Random House, London. Includes a chapter on e-sourcing.

Willcocks, L., Cullen, S. and Craig, A. (2011) *The Outsourcing Enterprise: From Cost Management to Collaborative Innovation.* Palgrave, London.

Willcocks, L., Feeny, D. and Islei, G. (1997) *Managing Information Technology as a Strategic Resource.* McGraw Hill, Maidenhead. Includes chapters on outsourcing strategy and retained capabilities.

Willcocks, L., Whitley and Venters (2014) *Moving to the Cloud Corporation*, Palgrave, London.

Refereed Journal Papers

Abbott, P., Zheng, Y. Du, R. and Willcocks, L. (2013) "From Boundary Spanning to Creolization: a study of Chinese software and services outsourcing vendors", *The Journal of Strategic Information Systems,* June.

Cordella, A. and Willcocks, L. (2009) "Outsourcing, bureaucracy and public value: Reappraising the notion of the contract state", *Government Information Quarterly*, September.

Cordella, A. and Willcocks, L. (2012) "Government Policy, Public Value and IT Outsourcing: The Strategic Case of ASPIRE", *Journal of Strategic Information Systems*, December.

Cullen, S. and Willcocks, L. (2004) "IT Outsourcing: Carving The Right Strategy", *General Management Review,* Jan-March.

Cullen, S., Seddon, P. and Willcocks, L. (2005) "Managing Outsourcing: The Lifecycle Imperative", *MISQ Executive*, June.

Cullen, S., Seddon, P. and Willcocks, L. (2005) "ITO Configuration: Research into Defining and Designing Outsourcing Arrangements", *Journal of Strategic Information Systems.* December, 14.

Cullen, S., Seddon, P. and Willcocks, L. (2008) "Outsourcing Success: Unique, Shifting, and Hard to Copy", *Research and Markets*, Dublin.

Currie, W. and Willcocks, L. (1996) "The New Branch Columbus Project at Royal Bank of Scotland: The Implementation of Large-Scale Business Process Reengineering", *Journal of Strategic Information Systems*, 5, 3.

Currie, W. and Willcocks, L. (1998) "Analysing IT Outsourcing Decisions in the Context of Size, Interdependency and Risk", *Information Systems Journal,* 8, 2.

Feeny, D. and Willcocks, L. (1998) "Core IS Capabilities for Exploiting Information Technology", *Sloan Management Review*, 39, 3 1.

Feeny, D. and Willcocks, L. (1998) "Redesigning the IS Function around Core Capabilities", *Long Range Planning*, June 32, 3.

Feeny, D. Willcocks, L. and Lacity, M. (2005) "Taking the Measure of Outsourcing Providers", *Sloan Management Review*, April.

Hindle, J., Willcocks, L., Feeny, D. and Lacity, M. (2003) "Value-added Outsourcing at Lloyds and BAE Systems", *Knowledge Management Review*, 6, 4, September/October.

Hirschheim, R., and Lacity, M. (2000) "Information Technology Insourcing: Myths and Realities", *Communications of the ACM*, Vol. 43, 2.

Kern, T. and L. P. Willcocks (2000) "Contracts, Control, and Presentation in IT Outsourcing: Research in 13 UK Organizations", *Journal of Global Information Management* 8(4).

Kern, T. and Willcocks L. (2002) "Exploring Relationships in IT Outsourcing: The Interaction Approach", *European Journal of Information Systems*, 11, 1.

Kern, T. and Willcocks, L. (2000) "Exploring IT Outsourcing Relationships: Theory and Practice", *Journal of Strategic Information Systems*, 9.

Kern, T. and Willcocks, L. (2002) "Exploring ASP as Sourcing Strategy: Theoretical Perspectives, Propositions for Practice", *Journal of Strategic Information Systems*, June.

Kern, T. and Willcocks, L. and Van Heck, E. (2002) "The Winners' Curse in IT Outsourcing: Strategies for Avoiding Relational Trauma", *California Management Review*, 44, 2.

Kern, T., Willcocks, L. and Lacity, M. (2002) "Application Service Provision: Risk Assessment and Mitigation",. *MISQ Executive,* June.

Khan, S., and Lacity, M. (2012) "Survey Results: Are Client Organizations Responding to Anti-Offshoring Pressures?", S*trategic Outsourcing: An International Journal*, Vol. 5, 2.

Kotlarsky J. Oshri I. and Willcocks, L. (2007) "Social Ties in Globally Distributed Software Teams: Beyond Face-to-Face Meetings", *Journal of Global Information Technology Management,* 10(4).

Kotlarsky, J., van Fenema, P.C. and Willcocks, L. (2008) "Developing a Knowledge-Based Perspective on Coordination: The Case of Global Software Projects", *Information & Management*, 45(2).

Lacity, M. (2002) "Global Information Technology Sourcing: More than a Decade of Learning", *IEEE Computer*, Vol. 35, 8.

Lacity, M. and Willcocks, L. (1996) "Interpreting Information Technology Sourcing Decisions from a Transaction Cost Perspective: Findings and Critique", *Accounting, Management and Information Technology*, 5, 3-4.

Lacity, M. and Willcocks, L. (1997) "IT Outsourcing - Examining the Privatization Option in US Public Administration", *Information Systems Journal*, 7, 2, June.

Lacity, M. and Willcocks, L. (1998) "An Empirical Investigation of Information Technology Sourcing Practices: Lessons From Experience", *MIS Quarterly*, 22, 3.

Lacity, M. and Willcocks, L. (2000) "A Survey of IT Outsourcing Experiences in USA and UK", *Journal of Global Information Management*, March.

Lacity, M. and Willcocks, L. (2013) "Outsourcing Business Processes for Innovation", *Sloan Management Review,* 54, 3.

Lacity, M. Solomon, S., Yan, A. and Willcocks, L. (2011) "Business Process Outsourcing Studies: A Critical Review and Research Directions", *Journal of Information Technology,* 26, 4.

Lacity, M. Willcocks, L. and Khan, S. (2011) "Beyond Transaction Cost Economics: Towards an Endogenous Theory of IT Outsourcing", *Journal of Strategic Information Systems,* 20.

Lacity, M., and Fox, J. (2008) "Creating Global Shared Services: Lessons from Reuters", *MIS Quarterly Executive*, Vol. 7, 1.

Lacity, M., and Hirschheim, R. (1993) "Implementing Information Systems Outsourcing: Key Issues and Experiences of an Early Adopter", *Journal of General Management*, Vol. 19, 1.

Lacity, M., and Hirschheim, R. (1993) "The Information Systems Outsourcing Bandwagon: Look Before You Leap", *Sloan Management Review*, Vol. 35, 1.

Lacity, M., and Rottman, J. (2008) "The Impact of Offshore Outsourcing on Client Project Managers", *IEEE Computer*, Vol. 41, 1.

Lacity, M., and Rottman, J. (2009) "Effects of Offshore Outsourcing of Information Technology Work on Client Project Management", *Strategic Outsourcing: An International Journal*, Vol. 2, 1.

Lacity, M., and Rudramuniyaiah, P. (2009) "Funny Business: Public Opinion of Outsourcing and Offshoring as Reflected in U.S. and Indian Political Cartoons", *Communications of the Association for Information Systems*, Vol. 24, Article 13.

Lacity, M., and Willcocks, L. (2003) "Information Technology Sourcing Reflections", *Wirtschaftsinformatik, Special Issue on Outsourcing*, Vol. 45, 2.

Lacity, M., and Willcocks, L. (2012) "The Practice of Outsourcing Business and IT Services: Evidence of Success, Robust Practices, and Contractual Challenges", *Legal Information Management*, Vol. 12.

Lacity, M., and Willcocks, L. (2013) "Legal process outsourcing: the provider landscape", *Strategic Outsourcing: An International Journal*, Vol. 6, 2.

Lacity, M., Carmel, E. and Rottman, J. (2011) "Rural Outsourcing: Delivering ITO and BPO Services from Remote Domestic Locations", *IEEE Computer*, Vol. 44.

Lacity, M., Hirschheim, R. and Willcocks, L. (1994) "Realizing Outsourcing Expectations: Incredible Expectations, Credible Outcomes", *Information Systems Management*, Fall.

Lacity, M., Iyer, V. and Rudramuniyaiah, P. (2008) "Turnover Intentions of Indian IS Professionals", *Information Systems Frontiers, Special Issue on Outsourcing of IT Services*, Vol. 10, 2.

Lacity, M., Kern, T. and Willcocks, L. (2005) "Netsourcing: Survey and Critique", *Journal of Global Information Management*, June.

Lacity, M., Khan, J. and Willcocks, L. (2009) "A Review of the IT Outsourcing Literature: Insights for Practice", *Journal of Strategic Information Systems*, 18.

Lacity, M., Khan, S., Yan, A. and Willcocks, L. (2010) "A Review of the IT Outsourcing Empirical Literature and Future Research Directions", *Journal of Information Technology*, 25, 4.

Lacity, M., Rottman, J. and Khan, S. (2010) "Field of Dreams: Building IT Capabilities in Rural America. *Strategic Outsourcing: An International Journal*, Vol. 3, 3.

Lacity, M., Willcocks, L. and Craig, A. (2014) "South Africa's Business Process Outsourcing Services Sector: Lessons for Western-based Client Firms", *The South African Journal of Business Management*, forthcoming.

Lacity, M., Willcocks, L. and Feeny, D. (1995) "IT Outsourcing: Maximise Flexibility and Control", *Harvard Business Review*, May-June.

Lacity, M., Willcocks, L. and Feeny, D. (1996) "The Value of Selective IT Sourcing", *Sloan Management Review*, 37, 3.

Lacity, M., Willcocks, L. and Feeny, D. (2003) Transforming a Back-Office Function: Lessons from BAE Systems' Enterprise Partnership. *MISQ Executive*, June.

Lacity, M., Willcocks, L. and Rottman, J. (2008) "Global Outsourcing of Back Office Services: Lessons, Trends and Enduring Challenges", *Strategic Outsourcing Journal*, 1, 1.

Margetts, H. and Willcocks, L. (1992) "La Technologie de L'Information Comme Instrument de Politique dans Le Systeme de Securite Sociale Brittanique", *International Review of Administrative Sciences*, Vol. 58, No. 3.

Margetts, H. and Willcocks, L. (1994) "Informatization in Public Sector Organizations: Distinctive or Common Risks? ", *Informatization and the Public Sector*, 3, 1.

Oshri I., Kotlarsky J. Rottman J.W. and Willcocks, L. (2009) "A Review of Recent Trends in Global Sourcing of IT and Business Services", *Information Technology and People,* August.

Oshri, I., Kotlarsky, J. and Willcocks, L. (2006) "Missing Links: Building Critical Social Ties for Global Collaborative Work", *Communications of The ACM*, Winter.

Oshri, I., Kotlarsky, J. and Willcocks, L. (2007) "Global Software Development: Exploring Socialization in Distributed Strategic Projects", *Journal of Strategic Information Systems*, 16(1).

Oshri, I., Kotlarsky, J. and Willcocks, L. (2007) "Managing Dispersed Expertise in IT Offshore Outsourcing: Lessons from Tata Consultancy Services", *MISQ Executive,* 6(2).

Oshri, I., Kotlarsky, J. and Willcocks, L. (2008) "Missing Links: Building Critical Social Ties for Global Collaborative Teamwork", *Communications of the ACM,* 51(4).

Rottman, J., and Lacity, M. (2004) "Twenty Practices for Offshore Sourcing", *MIS Quarterly Executive*, Vol. 3, 3.

Rottman, J., and Lacity, M. (2006) "Proven Practices for Effectively Offshoring IT Work", *Sloan Management Review,* Vol. 47, 3.

Rottman, J., and Lacity, M. (2008) A US Client's Learning from Outsourcing IT Work Offshore. *Information Systems Frontiers*, Special Issue on Outsourcing of IT Services, Vol. 10, 2.

Seddon, P., Cullen, S. and Willcocks, L. (2007) "Does Domberger's Theory of 'The Contracting Organization' Explain Why Organizations Outsource IT and the Levels of Satisfaction Achieved? ", *European Journal of Information Systems,* 16.

Whitley, E. and Willcocks, L. (2011) "Achieving Step-Change in Outsourcing Maturity: Towards Collaborative Innovation", *MISQ Executive,* 10, 3.

Willcocks, L. (1991) "Informatization in the UK Public Services: Toward a Management Era? ", *Informatization and the Public Sector,* Vol. 1 No. 3.

Willcocks, L. (1994) "Managing Information Systems in UK Public Administration - Trends and Future Prospects", *Public Administration,* 72, 2.

Willcocks, L. and Choi, C. (1995) "Cooperative Partnership and 'Total' IT Outsourcing: From Contractual Obligation To Strategic Alliance?", *European Management Journal,* 13, 1.

Willcocks, L. and Currie, W. (1997) "IT Outsourcing in Public Service Contexts: Towards The Contractual Organization? ", *British Journal of Management,* 8, S107-120, June.

Willcocks, L. and Fitzgerald, G. (1993) "Market as Opportunity? Outsourcing IT and Services in the United Kingdom", *Journal of Strategic Information Systems,* 1993, 2, 3.

Willcocks, L. and Griffiths, C. (1994) "Predicting Risk of Failure in Large-Scale IT Projects", *Technological Forecasting and Social Change,* 27, 2.

Willcocks, L. and Griffths, C. (2010) "The Crucial Role of Middle Management in Outsourcing", *MISQ Executive,* September, 9, 3.

Willcocks, L. and Kern, T. (1998) "IT Outsourcing As Strategic Partnering: The Case Of The Inland Revenue. *European Journal of Information Systems,* 7. Winner of best case award at Fifth European Conference in Information Systems, Cork, June.

Willcocks, L. and Lacity, M. (1999) "IT Outsourcing In Financial Services: Risk, Creative Contracting, Business Advantage", *Information Systems Journal,* September. Winner of best paper award at Seventh European Conference in Information Systems, Copenhagen, June.

Willcocks, L. and Lacity, M. (1999) "Information Technology Outsourcing: Practices, Lessons and Prospects," *ASX Perspective,* April.

Willcocks, L. and Margetts, H. (1993) "Information Systems in the Public Service - Disaster Faster?", *Public Money and Management* Vol. 6, No. 2.

Willcocks, L. and Margetts, H. (1994) "Risk Assessment and Information Systems", *European Journal of Information Systems*, Vol. 5 No. 2.

Willcocks, L. and Mark, A. (1988) "From Strategy to Implementation: Information Technology and Management in the National Health Service", *Public Money and Management*, 1, 2.

Willcocks, L. and Mason, D. (1987) "Computerising: Lessons from the DHSS Pensions Strike", *Employee Relations* Vol. 9 no. 1.

Willcocks, L. and Plant, R. (2003) "How Corporations E-Source: From Technology Projects to Value Networks", *Information Systems Frontiers*, 5, 2.

Willcocks, L. Hindle, J., Feeny, D. and Lacity, M. (2004) "Knowledge in Outsourcing: The Missed Business Opportunity", *Knowledge Management Journal*, November.

Willcocks, L. Reynolds, P. and Feeny, D. (2008) "Evolving IS Capabilities To Leverage The External IT Services Market", *MISQ Executive*, 6, 3.

Willcocks, L., and Feeny, D. (2005) "Implementing Core IS Capabilities at DuPont", *Information Systems Management Journal*, December.

Willcocks, L., Feeny, D. and Olson, N. (2006) "IT Outsourcing and Retained IS Capabilities: Challenges and Lessons", *European Management Journal*, February.

Willcocks, L., Fitzgerald, G. and Feeny, D. (1995) "IT Outsourcing: The Strategic Implications", *Long Range Planning*, 28, 5.

Willcocks, L., Fitzgerald, G. and Lacity, M. (1996) "To Outsource IT or Not? Recent Research on Economics and Evaluation Practice", *European Journal of Information Systems*, 5, 3.

Willcocks, L., Hindle, J. Feeny, D. and Lacity, M. (2004) "IT and Business Process Outsourcing: The Knowledge Potential", *Information Systems Management Journal*, Summer. Reprinted in *IT Management Select*, Winter, Vol. 11, 4.

Willcocks, L., Lacity, M. and Fitzgerald, G. (1996) "IT Outsourcing in Europe and the USA: Assessment Issues", *International Journal of Information Management*, 15, 5. An early version won the best paper award at the Third European Conference in Information Systems, Athens, June 1995.

Willcocks, L., Lacity, M., Kern, T. (1999) "Risk Mitigation in IT Outsourcing Strategy Revisited: Longitudinal Case Research", *Journal of Strategic Information Systems*, April, 8, 2.

Contributions to Books and Teaching Case Collections

Cullen, S. (2005) "Designing Successful Outsourcing Relationships - Selective Techniques from the Lifecycle", in Brudenall, P. (ed) *Technology and Offshore Outsourcing Strategies*. Palgrave, London.

Cullen, S. and Willcocks, L. (2007) "Measuring success", in *The FD's Guide to Outsourcing.* Caspian Publishing, London.

Feeny, D. and Willcocks, L. (1999) "The Emerging IT Function - Changing Capabilities and Skills", in Currie, W. and Galliers, R. (eds) *Rethinking MIS.* Oxford University Press, Oxford.

Feeny, D. and Willcocks, L. (2000) "Core Capabilities and Selective Sourcing. Leadership Strategies", in Davenport, T. and Marchand, R. *Mastering Information Management.* FT/Pitman, London.

Feeny, D. and Willcocks, L. (2000) "IT-Based Business Innovation. Leadership Strategies", in Davenport, T. and Marchand, R. *Mastering Information Management.* FT/Pitman, London.

Feeny, D. and Willcocks, L. (2004) *Managing Strategic IT Projects: CLASS (A) The Norwich Union Experience*. European Case Clearing House, Cranfield.

Feeny, D., Willcocks, L. and Fitzgerald, G. (1993) "Strategic Management of IT in the Nineties - When Outsourcing Equals Rightsourcing", in Rock, S. (ed.) *Director's Guide to Outsourcing*. Institute of Directors, London.

Feeny, D., Willcocks, L., and Lacity, M. (2006) "Business Process Outsourcing, Knowledge, and Innovation", in Hirschheim, R., Heinzl, A. and Dibbern, J. (eds) *Information Systems Outsourcing: Enduring Themes, New Perspectives, and Global Challenges*, Springer-Verlag, Berlin-Heidelberg-New York.

Griffiths, C. and Willcocks, L. (1994) "The Management of Major IT Projects", in *Beyond 2000: A Sourcebook for Major Projects.* Major Projects Association, Templeton College.

Griffiths, C. and Willcocks, L. (1995) "Evaluating Risk in Major IT Projects", in Farbey, B., Land F., and Targett, D. *Hard Money, Soft Outcomes: Evaluating and Managing the IT Investment.* Alfred Waller, Henley. Reprint.

Grint, K. and Willcocks, L. (1997) "Reinventing the Organization? A Critique of Business Process Reengineering", in McLaughlin, I. and Harris, M. (eds) *New Perspectives on Organisation, Technology and Innovation.* Macmillan: London. Reprint.

Hindle, J. Feeny, D. and Lacity, M. (2004) "Leveraging Knowledge through Outsourcing: Enterprise Partnering in the London Insurance Market", in Lawson, R. et al. (eds) *Achieving Competitive Advantage through Collaborative Partnerships.* CxO, London.

Kern, T. and Willcocks, L. (1999) "Cooperative Relationship Strategy in Global IT Outsourcing: The Case of Xerox Corporation's Relationship Locally", in Faulkner, D. et al. (eds) *Cooperative Strategies.* Oxford University Press, Oxford.

Kern, T. and Willcocks, L. (2002) "Contract, Control and 'Presentation' in IT Outsourcing: Research In Thirteen Organizations", in Tan, F. (ed.) *Advanced Topics in Global Information Management.* Idea Group Publishing, Hershey.

Kovasznai, D. and Willcocks, L. (2012) "The Escalation of Strategic Outsourcing Projects: The Expertrans-C&CBPO case", *JIT Teaching Cases,* March vol. 2 no 1.

Lacity, M. and Willcocks, L. (2000) "IT Outsourcing Relationships: A Stakeholder Perspective", in Zmud, R. *Framing the Domains of IT Management Research. Glimpsing the Future Through the Past.* Jossey Bass, New York.

Lacity, M. and Willcocks, L. (2002) "Survey Of IT Outsourcing Experiences. In US and UK Organizations", in Tan, F. (ed.) *Advanced Topics In Global Information Management.* Idea Group Publishing, Hershey.

Lacity, M. and Willcocks, L. (2014) "Sourcing of Information Technology Services", in Tucker, et al. (eds) *The Computing Handbook Set, Information Systems and Information Technology, Third edition: Volume II.* Chapman and Hall/CRC.

Lacity, M., Hirschheim, R. and Willcocks, L. (1997) "Realizing Outsourcing Expectations", in Umbaugh, R. (ed.) *Handbook of IS Management*. Auerbach, Boston. Reprint.

Lacity, M., Willcocks, L and Feeny, D. (2004) *Transforming A Human Resource Function Through Outsourcing: The BAE Systems - Xchanging Enterprise Partnership*. European Case Clearing House, Cranfield.

Lacity, M., Willcocks, L. and Feeny, D. (1996) "Sourcing Information Technology Capability. A Decision-Making Framework", in Earl, M. (ed.) *Information Management: The Organizational Dimension*. Oxford University Press, Oxford. Reprint.

Lacity, M., Willcocks, L. and Feeny, D. (1999) "IT Outsourcing: Maximizing Flexibility and Control", in *Business Value From IT*. Harvard Business Press, Cambridge, Mass.

Lacity, M., Willcocks, L. and Feeny, D. (2004) "Transforming Indirect Procurement Spend: The Case of BAE Systems and Xchanging's Enterprise Partnership", in Brudenall, P. (ed.) *IT and Business Process Outsourcing Strategies*. Heidelberg Press, London.

Norton, J. and Willcocks, L. (1999) "News Corporation: Managing Multinational Strategy", in Scholes, K. and J. Johnson (eds) *Exploring Corporate Strategy: Texts and Cases (4th edition)*. Prentice Hall, London.

Oshri, I. Kotlarsky, J. and Willcocks, L. (2008) "Expertise Management in Distributed Offshore Outsourcing", in Lacity M. and L. Willcocks (eds) *Information Systems and Outsourcing: Studies in Theory and Practice*. Palgrave, London.

Oshri, I., Kotlarsky, J. and Willcocks, L. (2008) "Socialization in a Global Context: Lessons from Dispersed Teams", in Panteli, N. and M. Chiasson (eds) *Exploring Virtuality within and Beyond Organizations*. Palgrave, London.

Oshri, I., Kotlarsky, J., van Fenema P.C. and Willcocks, L. (2007) "Expertise Management in a Distributed Context: The Case of Offshore Information Technology Outsourcing", in Crowston, K, Sieber, S. and Wynn, E. (eds) *Virtuality and Virtualization*. Springer.

Smith, G. and Willcocks, L. (1994) "Business Process Reengineering, Politics and Information Systems: From Methodologies to Processes", in Grover, R. and Kettinger, W. (eds) *Business Process Reengineering: A Managerial Perspective.* Idea Group Publishing,: Harrisburg. Reprint.

Willcocks, L. (1992) "Strategy Development and Delivery: Dealing with the IT Evaluation Question", in Brown, A. (ed.) *Creating Business-Based IT Strategies* Chapman and Hall, London.

Willcocks, L. (1994) "Managing IT Evaluation - Techniques and Processes", in Galliers B. and Baker, B. (eds) *Strategic Information Systems and Management.* Macmillan, London. Reprint.

Willcocks, L. (1999) "IT Evaluation: Techniques and Processes", in Galliers, R., Leidner, D. and Baker, B. (eds) *Strategic Information Management.* Butterworth-Heinemann, London. Reprint.

Willcocks, L. (2002) "Outsourcing IT and E-Business", in Remenyi, D. and Brown, A. (eds) *Make Or Break Issues in IT Management.* Butterworth, Oxford.

Willcocks, L. (2005) "Risk and ICTS", in Hoque, F. (ed.) *Winning The Three-Legged Race.* BTM/Prentice Hall, New York.

Willcocks, L. and Currie, W. (1998) "IT Outsourcing in Public Service Contexts: Towards the Contractual Organization? ", Reprinted in Mische, M. (ed.) *The High Performance IT Organization.* Auerbach Publications, Oxford.

Willcocks, L. and Feeny, D. (2004) *Managing Strategic IT Projects: CLASS (B) The IBM Experience.* European Case Clearing House, Cranfield.

Willcocks, L. and Fitzgerald, G. (1995) "Pilkington PLC: A Major Multinational Outsources its Head Office IT Function", in Turban, E., Mclean, E. and Wetherbe, J. (eds) *Information Technology For Management.* Wiley, New York.

Willcocks, L. and Fitzgerald, G. (1996) "The Changing Shape of the Information Systems Function", in Earl, M. (ed.) *Information Management: The Organizational Dimension,* Oxford University Press, Oxford. Reprint.

Willcocks, L. and Lacity, M (2000) "Strategic Dimensions of IT Outsourcing", in Marchand, D. and Davenport, T. (eds) *Mastering Information Management.* FT/Pitman, London

Willcocks, L. and Lacity, M. (1999) "Experience of Information Technology Outsourcing", in Angel, J. (ed.) *The Outsourcing Practice Manual.* Sweet and Maxwell, London.

Willcocks, L. and Lioliou, E. (2011) "Everything is Dangerous': Rethinking Foucault and Information Systems", in Currie, W. and Galliers, R. (eds) *Rethinking Information Systems.* Oxford University Press, Oxford.

Willcocks, L. and Mason, D. (1987) "The DHSS Operational Strategy 1975-86", in Roff, A. and Brown, D. (eds) *Business Cases in Information Technology.* Van Nostrand Reinhold, London.

Willcocks, L. and Plant, R. (2000) "Moving to The Net – Leadership Strategies", in Davenport, T. and Marchand, R. *Mastering Information Management.* FT/Pitman, London.

Willcocks, L. and Plant, R. (2002) "Pathways to E-Business leadership", in Brynjolfsson, E. et al.(eds) *Strategies For E-Business Success.* Jossey Bass, New York. Reprint.

Willcocks, L. and Plant, R. (2004) "E-Sourcing: From Projects to ASPs and Value Networks", in Currie, W. (ed.) *Value Creation For E-Business Models.* Butterworth-Heinemann, Oxford.

Willcocks, L. and Sauer, C. (2003) "Building a Platform for E-Business: Business and Technology Choices", in S. Chowdury (ed) *Next Generation Management.* Financial Times/Prentice-Hall, London.

Willcocks, L. Graeser, V. and Lester, S. (1999) "Cybernomics and IT Productivity: Not Business As Usual", in Galliers, R., Leidner, D. and Baker, B. (eds) *Strategic Information Management.* Butterworth Heinemann, London. Reprint.

Willcocks, L., Currie, W. and Jackson, S. (1997) "Reengineering in Public Services", in Taylor, J., Snellen, I. and Zuurmond, A. (eds) *Beyond Business Process Reengineering: Ideas, Cases and Opportunities.* IOS, Amsterdam.

Willcocks, L., Feeny D. and Lacity, M. (2013) "Transforming a Human Resource Function through Shared Services and Joint-Venture Outsourcing: the BAE Systems–Xchanging Enterprise Partnership 2001-2012", *JIT Teaching Cases* vol. 3, 1.

Willcocks, L., Feeny, D. and Lacity, M. (2006) "Outsourcing, Knowledge, and Organizational Innovation: A Study of Enterprise Partnership", in Markus, L., and Grover, V. (eds) *Business Process Transformation.* Idea Group Publishing, Hershey, PA.

Willcocks, L., Feeny, D. and Lacity, M. (2006) "Transforming HR and Business Processes at BAE", in Markus, L., and Grover, V. (eds) *Business Process Transformation.* Idea Group Publishing, Hershey, PA.

Willcocks, L., Fitzgerald, G. and Feeny, D. (1993) "Effective IT Outsourcing - The Evidence in Europe", in *The Management of Change: Market Testing and Outsourcing of IT Services,* Elite/ British Computer Society: London.

Willcocks, L., Lacity, M. and Cullen, S. (2007) "Outsourcing: Fifteen Years of Learning", in Mansell, R. (ed.) *Oxford Handbook of ICT.* Oxford University Press, Oxford.

Willcocks, L., Lacity, M. and Fitzgerald, G. (1995) "Information Technology Outsourcing: Economics, Contracting and Measurement", in Farbey, B., Land F., and Targett, D., *Hard Money, Soft Outcomes: Evaluating and Managing the IT Investment.* Alfred Waller, Henley. Reprint.

Executive Publications

Cullen, S. (1994) *Thought Leaderships Series: IT Outsourcing Survey - Exploding the Myths.* Ernst & Young, Sydney.

Cullen, S. (1997) *Information Technology Outsourcing Survey: A Comprehensive Analysis of IT Outsourcing in Australia.* Deloitte, Melbourne.

Cullen, S. (2005) "Due Diligence over Potential Outsourcing Deals", *Enterprise Risk Management and Governance Executive Report,* Vol 2 No 12. Cutter Consortium, Arlington.

Cullen, S. (2005) "Outsourcing Evolution: SWOT Assessments", *Sourcing and Vendor Relationships Executive Update,* Vol 6 No 20. Cutter Consortium, Arlington.

Cullen, S. (2005) "Preparing for Disengagement: What You Wished You had Put in Your Contract... and Still Can", *Sourcing and Vendor Relationships Executive Update,* Vol 6 No 16. Cutter Consortium, Arlington.

Cullen, S. (2005) "Relationship Values Charter: Managing Good Behaviors in Outsourcing Arrangements", *Sourcing and Vendor Relationships Executive Update*, Vol 6 No 13. Cutter Consortium, Arlington.

Cullen, S. (2005) "The Contract Scorecard: Designing and Measuring Successful Outsourcing Deals", *Sourcing and Vendor Relationships Executive Report*, Vol 6 No 12. Cutter Consortium, Arlington.

Cullen, S. (2005) "The Outsourcing Lifecycle: Womb to Tomb (and Back Again)", *Sourcing and Vendor Relationships Executive Update,* Vol 7 No 7. Cutter Consortium, Arlington.

Cullen, S. (2006) "Auditing Outsourcing Deals", S*ourcing and Vendor Relationships Executive Update,* Vol 3 No 14. Cutter Consortium, Arlington.

Cullen, S. (2006) "Competitive Bidding: Getting the Right Deal with the Right Supplier", *Sourcing and Vendor Relationships Executive Report*, Vol 7 No 9. Cutter Consortium, Arlington.

Cullen, S. (2006) "Designing Successful Outsourcing Relationships", *The Journal of Information Technology Management*, Vol 19 No 12. Cutter Consortium, Arlington.

Cullen, S. (2006) "Governing Documents: Making an Outsourcing Deal's Key Documents Work for You", *Sourcing and Vendor Relationships Executive Update,* Vol 7 No 10. Cutter Consortium, Arlington.

Cullen, S. (2006) "Pricing Models in Outsourcing Contracts: Options, Issues, and Solutions", *Sourcing and Vendor Relationships Executive Update,* Vol 7 No 5. Cutter Consortium, Arlington.

Cullen, S. (2006) "Profiling: Minimizing Your Outsourcing Risks", *Enterprise Risk Management and Governance Executive Update,* Vol 3 No 10. Cutter Consortium, Arlington.

Cullen, S. (2006) "Service Level Agreements: Articulating What Will Make a Successful Deal", *Sourcing and Vendor Relationships Executive Report*, Vol 7 No 5. Cutter Consortium, Arlington.

Cullen, S. (2006) "The 40 Fundamental Clauses in an Outsourcing Contract", *Enterprise Risk Management and Governance Executive Report*, Vol 3 No 8. Cutter Consortium, Arlington.

Cullen, S. (2006) "The Configuration Concept: Scope Grouping", *Sourcing and Vendor Relationships Executive Update,* Vol 7 No 17. Cutter Consortium, Arlington.

Cullen, S. (2006) "The Configuration Concept: Supplier Grouping", *Sourcing and Vendor Relationships Executive Update,* Vol 7 No 18. Cutter Consortium, Arlington.

Cullen, S. (2006) "Staff Transitions: Managing the Impact of Outsourcing on Staff", S*ourcing and Vendor Relationships Executive Update,* Vol 7 No 12. Cutter Consortium, Arlington.

Cullen, S. (2007) "Getting smart before you start – Outsourcing Choices with Foresight", *Enterprise Risk Management and Governance Executive Update,* Vol 4 No 7. Cutter Consortium, Arlington.

Cullen, S. (2007) "Negotiation Planning", *Sourcing and Vendor Relationships Executive Report,* Vol 8 No 7. Cutter Consortium, Arlington.

Cullen, S. (2007) "Outsourcing Success: Unique, Shifting, and Hard to Copy", *Sourcing and Vendor Relationships Executive Report,* Vol 8 No 8. Cutter Consortium, Arlington.

Cullen, S. (2007) "Preparing for the Next Generation Contract", *Enterprise Risk Management and Governance Executive Report,* Vol 8 No 5. Cutter Consortium, Arlington.

Cullen, S. (2007) "Staying out of court – dispute prevention and management in outsourcing contracts", *Enterprise Risk Management and Governance Executive Update,* Vol 4 No 14. Cutter Consortium, Arlington.

Cullen, S. (2007) "The AMCs of Modeling your Outsourcing Contract: Mitigating the Risk of the One-Size Fits All Contract", *Enterprise Risk Management and Governance Executive Update,* Vol 4 No 18. Cutter Consortium, Arlington.

Cullen, S. (2007) "The Configuration Concept: Commercial Relationship", *Sourcing and Vendor Relationships Executive Update,* Vol 8 No 10. Cutter Consortium, Arlington.

Cullen, S. (2007) "The Configuration Concept: Duration", *Sourcing and Vendor Relationships Executive Update,* Vol 8 No 3. Cutter Consortium, Arlington.

Cullen, S. (2007) "The Configuration Concept: Financial Scale", *Sourcing and Vendor Relationships Executive Update,* Vol 8 No 1. Cutter Consortium, Arlington.

Cullen, S. (2007) "The Configuration Concept: Outcomes", *Sourcing and Vendor Relationships Executive Update,* Vol 8: No 13. Cutter Consortium, Arlington.

Cullen, S. (2007) "The Configuration Concept: Pricing", *Sourcing and Vendor Relationships Executive Update,* Vol 7 No 5. Cutter Consortium, Arlington.

Cullen, S. (2007) "The Configuration Concept: Resource Ownership", *Sourcing and Vendor Relationships Executive Update,* Vol 8 No 6. Cutter Consortium, Arlington.

Cullen, S. (2007) "The Contract Management Strategy", *Enterprise Risk Management and Governance Executive Report*, Vol 4 No 8. Cutter Consortium, Arlington.

Cullen, S. (2007) "The Governance Charter: Managing the Outsourcing Arrangement", *Sourcing and Vendor Relationships Executive Report*, Vol 8 No 1. Cutter Consortium, Arlington.

Cullen, S. (2007) "The Outsourcing Contract – Seven Solutions to Minimize Risk", *Enterprise Risk Management and Governance Executive Report*, Vol 4 No 4, May. Cutter Consortium, Arlington.

Cullen, S. (2007) "Using a Performance Points Model for Your KPI "Incentive" Scheme", *Sourcing and Vendor Relationships Executive Update,* Vol 8 No 16. Cutter Consortium, Arlington.

Cullen, S. (2008) "Bargaining Power throughout the Outsourcing Lifecycle", *Enterprise Risk Management and Governance Executive Update*, Vol 9 No 8. Cutter Consortium, Arlington.

Cullen, S. (2008) "Benchmarking your Outsourcing Contract: Approaches and Opportunities", *Sourcing and Vendor Relationships Executive Update,* Vol 9 No 4. Cutter Consortium, Arlington.

Cullen, S. (2008) "Benchmarking your Outsourcing Contract: Clause Options. *Sourcing and Vendor Relationships Executive Update,* Cutter Consortium, Vol 9 No 1, Cutter Consortium, Arlington.

Cullen, S. (2008) "Core Competencies of the Outsourcing Lifecycle, Part 1", *Sourcing and Vendor Relationships Executive Update*, Vol 9 No 11. Cutter Consortium, Arlington.

Cullen, S. (2008) "Debriefing the Winner and Loser after a Bidding Process: Generating Goodwill and Future Success", *Enterprise Risk Management and Governance Executive Update,* Vol 5 No 12. Cutter Consortium, Arlington.

Cullen, S. (2009) "Core Competencies of the Outsourcing Lifecycle, Part 2", *Sourcing and Vendor Relationships Executive Update,* Vol 10 No 1. Cutter Consortium, Arlington.

Cullen, S. (2009) "Getting innovation in outsourcing contracts", *Innovation and Enterprise Agility Executive Update*, Vol 3 No 8. Cutter Consortium, Arlington.

Cullen, S. (2009) "Outsourcing Lifecycle Part 1", *Sourcing and Vendor Relationships Executive* Report, Vol 10 No 1. Cutter Consortium, Arlington. Part 2 - Vol 10 No 2. Part 3 - Vol 10 No 3. Part 4 - Vol 10 No 4.

Cullen, S. (2009) "Outsourcing Strategies to Weather a Recession", *Journal of Information Technology Management*, Vol 22 No 5. Cutter Consortium, Arlington.

Cullen, S. (2009) "Partnering in Outsourcing Deals: Is it a Myth or a Genuine Strategy?", *Sourcing and Vendor Relationships Executive Update*, Vol 10 No 11. Cutter Consortium, Arlington.

Cullen, S. (2009) "Performance Evaluations", *Enterprise Risk Management and Governance Executive Report*, Vol 6 No 3.Cutter Consortium, Arlington.

Cullen, S. (2009) "Show Me the Money: The use of Financial Metrics in Your Contracts", *The Journal of Information Technology Management*, Vol 22 No 3. Cutter Consortium, Arlington.

Cullen, S. (2009) "Special Considerations when Re-tendering an Outsourcing Contract", *Enterprise Risk Management and Governance Executive Update,* Cutter Consortium, Vol 6 No 4. Cutter Consortium, Arlington.

Cullen, S. (2009) "Team Chemistry: Are the individuals in the parties well suited?", *Sourcing and Vendor Relationships Executive Update*, Cutter Consortium, Vol 10 No 6. Cutter Consortium, Arlington.

Cullen, S. (2009) "The Contract Blueprint: Creating agreements that will work in practice", *Enterprise Risk Management and Governance Executive Update*, Cutter Consortium, Vol 6 No 6. Cutter Consortium, Arlington.

Cullen, S. (2009) "The Outsourcing Business Case – a focus on the financials", *Sourcing and Vendor Relationships Executive Update*, Cutter Consortium, Vol 12 No 11. Cutter Consortium, Arlington.

Cullen, S. (2009) "The Retained Organization: Managing the hybrid sourcing solution", *Enterprise Risk Management and Governance Executive Update*, Vol 6 No 11. Cutter Consortium, Arlington.

Cullen, S. (2009) The Outsourcing Lifecycle Communications Strategy. *Sourcing and Vendor Relationships Executive Update*, Cutter Consortium, Vol 10 No 10. Cutter Consortium, Arlington.

Cullen, S. (2012) *A study of contract management styles in Australia 2011-12: The different values and behaviours exhibited by the people who develop and manage contracts.* Chartered Institute of Purchasing and Supply, Melbourne.

Cullen, S. and Willcocks, L. (2007) "Measuring Success", *Financial Director's Guide to Outsourcing*, Caspian Publishing, London.

Cullen, S. et al. (2010) "The Debate Surrounding Offshoring and its Effect on Employment", *Sourcing and Vendor Relationships Executive Report*, Vol 11 No 3. Cutter Consortium, Arlington.

Cullen, S. et al. (2012) "Big Data Analytics: Outsourcing vs. Crowdsourcing", *The Journal of Information Technology Management*, Vol 25 No 10. Cutter Consortium, Arlington.

Cullen, S., Willcocks, L. and Seddon, P. (2001) *IT Outsourcing Practices in Australia.* Joint Deloitte /University of Melbourne study published in January.

Feeny, D., Willcocks, L. and Lacity, M. (2003) *Business Process Outsourcing: The Promise of Enterprise Partnership.* Xchanging sponsored research published as an Executive Research Briefing for Templeton College, Oxford.

Lacity, M. and Willcocks, L. (1996) "Best Practices In Information Technology Sourcing", *The Oxford Executive Research Briefings*, No. 2. Templeton College, Oxford.

Lacity, M. and Willcocks, L. (2000) *Inside IT Outsourcing: A State-of-the-Art Report.* Templeton College, Oxford.

Lacity, M. and Willcocks, L. (2012) Mastering High Performance BPO – The Case of Microsoft's One Finance. LSE Outsourcing Unit, London.

Lacity, M. and Willcocks, L. (2012) *Mastering High Performance BPO: Collaborative BPO Governance.* LSE Outsourcing Unit /Accenture, London.

Lacity, M. and Willcocks, L. (2012) *Mastering High Performance BPO: Domain Expertise and Analytics.* LSE Outsourcing Unit /Accenture, London.

Lacity, M. and Willcocks, L. (2012) *Mastering High Performance BPO: The Role of Transformational Leaders.* LSE Outsourcing Unit /Accenture, London.

Lacity, M. and Willcocks, L. (2012) *Mastering High Performance BPO: Dynamic Innovation.* LSE Outsourcing Unit /Accenture, London.

Lacity, M. and Willcocks, L. (2012) *Mastering High Performance BPO: Resolving Conflicts in BPO Relationships.* LSE Outsourcing Unit /Accenture, London.

Lacity, M. and Willcocks, L. (2012) *Mastering High Performance BPO: Technology as a Business Enabler.* LSE Outsourcing Unit /Accenture, London.

Lacity, M. and Willcocks, L. (2012) *The Legal Process Outsourcing: The LPO Provider Landscape.* LSE Outsourcing Unit, London.

Lacity, M., Feeny, D., and Willcocks, L (2006) "The Twelve Supplier Capabilities: Part 1. *Sourcing and Vendor Relationships Executive Update*, Vol. 7, No. 13, Cutter Consortium, Arlington. Part 2 - Vol. 7, No. 15.

Lacity, M., Willcocks, L. and Craig, A. (2012) *South Africa's BPO Service Advantage: Cases of Success.* LSE Outsourcing Unit, London.

Nievelt, G. van and Willcocks, L. (1997) "Benchmarking Organisational and IT Performance", *The Oxford Executive Research Briefings,* No. 7. Templeton College, Oxford.

Willcocks, L. (2004) *Eye Of The Market 1- The London Insurance Market: Modernisation or Muddle?* Knowledge Capital Partners: London.

Willcocks, L. (2005) *Eye Of The Market 2- Social Capital: The London Insurance Market's Secret Weapon?* Knowledge Capital Partners: London.

Willcocks, L. and Craig, A. (2007) *Outsourcing Enterprise 4: Retaining Core Capabilities,* Logica/LSE Outsourcing Unit, London.

Willcocks, L. and Craig, A. (2009) *Outsourcing in Difficult Times: Releasing Cost While Retaining Control.* Logica, London.

Willcocks, L. and Craig, A. (2009) *Step-Change: Collaborate to Innovate.* Logica/LSE Outsourcing Unit, London.

Willcocks, L. and Cullen, S. (2005) *The Outsourcing Enterprise 1: The CEO Role In Creating Strategic Advantage.* Logica, London.

Willcocks, L. and Cullen, S. (2005) *The Outsourcing Enterprise 2: The Power of Relationships.* Logica, London.

Willcocks, L. and Lacity, M. (2012) *Mastering High Performance BPO – Strategic F&A Partnering at BP.* LSE Outsourcing Unit, London.

Willcocks, L. and Lacity, M. (2012) *Mastering High Performance BPO: A Focus On Business Outcomes.* LSE Outsourcing Unit /Accenture, London.

Willcocks, L. and Lacity, M. (2012) *Mastering High Performance BPO: Value Beyond Cost.* LSE Outsourcing Unit /Accenture, London.

Willcocks, L. and Lacity, M. (2012) *Mastering High Performance BPO: Making Change Management A Priority.* LSE Outsourcing Unit /Accenture, London.

Willcocks, L., Craig, A. and Lacity, M. (2012) *Becoming Strategic: South Africa's BPO Service Advantage.* LSE Outsourcing Unit, London.

Willcocks, L., Cullen, S. and Lacity, M. (2006) *Outsourcing Enterprise 3 – Selecting Effective Suppliers.* Logica, London.

Willcocks, L., Griffiths, C. and Kotlarsky, J. (2009) *Beyond BRIC: Offshoring in non-BRIC Countries – Egypt a Growth Market.* ELSE/ITIDA, London.

Willcocks, L., Lacity, M. et al. (2012) *Achieving High Performance in BPO – Research Report.* LSE Outsourcing Unit/Accenture, London.

Willcocks, L., Oshri, I. and Hindle, J. (2009) *The Bundling of Services in Outsourcing.* LSE Outsourcing Unit/Accenture, London.

Willcocks, L., Venters, W. and Whitley, E. (2011) *The Cloud and the Future of Business*. LSE Outsourcing Unit/Accenture, London. Five papers on the promise, the challenges, the impacts, innovation, management.

Full listings of contributions to 12 City University Business School Working Papers and to 32 OXIIM Research and Discussion Papers, and also the Warwick University IS Research series are available from l.p.willcocks@lse.ac.uk.

Made in United States
North Haven, CT
28 March 2024

50618179R00285